M T W T F S S 24

8:

9:

10

11:

12:

1:

2:

3:

4:

5:

5

6

7

8

9

10

Using the *Sams' Teach Yourself in 24 Hours* Series

Welcome to the *Sams' Teach Yourself in 24 Hours* series! You're probably thinking, "What, they want me to stay up all night and learn this stuff?" Well, no, not exactly. This series introduces a new way to teach you about exciting new products: 24 one-hour lessons, designed to keep your interest and keep you learning. Because the learning process is broken into small units, you will not be overwhelmed by the complexity of some of the new technologies that are emerging in today's market. Each hourly lesson has a number of special items, some old, some new, to help you along.

10 Minutes

The first 10 minutes of each hour lists the topics and skills that you will learn about by the time you finish the hour. You will know exactly what the hour will bring with no surprises.

20 Minutes

Twenty minutes into the lesson, you will have been introduced to many of the newest features of the operating system. In the constantly evolving computer arena, knowing everything an operating system can do will aid you enormously now and in the future.

30 Minutes

Before 30 minutes have passed, you will have learned at least one useful task. Many of these tasks take advantage of the newest features of the operating system. These tasks use a hands-on approach, telling you exactly which menus and commands you need to use to accomplish the goal. This approach is found in each lesson of the *24 Hours* series.

40 Minutes

You will see after 40 minutes that many of the tools you have come to expect from the *Sams' Teach Yourself* series are found in the *24 Hours* series as well. Time Savers offer special tricks of the trade to make your work faster and more productive. Cautions help you avoid those nasty time-consuming errors.

50 Minutes

By the time you're 50 minutes in, you'll probably run across terms you haven't seen before. Never before has technology thrown so many new words and acronyms into the language, and the New Terms elements in this series will carefully explain each and every one of them.

60 Minutes

At the end of the hour, you may still have questions that need to be answered. You know the kind—questions on skills or tasks that come up every day for you, but that weren't directly addressed during the lesson. That's where the Q&A section can help. By answering the most frequently asked questions about the topics discussed in the hour, Q&A not only answers your specific question, it provides a succinct review of all that you have learned in the hour.

Who Should Read This Book

Although this book is geared toward beginning Windows users, advanced users will find it handy as well. Readers rarely believe that lofty claim for good reason, but the design of this book and the nature of Windows 98 make it possible for this book to address such a wide audience. Here is why: Windows 98 is a major improvement over the previous versions of Windows due to its ease of integration into the Internet's online technology. If you do not yet use the Internet, you'll still appreciate the new features and improvements that Microsoft put into Windows 98.

Readers unfamiliar with windowed environments will find plenty of introductory help to bring them up to speed quickly. This book teaches you how to start Windows 98, how to exit Windows 98, and how to manage almost every aspect of Windows 98. This book talks to beginners but does not talk down to beginners.

For readers who presently use Windows 95, this book also addresses you. Here is how: There are several sidebars labeled Step-Up that explain how a specific Windows 98 feature improves upon or replaces a Windows 95 feature. With your fundamental base of Windows 95 understanding, you'll appreciate the new Windows 98 feature. In addition to the Step-Ups, keep in mind that Windows 98 operates using a completely new style from previous versions. Windows 98 is similar to Windows 95 so you will feel comfortable learning Windows 98. But there are more than enough new features to keep Windows 95 users interested and happy for a long time.

Sams' Teach Yourself Windows 98 in 24 Hours, Preview Edition

Sams' Teach Yourself Windows 98 in 24 Hours, Preview Edition

Greg Perry

SAMS PUBLISHING

201 West 103rd Street
Indianapolis, Indiana 46290

This book is for a man who serves, does right, and risks the consequences:
Mr. Steve Largent.

Library of Congress Catalog Number: 97-69137

ISBN: 0-672-31313-8

Printed in the United States of America 1 2 3 4 5 6 7 8 9 0

Composed in AGaramond and MCPdigital by Macmillan Computer Publishing

Warning and Disclaimer

This book is sold as is, without warranty of any kind, either express or implied. While every precaution has been taken in the preparation of this book, the authors and Sams Books assume no responsibility for errors or omissions. Neither is any liability assumed for damages resulting from the use of the information or instructions contained herein. It is further stated that the publisher and authors are not responsible for any damage or loss to your data or your equipment that results directly or indirectly from your use of this book.

Trademarks

All terms mentioned in this book that are known to be trademarks or services marks have been appropriately capitalized. Sams Books cannot attest to the accuracy of this information. Use of a term in this book should not be regarded as affecting the validity of any trademark or service mark. Windows 98 is a trademark of Microsoft, Inc.

Executive Editor Grace Buechlein

Development Editors Fran Hatton
Brian-Kent Proffitt

Managing Editor
Sarah Kearns

Development Editor
Philip Wescott

Project Editors
Kevin Laseau
Mike LaBonne

Copy Editors
Julie Maclean
Nancy Albright

Technical Editors
Craig Brush
Jeff Perkins
John Charlesworth
Susan Charlesworth

Indexer
Kelly Talbot

Cover Designer
Gary Adair

Book Designer
Gary Adair

Production Team
Marcia Deboy
Jennifer Earhart
Cynthia Fields

Overview

Contents

Acknowledgments

I have the opportunity to work with the best people in the publishing business. My sincere thanks go to the editors and staff at Sams Publishing who strive to produce computer books that teach all levels of computer users from beginners to experts. The people at Sams Publishing take their jobs seriously because they want readers to have only the best books possible.

Sams' greatest, Grace Buechlein, puts up with far more than she should from me. I am ever so grateful for her kindness, patience, and diligence. In addition, the man who passes projects along my way, Dean Miller, deserves praises and raises. Dean has his hand somewhere in most of my successful books and I appreciate that more than he knows.

Other editors and staff at Sams who produced this book, namely Mike LaBonne, Julie Maclean, Nancy Albright and Kevin Laseau are also responsible for this book's excellence, and I alone am responsible for any problems if there are any.

My lovely and gracious bride, Jayne, stands by my side day in and day out. Thank you, my Dear Jayne. Thanks also to my Dad and Mom, Glen and Bettye Perry, who are my biggest fans. I love you all.

—Greg Perry

About the Author

Greg Perry is a speaker and writer on both the programming and the applications sides of computing. He is known for his skills at bringing advanced computer topics down to the novice's level. Perry has been a programmer and trainer since the early 1980s. He received his first degree in computer science and then a master's degree in corporate finance. Perry is the author of more than 50 computer books, including *Absolute Beginner's Guide to Programming, Absolute Beginner's Guide to C, Sams' Teach Yourself Office 97 in 24 Hours, C Programming in 12 Easy Lessons*, and the *Visual Basic Starter Kit*. He also writes about rental-property management and travels as a hobby.

Introduction

You probably are anxious to get started with your 24-hour Windows 98 tutorial. Windows 98 is the most exciting operating system produced to date by Microsoft and the wait was more than worth it.

This book's goal is to get you up to speed as quickly as possible. Take just a few preliminary moments to acquaint yourself with the design of this book described in the next few sections.

About this Preview Edition

This preview edition of *Sams' Teach Yourself Windows 98 in 24 Hours* uses a pre-release Windows 98 version called a "beta version." Software companies often distribute early test versions of software to a limited pool of special users called "beta testers." In this way the software companies receive valuable feedback which they can incorporate into the design of the product prior to its ultimate release to the public, and beta users can become familiar with the features of a product prior to its release. By learning from this preview edition of *Sams' Teach Yourself Windows 98 in 24 Hours* (which is based on beta version 3 of Windows 98), you will be able to get an early look at the likely features of Windows 98.

Because Windows 98 is still under development, it is possible that the final version of Windows 98 will differ in some respects from Windows 98 beta version 3. Therefore some features or screenshots presented this book may not match the ultimate release version of Windows 98. The official release version of *Sams' Teach Yourself Windows 98 in 24 Hours* will be updated for the final release of Windows 98.

What's New with Windows 98

Different, better, and still the same best describes how Windows 98 compares to previous versions of Windows. Despite the similarities, there are major differences in Windows 98 that you should know about ahead of time so that you can use Windows 98 the way it is supposed to be used. Microsoft designed Windows 98 so that you can concentrate on using your software and hardware rather than concentrate on using Windows 98.

Windows 98 improves upon the Windows 95 interface that has become the standard. If you are new to the Windows 95 and Windows 98 environments—perhaps because you upgraded from Windows 3 or from an Apple operating system—consider yourself fortunate! You are about to be impressed. Some of the Windows 98 key features are

- The Internet's online environment is more closely associated with the Windows 98 desktop.
- The Start menu is more operational and lets you make menu changes on the fly without messy dialog boxes.
- Advanced system tools now help protect your computer files and monitor your hardware.
- Improved Plug-and-Play features enable you to plug new devices into your computer without having to set hardware switches or determine appropriate interrupt settings. Windows 98 supports new hardware such as the Universal Serial Bus (*USB*) and advanced laptop docking and infrared ports.
- One of the benefits that current Windows users will appreciate is that Windows 98 does not require as many mouse clicks and double-clicks as previous versions of Windows did.
- Outlook Express is a new email manager that lets you organize your incoming and outgoing messages easily.
- Monitor newsgroups and make postings from Outlook Express's common interface.
- Your desktop now becomes an online access tool that lets you access Internet web pages as easily as you access your own PC's files.

What This Book Will Do for You

Although this is not a reference book, you'll learn almost every aspect of Windows 98 from the user's point of view. There are many advanced technical details that most users will never need, and this book does not waste your time with those. This book knows that you want to get up to speed with Windows 98 in 24 hours, and this book fulfills its goal.

This book presents both the background and the theory that a new Windows 98 user needs. In addition to the background discussions, this book is practical and provides more than 75 useful step-by-step tasks that you can work through to gain hands-on experience. The tasks guide you through all the common Windows 98 actions you'll need to make Windows 98 work for you, instead of you working to use Windows 98.

Can This Book Really Teach Windows 98 in 24 Hours?

Yes. You can master each chapter one hour or less (by the way, chapters are referred to as "hours" in the rest of the book). Although some chapters are longer than others, the material is balanced. The longer chapters contain several tasks, and the shorter chapters contain background material. The balance provided by the tasks, background, and insightful explanations and tips make learning Windows 98 using this book fresh at every page.

Conventions Used in This Book

Each chapter contains a glossary to explain the important new terms in the chapter. There is a question-and-answer section at the end of each chapter to reinforce ideas. This book also uses several common conventions to help teach the Windows 98 topics. Here is a summary of the typographical conventions:

- The first time a new term appears, the term is italicized.
- Commands and computer output appear in a special `monospaced` computer font.
- Words you type appear in a **`boldfaced`** computer font.
- If a task requires you to select from a menu, the book separates menu commands with a vertical bar. Therefore, this book uses File | Save As to select the Save As command from the File menu.
- Windows 98 uses underlining to indicate hot keys on the screen. (Hot keys are keyboard alternatives to using the mouse to choose menu items and dialog box options.) This book indicates hot keys with a boldface character. For example, in the menu commands File | Save As, the F and A are hot keys.

In addition to typographical conventions, the following special elements are included to set off different types of information to make them easily recognizable:

Just a Minute

Special notes augment the material you are reading in each hour. They clarify concepts and procedures.

Time Saver

You'll find numerous tips that offer shortcuts and solutions to common problems.

Caution

The caution sections warn you about pitfalls. Reading them will save you time and trouble.

Current Windows 95 users will advance quickly by reading the Step-Ups provided for them.

Review the Basics

Windows Minute

Windows Minutes are sections that provide background information for users who have never used a windowed operating environment before. Windows Minutes can be from a paragraph to a page or two long.

Although these sections are intended for beginners, experienced users may find them useful as a refresher course on the topic or procedure at hand.

PART I

Wake Up with Windows 98

Hour

1 What's Windows 98 All About?

2 Tour Windows 98 Now

3 Take Windows 98 to Task

4 Understanding the My Computer Window

Hour 1

What's Windows 98 All About?

Who says that a productive computer user cannot have fun being productive? Windows 98 from the Microsoft Corporation is fun, friendly, and powerful. This hour introduces you to Windows 98. You will learn some of the goals that the Microsoft programmers had in mind when they designed Windows 98. Also, you will learn how Windows 98 improves upon previous versions of Windows and other operating environments by fully integrating an online environment into the operating system.

The highlights of this hour include:

- How Microsoft designed Windows 98 to be as easy and intuitive as possible
- What makes Windows 98 more powerful than many other operating environments
- How to start Windows 98
- Why you might have to log on to Windows 98
- How to access and manipulate common Windows 98 controls, such as command buttons and check boxes
- When you need to perform a shutdown of Windows 98

Getting a Feel for Windows 98

Most users like the look and feel of Windows 98, and they appreciate the fact that Windows 98 is also enjoyable to use. Although Windows 98 is both fun and easy to master, it is also a computer interface system that offers tremendous power for anyone who uses PCs. With Windows 98 you can access your computer's hardware and data files easily, even if you are new to computers. As a matter of fact, Microsoft spent many hours and dollars streamlining the way Windows 98 helps people work.

Windows 98 contains a computer interface that attempts to please all groups of people, including novice computer users and advanced computer programmers. To achieve the lofty goal of pleasing a broad spectrum of users, Microsoft designed an interface that is intuitive without being intrusive. In addition to the usable interface, Windows 98 blurs the distinction between your home or office PC and other computers around the world. The Windows 98 operating environment incorporates the online world because the information you want is not always on your hard disk. Windows 98 helps you access the Internet as easily as you access the files on your own PC.

Figure 1.1 shows a typical Windows 98 screen that Windows 98 users might see. The Windows 98 screen is often called a *desktop*, which you will learn to manage just as you manage the desk at which you sit.

Just a Minute

> If you've used Windows 95, you will appreciate that Microsoft did not dramatically change the Windows 98 interface. Nevertheless, Microsoft did add considerable customization tools to Windows so that you can change the way the Windows 98 interface operates and looks, even making your desktop look much like a Web page.

The pictures on the background of the Windows 98 desktop are called *icons*. Figure 1.1 contains several icons along the left side of the screen. Icons also appear elsewhere throughout Windows 98, such as on the ribbon across the bottom of the desktop in Figure 1.1.

Caution

> Your Windows 98 screen might contain more or fewer icons than Figure 1.1's screen, depending on the way your version of Windows 98 is configured. For example, if your PC is connected to a computer network, you will see the icon labeled Network Neighborhood. In addition, you might see artwork in your Windows 98 desktop's background, as well as other windows, icons, and screen elements.

The artwork that forms the background for a Windows 98 screen is called *wallpaper*, which comes from a graphics file you can supply. In Hour 4, "Understanding the My Computer

Window," you will see how you can change or remove the wallpaper if you don't like the artwork on your desktop.

Figure 1.1.
The Windows 98 screen, like a clean desktop, is normally free of clutter.

Figure 1.2 shows the same Windows 98 desktop as before, except that the desktop contains a graphical wallpaper file to make things more interesting. In addition, notice a column of buttons at the right of the screen that gives you one-button access to popular Internet sites by using the *Internet Explorer Channel Bar*. The channel bar enables you to switch from Internet site to site by using a television's channel-button analogy.

Throughout this entire 24-hour tutorial, references will be made to *online services*, the *Internet*, *Web integration*, remote *computers*, and other terms that refer to you using your PC within the framework of an Internet connected environment. That Internet environment might come from a dedicated Internet connection at work, a modem at home, or another way you interact with the Internet community. If you don't use the Internet, that's okay. Windows 98 will not force you to do so. Windows 98 stands on its own as the best PC graphical environment on the market, and you don't have to be online to enjoy its benefits.

The Windows 98 screen acts like a desktop from which to work on your computer. If you want to write letters with a word processor, start the word processor program from the Windows 98 environment. Windows 98 always remains in the computer's memory to help you interact with your programs and with the computer hardware.

In ancient times (less than ten years ago!), people controlled computers by typing all kinds of cryptic commands to which the computer responded. MS-DOS is one such environment that requires typed, and sometimes difficult, commands. These commands take a long time to learn and are often difficult to remember.

Figure 1.2.
Wallpaper and online services can make your desktop less boring.

Computers controlled by graphical user interfaces, such as Windows 98, no longer require the tedium of typed commands. Windows 98 is extremely graphical in nature. Instead of typing a command that directs the computer to start a program, you use the mouse or keyboard to point to an icon on the screen to activate the matching program.

Microsoft developers proudly promote the effort they put into the Windows 98 interface. In designing Windows 98, Microsoft took people who had never before used a computer and placed them in front of other operating environments, such as previous versions of Windows, and asked the new users to perform certain tasks, such as starting game programs. As a result, Microsoft gained insight as to how people approach a visual environment. Windows 98 is the result of countless hours of this kind of usability testing.

If you are fairly new to computers, you might not understand why you would want to use Windows 98. Perhaps you've used a word processor or a spreadsheet but never have taken the time to learn about MS-DOS or find out what this Windows stuff is all about. Other newcomers to Windows 98 might have migrated to the PC world from a Macintosh, from Windows 3.1, or from a mainframe computer. In a nutshell, Windows 98 is all of the following:

- An operating system that manages your hardware and software interactions. Windows 98 provides uniform access to your system so that programs can more accurately use your system's resources (such as disks and printers).
- A graphical user interface that enables you to start programs, go online, and control hardware graphically.
- Total Web integration that blurs the distinction between the PC on your desk and the Internet.

- A Web-based desktop environment that complements or replaces your standard Windows 98 desktop. You can place Web pages right on your desktop instead of accessing the Internet solely from an Internet browser program. If you want help, you can search Windows 98 help files or access the Internet to locate a help topic—all from within your desktop environment (see Figure 1.3).

Figure 1.3.
The Windows help desk area searches both your PC and, optionally, the Internet to give you answers when you need assistance.

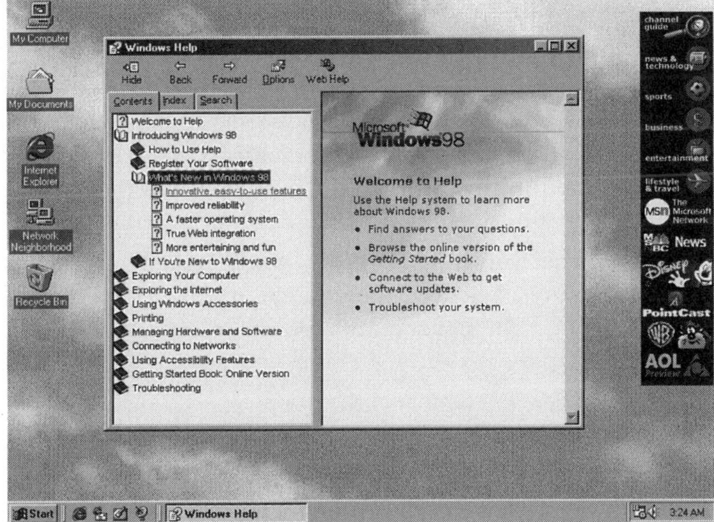

- A more efficient disk storage system called *FAT32* that makes your hard disks capable of holding almost twice as much as before.
- A *32-bit environment*, which means that Windows 98 utilizes your computer's internal architecture to its fullest, unlike Windows 3.1 and MS-DOS, which are only 16-bit environments. A 32-bit environment does not necessarily guarantee double-speed performance, but programs often run much faster than in 16-bit environments.
- A safer system security that protects against possible *virus programs* (programs that can destroy disk contents) and also keeps your system fine-tuned and running properly. With Internet access you will be able to do this without updating your Windows 98 system files, as Microsoft releases future enhancements.
- A network management system that helps seamlessly integrate a *network* (a wired connection to other computers) and the Internet into your work environment.

Possibly the single greatest reason to use Windows 98 is that: Microsoft designed Windows 98 so that you can concentrate on using your software and hardware—not so that you have to concentrate on using Windows 98 commands. As you'll see throughout this book, the keyboard and mouse complement each other to give you easy control over every aspect of Windows 98.

Mouse Around

The odds are good that you've used a mouse if you've used a computer before. Using the mouse involves following the mouse cursor around the screen. The *mouse cursor* is the pointing arrow that moves as you move your mouse. In Hour 4, "Understanding the My Computer Window," you learn how to change the mouse cursor shape from the arrow to something else.

Here's a quick review of the possible mouse actions you can perform:

- When you *move* the mouse, you physically move the mouse across your desk. (You might have a trackball, which remains stationary as you spin the trackball's sphere to move the cursor. Other mouse alternatives include touch pads that you point to and run your finger over to simulate mouse clicks and movements.) When you point to an object on the screen, you are moving the mouse to that object.
- When you click the mouse, you press and immediately release the left mouse button. To select graphical screen objects, you often click the left button. You use your right mouse button to display special pop-up menus. Hour 4 explains how to swap the left and right mouse button actions if you are left-handed.
- When you double-click, you press and immediately release the left or right mouse button twice in succession.
- When you drag screen objects with the mouse, you move the mouse cursor over an object that you want to move to another screen location. With the mouse cursor over the object, press and hold the left mouse button. The item under the mouse cursor is now temporarily welded to the mouse cursor. As you move the mouse (while still holding the mouse button), the screen object moves with the cursor. When you release the mouse button, Windows 98 anchors the object in the mouse cursor's new position. In Windows terminology, *drag and drop* refers to the action of moving a screen object (such as an icon) to a different location.

Just a Minute

> Later hours will teach you additional ways to use the mouse. For example, the mouse can help you create special links, called *shortcuts*, to programs you use often. In addition, you can use the mouse to copy objects, such as files, from one location to another.

You can almost always use the keyboard instead of the mouse to perform many Windows 98 operations. Using the mouse is often easier than using the keyboard for most operations. If you are uncomfortable using a mouse, don't fret—mouse actions soon become second nature.

1

If you've used Windows 95 or an earlier Windows version, you'll appreciate how Windows 98 enables you to use a single-click to select screen objects instead of the double-click so common in previous versions. Depending on your setup, you can even launch programs by resting the mouse over an icon without clicking at all! You learn how to add this one-click selection to Windows 98 objects in Hour 14.

First Things First

Windows 98 contains a complete native operating system (called the *kernel* because the operating system is the heart of everything you do on the computer), in addition to a graphical user interface. Except in rare cases in which someone configures his or her computer to run Windows 98 along with another version of Windows, Windows 98 starts automatically when you turn on your PC. Therefore, you don't have to learn how to start Windows 98; it automatically loads when you turn on your computer or *reboot* it (which means to reset the computer by using the Ctrl+Alt+Del keystroke sequence).

Just a Minute

To issue the Ctrl+Alt+Del key combination, press and hold down the keys sequentially: Press and hold down the Ctrl key, press and hold down the Alt key, and then press the Del key (you'll actually hold down all three keys). Release all three keys at once to begin the reboot process. A window appears, asking if you're sure and you must issue the reboot key sequence once more to activate the reboot. Unless your PC freezes completely, reboot sparingly. This lesson's final section explains how to shut down your PC properly.

Logging On

If you are not connected to a network, nothing in this section applies to you. Even if you access the Internet, you do not need to know this section's material if your computer is not part of a wired networking system. You may skip ahead to the next section entitled, "Welcome to Windows 98."

If your PC is connected to a network, you must log on to the network.

Task 1.1: Logging On to Windows 98

Step 1: Description

You will have to ask the person responsible for installing the networked Windows 98 on your PC for your username and password. After you receive the logon information, you can log on to the computer and access Windows 98. Figure 1.4 shows the logon screen that you might see if you are running in a networked computer environment.

Figure 1.4.
Network users must log on to Windows 98.

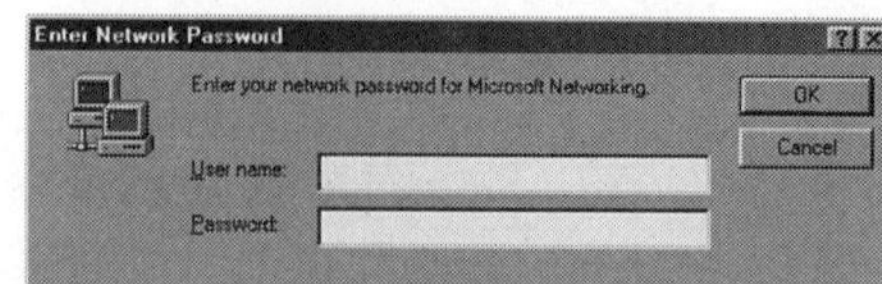

Step 2: Action

1. When you see the logon screen, type your username exactly as the System Administrator set it up. Often, your username is your full name or your first initial and last name.
2. Press the Tab key.
3. Type your password exactly as the System Administrator set it up. Asterisks appear in place of the actual password you type so that no one looking over your shoulder can read your password.
4. Press Enter to start Windows 98.

Step 3: Review

If you receive an error message, you must check with the System Administrator to make sure you are properly authorized to use the networked Windows 98. If this is the first time you or anyone else has logged on with your username, the initial password you enter will be the permanent password, unless you change the password later. Windows 98 requests that first password twice to be sure that you type the initial password exactly as it should be.

Just a Minute

By design, networks enable more than one user access to the same files. In other words, assuming that you have the proper electronic authorization, you can access files stored on any person's PC that is connected to your PC. The extra benefits that a network provides also require extra security precautions so that unauthorized users do not bother other people's files.

Your Network Administrator can set up different user profiles for each network user. A user profile defines your interface preferences and the file access you have. The Windows 98 interface is customizable, as you'll see throughout this book. When you log on, your custom interface—such as a particular desktop wallpaper you prefer—appears. If another user uses your computer, that user's profile determines that user's interface design.

You can change your password by double-clicking the Windows 98 Control Panel's Password icon and entering your current and new password. If you need further help with the Control Panel, turn to Hour 4.

Take a Windows 98 Tour

Windows 98 is helpful. In fact, Windows 98 is so helpful you can launch a Windows 98 introduction video right from your desktop!

Double-click the icon labeled, `Welcome to Windows`. The video starts when you first start Windows 98 unless you or someone else has removed the video from the Windows 98 Startup folder. If the video tour does not begin automatically, you should see the Welcome to Windows 98 icon on your Windows desktop. A multimedia tour begins with sound and video. Figure 1.5 shows a shot of the Welcome to Windows video. The tour enables you to register your copy of Windows 98 online, fine-tune your system, and read release notes for the product.

Figure 1.5.
Watch the video tour to see what Windows 98 can do.

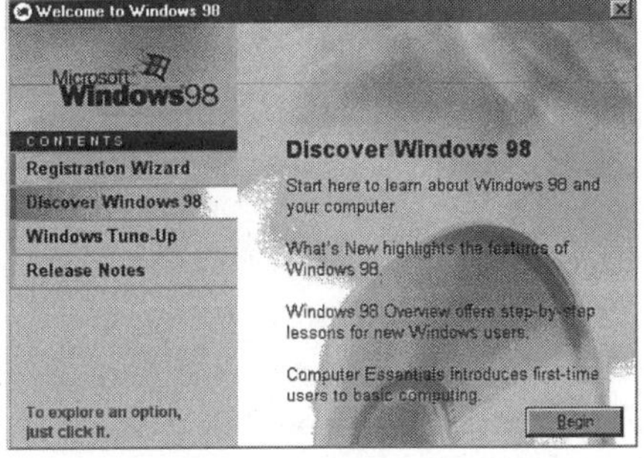

CAUTION

If you do not see the `Welcome to Windows` desktop icon, you must start the video tour another way. Before you finish this lesson, you'll be able to use the Windows 98 menu to start the tour from the Windows 98 menu system. The video is named *Tips and Tour*, and it's located on the Accessories menu. Return to this section to start the tour after you learn how to access the Windows 98 menu.

TIME SAVER

If you have not registered Windows 98, register now to receive updates and information on future enhancements. If you have Internet access, register online from the video tour's opening menu. If you don't register online, send the registration card that came with your new PC or Windows 98 to Microsoft.

Command Controls

As you work with Windows 98, you'll see all kinds of windows appear and disappear. A Window such as the one shown in Figure 1.6 is sometimes called a *dialog box*. Dialog boxes contain various *controls* with which to manage Windows 98. These controls can be *command buttons* that you click with your mouse to start or cancel a task; *check boxes* with a check mark, indicating an item you selected by clicking the mouse over the box; and *option buttons* that you select from a choice of options. Some dialog boxes contain multiple tabbed pages so that you can read and select from two or more pages of controls within the same dialog box.

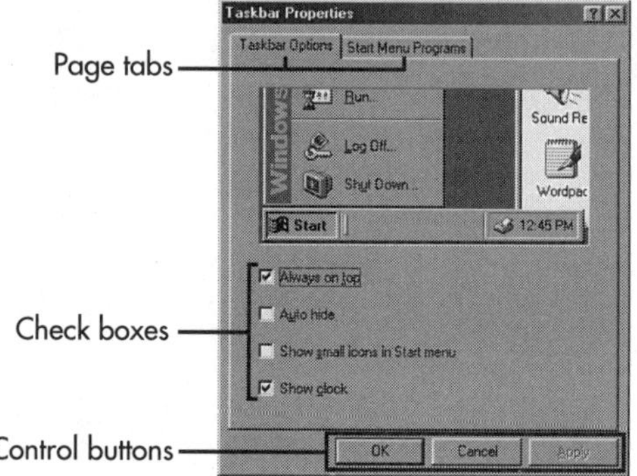

Figure 1.6.
Dialog box windows often contain several controls that select options and determine behavior.

Figure 1.6 shows a dialog box called the *Taskbar Properties* dialog box. You learn all about the taskbar in the next section. For now, concentrate on the various controls you see in the dialog box. Although you can use your keyboard to select any control, pointing and clicking your mouse is often much easier.

There are three ways to select an onscreen command button:

1. Click the button with the mouse.
2. Press Tab to highlight the buttons in succession. Shift+Tab moves backward. You will know that a button is highlighted when a dotted outline appears around the button's caption. Moving the highlight between onscreen controls is called *changing the focus*. As soon as the focus (the dotted highlight) appears on the button you want to select, press Enter to activate that button.
3. Press Alt plus the underlined letter on the button's caption. This combined keystroke is called a *hotkey*. Figure 1.6 contains only one command button with such a hotkey— the Apply key. You can select the Apply command button by pressing Alt+A.

Figure 1.6 contains four check boxes at the left of the dialog box. Certain windows need check boxes to indicate a yes or no possibility.

There are three ways to check (or uncheck) a check box:

1. Click either the check box or the message next to the check box with the mouse.

2. Move the focus to the check box text (by pressing Tab or Shift+Tab) and press Enter.
3. Press Alt plus the hotkey of the check box's message.

In Hour 2, "Tour Windows 98 Now," you will learn how to leave a window without completely closing the window; it will be out of your way, but you will be able to return to it whenever you want.

Save Before You Quit

You are probably anxious to get started, but before you learn more about using Windows 98, you must learn how to quit Windows 98 properly. Due to the integration of Windows 98 and your computer's hardware and software, you must take a few extra steps when quitting your Windows 98 session and turning off your computer.

CAUTION

If you do not properly shut down Windows 98, you can lose work that you just completed. At the worst, you can damage a Windows 98 configuration file and cause problems for Windows 98 the next time you start your PC.

Surely you've noticed the button in the lower-left corner of the Windows 98 screen labeled Start. This area of the screen is known as the *taskbar*, and this button is called the *Start button*. The taskbar is perhaps the most important element in Windows 98 because you'll use it to launch and switch between running programs. Windows 98 *multitasks*, which means you can run more than one program at the same time. In other words, you can download a file from another computer, print a spreadsheet, listen to an opera on an audio CD, and type with a word processor, all at the same time. The taskbar lists each program currently running. Figure 1.7 shows a taskbar that lists two programs and the My Computer window in memory at the same time.

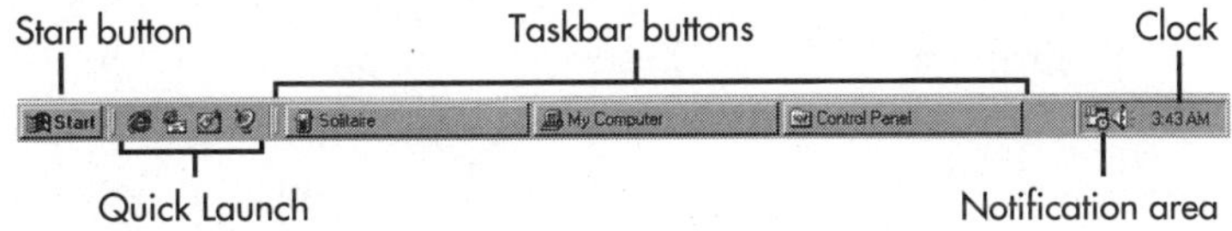

Figure 1.7.
The taskbar lists every program running.

TIME SAVER

Think of the taskbar as a television channel changer. On a television, there are several channels with programs going at the same time; you can switch between the channels by using the remote control. When you run more than one Windows 98 program, you can switch among the programs by clicking the program buttons in the taskbar.

The taskbar does more than list and manage running programs—it is the starting point for just about everything you do in Windows 98. If you want to rearrange files, start programs, change screen colors, modify the mouse, or view the contents of files, the taskbar contains the power to do all those things. In addition, you can add tools to the taskbar that enable you to traverse recently surfed web sites, bring up documents you recently edited, as well as more powerful controls called *ActiveX* controls (miniature programs that can run outside a window to help you work) such as stock tickers that scroll across your taskbar. The taskbar is the launch pad for just about everything you'll want to do in Windows 98.

The taskbar also contains the commands you need to shut down Windows 98 and your computer. In Hour 3, "Take Windows 98 to Task," you'll delve much more deeply into the operations of the taskbar. At this point though, you will learn just enough to master the Windows 98 shutdown process because without the proper shutdown, you face the risky consequences of data loss, as you learned at the start of this section.

TIME SAVER

Place the mouse cursor over the Start button, but do not click the mouse button. After a brief pause, Windows 98 displays a small *ToolTip* caption box next to the mouse cursor that reads, "Click here to begin." If you are unsure as to what a Windows 98 button does, move the mouse cursor over the button and wait a moment.

When you click the Start button on the taskbar, the Start menu pops up, as shown in Figure 1.8. The Start menu gives you access to every part of your computer. Table 1.1 describes what each option of the Start menu does. From the Start menu, you can start programs, check disk space, manage files, and properly shut down the computer. You might also add additional programs at the top of the taskbar to launch those programs more quickly. For now, you should master how to shut down your PC.

Table 1.1. Common Start menu commands

Command	Description
Programs	Displays lists of program groups and names that you can run.
Favorites	Displays a list of your stored favorite locations. Those locations might be files on your PC, files on a networked PC, or Web pages.
Documents	Displays a list of documents, or data files, that you've recently opened and might want to return to. Windows 98 works from a data-driven viewpoint and enables you to work on your data without worrying about tedious program-starting details. Selecting a document, no matter which program created that

1

Command	Description
	document, launches the program and loads that data document into the program.
Settings	Enables you to change the configuration of Windows 98.
Find	Enables you to search your PC's and other computer files for specific data.
Help	Provides online help for the various tasks you can perform in Windows 98.
Run	Gives you the ability to execute programs or open program group folders if you know the proper MS-DOS commands.
Log Off User	If you work in a multi-user environment, you and others can log on to Windows 98, and Windows 98 behaves the way you set up in your personal profile. Some Windows 98 Start menus do not contain a Log Off User option.
Shut Down	Enables you to safely shut down your computer without losing data that you might otherwise lose if you did not shut down properly.

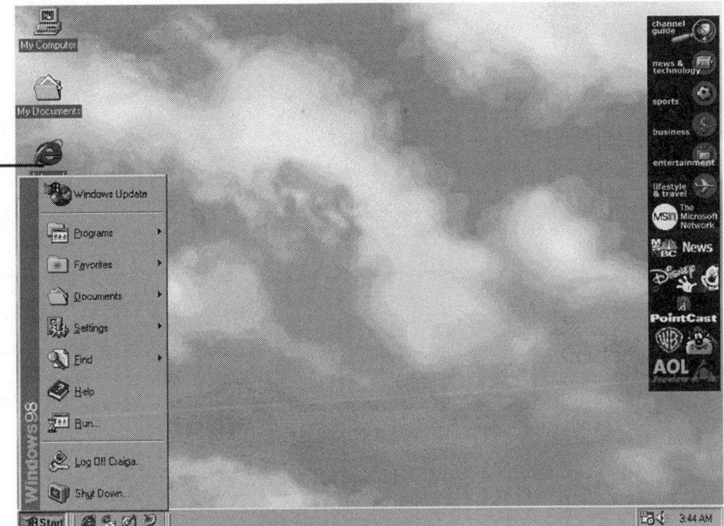

Figure 1.8.
The Start menu is the command center for the rest of Windows 98.

You can add programs here

Although you can select the various Start menu commands, please understand that the most important command on the start menu is the Shut Down command. Before you do too much, even before you really master the ins and outs of the Start menu, you should read the rest of this section to learn how to shut down your computer safely. You don't want to write the first chapter of a best-selling novel only to find that Windows 98 sent the chapter into oblivion because you did not shut down the computer properly before turning off the power.

Just a Minute

Actually, the data on your computer is fairly safe in most cases. If you do not shut down the computer properly, you probably won't lose any data 99 times out of 100. Why take the chance, though? Shut Down is quick and easy to use and ensures that all data and Windows 98 settings are safely recorded so that you can turn off the computer without the worry of data loss.

Windows Minute

Activating Menu Commands

Windows 98 menus list various options and commands available to you at the time. When confronted with a menu, such as the Start menu, there are several ways you can select the item you want.

You can point to an item on the menu with the mouse. As you move the mouse cursor over the menu items, a highlight follows the mouse cursor through the menu, clearly showing you which menu item the mouse cursor is over. If your hands are on the keyboard when you display a menu, you can press the up and down arrow keys to move the highlight through the menu's commands.

Some menu commands, such as the Shut Down command, contain ellipses (...) to the right of the command name. The ellipses indicate that if you choose this command, a dialog box appears, requiring additional information.

Just a Minute

If a menu does not fit within the screen boundaries, Windows 98 adds up and down arrows to each end of the menu. Click the arrows to see the menu items that appear offscreen.

Some menu commands, such as the Start menu's Programs and Documents commands, display arrows to the right of the command names. The arrows indicate that other command menus appear if you select from those commands. Sometimes Windows 98 menu commands *cascade* (trigger additional menus, often called *submenus*) several levels deep, such as the one shown in Figure 1.9. You can decrease the cascade, removing one or more of the extra cascaded menu levels, by moving the mouse one menu to the left or by pressing the Esc key. (Esc always removes the current menu.)

Figure 1.9.
Some menus trigger other menus, producing a cascaded menu look.

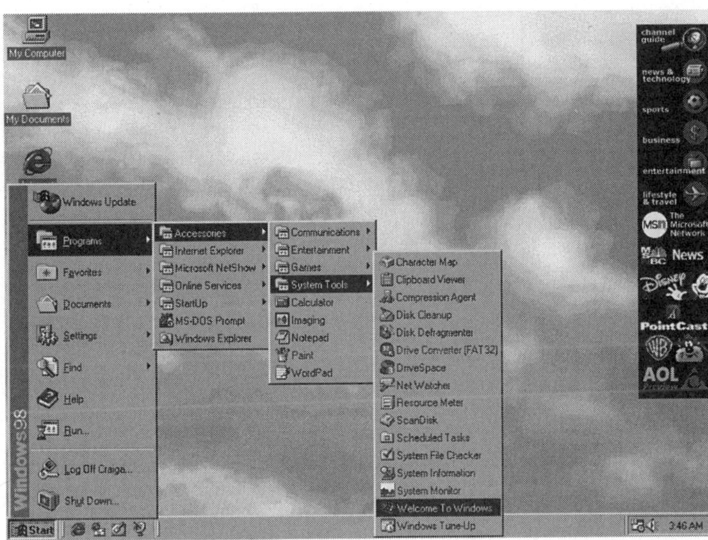

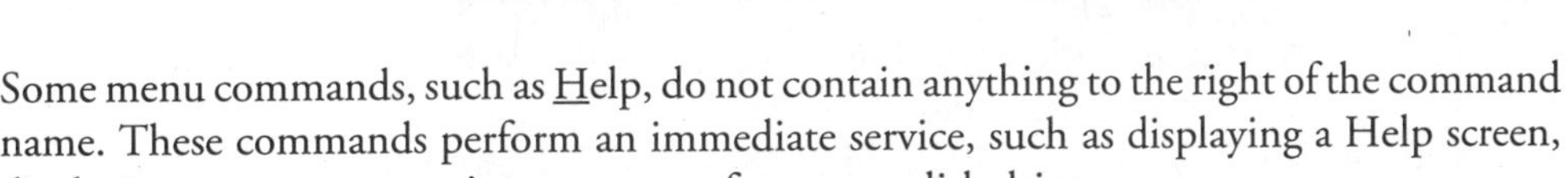

Some menu commands, such as Help, do not contain anything to the right of the command name. These commands perform an immediate service, such as displaying a Help screen, displaying a menu, or starting a program from your disk drive.

If a menu command contains an underlined letter, such as Help, you can select that menu command by pressing Alt plus the letter. Alt+H is the hotkey that activates the Help menu command.

If you explore a bit and display a cascaded menu or select another command from the Start menu, press Esc until the Start menu disappears, and the Start button returns to normal. As mentioned earlier, this is an important time to learn about the Shut Down command.

Press the Start button once again and select the Shut Down command. The ellipses after the words Shut Down indicate that a dialog box window will appear. Figure 1.10 shows the resulting Shut Down window. There is more than one way to shut down your computer, however, depending on your current need. In addition, your Shut Down menu might contain more or fewer options depending on your PC's configuration.

Figure 1.10.
You must decide how you want to shut down the computer.

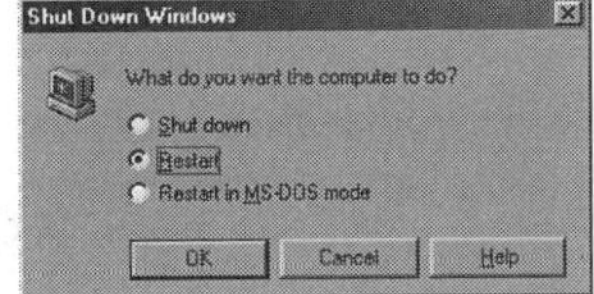

Shut Down Options

The Shut Down window demonstrates the use of option button controls. A dot inside one of the option buttons indicates that this option is the selected option. When you first display the Shut Down window, the option, "Shut down" is the selected option. If you were to select another option, Windows 98 would deselect the first option, thereby ensuring that only one is active at any one time.

Here are three ways to select an option from a list of option button choices:

- Point to one of the options with the mouse and click the mouse button.
- Use the keyboard's up and down arrow keys to move the focus (the focus's dotted line surrounds the selected option button) among the selections.
- Press Alt plus the underlined letter of the option you want to select. For example, Alt+R is the hotkey sequence for "Restart."

Simply selecting an option does not trigger any action. After you select the desired option, you must activate the OK command button to execute that option's command. If you choose Cancel, Windows 98 removes the Shut Down window and returns you to the Windows 98 environment. If you push the Help command button, Windows 98 displays online help that describes the options in more detail.

If you want to restart Windows 98 without rebooting your PC, hold down a Shift key when you select the Restart option. Continue holding Shift until you see the message, `Restarting Windows 98`. Windows 98 will restart, but your computer won't go through the time-consuming power-up reboot and memory test.

Table 1.2 describes the four shut down options. Most of the time, you will select the first one because you are turning off the computer. When you select the first option, Windows 98 pauses briefly and then displays a message telling you that you can turn off the computer's power. Select the first option now. Select the first option button and click the Yes button to initiate the shut down.

When you see command buttons, Windows 98 highlights one of them by darkening the button's edges, as shown on the OK button in Figure 1.10. If you press Enter, Windows 98 activates the OK button for you. As a shortcut to using Windows 98 and command buttons, you can always

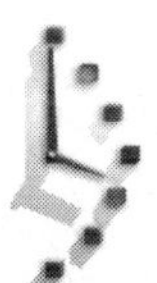

press Enter to trigger the activation of the highlighted button instead of using the mouse or keyboard to find and press that same button. The highlighted button is known as the *default button* because that's the button Windows 98 selects if you don't click another button before pressing Enter.

Table 1.2. The Shut Down Commands and Their Descriptions

Command	Description
Stand by	Powers down everything but enough electrical current to keep the memory intact. Laptop users can quickly return to their previous computing session from a standby mode. You can restart Windows 98 quickly from the standby state without the time-consuming Windows 98 reload required if you shut down completely.
Shut down	Writes all unsaved information to disk and prepares Windows 98 so you can turn off your PC. If your hardware supports the feature, your PC can power down automatically when you select the Shut Down option.
Restart	Performs a shut down but then reboots the computer for you. Sometimes, you will be instructed to restart Windows 98 after installing a new program or after changing a Windows 98 option.
Restart in MS-DOS	Performs a shut down but then restarts the computer in MS-DOS mode without putting you directly into Windows 98. Only those users who understand MS-DOS commands would want to use this command. Some games require the MS-DOS mode. From the MS-DOS mode, you can type the word **exit** to leave MS-DOS and enter Windows 98.

JUST A MINUTE

If you see a Hibernate option, Windows 98 saves everything to disk and powers off your PC. When you power back on, whatever programs you were running will still be active. Some laptops automatically enter the hibernate mode when you shut down their screens and, for those, you have no need to shut down before closing the screen. Hibernate only appears if you request the option in the Control Panel's Power Management section. You will learn about the Control Panel in Hour 4.

You might have to develop the habit of shutting down Windows 98 properly before turning off the computer. Perhaps you can stick a note to the computer's on/off switch until you get used to running the Shut Down command. Again, the Shut Down command is cheap insurance against data loss, and the Shut Down habit is a good one to develop.

Ten Good Reasons to Switch to Windows 98

Still not convinced that you want to move to Windows 98? Here are ten good reasons to make the switch:

- Windows 98 is faster than previous Windows versions. Windows 98 requires fewer keystrokes and mouse clicks to get work done. Most applications run faster, as well.
- Windows 98 includes an *active desktop* that blurs the distinction between your desktop PC and an Internet connection. You can place virtually anything on the Windows 98 desktop, including Web pages, ActiveX controls, and *push content* (Web content you've requested to be sent to your browser).
- Windows 98 includes support for broadcast television! Why not watch a tennis match while crunching numbers for the accounting department upstairs?
- Windows 98 contains integrated networking capabilities if you work in a networked environment. As a matter of fact, for those on a budget, Windows 98 offers a direct-connect pseudo-networking feature that enables you to connect two PCs together with just a serial or printer cable.
- Windows 98 includes Internet Explorer 4.0, which vastly improves the way you surf the Web.
- You will not have to match switch settings or worry about those pesky things called DMAs and IRQs when installing new hardware. With its *Plug and Play* feature, Windows 98 detects when you add or change hardware and adjusts all the computer's settings automatically. (Not all hardware is approved for Plug and Play compatibility.)
- Windows 98 has the capability to detect when you insert a CD-ROM in the drive and start (or install) the software stored on the CD-ROM. This AutoPlay feature eliminates the need for users to issue start-up instructions when they want to run a program from a CD-ROM. In addition, other areas of multimedia are more integrated into Windows 98 than before. For example, you can place a volume control at the bottom of the screen to control the speaker volume for audio playback of CDs.

- Windows 98 utilizes the right-hand button on your mouse. Clicking the right-button pops up a context-sensitive menu that gives you instant access to common tasks you might want to perform.
- Windows 98 automatically upgrades itself. When Microsoft releases a bug fix or Windows update, Windows 98 logs on to the Internet and takes care of updating itself when you request the update.
- Perhaps the most important improvement are Windows 98's cleanup and fine-tuning wizards that keep your system working at its fastest automatically.

Summary

You are off to a great start! It's time to push your own Start button, gear up your mind's memory chips, and begin exploring Windows 98 to learn what it can do for you. Over the next 23 hours of study and tutorial, you will master the Windows 98 environment and learn many shortcuts.

Keep in mind that Windows 98 is not an end in itself. The application programs that you want to run are the most important parts of using your computer. It is Windows 98's job to help you work with your applications as painlessly as possible.

Q&A

Q When will I have to log on to Windows 98?

A If your computer is connected to a network, chances are good that you will have to log on before you can use Windows 98. In a network environment, computers have connections to each other so users have physical access to other people's files. By delegating usernames and passwords, the system administrator assigns protection and privileges to all users on the system.

Q Why do asterisks appear when I enter my network password?

A Asterisks appear in place of the actual characters that you type so that someone looking over your shoulder cannot steal your password.

Q What happens if I do not use the Shut Down procedures for my computer?

A If you do not shut down your computer before turning off the power, you can lose data files or even system configuration files. Most of the time, you probably will be okay if you do not shut down the computer properly, but your data is worth too much not to get into the habit of properly shutting down the system and safely storing all data.

Workshop

Key Terms

Please review the following list of terms:

- ☐ *ActiveX controls* Small embedded programs that appear in Web pages.
- ☐ *AutoPlay* The Windows 98 feature that starts the loading and execution of CD-ROMs as soon as you place the CD-ROM in your computer's CD-ROM drive.
- ☐ *check box* A Windows 98 control that appears next to each item in a list that you use to select one or more items from the list.
- ☐ *command button* A Windows 98 control that appears and acts like a push button on the screen.
- ☐ *cursor* A pointing device, such as the arrow that represents the mouse pointer location and the insert bar that represents the Windows 98 text location. The cursor moves across the screen as you type or move the mouse.
- ☐ *desktop* The Windows 98 screen and background.
- ☐ *dialog box* A window containing text and one or more screen controls that you use to issue instructions to Windows 98.
- ☐ *disk operating system* The program inside memory that controls all the hardware and software interactions.
- ☐ *focus* The highlighted command button or control in a dialog box that Windows 98 automatically selects when you press enter.
- ☐ *hotkey* The combination of an Alt keypress combined with another key that selects command buttons. The key you press with Alt is displayed with an underlined letter.
- ☐ *icons* Small pictures that represent commands and programs in Windows 98.
- ☐ *kernel* The internal native operating system that controls the hardware and software interaction.
- ☐ *log on* The process that enables you to gain access to a networked computer.
- ☐ *multitasking* The process of a computer that is running more than one program at the same time.
- ☐ *option buttons* A Windows 98 control that appears next to each item in a list that you use to select one and only one item from the list.
- ☐ *Plug and Play* The feature that detects and automatically configures the operating system to match new hardware that you install in your computer system.
- ☐ *Push content* Information you've requested to be sent to your Web browser.

1

- *reboot* The process of restarting your computer through the keyboard (by pressing Alt+Ctrl+Del).
- *Start button* The button at the left of the taskbar that displays the Windows 98 cascading menu of choices. When you click the Start button, the Windows 98 Start menu appears.
- *Start menu* A Windows 98 system and program menu that appears when you click the taskbar's Start button.
- *System Administrator* The person in charge of assigning usernames and setting up new users on networked environments.
- *taskbar* The bar at the bottom of a Windows 98 screen where running program icons appear along with the system clock.
- *ToolTips* Popup messages that describe buttons under the mouse cursor.
- *user profile* The customized interface and file-access rules setup for each networked user.
- *wallpaper* The background graphics that appear on the Windows 98 desktop.

PART I

Hour 2

Tour Windows 98 Now

In this hour, you are going to learn a lot about the Windows 98 interface and become comfortable with managing windows and icons.

To help you learn the Windows 98 interface, you will follow along with several practice examples in this hour. The coverage is so complete that some people who have used Windows for years might not know more than you'll learn in these pages. This hour's techniques will help you manage almost every aspect of Windows 98 that you will work with in the future. In other words, after you master the basics of the window and screen management tools, you'll use those abilities in all your Windows 98 applications work.

The highlights of this hour include the following:

- Why windows management is important
- What the parts of a window are called
- How to resize and move windows
- When the System menu is useful
- How to change the appearance and behavior of windows and toolbars

Just a Minute

Windows appear all over the place when you work with Windows 98—that's why it's called Windows! Therefore, learning proper windows management now will reap big-time savings and reduce confusion in the future.

I Do Do Windows!

The first window that you will work with is called the My Computer window. This lesson focuses on managing the window, whereas Hour 4, "Understanding the My Computer Window," explains how to use the contents of the My Computer window. First, locate the My Computer icon on your Windows 98 desktop. Double-click the icon to open the My Computer window. Most icons on the desktop open to windows when you double-click them, as you'll see throughout this book. Some icons produce program windows, whereas others produce windows from which you select additional items.

Figure 2.1 shows the My Computer window with all its control buttons and window components labeled. You will find this same window structure in almost every window that you open, as well as in applications that you run, such as a database program. Although you saw simpler windows (dialog boxes) in the previous hour, the window in Figure 2.1 is more typical of the windows with which you will work.

Figure 2.1.
Use a window's controls and menus to manage the window.

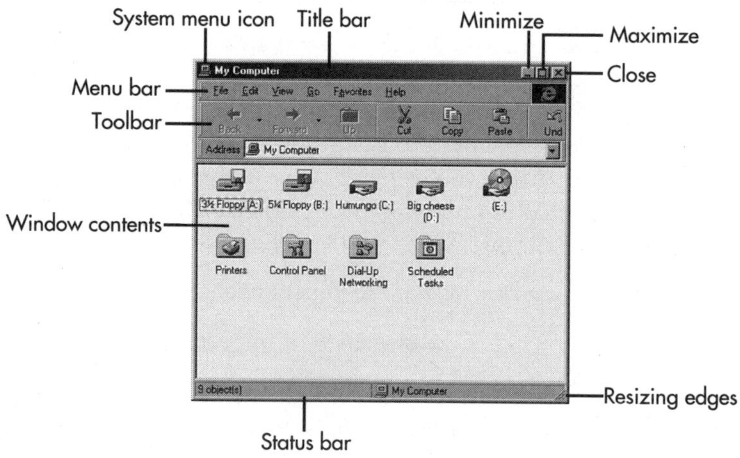

Time Saver

Tooltips appear throughout Windows 98. For example, if you rest the mouse over a window's Close button, the Close Tooltip description appears.

Familiarize yourself with the buttons and window sections pointed out in Figure 2.1 because almost every window contains these window controls or a subset of them. If you've worked with previous Windows versions, notice that the toolbar is new to Windows 98. Here are some of the more general things you can do with such a window on the screen:

- *Minimize* the window down to an icon on the taskbar, eliminating the window from the screen, while keeping it active.
- *Maximize* a minimized window to partial- or full-screen size.
- Move a window from one location to another on the screen.
- Bring a window to the top of a stack of windows so that you can work within that window. (Due to Windows 98 multitasking capability, hidden windows can still perform data processing, such as calculating and printing.)
- Display different contents in the window by selecting a new address from the toolbar's Address field. If you display new window contents, you can click the back toolbar button to return to the window's previous contents.
- Drag items, with the mouse, from one window to another or to a different location within the same window.
- Close a window completely, removing its icon from the taskbar and stopping the application that is running inside the window.

You can have one or more windows on your screen, some overlapping other windows, some completely covering others, and you will sometimes see windows side by side or above others. In a typical Windows 98 user's day, the user might have two or more applications running at the same time. Each of those applications might display one or more windows of its own.

You must learn how to manage windows if you want to be as productive as possible. Don't jump to the conclusion, though, that multiple windows result in confusion. On a typical desk, even the desks of the most organized people (the author not being one of them!), you'll find all sorts of paper stacks, and those stacks don't imply disorganization. The desk's user simply has to know how to organize the stacks and bring the most important stacks to the forefront when he or she wants to work on them. It is the same with Windows 98.

JUST A MINUTE

When you start a program or open a window, the taskbar gets a new button with the name of that program or window appearing on the taskbar button.

Some applications display single windows. Other applications might display multiple windows. For example, there are word processors that can display two documents side by side in two different windows.

Minimizing Windows

If you temporarily finish working with a window, you can minimize that window by pressing the window's Minimize button. Minimizing a window keeps the program in the window loaded and active but puts it out of the way until you are ready to return to that program again. Even if you minimize a window, the window's icon and description remain on the taskbar at the bottom of the screen. The taskbar continues to hold the application's button until you completely close the application.

To Do

Task 2.1: Minimizing a Window

Step 1: Description

The Minimize button clears the window from your desktop. The program running inside the window is still loaded and active, but the program no longer takes up screen space. The taskbar continues to list the it because it is still active. Double-click your My Computer window to follow this task's steps.

Step 2: Action

1. Find the Minimize button on your My Computer window.
2. Click the button. Look closely at the screen as you minimize the window. Notice that Windows 98 graphically and quickly shrinks the outer edges of the window down into the taskbar button labeled My Computer.

Step 3: Review

When you minimize a window, whatever window or icon behind it appears. Remember that a window is active when its icon and description still appear on the taskbar, as shown in Figure 2.2.

Figure 2.2.
The window's taskbar button still appears after you minimize a window.

The taskbar button in Figure 2.2 contains the caption My Computer because the minimized window's title bar contained the title My Computer. The taskbar button usually contains the same title listed in the application's title bar.

Just a Minute

Some window titles are too long for Windows 98 to fit the entire title in the taskbar's button. Depending on the length of the title and the number of items in the taskbar, the taskbar may only show the first few letters of a window's title followed by an ellipsis.

2

TIME SAVER

Click the taskbar's Show Desktop icon to minimize *all* open windows at once and return to the Windows 98 desktop screen.

Enlarging Windows

Windows 98 supplies several ways to enlarge a window. You can enlarge a minimized window from its taskbar status to the window's regular size. You can also maximize a window that's already showing, to take up the entire screen space. You can alter the size of a window by doing one of the following:

- Click the window's taskbar button when the window is minimized.
- Click the window's Maximize button to enlarge the window to full screen (the Maximize button changes to a Restore button as soon as you maximize a window).
- Drag one of the window's corners or edges outward to increase the size of the window or inward to shrink the size of the window manually.

The next task discusses the first two window enlarging methods that utilize buttons, and the next task explains how to enlarge a window manually.

To Do

Task 2.2: Restoring a Minimized Window

Step 1: Description

Use the taskbar buttons to display minimized windows. In other words, if you have one or more minimized windows and want to work with one of those window's programs, click the matching taskbar button, and the window reappears at its original size before you minimized the window.

Step 2: Action

1. Click the My Computer taskbar button. The My Computer window reappears.
2. Notice how the window quickly and visually grows from the taskbar back to its original size? Perhaps you want to see that again. Minimize the now enlarged My Computer window once again to shrink the window down into the taskbar.
3. Click the My Computer taskbar button and watch the window return to its original and enlarged state.

Step 3: Review

The taskbar lists windows that represent all running programs. Some of those programs might have their windows showing on the screen; other programs are minimized so that they take no screen space but are still loaded. Clicking a taskbar button causes a minimized window to return to its original size.

Just a Minute

> Not all taskbar icons are open windows. The taskbar also contains the Show Desktop button and, often, Internet-related buttons. If you click the taskbar button of a window that's open, Windows 98 minimizes that window.

To Do

Task 2.3: Maximizing a Window

Step 1: Description

As long as a window contains a Maximize button, you can maximize that window to the screen's full size. (Some windows are designed to be no larger or smaller than a preset size; these windows have Maximize or Minimize buttons that are disabled, indicated by grayed-out buttons.) When you want to dedicate the entire screen to a window, you can usually maximize the window by clicking the window's Maximize button.

Time Saver

> You also can maximize a window by double-clicking the window's title bar. Double-click once again, and the window returns to its previous size.

Step 2: Action

1. Click the My Computer window's Maximize button. The window grows to consume the entire screen. Figure 2.3 shows what you will see when you click the My Computer window's Maximize button. The My Computer window does not contain many items, so maximizing it is not very beneficial other than for this practice. The more a window contains, the larger you will want to make that window so that you can see contents that might not fit in a non-maximized window.

   There is no need for Windows 98 to keep a Maximize button on a window that's already maximized; thus, the Restore button takes the Maximize button's place when maximized. The Restore button always restores the window to the size it measured before you maximized it.
2. Click the My Computer window's Restore button. The window resizes (down) to its original size. As soon as you restore the window's size, you will see that the Restore button switches back to a Maximize button once again.
3. This time, double-click the My Computer window's title bar (point the mouse anywhere over the title in the window's title bar before double-clicking). Double-clicking the title bar maximizes a window just as pressing the Maximize button does.
4. Restore the My Computer window's original size again by clicking the Restore button.

2

Figure 2.3.
A maximized window fills the entire screen.

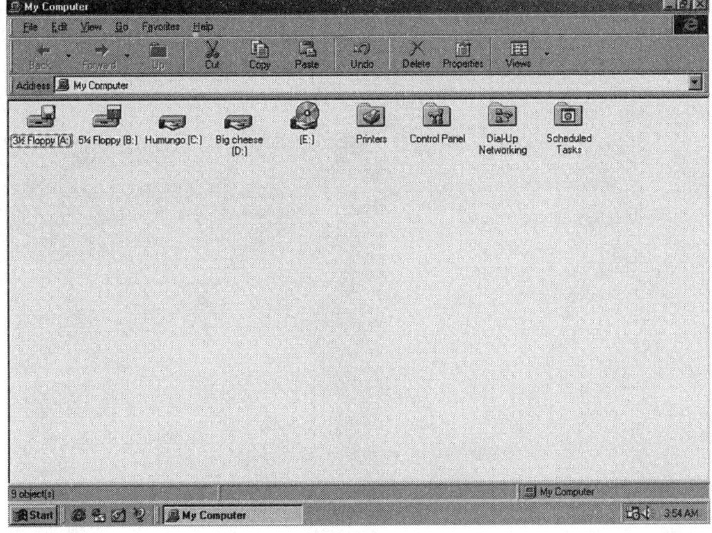

Step 3: Review

You will often want to maximize a window if you are doing a lot of work within that window's program. For example, most word processor users maximize the word processing window while typing a document so that more screen real estate goes to that document and, therefore, more of it appears on the screen at one time.

Time Saver

If you have loaded several programs and one program's window is covering up another program, you can click the hidden program's taskbar button to bring that covered window to the top of the window stack and into view.

Manually Changing Window Sizes

This section shows you how you can resize a window by dragging the mouse.

When you point to any window's edge or corner, the mouse cursor changes from its default shape (the pointing arrow) to a bidirectional arrow. The bidirectional arrow indicates that you are at one of the edges of the window and that you can drag that edge or corner inward or outward to change the size of the window.

When you drag one of the four straight edges, the window grows or shrinks left, right, up, or down. When you drag one of the four window corners, the window grows or shrinks in both height and width in the direction of the cursor's bidirectional diagonal shape.

Task 2.4: Manually Resizing a Window

Step 1: Description

Figure 2.4 shows the My Computer window after it is expanded down and to the right. In this task, you duplicate the figure's window size by manually enlarging your own My Computer window's size.

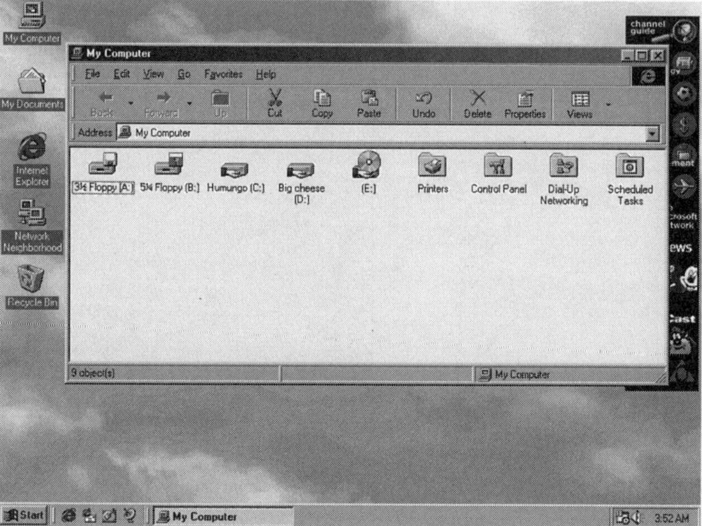

Figure 2.4.
You can manually enlarge a window with the mouse.

Step 2: Action

1. Point to the right edge of the My Computer window. Notice that the cursor changes to a horizontal bidirectional arrow. The horizontal arrow indicates that you can manually resize the window by dragging the right edge inward or outward.
2. Now point to the lower-right corner of your My Computer window. Notice that the cursor changes to a diagonal, bidirectional arrow.
3. Drag the corner down (be sure that the cursor is a diagonal bidirectional arrow before pressing the mouse button) and to the right until your My Computer window is approximately the same size as Figure 2.4. Release the mouse button when the window obtains the desired size.

Step 3: Review

When you touch the corner of the window, the mouse cursor's shape changes to a bidirectional arrow that indicates manual resizing is now available. When the bidirectional arrow appears, you can drag the mouse left, right, up, down, or diagonally to move that edge or corner of the window and resize the window.

Just a Minute

Some windows enlarge or shrink only to dimensions pre-set by the window's programmers. Therefore you will not be able to resize every window that appears on your monitor.

Moving Windows

The windows that appear on your Windows 98 desktop don't always appear in the location you want. That's okay. By using the mouse, you can easily drag a window to another location on the screen. The title bar acts like a handle for the window—to move the window, you drag the window's title bar.

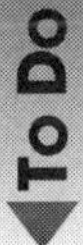

Task 2.5: Moving a Window

Step 1: Description

Sometimes, you need to rearrange the windows on your screen so that they form a more logical appearance as you work. To move a window, drag its title bar. As you move the window by dragging the title bar, an outline of the window follows the mouse. When you release the mouse button, the window appears in the new location.

Time Saver

When you run multiple programs at the same time, monitors measuring 17 inches diagonally and larger make window management easier. The bigger size enables you to read the text in multiple windows more easily. Although you can work in high-resolution graphics comfortably from a 15-inch monitor, a 17-inch monitor gives you more viewing room and enables Windows 98 to display more text at one time inside a window.

Step 2: Action

1. Move the My Computer window by dragging the title bar and moving the mouse. The window moves with the mouse.
2. Release the mouse button to end the dragging session and anchor the window in its new location.
3. Move the window once again. Move the window off the edge of the screen. As you can see, when you move a window over the screen's edge, Windows 98 clips (chops off) a portion of the window. When you move the window back into full view, it reappears in its entirety.

Step 3: Review

Any time your screen's window arrangement is inappropriate, move one or more open windows to different locations.

Closing a Window

Windows 98 is obviously full of windows that contain executing programs that work with data values of all kinds. This windowed concept gives you a flexible and manageable way to run and control several programs at once.

When you're finished with an open window you must close the window. Closing a window eliminates the window from view, and if that window contained a running program (as most do), that program will cease executing. The window's taskbar button will no longer appear on the taskbar.

CAUTION

> Remember that closing a window differs from minimizing the window. Closing a window stops a program; minimizing a window keeps it running in the background and on the taskbar.

If you open a window from an icon, as you did when you first opened the My Computer window, closing the window eliminates it from your desktop area, but the icon remains on the screen in its original place. Unless you take some advanced steps to erase the icon and its contents, it remains on your Windows 98 desktop area whether the corresponding window is open or closed.

TIME SAVER

> You can rearrange icons on your screen by dragging them with the mouse just as you rearrange windows. In addition, if you right-click over your desktop and select Arrange Icons, a pop-up menu appears that enables you to select the order of your desktop icons (alphabetically, by type, size, date, or automatic arrangement).

Keep in mind that some windows contain running programs (such as the window you see when typing in a word processor program), while other windows contain icons and even more windows (such as the My Computer window). You can close both types of windows by clicking the Close button. When running a program, you also can close its primary window and terminate the entire program by double-clicking the program's icon in the upper-left corner of the window or by selecting File | Exit (for programs) or File | Close (for windows) from the program's menu.

When you double-click a folder icon inside a window such as the My Computer window, more folders or windows of icons appear. Folders often represent directories on your disk.

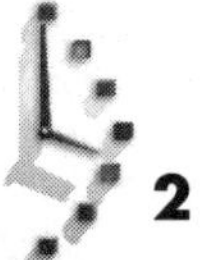

Task 2.6: Closing a Window by Using the Mouse

Step 1: Description

When you're finished with a window, you can close the window by clicking the Close button, by double-clicking the window's icon, or (if the window represents a running program) by using the program's termination commands to close the program and the window.

Step 2: Action

1. Click the Close button on the My Computer window. The window instantly disappears from view.
2. Look at the taskbar for the My Computer icon. You will see no My Computer icon! Remember that a closed window is different from a minimized window because it is still active and loaded.
3. Open the My Computer window once again by double-clicking the My Computer icon on your desktop.

Step 3: Review

Closing a window is like taking a paper file off your desktop and storing that file away in a file cabinet. The window is completely gone from your work area just as the paper file would be. If you want to work in the window again, you must reinitiate the commands that displayed the window to begin with (usually by double-clicking an icon that represents the window).

Using the System Menu

All windows contain icons in the upper-left corner. The icon is the same one you see when the window is closed. For example, you clicked a large PC icon on the Windows 98 desktop to open the My Computer window. When opened, the My Computer window contains a small icon that matches the startup icon you double-clicked to start the program.

Earlier (in the section labeled "Closing a window") you learned to double-click this icon to close a window. The icon also represents a System menu with which you can control the window's size and placement. Figure 2.5 shows the My Computer window's System menu. Almost every Windows 98 program contains this menu.

WINDOWS MINUTE

What's on the System Menu?

Just as a menu in a restaurant is a list of food items you can choose, a Windows menu is a list of commands you can select. The System menu is a typical Windows 98 menu. Many menus operate as the System menu operates—the list of menu choices stays out of the way until you are ready to choose from it. You learned about another kind of menu in Hour 1: the Start menu. After you display a menu, you can move through the selections by using the keyboard's up and down arrow keys, as well as with the mouse.

> You can quickly display the System menu by pressing Alt+Spacebar. The first thing you will notice about Figure 2.5 is that the top choice, Restore, is grayed out. Often one or more menu items is grayed out, meaning that the choice is unavailable at this time but, depending on circumstances, might be available from this menu at a later time.

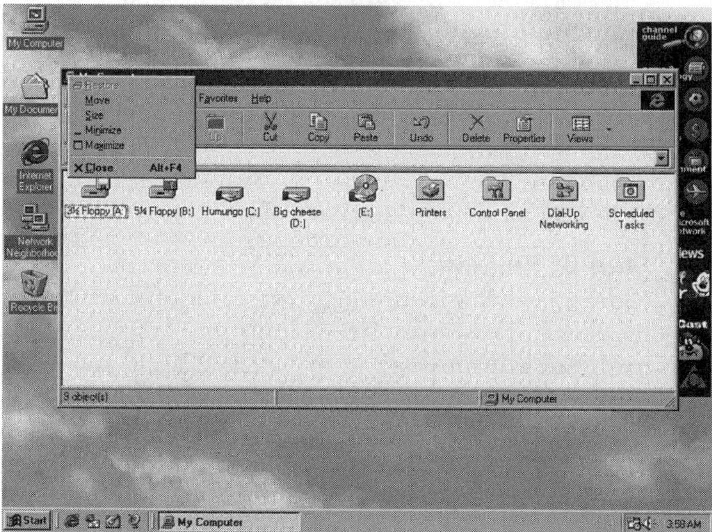

Figure 2.5.
You can control a window's size and placement through the System menu.

Just like the Start menu, the System menu offers a list of shortcut keys with which you can quickly select a menu item. For example, N selects the System menu's Minimize command as long as the System menu is shown at the time you press N.

There's another kind of shortcut key on the System menu. Alt+F4 selects the System menu's Close command. The Alt+F4 key, unlike a hotkey, is an *accelerator key*, which means that the System menu does not have to be visible when you press Alt+F4 to close the window. Accelerator keys generally involve Alt or Ctrl keys and appear to the right of their associated menu choices.

As with the Start menu, you also can select from the System menu by clicking the mouse. Remember that the Esc key closes an open menu and so does another Alt keypress. You now know everything there is to know about using and choosing Windows 98 menus!

TIME SAVER

When you use a window's menu bar (shown previously in Figure 2.1), you select commands and shortcut keys from the menu bar just as you do from the System menu. The only difference is that the commands on the menu bar always appear at the top of the window, whereas the System menu appears only when you click the System menu icon.

Table 2.1 explains what each System menu command does.

Table 2.1. The System menu commands.

Command	Description
Restore	Restores a window that you've maximized. The Restore command is available only when the window is maximized or completely minimized.
Move	Moves a window on the screen to a different location.
Size	Resizes a window by enlarging or shrinking the window.
Minimize	Shrinks the window to the taskbar icon.
Maximize	Enlarges the window to full-screen size.
Close	Closes the window and terminates the window's running program.

A Window's Menu

Most Windows 98 windows contain a menu bar. Even non-program windows that display information such as the My Computer window display a menu bar. You can use the menu bar to close the window, open additional windows, copy, cut, and paste information from one window to another, get help, and even access the Internet for related information. (The Internet's never far away in Windows 98.)

As you progress over the next 22 lessons, you'll learn ways to use the window menu bar options to traverse windows and to find the information you need. When you select an option from a menu bar, that option's menu pulls down to display a list of actions. For example, Figure 2.6 shows an open View menu. Throughout the remaining lessons, when asked to select View | Details, for example, you will click the View menu bar option and select Details with your mouse or arrow keys.

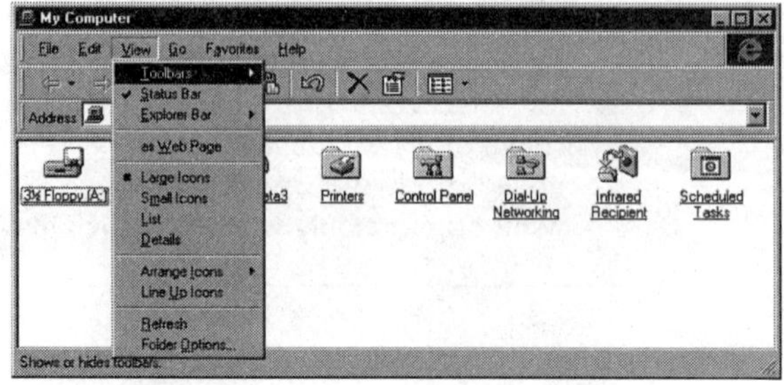

Figure 2.6.
Windows contain menus that enable you to control operations on and within the window.

Task 2.7: Working with a Window's Menu Bar

Step 1: Description

The menu bar enables you to control the way the window looks and behaves. If the window's icons are too large to hold all of a window's contents, you can select smaller icons or change the window to a list view format.

Step 2: Action

1. From the open My Computer window, select View | Small Icons. The window's icons become smaller so that they can display in a smaller space.
2. Select View | Details to see the window's contents compacted even further. The list view shows extra information about the window's contents such as the size, date created, free disk space, and other statistics relative to the item in the window.

Step 3: Review

Use a window's menu bar to change the window's appearance and behavior. More of the menu bar options will come in handy as you learn more about Windows 98.

A Window's Toolbar

A *toolbar* is a ribbon of buttons across the top of a window. Some programs have multiple toolbars. The toolbar you see atop the My Computer window is fairly common and appears throughout most windows that appear in Windows 98. Toolbar buttons give you push-button access to common actions you perform with the window.

As you work within a window, the toolbar changes to reflect actions that become available. For example, if you open a folder icon located in a window, not only does the clicked folder's contents replace the window's original contents, but the toolbar changes, as well.

All of the window toolbars in Windows 98 are known as *Explorer toolbars* because they mimic the actions of Internet Explorer, a Web browser that comes with Windows 98. Many toolbar buttons are standard across applications and windows, so you will learn to recognize them quickly.

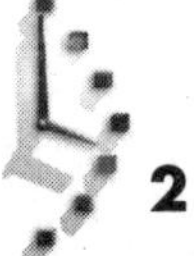

To Do

Task 2.8: Working with a Window Toolbar

Step 1: Description

Toolbars change as you work within the window. In addition, you might want to modify a toolbar's behavior to access its benefits more efficiently. Although total toolbar management is a lengthy topic, simple toolbar management is easy, as you will learn in this task.

Step 2: Action

1. Maximize the My Computer window. Notice the Back toolbar button (the button with the left-pointing arrow) is grayed out.
2. Double-click the Printers folder. The Printers folder contains an icon, enabling you to set up a new printer that you might add to your system, as well as icons for existing printers you've already designated. Notice that the Back toolbar button is now available, enabling you to return to the previous window contents.
3. Click the Back button and the original My Computer contents return. (Forward takes you to the Printers folder.) No matter how many windows and sub-folders you open within a window, you always can retrace your steps backward and forward with the Back and Forward buttons.
4. Modify the way the toolbar looks. Right-click over the right-end of the toolbar (an area where no buttons appear) to display the toolbar's menu. Select Text Labels. As Figure 2.7 shows, the window's toolbar buttons now display textual descriptions so that you know at a glance what the buttons do. (You also can control the toolbar's appearance from the View | Toolbar menu bar option.)

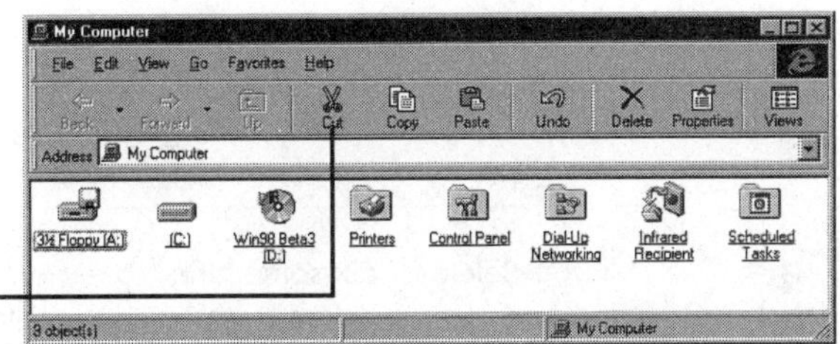

Figure 2.7.
Text labels help you learn the toolbar buttons more rapidly.

5. The text labels make the toolbar grow to accommodate the labels. Many of the toolbar areas have *Toolbar handle controls* (see Figure 2.7) that enable you to slide that portion of the toolbar left or right to make room for something else. Drag one of the sliders left or right to see how the toolbar adjusts to the Toolbar handle control. If you double-click a toolbar's slider, the tools on the slider come into view (and cover up other items) or hide to bring hidden items into focus once again.
6. A window's contents don't dictate what you view in the window. The area of the toolbar labeled `Address` is not a button but instead describes the white box to the right of `Address`. The box is a *drop-down listbox* that can display choices you might want to use. Click the listbox's down arrow (at the right of the listbox) to see a list

of areas you can go to from the window. Whether you choose a disk drive or the Internet (by dragging the mouse or using the keyboard), the contents you pick will appear inside the window and replace the window's original My Computer contents. As always, the Back button returns you to where you started.

Just a Minute

The Address listbox, as well as the other traversal features of the toolbar such as the Back and Forward buttons, means that Windows 98 doesn't limit you; just because you open a window doesn't mean that you want to stay with that window. The toolbar enables you to move from one window's contents to a totally unrelated window and even to an Internet site (that will display in the window) if you've got a connection.

Time Saver

You can remove the Address listbox if you don't want to consume the toolbar space. Select View | Toolbar and click Address bar to remove the check mark next to the entry and hide the Address bar. (Repeat this tip to bring the bar back once again.)

Step 3: Review

A window's toolbar is a new feature with Windows 98 that enables you to traverse any part of your PC or a networked file or the Internet from any window. Customize the toolbars so that they display the information that helps you most. The toolbars are plentiful with push-button uses, and even contain the standard Windows capabilities to copy, cut, and paste information from the window to elsewhere in your system.

Time Saver

If you delete or cut something from a window accidentally, click the toolbar's Undo button to restore the mistake.

One Last Note About Windows

You can completely change the way a window looks by selecting View | As Web Page from the menu. The window changes from an icon or list view to a view that acts like an Internet Web browser. Figure 2.8 shows the My Computer window shown in its Web page format. The details appear at the right side of the window, and the description of the selected item shows at the left.

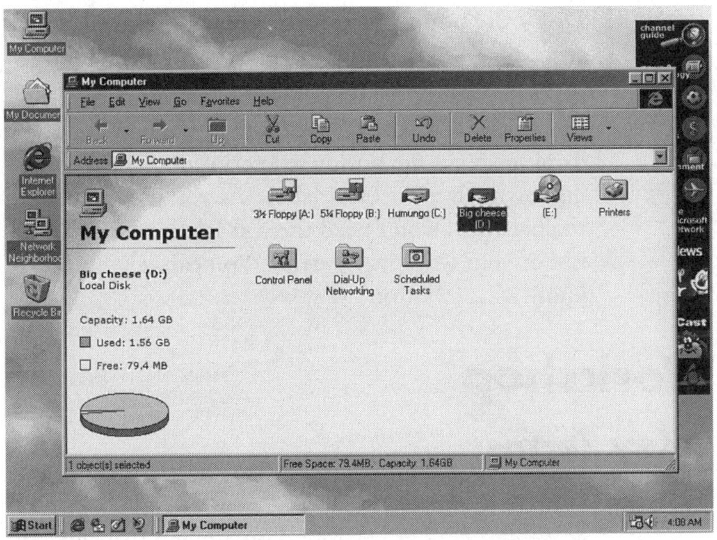

Figure 2.8.
You might prefer to view your windows in a Web page format.

Summary

This hour taught you the ins and outs of windows management. Learning how to manage windows is a fundamental skill that Windows 98 users must understand. Windows 98 enables you to open, resize, move, and close windows. The windows on your desktop contain the running applications, and part of running Windows 98 programs requires being able to position those windows where you want them.

Mastering fundamental windows management, as you've done so far this hour, is like learning to drive a car. You have to learn the basics before getting into traffic. Now you are ready to begin racing down the road by seeing what Windows 98 can really do.

Q&A

Q What's the difference between a shortcut key and an accelerator key?

A Both shortcut (or hot) keys and accelerator keys involve selecting commands from Windows 98 menus. The shortcut keystrokes appear as underlined letters in menu commands. When you use the hotkey (such as R to select Restore), the matching menu item executes.

Accelerator keys have the added distinction of enabling the user to select menu commands by pressing keystrokes without first having to display a menu. For example, you can often press Ctrl+O instead of selecting File | Open from most menus. Accelerator keys appear at the right of their corresponding menu commands.

Q Don't the pop-up Tooltips replace the need for text labels?

A When you hide a toolbar's text labels, you make room for more buttons and you get more screen real estate for the window's contents. If you forget what a button is for, rest your mouse cursor on the button without clicking the button, and the Tooltip shows the button's description. The Tooltips don't appear when you display the buttons' text labels. As you grow more familiar with Windows 98 toolbars, you won't need the text labels and you'll want to make more room for the rest of your window elements. You can rely on the Tooltips when you need to know what a button does.

Workshop

Key Terms

Review the following list of terms:

- ☐ *accelerator key* A key found on a menu (usually a function key used in conjunction with the Alt key, such as Alt+F4) that enables you initiate a menu command from the keyboard without first having to display the menu.
- ☐ *drop-down listbox* A list of choices that opens when you click the down arrow to the right of the listbox.
- ☐ *folder* A special icon containing other icons that display when you double-click the folder icon; a grouping of related files stored under the same subdirectory.
- ☐ *opening a window* The process of starting a program in a window or double-clicking an icon to display a window.
- ☐ *shortcut key* An underlined letter on a menu that you can combine with the Alt key to issue a menu command.
- ☐ *system menu* A menu available on all windows that enables you to move and resize windows with the keyboard.
- ☐ *toolbar* A strip of buttons across a window that offers one-button access to common commands and tasks.
- ☐ *toolbar handle control* A toolbar control that lets you move areas of a toolbar left or right to make room for the items you need to see.

PART I

Hour 3

Take Windows 98 to Task

The taskbar and the Start button are closely related. Most Windows 98 users use the Start button to display the Start menu, then execute a program. When the program begins running, the taskbar displays a button with an icon, along with a description that represents that running program.

The taskbar, Start button, and Start menu are the most fundamental components in Windows 98. The taskbar is the cornerstone of Windows 98. This hour explains how to customize the taskbar to best suit your computing style. Along the way you also learn how to make your desktop items mimic the one-click operation of the taskbar.

The highlights of this hour include the following:

- Where the Start menu comes from
- How to move, resize, and change the appearance of the taskbar
- Why the Start menu's Programs command may not execute all programs
- How to simplify icon selection

A Quick Taskbar and Start Button Review

In Hour 1, "What's Windows 98 All About?," you saw the Start menu and used it to shut down your computer properly. Clicking the taskbar's Start button produces the Start menu. The Start menu does all these things and more:

- It makes itself available to you no matter what else you are doing in Windows 98. Even if you work inside a full-screen MS-DOS session, you can display the Windows 98 Start menu.
- It displays a list of programs on your system using the Start menu's cascading system.
- It enables you to return to your favorite places, whether those places are Internet Web pages or programs on your local hard disk.
- It provides easy access to recently opened data documents that you can look at or edit.
- It provides a search engine that navigates through all your files looking for the one you need.
- It activates the Windows 98 help engine, which provides online help for working within Windows 98.

The next few sections explain how you can customize the taskbar and its associated Start menu so that the Start menu acts and looks the way you expect.

TIME SAVER

Sometimes the Start button temporarily disappears (when you're working in a full-screen MS-DOS session, for example). Press Ctrl+Esc to display the Start menu when you cannot see it. If your keyboard contains a key with the Windows logo, that key also displays the Start menu. If you are working in a full-screen MS-DOS session when you press Ctrl+Esc, Windows 98 switches back to the Windows 98 desktop to display the Start menu, but the MS-DOS session remains active.

Moving the Taskbar

The taskbar does not have to stay at the bottom of your screen. You can move the taskbar to either side of your monitor or even to the top of your screen. The taskbar placement is easy to change.

JUST A MINUTE

Figure 3.1 shows that a side taskbar does not have the width necessary to display lengthy descriptions. When you place the taskbar at the bottom or top of the screen, the taskbar has more room for longer descriptions.

Figure 3.1.
You can place the taskbar on any edge of your screen.

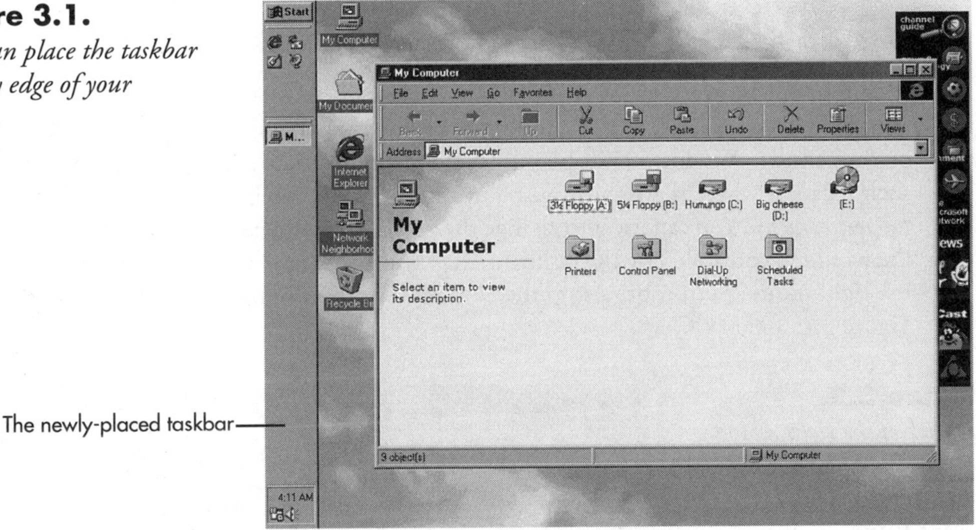

If you place the taskbar at the top of the screen, the Start menu falls down from the Start button, whereas the Start menu pops up from the Start button when you place the taskbar at the bottom of the screen.

Time Saver

When working on a wide spreadsheet or document, you may want as much screen width as you can get. You then want the taskbar at the bottom or top of your screen. When working with graphics, you usually need more vertical screen space, so you can move the taskbar to either side of the screen.

To Do

Task 3.1: Moving Your Taskbar

Step 1: Description

Moving the taskbar to any of the four edges of your screen is easy. Simply drag the taskbar to the new location.

Step 2: Action

1. Find a blank spot on your taskbar and point to the spot with the mouse cursor. Be sure that you are pointing within the taskbar and not over a button.
2. Drag the taskbar to another edge of the screen. As you drag the mouse, the taskbar moves with the mouse and appears at the edge of the screen where you release the mouse.
3. Release the mouse button to anchor the taskbar at its new position.

Step 3: Review

The taskbar does not have to stay at the bottom of your screen. If you like, drag the taskbar to another location. You can move the taskbar any time, even after you've started one or more programs.

The Taskbar Properties Menu

A right mouse button click often displays a *context-sensitive menu* of options available to you. Windows 98 looks at what you are doing when you click the right mouse button. Depending on the context, Windows 95 displays commands appropriate to that task. The taskbar is one such location where the right mouse button brings up a helpful menu, called the *taskbar properties menu*. You can use it to change the appearance and performance of the taskbar and the windows controlled by the taskbar. After finding a blank spot on your taskbar, clicking the right mouse button brings up the context-sensitive taskbar properties menu shown in Figure 3.2.

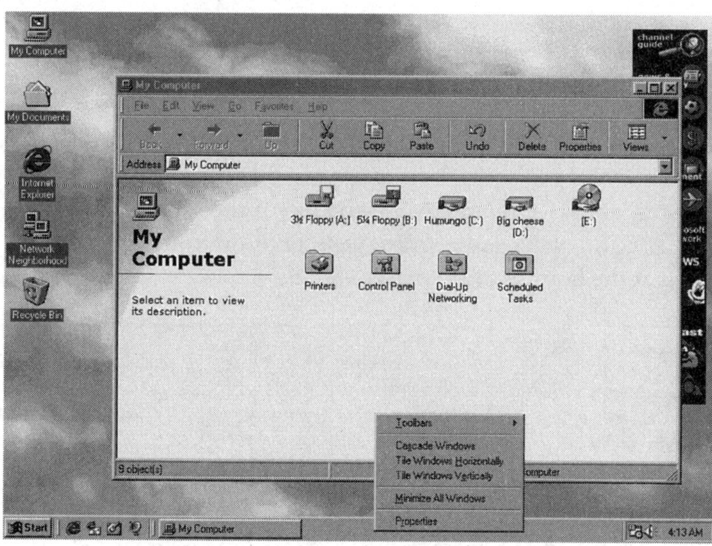

Figure 3.2.
A click of the right mouse button on a blank space on the taskbar displays a context-sensitive menu.

CAUTION

Do not click the right mouse button over one of the taskbar programs unless you want to activate that button's program or window (known as bringing the program into focus). For example, suppose you load these three programs: a word processor, a spreadsheet, and a database. The taskbar will list each program's taskbar button.

If you are typing with the word processor and decide that you want to change the taskbar's properties through the right mouse button's taskbar menu, don't click the right mouse button when the mouse pointer points to the database or spreadsheet button. If you do, Windows 98 will give that program's window the focus and will display a menu that controls the size and location of the window—not at all what you had in mind. (If you right-click over a taskbar button whose window is minimized, the window will not appear; its pop-up taskbar menu does appear, however, so you can select from the menu.)

The taskbar properties menu is not necessarily a menu you want to display often. Most users play around with different taskbar and window settings for a while until they find preferences that suit them best. Thereafter, those users may rarely use the taskbar properties menu.

The first menu option, Toolbars, enables you to customize your toolbar by selecting which items you want to see. Table 3.1 explains each kind of element you can place on the taskbar. Many will now be familiar to you after Hour 2, "Tour Windows 98 Now."

Table 3.1. You can add these toolbar elements to your Windows 98 taskbar.

Toolbar Element	Description
Address	Displays a drop-down listbox on your taskbar that you can click to return to recent Web and file locations.
Links	Displays popular Web links that you can quickly return to with the click of a button. You can modify the list of links.
Desktop	Displays a ribbon of icons that match those on your Windows 98 desktop. You can click on one of the icons to start that icon's program or open that icon's window instead of having to return to your desktop to locate the icon.
Quick Launch	Adds Internet access control buttons so you can quickly get on the Web. In addition, the Show Desktop icon appears in the Quick Launch section so you can minimize all open windows with a single taskbar click. Other items appear on the taskbar's right-click menu when you activate the Quick Launch taskbar icons.
New Toolbar	Enables you to select a disk drive, folder, or Web location whose contents appear as a secondary toolbar slider control on the taskbar. Subsequently, the taskbar's right-click menu contains that new toolbar that you can deselect to hide once again.

The next three menu options are important when you want to work with more than one open window. These three menu options offer three ways of arranging your open windows so they are more manageable. If you open two or more windows at once, all those windows can be difficult to manage individually. You could maximize each window and display only one window at a time. There are many reasons, however, to keep more than one window open and displayed at the same time, such as when you want to copy data from one window to another. (Hour 5, "Explore the Windows 98 System," explains how to copy between windows.)

Tiling Windows

When you want to see more than one open window at a time, the taskbar properties menu gives you tools that provide quick management of those windows so you do not have to size and place each window individually. Figure 3.3 shows how too many windows open at the same time can be confusing. You'll see in the Task section that follows how to use the taskbar properties menu to straighten up such a mess.

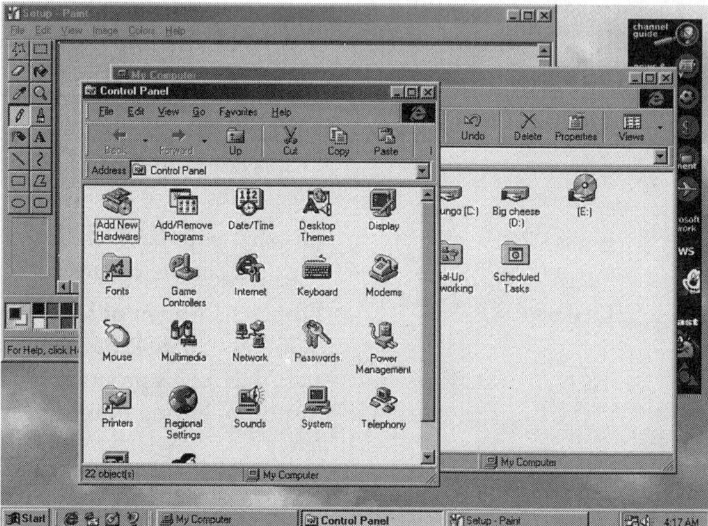

Figure 3.3.
Too many open windows can quickly cause disorganization.

To Do

Task 3.2: Organizing Multiple Windows

Step 1: Description

The taskbar properties menu provides a way to organize several open windows with the click of a mouse. There are three ways to organize the windows: You can cascade them, horizontally tile them, or vertically tile them.

Step 2: Action

1. Double-click the My Computer icon to open the My Computer window.
2. Double-click the Recycle Bin icon to open that window as well. Although you may not understand the Recycle Bin until Hour 5, the open window helps show the effects of the taskbar's properties menu.
3. Display the Start menu and select the Help option. Shortly, you'll see a help window open. Again, this window is just to put more on your desktop to work with for this task.
4. Now that you've opened three windows, ask Windows 98 to organize those windows for you. Display the taskbar's properties menu by right-clicking the mouse button after pointing to a blank spot on the taskbar.
5. Select the menu item labeled Cascade Windows. Windows 98 instantly organizes your windows into the cascaded series of windows shown in Figure 3.4.

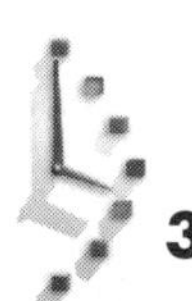

Figure 3.4.
The windows are now more manageable.

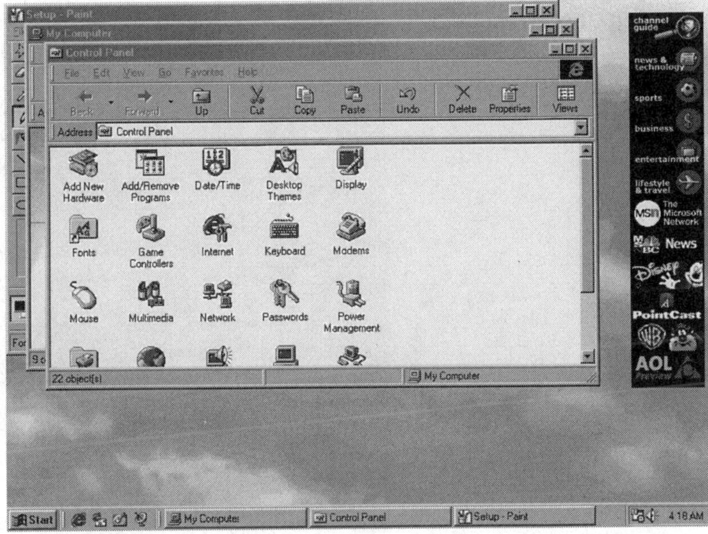

Notice that the title bars of *all* open windows appear on the Windows 98 desktop area. When you want to bring any of the hidden windows into focus, click that window's title bar, and the window will rise to the top of the window stack. The cascading effect always gives you the ability to switch between windows. As long as any part of a hidden window is peeking out from under another, you can click the title bar to bring that hidden window into focus.

6. Sometimes, you need to see the contents of two or more windows at the same time. Windows 98 enables you to *tile* the open windows so you can see the actual body of each open window. Windows 98 supports two kinds of tiling methods: horizontal tiling and vertical tiling. Display the taskbar's properties menu and select Tile Windows Horizontally. Windows 98 will properly resize each of the three open windows, as shown in Figure 3.5. (If a window's title bar is hidden but another part of the window is visible, you can bring that window into focus by clicking over the part of the window that is visible.)

CAUTION

Your windows may differ in size and placement, depending on your monitor size and graphics card settings.

Figure 3.5.
The windows are now tiled horizontally.

At first glance, the tiling may seem too limiting to you. After all, to fit those three open windows on the screen at the same time, Windows 98 cannot show you a *lot* of any one of the windows. Keep in mind that all the window resizing and moving tools that you learned about in Hour 2 work even after you've tiled windows. Therefore, you can move the Help window toward the top of the screen, after tiling the windows, if you want to see more of that window. (Scrollbars automatically appear in tiled windows if the contents of the window consume more space than can be displayed at once. Click the arrows at each end of the scrollbar to move window contents into view.)

7. The vertical tiling method produces side-by-side windows that are fairly thin but offer yet another kind of open window display. Select Tile Windows Vertically and Windows 98 will reformat the screen to look something like Figure 3.6.

   After changing the look of your open windows by using the taskbar properties menu, you can revert the windows to their previous state through the taskbar properties menu. Now that you've vertically tiled the open windows, you can restore the original placement of the windows by selecting Undo Tile. (The Undo option appears only after you've selected the Cascade, Tile, or Minimize option.)

9. The Minimize All Windows taskbar properties menu option attempts to minimize all open windows at the same time. The problem with the Minimize All Windows option is that not all windows can be minimized. Therefore, the option minimizes only those windows that have a minimize button (most do). The Show Desktop icon minimizes all open windows in one step. The Show Desktop icon appears on the Quick Launch taskbar toolbar, so you must display that toolbar before you see the Show Desktop icon. Don't minimize any windows now, however, because you need them open for the next task.

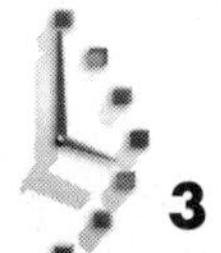

Figure 3.6.
The windows are now tiled vertically.

JUST A MINUTE

No matter how you tile or cascade the windows, each window's Minimize, Maximize, and Restore buttons work as usual. Therefore, you can maximize any cascaded window at any time by clicking that window's Maximize button.

Step 3: Review

You can use the taskbar's properties menu to control the appearance of the open windows on your screen. The nice thing about using the taskbar to manage open windows is that you don't have to size and place each window individually.

Working with Taskbar Properties

The taskbar properties menu not only controls the appearance and performance of open windows, but also controls the appearance and performance of the taskbar. The Properties menu option displays the Taskbar Properties tabbed dialog box shown in Figure 3.7. (This same dialog appears when you select Start | Settings | Taskbar & Start Menu.) With the Taskbar Properties dialog box, you can change the way the taskbar appears and performs, and you also can change the contents of the Start menu.

JUST A MINUTE

In Hour 7, "Manage Your Desktop," you'll learn how to use the Taskbar Properties dialog box to change the contents of the Start menu.

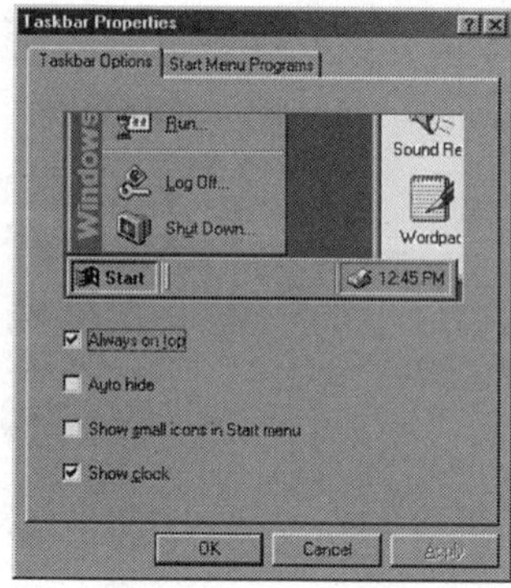

Figure 3.7.
You can change the taskbar's appearance and performance by using the Taskbar Properties dialog box.

WINDOWS MINUTE

Using Dialog Boxes

The pages in a tabbed dialog box are often called *property sheets*. Before you can understand a tabbed dialog box, you should know what a dialog box is all about.

When Windows 98 needs one or more items of information from you, you see a dialog box window. Dialog boxes can capture all kinds of information that Windows 98 needs. Windows 98 might put command buttons, option buttons, checkmarks, text boxes, or other kinds of controls together in a dialog box. You can choose to respond to one or more of those controls, depending on the information you want to provide at the time. When you click the dialog box's OK button, Windows 98 closes the dialog box and your dialog box settings go into effect.

When Windows 98 displays a tabbed dialog box, it is offering you more than one dialog box at the same time. Instead of displaying two or more dialog boxes on the screen at the same time, the tabs give you a way to select which dialog box you want to respond to. You can even respond to one dialog box and then click another tab, and that tab's dialog box then appears so that you can respond to it. Windows 98 often puts an OK command button on a dialog box that you can press when you are finished responding to the dialog box's controls.

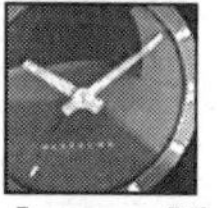

JUST A MINUTE

In addition to the OK button, some dialog boxes have an Apply button. Generally, these dialog boxes change a Windows 98 setting, such as the font size. If you click Apply, Windows 98 puts your dialog box settings into effect but does not close the dialog box. Therefore, you can see the results of your dialog box settings without getting rid of the dialog box.

To Do

Task 3.3: Using the Taskbar Properties Dialog Box

Step 1: Description

The Taskbar Properties dialog box accepts information that controls the way the taskbar appears on the screen. You can allow (or disallow) windows to overlap the taskbar if those windows are large enough to do so, you can eliminate the clock from the taskbar, and you can even minimize the taskbar so that it does not appear until you need it.

Step 2: Action

1. With the three windows still open on your screen from the previous task, display the Taskbar Properties menu once again by right-clicking the mouse button on the taskbar.
2. Select the Properties command to display the tabbed Taskbar Properties dialog box shown in Figure 3.7.
3. The first checkmark option, Always on top, is normally checked because Windows 98 by default displays the taskbar at all times. The taskbar is most helpful when it appears on the screen, right? The only problem with the taskbar's being on the screen at all times is that one complete row of the screen is consumed by the taskbar instead of by your own windows. Uncheck the option by clicking over the checkmark or anywhere on the words beside it. The graphic inside the dialog box actually changes when you remove the checkmark to show a window overlapping the clock in the taskbar.
4. Click the OK command button to see the results of the unchecked option. (If you clicked the Apply command button, Windows 98 would have changed the taskbar immediately while still displaying the dialog box.)
5. Display the Taskbar Properties dialog box again. Check the Auto hide option and click the OK button. Where did the taskbar go?
6. The taskbar is now out of sight and out of the way except for a thin horizontal line across the bottom of your screen. The taskbar hasn't gone far—point the mouse cursor to the bottom of the screen and the taskbar will reappear. You can now have your taskbar and hide it, too!

Time Saver

> If you display the Taskbar Properties dialog box but decide that you don't want to make any changes after all, click the Cancel command button; Windows 98 will remove the Taskbar Properties dialog box and leave the taskbar unchanged.

7. Although only a little of the taskbar is still showing, you can display the Taskbar Properties dialog box once again and check the Always on top option and uncheck the Auto hide option.

8. The third checkmark option controls how the Start menu's icons are displayed. If you want to save some screen room when you display the Start menu, you can request small icons, and the Start menu will consume less screen space. If you uncheck the last option, labeled Show Clock, the clock goes away after clicking the OK command button on the dialog box.

JUST A MINUTE

If you see a speaker icon at the right of your taskbar, check out Hour 23, "Multimedia and Sound." You'll learn how to use the speaker icon there.

9. Display the Taskbar Properties tabbed dialog box once again and set the checkmark options to your desired values. Before clicking the OK command button, click the tab labeled Start Menu Programs (at the top of the dialog box). You see the second dialog box, which is shown in Figure 3.8.

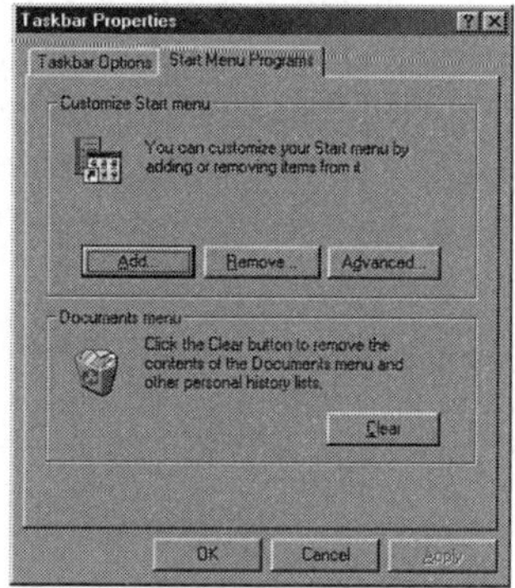

Figure 3.8.
The second dialog box appearing from behind the taskbar options.

The Start Menu Programs page enables you to change the appearance of the Start menu. Because you have yet to really learn what the default Start menu is all about, let's save the discussion of this dialog box until Hour 7.

The second half of this dialog box controls the contents of the Start menu's Documents command. When you select Start | Documents, Windows 98 displays a list of your most recent data files. All data files are known as *documents* to Windows 98. If the list gets too full, you can erase it by clicking the Clear button.

10. Click the Cancel command button to close the dialog box and return to the regular Windows 98 desktop. Close all windows that are now open by clicking the Close button in the window's upper-right corner.

Step 3: Review

There are several ways to change the taskbar's properties and performances through the taskbar properties menu. The menu appears when you click the right mouse button. The menu contains commands to modify the appearance of all the following:

- The open windows on the screen
- The taskbar
- The Start menu's commands

Sizing the Taskbar

What happens if you open a number of windows by starting several programs? The single-line taskbar fills up very quickly with buttons and icons and descriptions that represent those open windows. The taskbar can get extremely full if you display multiple toolbars on the taskbar. Figure 3.9 shows such a taskbar. If you're doing a lot of work, the taskbar gets squeezed for space. However, you can solve that problem rather easily.

Figure 3.9.
The taskbar needs more room.

Just as you can resize a window, you also can resize the taskbar. When you enlarge the taskbar, it can more comfortably hold several buttons for open windows, and the descriptions on those buttons can be longer. Use the pop-up Tooltips if you need a reminder of the purpose of the taskbar buttons, such as the Show Desktop button. Figure 3.10 shows the same taskbar as the one shown in Figure 3.9. This time, the taskbar is larger, and you can better tell what each program is by the descriptions on the taskbar buttons.

Figure 3.10.
The taskbar now has more breathing room.

CAUTION

> You also can add too much height to the taskbar. Keep in mind that the more space you devote to the taskbar, the less space you have for your application windows. The taskbar exists to help you do your real work, so don't make it too large, or you won't have screen space for the rest of your work. If you see an up and down arrow appear on the taskbar, you can click either arrow to scroll through the list of applications currently running. Windows 98 adds the arrows because not all the applications will fit at one time.

Task 3.4: Resizing the Taskbar

Step 1: Description

If you need to expand (or shrink) the taskbar, you can drag the top of the taskbar up the screen until it reaches the middle of the Windows 98 desktop. The taskbar then has more room for more open window buttons and descriptions. Of course, if you've moved the taskbar to one of the other edges of the screen, you drag the innermost edge of the taskbar toward the middle of the screen to increase its size. If you want to shrink the taskbar, you can reverse the dragging.

Step 2: Action

1. Move the mouse cursor to the top edge of the taskbar. The cursor will change to a bidirectional resizing arrow that looks like the window-resizing cursor shape you saw in Hour 2.
2. Drag the taskbar toward the center of the screen. As you drag, it expands one row at a time until you complete the dragging operation.
3. Release the mouse button and you see the resulting (and larger) taskbar with more room for descriptions and open window buttons.
4. You can leave the taskbar at its present size or shrink it back again by dragging the top edge toward the outer edge of the screen.

TIME SAVER

If you drag the top of the taskbar down to the bottom of your screen, it goes away. In the previous section, you learned how to hide the taskbar by first displaying the taskbar properties menu and then selecting Auto hide from the dialog box. It is easier to shrink the taskbar with the mouse than to use the dialog box to hide it. To bring the taskbar into view, move the mouse to the bottom of the screen until the mouse cursor changes to the bidirectional arrow; then drag the arrow up the screen so the taskbar reappears.

Step 3: Review

When you need more room for the taskbar, drag the taskbar's edge until it is the size you need.

You can expand or shrink the taskbar by dragging its innermost edge with the mouse.

TIME SAVER

Right-click over any taskbar button to see that button's System menu. You can close the window by clicking Close without going to the window itself, if the window happens to be covered by other windows.

Starting Programs with Start

The Start menu offers an extremely simple way for you to start the programs on your computer. Two or three clicks start virtually any program on your disk drive. The Programs command on the Start menu launches your programs. To start a program, you display the menu that contains that program and then click the program's name or icon.

To Do

Task 3.5: Starting Solitaire

Step 1: Description

Microsoft gives you a Windows 98–based version of the Solitaire card game. Solitaire is considered an *accessory program*. Accessory programs are programs Microsoft includes with Windows 98 that fall under several categories, such as multimedia programs, text editors, and games. For this hour, you learn how to start and stop Solitaire.

Step 2: Action

1. Display the Start menu.
2. Select the Programs command. A cascaded menu will appear next to the Start menu. Your computer is unique, and a different set of commands might appear here. Figure 3.11 shows the screen from a computer with many program folders displayed by the Programs command.

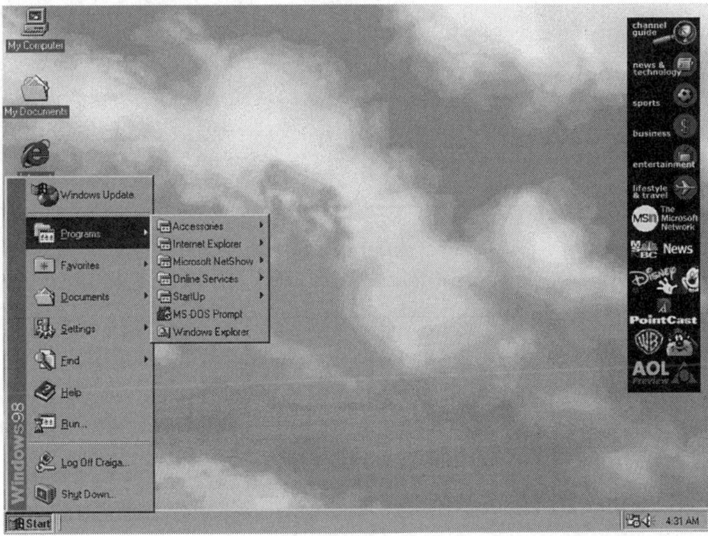

Figure 3.11.
You will see a list of several programs on your system.

Each of these items in the second menu represents either a program or a folder of programs. When you buy a program such as a word processor, the word processor might come with several related programs that help you manage the word processor

environment. The word processor folder opens to yet another window (you can tell by the presence of an arrow at the right of the word processor's folder) that then lists all the related programs in that folder.

3. Select the Accessories command to display the programs in the Accessories folder. Search down until you see the Games menu. Select Games to see the Solitaire game (look for a card deck icon).
4. Click the Solitaire game. You see the opening Solitaire screen, shown in Figure 3.12.

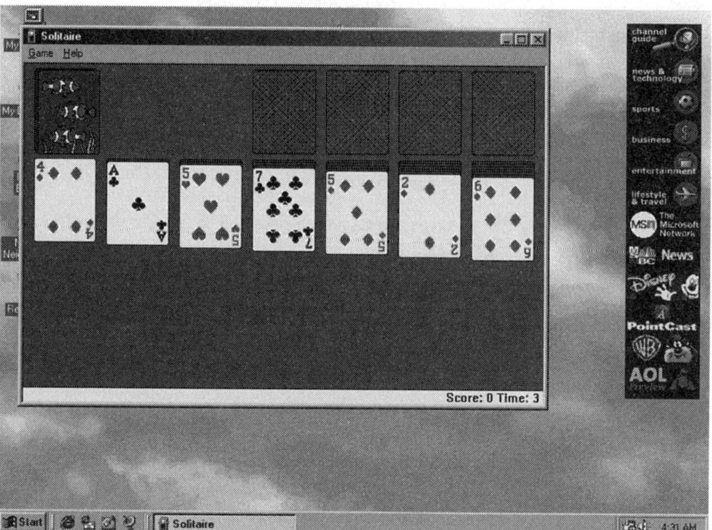

Figure 3.12.
Get ready to have fun!

JUST A MINUTE

Your Solitaire screen may differ slightly from the one in the figure because your default card deck may be set to have a different picture backing.

5. There's no time to play right now! This hour's closing quickly. Therefore, terminate the Solitaire program by clicking the window's Close button (the button with the X, as you learned in Hour 2). Solitaire goes away and you are back to the regular Windows 98 desktop.

Step 3: Review

The Programs command launches any and all programs on your system. Depending on the way your programs are set up and because many Windows 98 programs are stored in folders, you may have to display one or more menus to access individual programs that you want to execute.

If you didn't upgrade from a previous Windows version, your Start menu may not have many items. Only those programs that come with Windows 98 will appear. To add other programs on your system, if you have other programs, you have to install those programs again using Windows 98. (Hour 9, "Giving Windows 98 Your own Programs," explains how to add new programs.) When you reinstall the program, Windows 98 adds the program to the Start menu.

Generally, you don't need to worry about adding programs to the Start menu because Windows 98 does the work for you as you install each program.

Using the Run Command

In addition to the Start menu's Programs command, you can use another method to start programs that aren't set up on the Programs' cascade of menus. The Run command on the Start menu provides a way for you to execute specific programs.

3

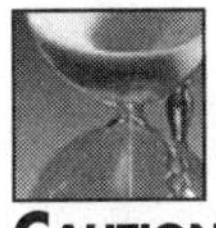

CAUTION

Before using Run, you must understand the basics of file pathnames (such as `C:\WORD\DEC97`). You must also know the exact name of the program you want to run. Most newcomers to Windows 98 stay away from the Run command for good reason: Run requires a comprehensive understanding of the program you are trying to start. Many Windows 98 users will work for years and never need Run because Windows 98 programs install their own icons on the Start menu.

WINDOWS MINUTE

Reaching Your Files

A pathname is the exact computer system location of a file. The document and folder concept in Windows 98 makes working with paths much easier than before Windows. Most often, you specify pathnames visually by clicking folder icons instead of typing long pathnames, as you had to do before Windows.

The folders in Windows 98 used to be called *directories*. A directory is just a collection of files and other directories. In file listings, Windows 98 often displays a folder icon with a name to represent a directory that holds other files. Folders can hold subfolders, so the location of a file, the file's path, may be deep within several nested folders on a disk or CD-ROM drive.

A full pathname begins with a disk drive name followed by a colon (:)followed by a backslash (\). If the file resides in the disk drive's top folder (called the *root directory*), you then type the filename. If, however, the file resides in another folder, you must list the folder after the backslash. If the file resides in several nested folders, you must list each folder in order, from the outermost to the innermost, and separate each folder name with a backslash. Both of the following are full pathnames to specific files:

c:\autoexec.bat

d:\Sherry\WordProc\Home\Insure\Fire and Casualty

The first filename is `autoexec.bat` located in the root directory. The second filename is `Fire and Casualty` located within a series of nested directories.

Task 3.6: Running with Run

Step 1: Description

The Start menu's Run command offers a tedious way to execute any program on your computer. If you want to run a program that would not properly set up in Windows 98 (perhaps the program is an old MS-DOS-based program), you have to execute the program using Run. This task uses Run to execute Solitaire.

Just a Minute

> Hour 5 shows you how to use Windows Explorer, a program that gives you simpler access to programs than the Run command gives. The Run command, however, does offer the advantage over other program starting methods, such as Windows Explorer, because the Run command is always on the Start menu. As you will see, you must load Windows Explorer before you can start programs with Windows Explorer.

Step 2: Action

1. Display the Start menu and select the Run command. Windows 98 displays the dialog box shown in Figure 3.13.

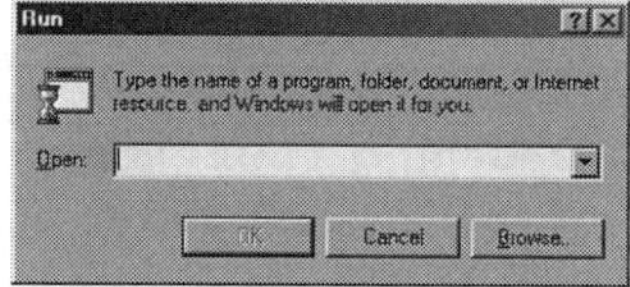

Figure 3.13.
You can run programs directly from the Start menu.

There may or may not be text next to the Open text prompt. Windows 98 needs to know the exact name and path of the program you want to open (and run).

Almost all users install Windows 98 on drive C. If your Windows 98 system is installed on another drive, substitute your drive name for the `C:` listed in the subsequent steps.

2. Type the following exactly as you see it (using either uppercase or lowercase letters): C:\WINDOWS\SOL

   The Solitaire game is normally installed on the Windows directory on drive C. The name of the program is `SOL.EXE`. To execute any program with an `.EXE` filename extension, you need to type only the first part of the filename, such as `SOL`. If Solitaire does not start, you may have typed the line incorrectly. Try again and be sure that you use backslashes and not forward slashes. (UNIX users, take note!)

3. After you get Solitaire to load and run, close the program and return to the Windows 98 desktop.

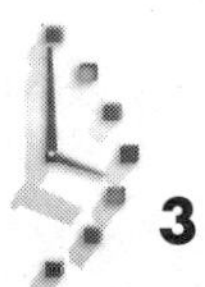

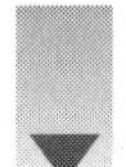

Step 3: Review

You may be one of the lucky few who never needs the Run command. Nevertheless, there are many programs on the market that Windows 98 cannot execute in its environment. Using Run, you can execute any program on your computer as long as you know the program's pathname and filename.

TIME SAVER

Windows 98 supports a strong data document concept. It is data-driven more than program-driven. If you type a data file (such as a Microsoft Word document) instead of a program name with the Run command, Windows 98 automatically starts the program needed to work with that data file and loads the data file for you. Therefore, you worry less about your programs, and you can concentrate more on your data. In addition, you can type an Internet address (often called a *URL*) at Run and Windows 98 automatically starts your Internet browser and takes you to the Web site you entered.

Introduction to Your Active Desktop

Windows 98's Active Desktop not only changes Windows 98 looks but also the way you work with Windows 98. Your Windows 98 desktop can display icons, text, and windows, but also more active content. You can display *HTML-based* documents on the Windows 98 background (HTML is the language behind Web pages).

JUST A MINUTE

This section serves only as an introduction to the Active Desktop that's so important to Windows 98. Complete chapters of this book are devoted to exploring the Active Desktop concepts. If you are new to the Internet, and especially if you are new to Windows, you may not see the full purpose of the Active Desktop at this time. Before this 24-hour tutorial is over, you'll know all you need to know to use Windows 98 efficiently and effectively.

You can place Web pages on the Windows 98 background's wallpaper. If those Web pages contain the special ActiveX controls that some Web pages contain (ActiveX controls energize Web pages with sound, videos, and interactive features), that active content will appear as well. If you've set up special push content, your Internet provider will bring your requested Internet information directly to your Windows 98 desktop. Hour 16, "The Internet's Push and Channel Content," explores the push content in more detail.

Just a Minute

If you're not connected to the Web, you can still benefit from the Active Desktop features, such as the single-click selection described next.

If you've used a Web browser before, you know that you can select Web page items just by resting your mouse over the item, and you can open items with a single-click. In pre-Windows 98 versions, you had to click once over a Windows item to select it and double-click the item to open that item. You've already opened windows in these lessons by double-clicking them. By providing the same kind of select and open capabilities as the Web provides, Windows 98 moves one step closer to integrating your desktop with the online world.

Time Saver

Using the Active Desktop means that you don't have to start a Web browser and request information, such as current stock prices, to see that data while you work in Windows 98. You can even set up the Web content to appear as a screen saver.

Task 3.7: Setting Up Web-like Mouse Selections

Step 1: Description

Hour 14, "Windows 98's Tight Web Connection," explains how to integrate Windows 98 and the Web to prepare you for the Active Desktop. In the meantime, you may want to convert your Windows 98 desktop to the Web-like desktop that simplifies the way you select desktop items and open windows. This task explains how to change your single- and double-mouse clicks to the Web-browser equivalents.

Step 2: Action

1. You can change the way you select objects from any open Windows 98 window. Therefore, open your My Computer window to gain access to window options.
2. Select View | Folder Options. The first dialog box page, the one with the General tab, contains three options that determine how your desktop items respond to your mouse selections. The Classic style option, the Windows 95 way, requires that you click once to select (highlight) an icon and double-click to open an icon's window. Web style gives you a Web-like selection ability so that the window's contents (as well as your desktop itself) display in a Web-like browser style, complete with a left window pane for descriptions and a right window pane for details. The Custom option activates the Settings button so you can control a combination of Web-like and normal Windows 98 selections.
3. Click the Web style option and then click OK to close the Options dialog box. Windows 98 asks once more, with a Yes or No dialog box, if you want to convert your icon selections to single-click selections. Answer Yes, and your Windows 98

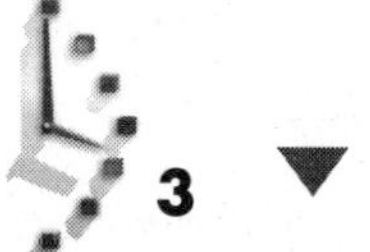

desktop changes immediately and the icons there now have underlined labels. (Resize the My Computer window so you can see the left part of your Windows 98 desktop.) Although your desktop changes immediately, you must make one more change to activate the Web style icons in the open window.

4. Select My Computer window's View menu bar option and then select the as Web Page menu option to place a checkmark next to that option. (Maximize the window to see the full effect.) The My Computer window now changes to the Web style view to complement your desktop. Figure 3.14 shows the result.

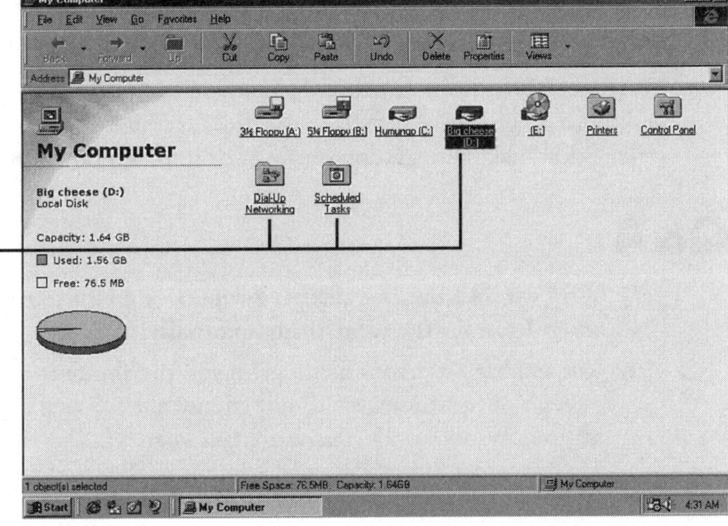

Figure 3.14.
You can now select items by pointing to them and open items with a single mouse click.

Examples of underlined descriptions

Step 3: Review

After you change your window and desktop view to a Web style view, you can select items by pointing to them with your mouse and open windows by clicking once instead of double-clicking over their icons. Your desktop now more fully mimics the Web. When you integrate Web pages into your Active Desktop, Windows 98 responds more uniformly.

Just a Minute

> You can revert to the classic view by once again selecting a window's View | Folder Options | Classic style menu option.

Summary

This hour concentrated mostly on the taskbar. The taskbar gives you a play-by-play status of the open windows on your system. As you open and close windows, the taskbar updates with new buttons to show what's happening at all times. If you start more than one program, you can switch between those programs as easily as you switch between cable TV shows: Click a button on the taskbar.

The taskbar works along with the Start menu to start and control the programs running on your system. Use the Programs command on the Start menu to start programs with a total of two or three mouse clicks. Although you can use the Run command to start programs, the Programs menu is easier to use as long as the program is set up properly in Windows 98.

To reduce your selection requirements, you can also change your desktop to a Web style desktop. You are then able to open windows as easily as you select from the taskbar. The Web style option makes integration of the Web into Windows 98 more seamless.

Q&A

Q Why would I use the taskbar properties menu to organize my open windows when I can do the same thing manually?

A The taskbar properties menu gives you the ability to adjust the appearance of your screen's open windows with one mouse click. If you select a cascading window scheme, Windows 98 ensures that all open window title bars appear on the screen, with the most recently opened window as the front window of focus. You can bring one of the hidden windows into focus by clicking the window's title bar. If, instead, you select the horizontal or vertical tiling options, Windows 98 displays a little of all open windows on top of each other or side-by-side.

If you normally work in only one window at a time, you won't use the taskbar properties. However, you may use the taskbar properties menu to change the appearance of the taskbar itself.

Q How can I use the taskbar properties menu to change the appearance or performance of the taskbar?

A The taskbar is set by default to appear, no matter what else is on your screen. Microsoft thought it best to keep the taskbar on the screen so that you can switch between programs and adjust the Windows 98 performance easily. However, to maximize the screen space and clear away as much as possible, you can change the taskbar's performance so that onscreen windows cover the taskbar, giving you an additional line for the open window. In addition, you can select that Windows 98 always hide the taskbar completely, showing you the taskbar only when you point

to the bottom of the screen with the mouse cursor. If you increase the size of the taskbar, you can still hide it through the properties' Auto hide feature. The increased size will appear when you show the taskbar, but the taskbar will not be in the way when hidden.

The taskbar properties menu also controls the size of the Start menu's icons, so you can decrease the width of the Start menu if you prefer. You also can eliminate (or add) the clock from the taskbar so that the taskbar has room for another window's button.

Q Help! My taskbar has fallen and I can't get my Start menu up! What did I do and how can I fix it?

A You've changed the options in the Taskbar Properties dialog box to hide the taskbar, or you've dragged the top of the taskbar to the bottom of your screen to shrink the taskbar. The taskbar is not gone for long, however. To see the taskbar again, all you need to do is point to the bottom of the screen with the mouse, and the taskbar appears once again.

Workshop

Key Terms

accessory programs Programs that Microsoft included with Windows 98 that fall into several categories, such as multimedia programs, text editors, and games (for example, Solitaire).

Active Desktop The Web-based desktop you can create for Windows 98 that contains active content direct from the Internet.

cascade The effect of neatly stacking all open windows on the screen so that each window's title bar appears.

context-sensitive The process Windows 98 uses to respond to what you're doing.

taskbar properties menu The menu that appears when you click the right mouse button over an empty spot on the taskbar. You can control the performance and appearance of the taskbar and Windows 98 through the taskbar properties menu.

tiling The effect of placing all open windows on the screen so that the body of each window appears next to, above, or below the other windows.

URL The address of an Internet Web site. URL is an acronym for uniform resource locator.

PART

I

Hour 4

Understanding the My Computer Window

The My Computer icon opens to a window, as you learned in Hour 3, "Take Windows 98 to Task," and contains information that relates to your computer's hardware and software. You will often open the My Computer window when you add or remove both hardware and software. The My Computer window provides access to many different areas of your computer.

Many computer beginners and advanced users ignore the My Computer window more than they should. The My Computer window, which always appears on your Windows 98 desktop, enables you to access every hardware device on your system in a uniform fashion.

In this hour, you use the My Computer window to change the behavior of your mouse and also to modify the screen background that you see. You must look at the desktop often, so changing the graphics behind the desktop can break the monotony that you might otherwise face with a dull Windows 98 desktop screen. People often spend the first few sessions with any new operating environment getting to know the environment and modifying the appearance to suit their preferences. In this hour, you learn about the My Computer window while you modify your work environment.

The highlights of this hour include the following:

- ☐ The contents of the My Computer window
- ☐ Where to go for mouse control changes
- ☐ How to change the screen's wallpaper
- ☐ How to test your modem
- ☐ Why a startup disk can help you locate system problems

Searching My Computer

Your computer system is a mixture of hardware (the system unit, monitor, keyboard, CD-ROM, and so on), firmware (the internal memory), and software (for example, Windows 98, MS-DOS, word processors, spreadsheets, and games). There are several ways to access your computer's hardware and software through different areas of Windows 98. The My Computer window contains one of the most helpful hardware and software management resources available in Windows 98.

If your My Computer window is not still open from Hour 3, open it now by double-clicking the icon. (Of course, if you changed your window-open command to a single-click, you need to click only once.) When you double-click the My Computer icon, Windows 98 displays the My Computer window, shown in Figure 4.1. Depending on your window's size and the style you've selected, your My Computer window might differ somewhat from the figure's.

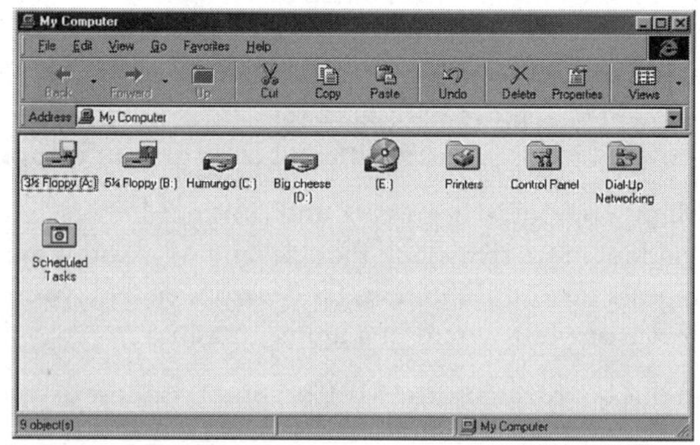

Figure 4.1. *The My Computer window displays the contents of your computer system.*

Introducing the My Computer Window

The My Computer icon is important or Microsoft would not have put it at the top of the opening Windows 98 screen. Its importance will become apparent throughout this book and in your own work as you learn more about Windows 98.

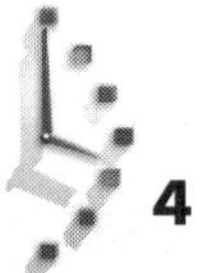

People's needs for the My Computer window differ greatly, depending on which systems they use to run Windows 98. For example, a network user probably displays the My Computer window more often than a single user working primarily on a spreadsheet program. The network user might have more reason to check the properties of a shared printer or a shared disk drive.

TIME SAVER

> If you have a computer that is compatible with Plug-and-Play and you add Plug-and-Play hardware to the computer, such as a new internal high-speed modem, Windows 98 should be able to detect that you've installed that new modem the next time you start your PC. Some devices, such as PC card devices that plug into most laptops and some desktop systems, automatically configure themselves when you insert the cards; they don't require that you first turn off your computer.

Before looking at a sample My Computer window work session, you should understand that there are three ways to view the My Computer window, as well as most other Windows 98 windows:

- As a Web page, as you learned in Hour 3
- In the icon view (with large or small icons)
- In the list view (with or without detail)

4

The icon view is the default view that is set when you install Windows 98. The My Computer window figures in this hour show the icon view format. Newcomers prefer the familiarity that an icon view provides. Later, you will learn how to move files from one disk drive to another by dragging a file to the disk icon where you want to put that file instead of typing a disk drive name as computer users of older operating systems have to do.

As you progress, you may prefer to switch to a list view. A list view lists window contents down the screen in a list of items more like a table of contents. Although small icons still appear next to most of the items in a list view of the My Computer window, the icons are extremely small. The list view gives you the ability to see more items at once without the clutter of icons filling the screen.

When you first open the My Computer window, the difference between the views is not extremely important because the My Computer window shows a high-level overview of the system with rarely more than a few icons. Nevertheless, as you add hardware and as you traverse additional windows from within the My computer window, your current view may no longer be adequate to display the data. For example, for only a few icons, the large icon view works well. If you open windows with additional icons, however, you may want to switch to the small icon view (by selecting View | Small Icons).

Often, the list views work better than the icons, depending on the information you've displayed inside the My Computer window. Figure 4.2 shows the same information from Figure 4.1's icon view as a details view. The detailed list view (available from the View menu) means that descriptions for the icons appear to the right and that the icons appear in a smaller format.

The detailed view becomes even more important if you display additional information in a window such as that shown in Figure 3.3. The detailed list view shows the filename, size in bytes, file type, and the most recent date modified.

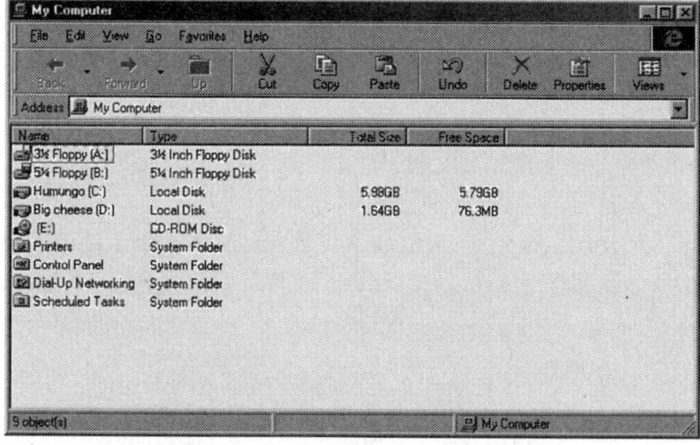

Figure 4.2.
The My Computer window shown in a detailed list view.

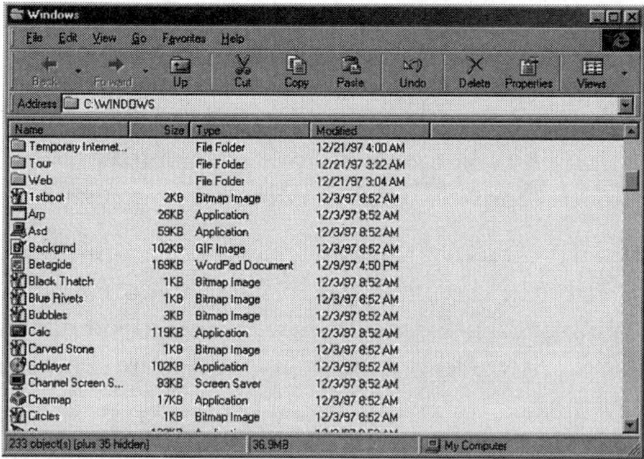

Figure 4.3.
A full window shown in a detailed list view.

When you first explore the My Computer window, just look around for a bit. The next task walks you through a sample exploration session of the My Computer window so that you'll quickly get acquainted with some of the window's more useful investigative features.

4

To Do

Task 4.1: Navigating the My Computer Window

Step 1: Description

The best way to begin learning about the My Computer window is to work within it. Follow the steps in this task to see some of the things that are possible with My Computer and, therefore, with all windows that you need to manage.

Step 2: Action

1. Open the My Computer window if you don't have it open already.
2. From the menu bar, select View | List. The view instantly changes to the list view.
3. Select View | Details. The list view expands to tell you more about each item, such as free space and total space on the disk and CD-ROM drives.
4. Go back to the View | Large Icons display. (The View | Small Icons display provides extremely small icons on most systems that do not add any readability over the list view.)
5. Maximize the My Computer window by clicking the Maximize button or by double-clicking the title bar.
6. Double-click the C disk drive icon. When you do, you should see a window of folders and other icons appearing similar to the one shown in Figure 4.4. Each folder represents a folder on your disk drive named C. A folder is a list of files (and subfolders) stored together in one group. The folder name appears under each folder icon. If you also see a hand holding the folder, the folder is known as a shared folder available to others on the network you're working on.

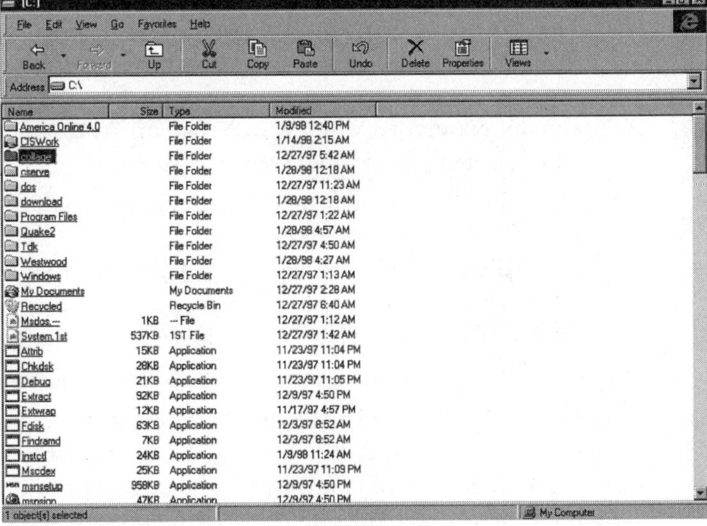

Figure 4.4.

Looking at the directories on drive C.

The grayed-out icons you might see are hidden or system files and folders. Depending on your window options, you may or may not see these icons. Select View | Options and click the View tab to designate whether you want to see all files (in which case Windows 98 grays out the system and normally hidden files and folders), all files except the hidden ones, or all files except both the hidden and system files. You generally won't work with system or hidden files, and by turning off their display you clean up your file listings considerably.

JUST A MINUTE

Folders enable you to group similar files together so that you can work with the entire group at once instead of having to work with individual files. For example, you may keep all your personal correspondence in a single folder so that you can copy it more easily to a disk when you want to back up that set of files.

The icons that look like pieces of paper are document icons that represent individual files, including programs and text files, on your system's C drive. You find other kinds of icons as well. If you see the list view when you display the C disk drive, use View | Large Icons to see the icons.

The window you're now looking at is a completely different window from the My Computer window. The window contains your C drive's contents. Anytime you want to traverse your C drive, or any other drive, and look at its contents you can do so from the My Computer window. Minimize the window to see the My Computer window, which was originally hidden, come back into view.

7. Maximize the C window (click the taskbar button). As you can see, the My Computer window remains on your desktop while you work with the C drive's window. To look at the contents of a file folder, double-click the file folder. When you do, yet another window will open up. You are leaving a trail of windows on your system that describes your hard drive.
8. Close the folder's window so that you return to the drive C window. If you have lots of files on drive C, and most people do, you may have to use the scrollbars to see all the window's contents. As you open additional windows by opening new folders, you can always return to the previous folder window by clicking the toolbar's Up icon, which shows a folder with an arrow in it).
9. Close the C window to return to the My Computer window.
10. Every time you open a window from the My Computer window by clicking an icon such as the C drive icon, another window appears. You can limit the open windows by pressing Ctrl when you open an icon. Press and hold Ctrl and open the C drive icon. The original My Computer window's contents are now replaced

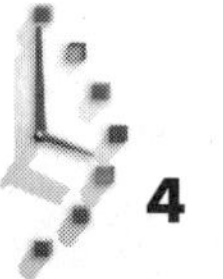

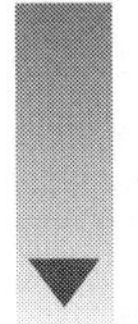

with the C drive's contents. As you open additional windows while pressing Ctrl, the new windows replace the original window. You can traverse right back through all your windows and return to the My Computer window contents by pressing the Back button on the toolbar, just as you do to traverse back through Web pages you may have traveled.

TIME SAVER

Click the arrow next to the My Computer toolbar's Views button. A view list drops down from which you can quickly select large icons, small icons, a list, or a detailed list view without having to first open the Views menu.

Step 3: Review

The My Computer window displays information about your computer and its contents. All the computer's hardware and files are located on the disk. As you add more hardware, you see more icons appearing in the My Computer window. The view that you select determines how much information you can see at one time and how that information appears with a corresponding icon. If you press Ctrl while opening icons, the new contents replace the current window's.

4

Other My Computer Folders

You will master some folders residing inside My Computer as you learn more about Windows 98. The Printers folder contains information about the printer or printers attached to your computer. If you add a non–Plug-and-Play printer to your system, you need to set it up by opening the Printers folder and selecting Add Printer. In some cases, however, the printer's installation requires more power than the Printers folder can provide. You need to check with your printer's documentation to learn how to make the printer work with Windows 98. The Control Panel folder, discussed later in this hour, describes the nonprinter devices connected to your PC, such as your modem, as well as system-setting options that determine how Windows 98 responds to you.

The Dial-Up Networking folder enables you to change your modem connection settings if you use a dial-up service to connect to the Internet. Fortunately, most Internet installations automatically make these setting changes for you because the Dial-Up Networking options can be tedious. You learn about the other nondrive icons in the remaining sections of this hour.

As you'll learn in Hour 22, "Windows 98 Advanced System Tools," the folder labeled Scheduled Tasks enables you to set up programs that you want to run at preset times. For example, you may want to back up your hard disk at the same time each evening or retrieve your email every morning at 7:00.

WINDOWS MINUTE

Scrolling Along

Your computer screen has a limited amount of display area. Within that area, you open one or more windows that each have even smaller display areas. Many times, there is simply too much information to display everything in a window at once. When Windows 98 senses that the available screen space will not hold all the contents of the window, it attaches scrollbars to that window's borders. Windows 98 may attach a vertical scrollbar, horizontal scrollbar, or both, depending on the direction the window holds the data being displayed.

With scrollbars, the window works like a camera panning all around a large scene. You can scroll up and down with a vertical scrollbar or left and right with a horizontal scrollbar. Figure 4.5 shows a resized My Computer drive C window with one vertical scrollbar. The figure tells the names of the scrollbar parts.

Clicking on either scroll arrow moves the window up, down, left, or right by a small amount. If you want to scroll the window farther than the scroll arrows allow, click within the scrollbar shaft for a larger scrolling jump. Press PageUp and PageDown to scroll up or down a window at a time.

The scroll box is sometimes called a "thumb" because you can drag the scrollbar to a specific position anywhere within the scroll shaft, and Windows 98 will instantly scroll the window directly to that exact position without your having to scroll incrementally with the scroll arrows. The size of the thumb is large when the majority of the window's contents is within view, and the thumb shrinks if the window is showing only a small portion of the window's contents.

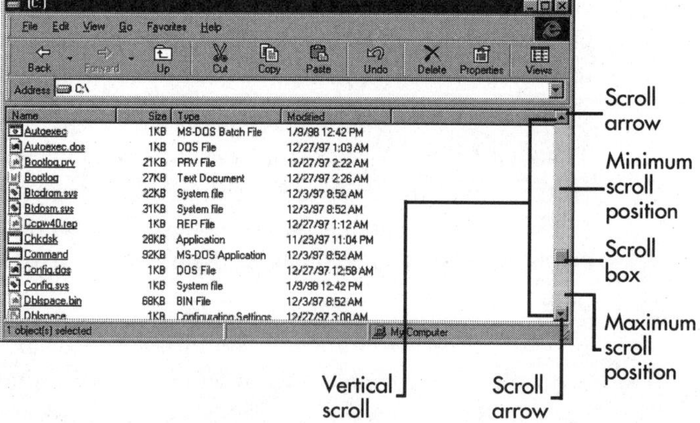

Figure 4.5.
Scrollbars let you look at lots of data.

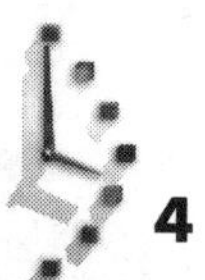

TIME SAVER

All the windows view commands you've learned so far work throughout the Windows 98 environment. Therefore, you can now change views for all windows you work with.

Introducing the Control Panel

The Control Panel icon enables you to adjust and manage the way hardware devices are attached to and respond to your computer. From the My Computer window, open the Control Panel icon, and you see a window like the one in Figure 4.6. The Control Panel's toolbar and menus are similar to those of the My Computer window. When you master windows basics for one kind of window, you can apply that talent to all other windows. From the Control Panel, you can change or modify system and hardware settings.

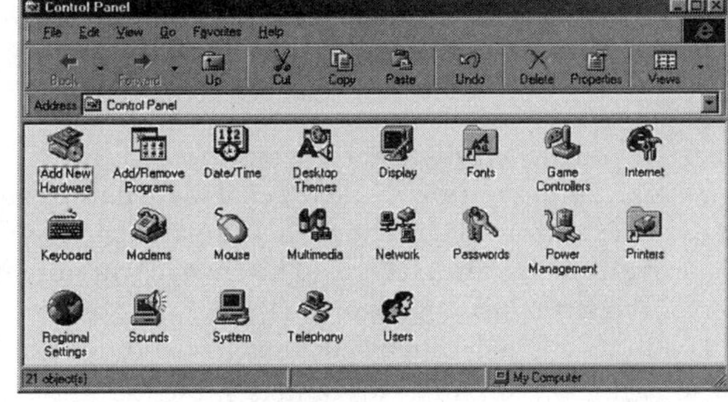

Figure 4.6.
Modify the system settings from within the Control Panel.

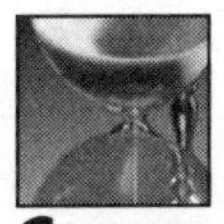

CAUTION

Be very sure that you know what to change before modifying values within the Control Panel. You could change a required setting that might be difficult to reverse later.

Some operations inside the Control Panel are complex and could violate your system's setup. Nevertheless, the next task demonstrates one safe use of the Control Panel so that it will not be foreign to you.

To Do

Task 4.2: System Modification with the Control Panel

Step 1: Description

One of the safest ways to explore the Control Panel is to modify the behavior of your mouse. This task changes the mouse cursor's default shape and enables you to reverse the buttons on your mouse.

Step 2: Action

1. Open the Control Panel window within the My Computer window if you have not yet done so.
2. Open the Mouse icon. The icon indicates that the mouse settings are found here. You see the Mouse Properties dialog box appear, as shown in Figure 4.7.

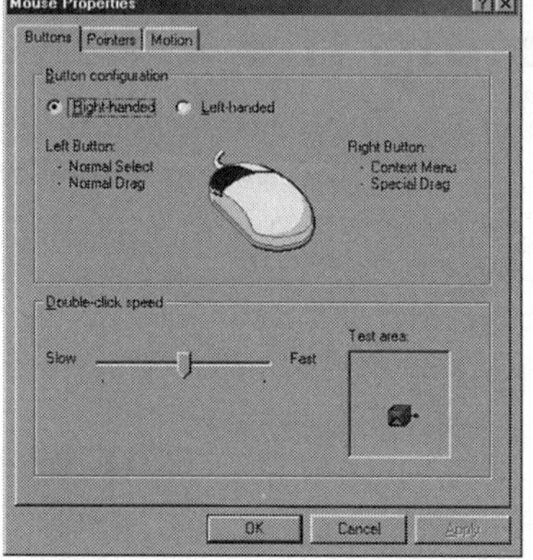

Figure 4.7.
You can change the behavior of the mouse.

3. If you are left-handed but your mouse is set for a right-handed user, you can select the option button marked Left-Handed to change the mouse button functions. The buttons then change their functionality as described in the text beneath each button after the change. (The change will not take effect until you close the Mouse Properties dialog box or click the Apply button.) You can change the button back to its original state by clicking on the other hand.
4. Click the tab marked Pointers at the top of the Mouse Properties dialog box. From the Pointer portion of the dialog box, you can change the default appearance of the mouse. A scrolling list of mouse shapes indicates all the kinds of cursor shapes that appear when certain Windows 98 events take place.
5. To change the normal mouse cursor (called the Normal Select shape), double-click the row with the Normal Select text. Windows 98 displays another screen, shown in Figure 4.8. Different mouse cursors appear for different reasons. The Pointers dialog box enables you to select shapes for the various mouse cursors that can appear. The shapes that end with an `.ani` filename extension are animated cursors that move when they appear.
6. Windows 98 needs to know the name of the file that holds your new mouse cursor. (This screen is not the easiest screen in Windows 98 to figure out, by the way.) Just for grins, double-click the Hourglass row in the choices listed under Look in, after scrolling the horizontal scrollbar so the `Hourglass.ani` file appears. Windows 98 changes the pointing cursor arrow to an hourglass. Click Open to open the `Hourglass.ani` cursor file and assign the file to your mouse cursor. If your cursor name display does not show filename extensions, click on the cursor names and look at the Preview area of the dialog box to see whether the cursor provides movement.

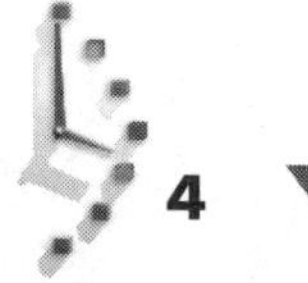

Figure 4.8.
Select a mouse cursor shape file.

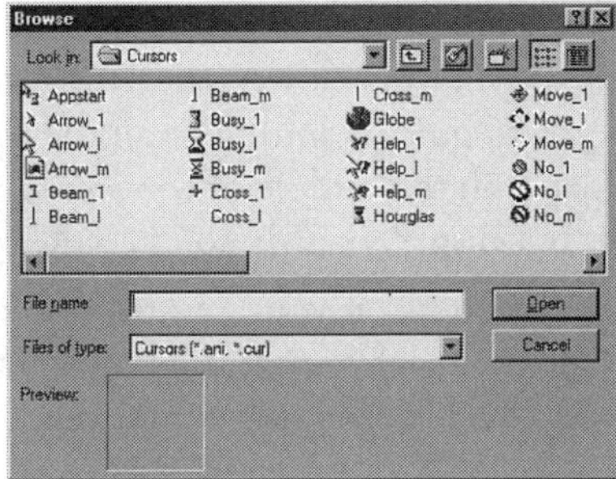

CAUTION

It's best to stick with the default cursor shape and not keep this change permanent so that others who use your computer will know what the cursor indicates. Even you may get confused if you change the mouse cursors to other shapes.

7. Before leaving the Mouse Properties window, click the Use Default button to return the standard mouse cursor to its default pointer shape. If you've already returned to the Control Panel, you have to click the Mouse icon again to set the cursor back to its default shape.
8. Click OK and close the Control Panel. You can now close the My Computer window as well.

Step 3: Review

Through the Control Panel located in the My Computer window, you can change various hardware settings so that Windows 98 interacts with your computer's hardware differently. This task peeked into the Control Panel by showing you how to reverse the mouse buttons and change the default mouse shapes.

The Right Mouse Button

Windows 98 uses the right mouse button to display context-sensitive menus with choices you can select at that time.

Task 4.3: Using the Right Mouse Button

Step 1: Description

This task shows that you don't always need the My Computer window to make changes to your system. In Hour 1, "What's Windows 98 All About?," you learned that wallpaper is the name for the background you see on the screen when you start Windows 98 and work within its windows. You can change that wallpaper to a different picture or eliminate the wallpaper altogether with a right mouse-click.

Step 2: Action

1. With all windows closed (click the toolbar's Show Desktop button, if the button appears, to quickly minimize all the windows), move the mouse cursor over the wallpaper in the middle of the screen. If your screen has no picture behind the icons but displays only a solid color, you do have wallpaper, but it's boring!
2. Point anywhere on your desktop and click the right mouse button. Windows 98 looks to see that your mouse is pointing to the wallpaper and displays a menu of choices that are relevant to your position.
3. Select the Properties command from the menu. Windows 98 opens the Display Properties screen, shown in Figure 4.9.

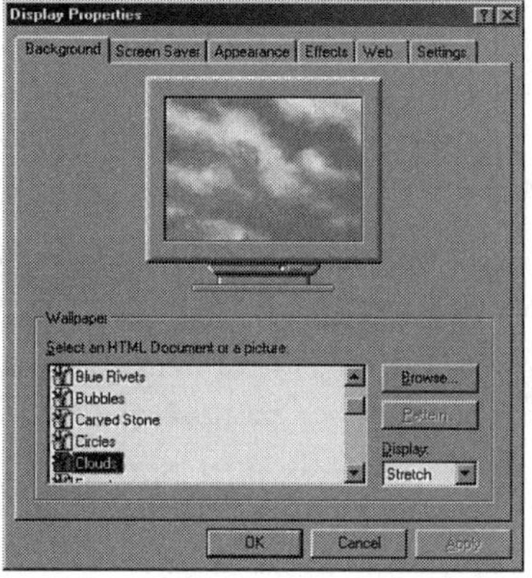

Figure 4.9.
A right click displays a wallpaper selection screen.

Find the bottom section, entitled Wallpaper. Scroll through the list of choices looking for an interesting name, such as Red Bricks, and click on that selection. Windows 98 models the new wallpaper style in the small screen to give you a preview of that style. You can go with that selection or choose another.

5. When you are happy with your selection, click the OK button, and presto, you've hung new wallpaper without messy cutting or gluing!

Step 3: Review

You'll learn other uses of the right mouse button as you progress through this book. You learned here how to change the wallpaper pattern so that you don't get too bored by the same old look.

Test Your Modem

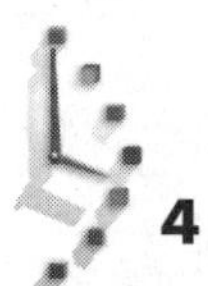

4

Due to its technical nature, communications can be difficult to understand and troubleshoot. If you are having trouble communicating with another computer, the first place to look is the My Computer's Control Panel folder. Learn how to diagnose your modem problems now so that you will know what to do if you experience the problems that invariably come with modem usage.

Time Saver

> You can open the Control Panel without first opening the My Computer window by selecting Start | Settings | Control Panel.

Task 4.4: Using the Modem Diagnostic Tool

Step 1: Description

This task shows you how to let Windows 98 find a potential problem. Windows 98 includes a modem diagnostic tool that tests your modem connection and tells you whether everything is fine or whether a problem exists.

Step 2: Action

1. Double-click the My Computer window.
2. Double-click the Control Panel folder to open the Control Panel window.
3. Double-click the Modems icon to open the Modems Properties tabbed dialog box.
4. Click the Diagnostics tab.
5. Click your modem's port name (such as COM1 or whatever port is to the left of your modem description) to highlight the proper port.
6. Click the More Info button. After a brief pause, Windows 98 displays a More Info dialog box similar to the one in Figure 4.10. If the More Info dialog box found an error, you will see the error.

Figure 4.10.
The modem is responding properly.

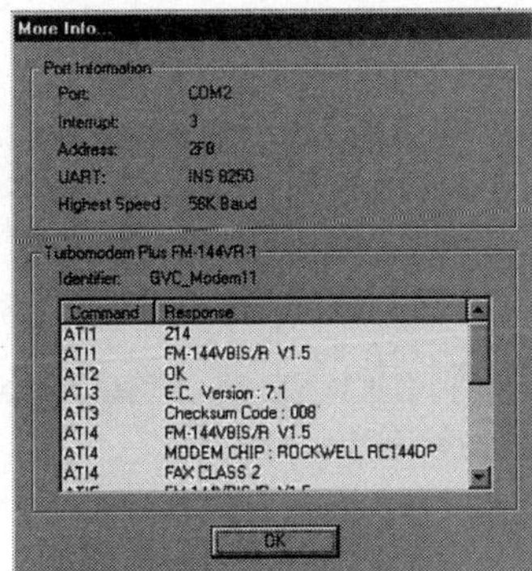

7. Click the OK button to close the More Info dialog box.
8. Close the Modem Properties dialog box and the My Computer window.

Step 3: Review

The Windows 98 modem test is another one of those nice features that even Windows 98 gurus often forget exists. Although the modem test will not describe detailed problems that might exist, you will learn whether Windows 98 recognizes your modem properly when you experience communications troubles.

Startup in Emergencies

Now that you've familiarized yourself with Windows 98, its environment, and the Control Panel, this is a great time to ensure against a minor or major disaster. During the course of using Windows 98, you will add hardware and software. Windows 98 makes adding such components relatively easy, but in some cases, problems may occur. Perhaps you receive a bad installation disk, or a hardware conflict arises that freezes up Windows 98.

By making a startup disk, you can safely get your computer started and access your hard disk when you otherwise cannot start your machine. The startup disk is little more than an MS-DOS boot disk, although the disk does contain several MS-DOS and Windows 98 utility programs (such as the Scan Disk utility explained in Hour 22) that can help you locate disk and memory troubles that can cause boot problems.

Just a Minute

If you upgraded Windows 98 from an earlier version of Windows, the Windows 98 installation gave you the option of creating a startup disk at that time. Therefore, you may already have a startup disk. If not, the Control Panel makes it easy to create a startup disk, as you see here.

Caution

If you use a laptop on the road, always carry a startup disk with you! The startup disk will help save you when you do not have Windows 98 installation disks, MS-DOS disks, or utility programs readily available.

Task 4.5: Making a Startup Disk

Step 1: Description

This task shows you how to create a startup disk. Before beginning this task, locate a high-density formatted disk. Make sure the disk contains no data that you need because the startup process overwrites all data on your disk.

Step 2: Action

1. Click the Start button.
2. Select Settings | Control Panel to display the Control Panel window.

3. Double-click the Add/Remove Program icon.
4. Click the Startup Disk tab to display Figure 4.11's Startup Disk page.

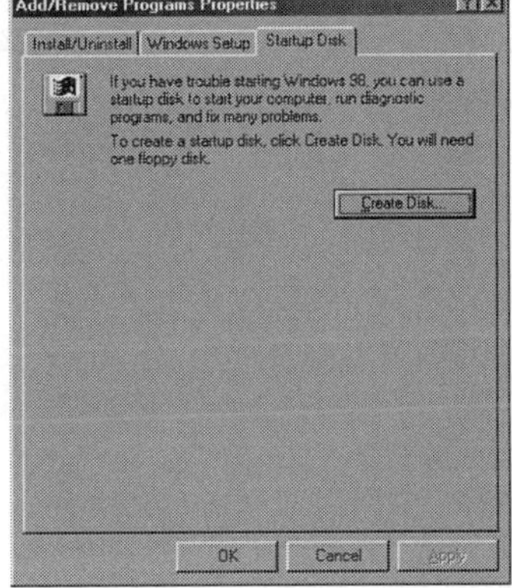

Figure 4.11.
Create a startup disk for emergencies.

5. Click the Create Disk button. The dialog box will tell you when you need to insert the disk you use for the startup disk.
6. After the startup disk creation process ends, close the Control Panel and put the startup disk in a safe place.

Step 3: Review

After you create a startup disk, you have a disk in case of emergencies. If you find that you cannot access your hard disk or boot your computer because your system files are corrupt, you can regain hard disk access by inserting the startup disk and rebooting your computer. The startup disk will not be able to cure any problems, but you will have system access once again so that you may begin tracing the difficulties.

Change the My Computer Icon

Windows 98 makes customization simple. Your desktop is not static, and you can move the icons and even change those you don't like. Here's a quick way to change the icon used for the My Computer window:

1. Right-click over your desktop wallpaper to display the Display Properties window.
2. Click the Effects tab to display the page shown in Figure 4.12.
3. To change the My Computer icon, click the My Computer icon in the Desktop icons section (if My Computer is not already selected) and then click the Change Icon button.
4. Scroll through the icons listed to find one you'd like to use for the My Computer desktop icon. Click that icon to select it.

5. Click OK to close the icon-selection window, then OK again to close the Display Properties dialog box. After a brief pause, your My Computer icon will be customized to your specifications.

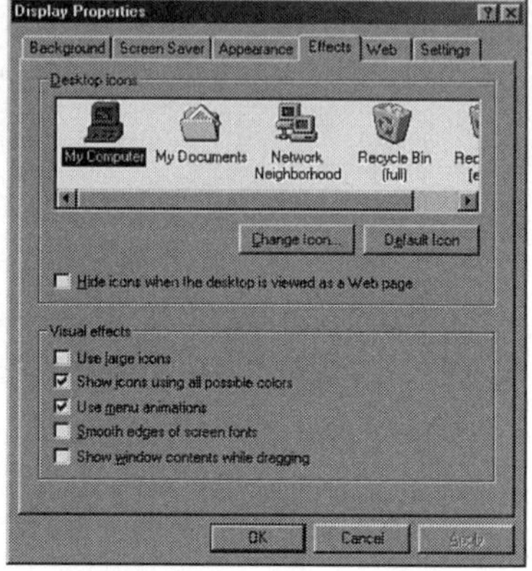

Figure 4.12.
You can select your own icon for the My Computer desktop window.

Summary

This hour taught you how to use the My Computer window. Don't be dismayed that this hour just skimmed the surface of what's available in the My Computer window because the My Computer icon provides a launching point for many powerful hardware and software interactions that sometimes take a while to master. The typical Windows 98 user does not have to know all the details of the My Computer window to use Windows 98 effectively.

Q&A

Q Will I use the My Computer icon a lot?

A This question's answer differs with different people. Some people use their computers primarily for one or two application programs. These people don't modify their computers very often and do not perform a lot of file interaction or system management, so they would rarely, if ever, need to open the My Computer window.

On the other hand, if you modify the hardware on your computer often, you might have to access the My Computer window often. As described in Hour 3, Windows 98 is designed for use with Plug-and-Play hardware, which means that you don't have to configure Windows 98 every time you change hardware on your computer. Not all hardware devices are compatible with Plug-and-Play, however, and you may have to modify some Windows 98 system settings using the My Computer window when you install new computer hardware, such as a second printer.

Q I like the animated cursors, but will they slow down my computer?

A If you use a slow computer, you don't want to do anything that will drain more speed from the processor. Nevertheless, the animated cursors do not seem to cause much of a drain on the processor's resources. The animated cursor icons are small and efficient. Therefore, you should feel free to use whatever cursors you want to use.

Q What do I do if the modem test fails?

A Unfortunately, this book cannot answer that question because the answer could come from myriad sources. The Windows 98 modem test is nice to remember because it gives you a first-step approach to tracing communications problems. If your modem test goes well but you experience communications problems, the problems are either with your software or with the computer on the other end of the telephone line. If the modem diagnostic fails, look into reinstalling the modem drivers that came with your modem. You can also try a different modem, which will solve the problem if the original modem you used is bad.

Workshop

Key Terms

animated cursors Cursors that display movement during the cursor's display, such as a cursor showing a picture of a running horse or a playing piano.

Control Panel A folder window within the My Computer window that enables you to change your computer's system settings.

desktop The Windows 98 screen and background.

folder A special icon that contains other icons that are displayed when you double-click the folder icon; a grouping of related files stored under the same subdirectory.

scrollbars Windows 98 controlling tools that enable you to view a window's contents more fully.

startup disk A disk you create from the Control Panel so that you can start your computer when your hard disk's system files get corrupted due to a hardware or software problem.

Part II

Morning Windows 98 Desktop Exploration

Hour

PART

II

Hour 5

Explore the Windows 98 System

Windows 98 includes a comprehensive program that you might use every time you turn on your computer, the Windows 98 *Explorer,* which graphically displays your entire computer system in a hierarchical tree structure. With Explorer, you have access to everything inside your computer (and outside if you are part of a network or on the Internet).

This hour demonstrates the Windows 98 Explorer, which enables you to manipulate all of your computer's software and hardware. After you've learned about Explorer, the hour wraps up by showing you some time- and disk-saving features of Windows 98.

The highlights of this hour include the following:

- ☐ How to change the various displays of the Windows 98 Explorer
- ☐ Why Explorer makes managing your computer painless
- ☐ What "shortcuts" are all about
- ☐ How to use the Recycle Bin

Hello, Windows 98 Explorer!

You can find the Windows Explorer program listed on the Start menu's second cascaded menu. Click the Start button to display the Start menu. Select Programs, and then select Windows Explorer. The Explorer window opens to look like the one shown in Figure 5.1. Although the figure shows the Explorer screen fully maximized, you can run Explorer in a smaller window if you want something else to appear on your screen as well.

Figure 5.1.
Explorer's opening window.

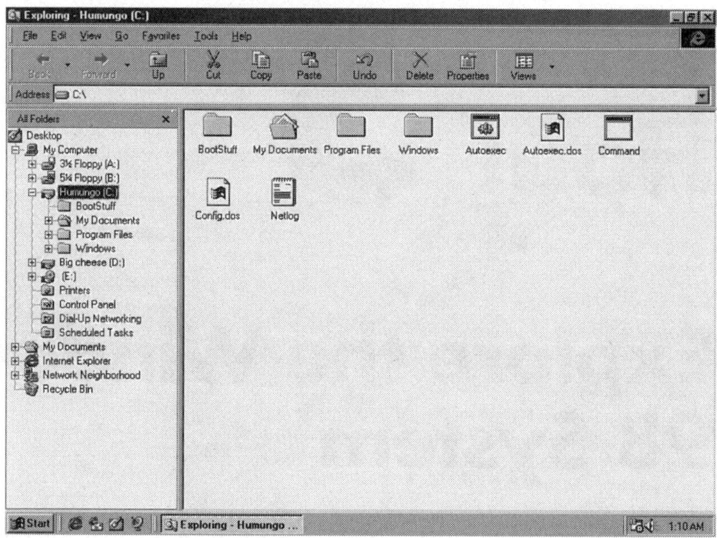

Just a Minute

Your Explorer screen might look slightly different, depending on your Windows 98 configuration. You can see how to change your Explorer's view in the next task.

Time Saver

You can quickly start Explorer by right-clicking over the Start menu and selecting Explore from the pop-up menu that appears. Explorer opens to the Windows\Start Menu directory. If you have a Windows keyboard, one with the flying Windows logo on a key (called the *Windows* key), you can start Explorer even faster by pressing Windows+E.

The left side of the Explorer screen contains a hierarchical overview of your computer system. You will recognize many of the icon entries from your My Computer window. If a vertical

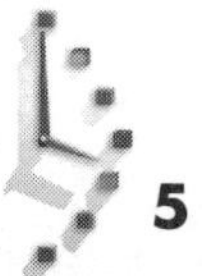

scroll bar appears on the left window, scroll to see the rest of the hierarchical system tree.

JUST A MINUTE

> If a folder icon appears with a plus sign to the left of it, as the Windows folder does, that folder contains additional folders. Folder icons without the plus sign contain only data files (called *documents* throughout Windows 98) but not additional folders. When you open a folder and display its contents, the plus sign changes to a minus sign, as you'll see in the first task.

The right window contains a pictorial overview of the contents of whichever device or folder you select in the left window. The overview might contain large or small icons or a list view, depending on the view you that select. As you select different items in the left window, the right window changes to reflect your changes. Task 5.1 guides you through an initial exploration of Explorer.

TIME SAVER

> The Windows 98 Explorer is not limited to directories and files but displays folders, including your networked folders, as well as Internet services.

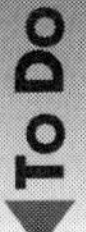

Task 5.1: Changing Explorer's View

Step 1: Description

This task teaches you how to adjust Explorer's display to see the Explorer screen in different ways. As you use Explorer, you can change the display to offer the best option for the information you're looking for at the time.

This task assumes that you've already started Explorer, as requested in the previous section.

Step 2: Action

1. Scroll through the left window pane until you see the icon for the C: drive in the window.
2. If you see a plus sign next to your C: icon in the left window (you might have to scroll the window's scroll bar to see the C: icon), click the plus sign to display the contents of the C: drive. The plus becomes a minus sign, and the left window opens the C: icon showing the list of folders and documents on the C: drive. Click the drive's minus sign again to close the window. Click once more to turn the plus to a minus and watch the right window. As you change between these two views of the C: drive (detailed and overview), watch the right window.

Just a Minute

Notice that the right window does not change as you click the C: icon in the left window. The reason is that the right window always displays the contents of whatever you highlight in the left window. Whether or not the C: icon is open (with a minus sign) or closed (with a plus sign), the C: icon is highlighted. The right window displays that selected C: drive's highest level folders and documents. If you were to click one of those documents on the C: drive, the right window would then update to show the contents of that folder (don't click a folder just yet).

3. Click the highest level in the left window, labeled Desktop, and Windows 98 displays the contents of your desktop in the right window. See Figure 5.2.

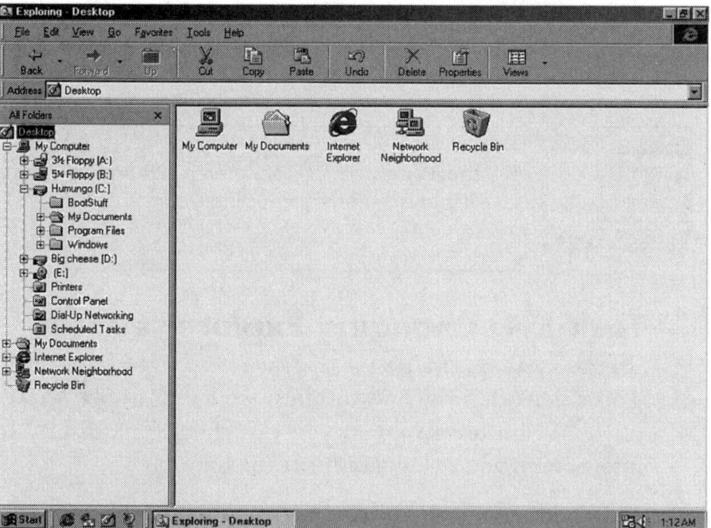

Figure 5.2.
You can view the desktop contents in the Explorer.

4. Click the C: icon to display the contents of the C: drive. Depending on the contents and size of your C: drive, the right window can contain a few or several document files.
5. Press Alt+V to open the View menu on the menu bar. Select Toolbar to display a list of tools you can display on your toolbar. You will recognize the tools from the My Computer window. For example, you can add text labels to the toolbar icons.

   Click the dropdown listbox on the toolbar, labeled Address Bar (display the Address Bar item from View | Toolbar if you don't see the listbox) to see another access method for swapping between devices, folders, and files on your computer. If you ever display more information than can fit in the left window, the Address drop-down listbox compacts the list so that detail does not appear in your viewing area.

6. Display the View menu once again. The Large Icons window (the default display view) consumes most of the right window. Therefore, select View | Small Icons to gather more room in the right window. The View | Small Icons command shrinks the size of the icons to show more items in the right window.
7. Select View | List. Windows 98 Explorer retains the small icon sizes and displays the items by type of item (folders first and then documents).
8. Select View | Details. Windows 98 Explorer displays the items in a detailed format that describes the name, type, and modified date of each item, as shown in Figure 5.3. Actually, given the detail that you normally have by using Explorer, you will almost always want to display the right window in this detailed list view. When you work with files, you will often need to know their size, type, or last modified date.

   Adjust the column widths of the three detailed columns in the right window by dragging the column title dividers left or right with your mouse.

   Click Name, the title of the first detailed column in the right window. Watch the window's contents change as you then click Modified. Explorer sorts the display to appear in date order (earliest first). Click Modified again and Explorer displays the items in reverse date order from the oldest to the most recent. If you click any column twice in a row, Windows 98 sorts the column in reverse order. You can always sort columns in order or reverse order by clicking the column's name when working in a columnar Windows 98 window.

Figure 5.3.
Sometimes you want more detail about the Explorer items.

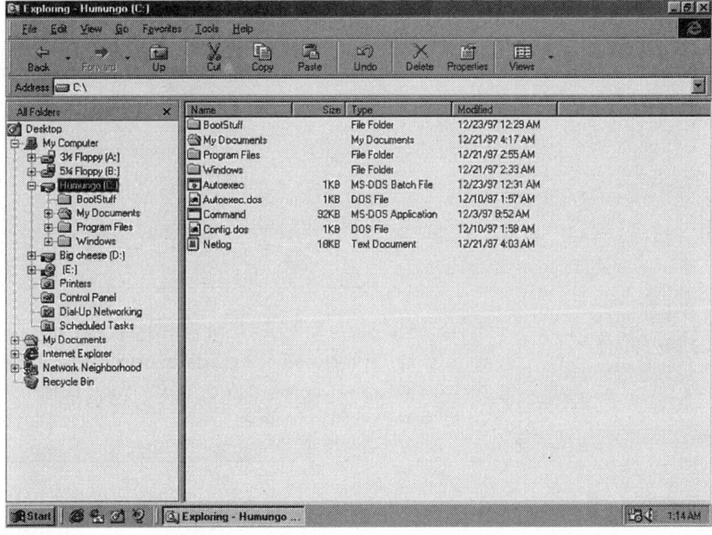

9. If you want to see more of one of Explorer's windows, you can drag the vertical dividing line that falls between the two windows to the left or right. For example, if you want the left window to be smaller to make room for more large icons, drag

the center column to the left and release the mouse when the left window is as small as you want it. (Remember that the mouse cursor changes shape when you place it at the proper position on the dividing column.)

Explorer does not update the display every time you resize a window. Therefore, if you enlarge the right window while in an icon view, Explorer does not automatically rearrange the right window's icons to fill up the newly enlarged space. The View | Refresh command adjusts the icons to fill the space evenly. You will almost always want to select View | Refresh after modifying Explorer's window sizes. Figure 5.4 shows an Explorer screen with a small left window. Perform Refresh when you open Explorer in a window and then add or delete files from another window. When you select View | Refresh, Explorer updates its file list and changes the display to reflect the new file status.

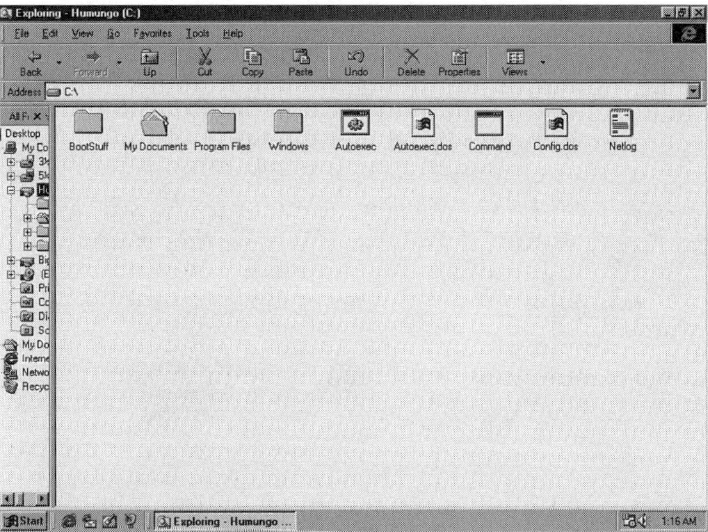

Figure 5.4.
Adjust the Explorer window sizes if you need more room.

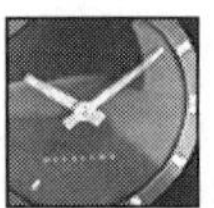

JUST A MINUTE

If you make the left or right window too small (such as Figure 5.4's left window), Windows 98 adds a horizontal scroll bar to the small window so that you can scroll its contents back and forth to see what's highlighted or to select another item.

10. The Explorer environment is always updating itself to reflect your current actions. Therefore, the right-click menu commands change, depending on whether you select a text document, folder, sound document, graphics document, disk drive, or network drive. Click a folder and click the right mouse button to see the menu that

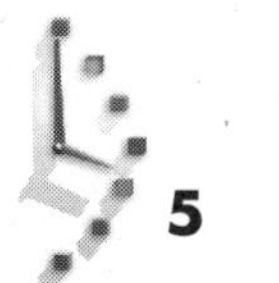

appears. Now, click the right mouse button over a document file to see a slightly different menu. The actions you might want to perform on a document are often different from the actions you might want to perform on a folder, and the menu reflects those differences. The right-click's pop-up menus are context-sensitive, so they contain only the options you can use at the time.

TIME SAVER

Open a folder by double-clicking it, and then return to the previous (parent) folder by clicking the Up One Level icon on the Explorer's taskbar. Use the Up toolbar button to return to your previously open Explorer window. You can return to the previous folder you opened (which is not necessarily the parent folder) by clicking the Back button.

11. Many Explorer users copy files to and from disk drives and other kinds of drives, such as networked drives.

    You can use Explorer to copy and move individual files or multiple files at once. Often, you want to put one or more files on a disk to use on your home computer for weekend overtime (sure, you want to do that a lot!).

    To select a Windows 98 file (called a document, remember), click that document or point to it if you've turned on the Web-like file-selection scheme. To select more than one document at a time, hold down the Ctrl key while clicking each document that you want to select. You can select folders, as well as documents. When you select a folder and other document files to copy to a disk, for example, Windows 98 copies all of the document files within the folder, as well as the other document files you've selected, to the disk. Figure 5.5 shows an Explorer screen with several document files and a folder selected. The File | Send To command is about to send those files to the disk in the A: drive. The Send To command is useful for sending copies of selected files and folders to a disk, a fax recipient, or one of several other destinations you've set up. You will learn more about the Send To command in the section called "Manage Documents with a Right Mouse click."

5

TIME SAVER

If you want to select all but one or two documents and folders inside a window, first Ctrl-click the one or two that you don't want to select (which selects those) and choose Edit | Invert Selection to reverse the selection. All the items that were not selected are now selected, and the one or two that were selected are not selected anymore.

Figure 5.5.
Select multiple documents and folders if you need to copy several at a time.

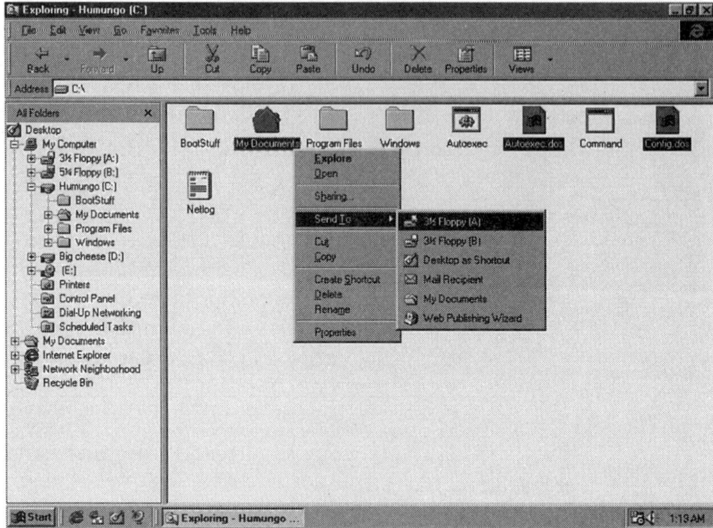

12. When you want to move or copy a file to another location (the Send To command works only for disks and other non-hard disk devices), select the file (or select a group of files) in the right window and drag while holding down the *right* mouse button to the folder or disk where you want to move or copy the file. Windows 98 opens a pop-up menu when you release the files from which you can select a move or copy operation.
13. Rename files and folders if you need to by selecting the file or folder and pressing the F2 shortcut key. (F2 is the shortcut for the File | Rename menu command.) Windows 98 highlights the name, so you can edit or enter a new name. When you press Enter Windows 98 saves the new name.

Step 3: Review

The Explorer windows give you both high-level and detailed overviews of your computer system and the computer's files. Explorer offers two windows for two different views: A computer-level view and a folder view, if you need one. Clicking folder icons inside either window opens those folders and gives you a view of more documents and folders deeper within your computer system.

After you display documents and folders, you are free to copy, move, delete, and rename those items.

The strength of Explorer is that your entire computer system appears in the left window at all times. When you want to drag a document or folder to a different directory on a completely different drive (or even to another computer on the network if you are connected to a

network), the target disk drive always appears in the left window. As long as you've clicked the disk drive's plus sign to display that disk's directories, you can drop a file into that directory from elsewhere in the system.

The Explorer Options

Explorer supports various display options for the items inside its windows. Recall from previous hours that Windows 98 supports the use of filename extensions. The View | Folder Options command displays tabbed dialog boxes that enable you to control the items in the Explorer display.

To Do

Task 5.2: Changing Explorer's Options

Step 1: Description

Different users require different output from the Explorer program. There are types of documents that you simply don't need to display during normal work inside Explorer. The system files are good examples of files that the typical user does not need to see.

In addition, the actual location of the file—its pathname—does not always match the system of embedded folders. (See Hour 3, "Take Windows 98 to Task," for more information on pathnames.) In other words, a document might be located inside two embedded folders shown with the Explorer display, but the actual file might be embedded three levels deep on your hard disk. The system of folders—usually but not always—matches the system of directories on your disk. If you need to know exactly where folders and documents are located on your disk drive, you can request that Explorer display the full pathname of those folders and documents.

Step 2: Action

1. Select the View | Folder Options command to display the Options tabbed dialog box shown in Figure 5.6.

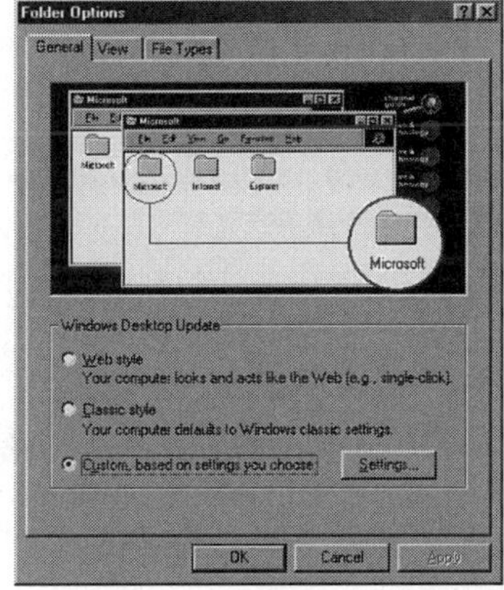

Figure 5.6.
The Options dialog box determines the appearance of Explorer.

2. Click the View tab to see the folder display options.
3. If you click Display the full path in title bar, Explorer displays a full pathname of selected documents in the title bar every time you select one of the items in the left window.
4. The next option, Hide file extensions for known file types, determines how Windows 98 responds to known file types. Windows 98 comes installed with several types of files already *registered*, and you might not ever need to register additional types. Registered files are files that Windows 98 recognizes by their filename extensions.

   When you register a file type (as described in Task 5.3), you tell Windows 98 the program for all files with that extension to associate to. Once registered, when you double-click that file's icon, Windows 98 starts the program you've associated with that file. For example, when you double-click a file with a .CDA extension, Windows 98 starts the CD Player application because CD Player is the application associated to all files that end with the .CDA extension.
5. Look through the remaining items to see the other folder options that Windows 98 provides.

TIME SAVER

If you are familiar with MS-DOS and filenames, you might feel more comfortable if you display the file extensions on the Explorer screen documents. Hiding the extensions reduces clutter in the right window, but with the extension, you can determine the exact name of the file when you need the exact name. Fortunately, with or without the extensions, the icons next to the filenames help remind you of the file's type.

CAUTION

If you hide filename extensions in Explorer, Windows 98 hides those extensions in almost every other file listing. For example, if you hide Explorer's extension display, you will no longer see extensions in WordPad's Open dialog boxes. You won't even see them in applications that you purchase in addition to Windows 98 applications, such as Microsoft Excel.

Step 3: Review

If you don't like the way Explorer displays information, you can probably change the display. Explorer's options enable you to determine how documents appear, how large their windows are, and whether or not filename extensions should appear.

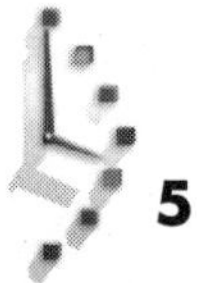

To Do

Task 5.3: Registering File Types

Step 1: Description

As the previous hour explains, Windows 98 makes the document, rather than the program, the focus of everything you do. When you want to edit a graphic image, you should be able to click that image instead of starting a graphics program and then load the image from there. By registering file types and the file's extension, you teach Windows 98 how to work with all files of that extension.

Suppose that someone designs a new graphics format after you begin using Windows 98 that increases the computer's graphic compression capability and enables you to store huge graphics files in a small amount of space. Suppose these compressed graphic files have an extension of .CPR, and the program that displays these graphics is called Compress Graphics. You can associate the .CPR filename extension to the Compress Graphics program name so that when you click any file with that extension, even if it is not showing in the Explorer window, Windows 98 knows to start the Compress Graphics program and automatically loads the image you double-clicked.

This task shows you how to view and change any associations that currently reside on your system.

CAUTION

> You are probably better off not changing any file associations unless you are very comfortable with files and programs. The only reason to change a current association is if you install a program that works with a certain type of file better than one already registered for that type. Most Windows 98 installation programs automatically register their file types when you install the programs. Therefore, this task is more informative than active, so you can better understand the purpose of file associations.

5

Step 2: Action

1. Select the View | Folder Options tabbed dialog box again if the dialog box from the Task 5.2 is not still showing.
2. Click the File Types tab to see the File Types dialog box shown in Figure 5.7.
3. Click the item in the scrollable listbox labeled CD Audio Track. In the File type details portion of the dialog box, you can see that the extension associated with this file type name is .CDA and that CDPLAYER is the name of the program that automatically starts when you double-click any file with this .CDA extension. The icon you see also serves to identify the file type.

JUST A MINUTE

> When double-clicking a file to start that file's associated program, remember that the file's extension does not have to show on the screen. If you've turned off the filename extension's display, Windows 98 still correctly associates the file properly with its registered program.

Figure 5.7.
You register file types in the File Types dialog box.

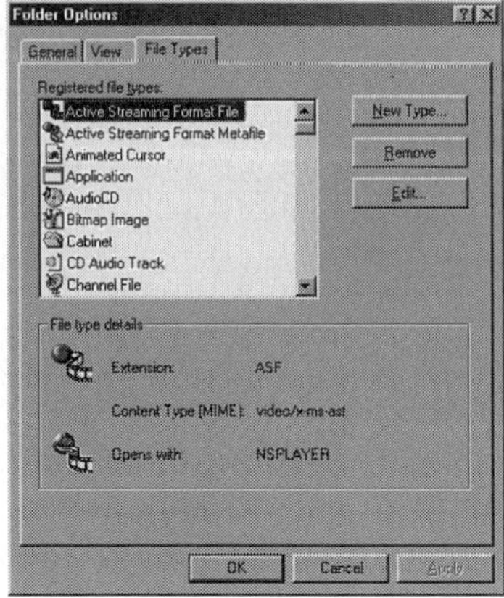

4. Click the Edit command button to see more information on .CDA file types. An additional dialog box, called the Edit File Type dialog box, appears, as shown in Figure 5.8.

Figure 5.8.
The Edit File Type dialog box controls the details of file associations.

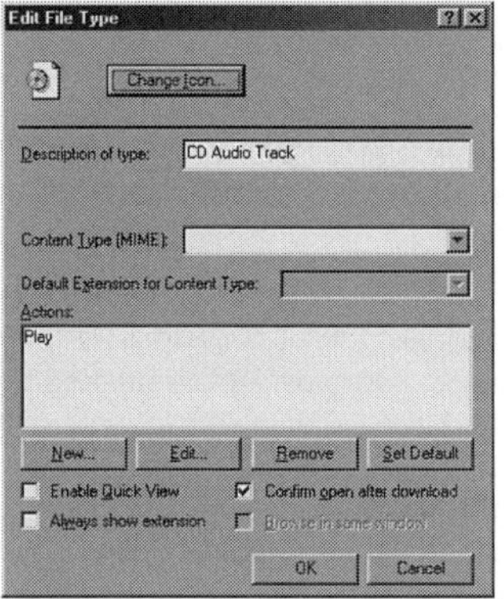

Here is where you select or change icons associated with registered file types. Every .CDA file appearing in Explorer has the same icon. You can select a different icon if you want (don't do so now). The Description of type prompt displays a description of the file type for reference purposes. Actions describe the first thing the program must do. Given the screen shown in Figure 5.8 (your screen should not be too different), the .CDA files have an icon that contains a compact disc over a document. The description of this file type is *CD Audio track*, and the first thing the CDPLAYER program will do automatically, upon loading itself after you double-click a .CDA file, is execute the Play command. This plays the .CDA song file you've selected.

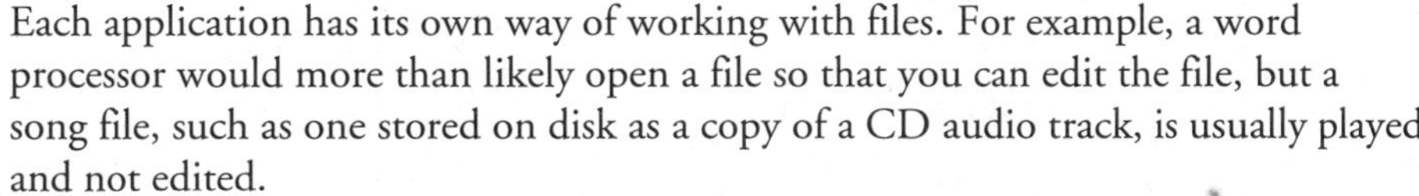

Each application has its own way of working with files. For example, a word processor would more than likely open a file so that you can edit the file, but a song file, such as one stored on disk as a copy of a CD audio track, is usually played and not edited.

5. Click Edit to see the lowest-level of detail available for file type associations. The Editing action dialog box appears, as shown in Figure 5.9.

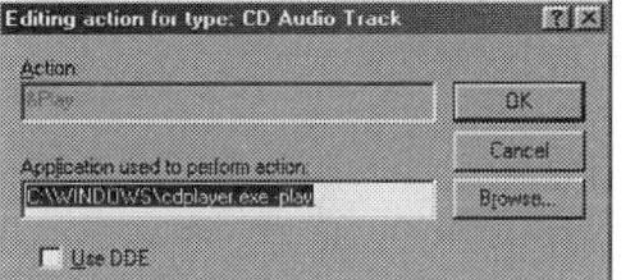

Figure 5.9.
This is the lowest level of detail available when you associate a file type.

6. Now that you've seen what's involved with registering file types, press the Esc key three times to return to Explorer. Leave Explorer loaded for the next task.

Step 3: Review

The file type registration is fairly complex. Rarely will you have to associate files with applications because the application's installation program should register its file types automatically.

JUST A MINUTE

Want to know what those song files are all about? Hour 23, "Multimedia and Sound," describes the multimedia capabilities of Windows 98, including the CD Player program and audio files stored on your system.

5

To Do

Task 5.4: Manage Documents with a Right Mouse Click

Step 1: Description

After you display the Explorer (or any other file list in Windows 98), you can point to any folder or document and click the right mouse button to perform several actions on the document. Here's what you can do with documents:

- Select the document
- Play sound documents or open graphics documents
- Print the document
- Copy the file to a disk
- Cut or copy selected text to the Windows 98 Clipboard
- Create a shortcut access to the file so you can later open the file without using the Open dialog box
- Delete the document
- Rename the document
- Change the document's system attributes

Right-clicking a folder's name produces a menu that enables you to perform these actions.

The following task walks you through many of these right-click actions.

Step 2: Action

1. Point to a text file on your C: drive. Text files use a spiral notepad icon. (Open your Windows folder if you see no text files in your C's root folder. Point to the file and click the right mouse button. A pop-up menu opens to the right of the document, as shown in Figure 5.10.

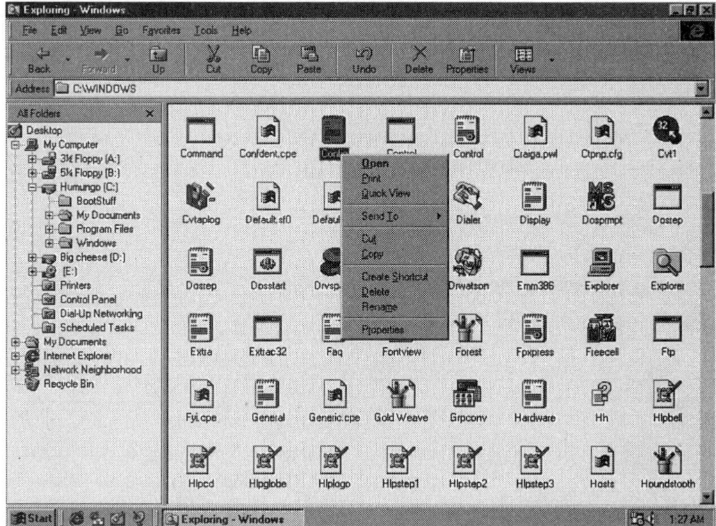

Figure 5.10.
The right mouse displays a pop-up menu.

The Open command always attempts to examine the document's native format and open the document with an appropriate program such as the Windows's Notepad program. Although the first command is Open for text files, the command is Play if you right-clicked a sound file. For now, don't select Open.

2. Find a blank formatted disk. Insert the disk in the A: drive. Click the right mouse button over the text document and select the Send To command. The disk drive appears in the list that appears when you select Send To. When you select the disk drive, Windows 98 begins sending an exact copy of the text file to the disk. Windows 98 graphically displays the sending of the document to the A: drive with a flying document going from one folder to another.

JUST A MINUTE

If you attempt to copy a document over another one that already exists with the same name, Windows 98 warns you that you are about to overwrite the existing document.

3. Point to the text file once again and click the right mouse button. Select Delete. Windows 98 displays the message box shown in Figure 5.11. Don't choose Yes because you need to keep the text file where it is.

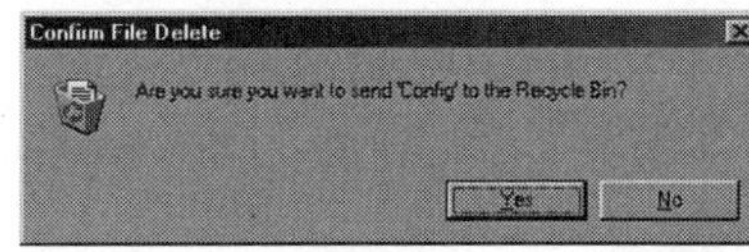

Figure 5.11.
The Recycle Bin holds deleted documents for a while.

The *Recycle Bin* is a special location inside Windows 98 that holds the documents you delete. Recycle Bin's icon appears on your Windows 98 desktop. Windows 98 gives you one last chance to recover deleted documents. When you delete a document file of any type, Windows 98 sends that file to the Recycle Bin. The documents are then out of your way but not deleted permanently until you empty the Recycle Bin. You will learn all about the Recycle Bin in the section entitled, "Where Do the Deleted Files Go?" For now, remember that you can delete documents directly from any Open dialog box.

TIME SAVER

The File | Save and File | Save As menu commands in Windows 98-compatible programs also display dialog boxes that act just like the Explorer window. All of the right-mouse-click commands described here are also available in those dialog boxes.

4. Click No because you should not delete the text file now.
5. It's extremely easy to rename a document. Click the right mouse button to display the document's menu and select Rename. Windows 98 highlights the name, and you can edit or completely change the name to something else. Change the filename now to **XYZ**. Press Enter to keep the new name. (If you want to cancel a rename operation you've started, press Esc.

CAUTION

Do not supply an extension when you rename the file unless you've turned on the filename extension display. For example, if you renamed a Readme document (that is really named Readme.txt) to NewName.txt, the document would actually be named NewName.txt.txt! Fortunately, Windows 98 warns you if you change a file's extension, so you can accept or reject the change before it becomes permanent.

6. Try this: Move the mouse pointer to an area of the Explorer's right pane where no icon appears and click the right mouse button. A new menu appears, as shown in Figure 5.12.

5

The Undo Rename command reverses the previous renaming of the document. Select Undo Rename and the XYZ text file you just renamed reverts to its original name.

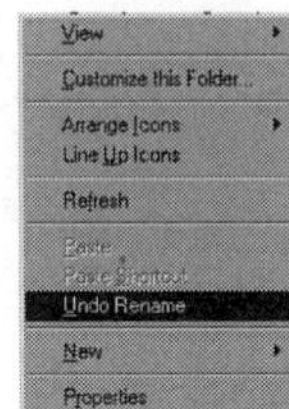

Figure 5.12.
You can undo the renaming of a file.

TIME SAVER

> Undo Rename remembers a long list of past names. For example, if you change a document's name three times in a row, and then select Undo Rename three times, Windows 98 reverts the name to its first and original name!

Step 3: Review

This task covered the most important commands in the Open dialog box's right-click document menu. This menu differs slightly depending on the kind of document you click (folder, sound, graphic, program, text, word processor document, and so on), but the fundamental menu of commands stays the same and works the way this task described. If you want to make copies of files on the hard disk or move the file to a different location, you should master the techniques described in Task 5.5.

To Do

Task 5.5: Copy and Move Documents

Step 1: Description

A file icon's right-click menu offers advanced copying and moving of files. The *Clipboard* is the go-between for all Windows 98 copy, cut, paste, and move operations. When you want to copy a file from one place to another, you can place a copy of the file on the Windows 98 Clipboard. When you do, the file is on the Clipboard and out of your way, until you go to where you want the file copied. You'll then paste the file to the new location, in effect copying from the Clipboard to the new location. When you copy a file to another location, the file remains in its original location and a copy is made elsewhere.

JUST A MINUTE

> The Clipboard holds one item at a time. If you copy a document to the Clipboard, a subsequent copy overwrites the first copy.

TIME SAVER

If you want to copy a file to disk, use the Send To command explained in Task 5.4 because Send To is easier to use than copying to a disk.

When you move a file from one location to another, Windows 98 first performs a cut operation. This means that Windows 98 deletes the file from its current location and sends the file to the Clipboard (overwriting whatever was on the Clipboard). When you find the location to which you want to move the file, Windows 98 copies the Clipboard's contents to the new location (such as a different folder or disk drive).

WINDOWS MINUTE

The Clipboard

In a way, the Clipboard is like a short-term Recycle Bin, which holds all deleted files until you are ready to remove them permanently. The Clipboard holds deleted (or copied) documents and pieces of documents, but only until you send something else to the Clipboard or exit Windows 98 and turn off your computer.

Step 2: Action

1. Right-click a text file's icon.
2. Select the Copy command. Windows 98 sends a complete copy of the document to the Clipboard. The Clipboard keeps the document until you replace the Clipboard's contents with something else or until you exit Windows 98. Therefore, you can send the Clipboard document to several subsequent locations.
3. Right-click a folder in Explorer's right window. The menu appears with the Paste command. Windows 98 knows that something is on the Clipboard (a copy of the text file), and you can send the file's copy to the folder by clicking Paste. Don't paste the file now, however, unless you then open the folder and remove the file. There is no need to have two copies of the text file on your disk.
4. Right-click once again over the text file. This time, select Cut instead of Copy. Windows 98 erases the document file from the Windows folder and places the file on the Clipboard.

CAUTION

Windows 98 keeps the name of the document in place until you paste the document elsewhere. The name is misleading because it makes you think the document is still in the Windows folder. A ghost outline of an icon appears where the document's icon originally appeared. As long as the name still appears in the Windows folder, you can open the file and do things with it, but as soon as you paste the Clipboard contents elsewhere, the file permanently disappears from the Windows folder.

5

5. Right-click a folder. If you select Paste, the text document leaves its original location and goes to the folder. Don't paste now but press Esc twice (the first Esc keypress removes the right-click menu, and the second restores the cut file).
6. Windows 98 is as safe as possible. If you change your mind after a copy or cut operation, you can always reverse the operation! Right-click the icon area and the pop-up menu contains an Undo command that reverses the most recent copy or cut.

TIME SAVER

Here's a much faster way to move a document to another folder listed in the Explorer windows: Drag the document to the folder! Try it by dragging a test file over to another hard disk or to another folder on the same disk. An outline of the document travels with the mouse cursor during the drag. When you release the mouse button, the file anchors into its new position. Want to restore the item? Right-click the mouse and select Undo Move or Undo Copy. Windows 98 always enables you to undo copies and moves, no matter how you perform the move, through menus or with the mouse.

If you want to use the drag-and-drop shortcut method for copying documents, hold down the Ctrl key while dragging the document to the other folder. (The key combination is easy if you remember that both copy and Ctrl begin with the same letter.) As you drag an item, Windows 98 displays a plus sign at the bottom of the icon to indicate that you are copying and not moving. To cancel a copy you've started, drag the item back to its original location before releasing your mouse button or press Esc before releasing your mouse button. In addition, if you drag the item while holding the right mouse button, Windows 98 displays a pop-up menu, enabling you to specify that you want to move or copy the document.

CAUTION

You cannot drag an item such as a document to just anywhere. Windows 98 changes the mouse cursor to a circle with a slash through it (the international "Do Not" symbol) when you drag the document over any area of the screen that cannot accept it.

7. Sometimes, you might need a document for a program outside of the program in which you're currently working. You can place a document on the Windows 98 desktop. Select a text file and copy the document to the Clipboard by right-clicking and selecting Copy. (You also can use drag-and-drop if you want. Hold down Ctrl and drag the document out of the Explorer window, if you've resized Explorer so you can see part of the desktop, and continue with step 8.)

8. Move the cursor on the Windows 98 desktop to an area of the wallpaper that has no icon on it. Click the right mouse button to display a menu and select Paste. The document's file will now have an icon on your desktop along with the other icons already there.

   To copy or move the wallpaper document, use the right click menu or drag the document with the mouse, as explained earlier in this hour.

Windows Minute

Placing Documents on the Desktop

The items you place on the desktop, whether by copying or by moving, stay on the desktop until you remove them from the desktop. Even after shutting down Windows 98 and turning off your computer, a desktop item will be there when you return.

Although you shouldn't clutter the desktop with too many documents, you might want to work with a document in several different programs over a period of a few days. By putting the document on the desktop, it is always easily available to any application that's running. Of course, if you run an application in a maximized window, you must shrink the window to some degree to retrieve the document because you have to see the desktop to copy and move the items on it. Also, you can drag Web pages to your desktop if you've activated the Active Desktop feature.

Step 3: Review

Managing documents often involves moving or sending copies of those documents from one location to another. Perhaps you want to work with a document in two or more applications. If so, you can copy that document into each application's folder.

5

Windows 98 supports a complete set of menu-driven cut, copy, and paste commands from the right mouse click. With these commands, you can copy or move files from one place to another. If you can see the target location of the copy or move, such as another window's folder on the screen or the desktop, use the mouse to copy or move the document and save time.

Where Do the Deleted Files Go?

When you delete files by using dialog boxes or Explorer, you now know that those files go to the Recycle Bin. While in the Recycle Bin, those files are out of your way and deleted in every respect except one: They are not really deleted! Those files are not in their original locations, but they stay in the Recycle Bin until you empty it.

Periodically, you will want to check the Recycle Bin for files that you can erase completely from your hard disk. The following task explains the Recycle Bin in more detail.

TIME SAVER

> The Recycle Bin icon changes from an overflowing bin to an empty one when you empty the Recycle Bin enabling you to tell at a glance whether or not your Recycle Bin is empty.

Task 5.6: Using the Recycle Bin

Step 1: Description

The Recycle Bin appears on your Windows 98 desktop. Any time you want to view or delete items from the Recycle Bin, display your desktop and access the Recycle Bin icon.

TIME SAVER

> If your desktop is completely covered up with running applications, you don't have to close those applications to see the desktop. Click the taskbar's Show Desktop icon to minimize your applications' windows.

Step 2: Action

1. Display your desktop by minimizing any open windows you might have on the screen.
2. Double-click the Recycle Bin icon. The Recycle Bin window opens, as shown in Figure 5.13.

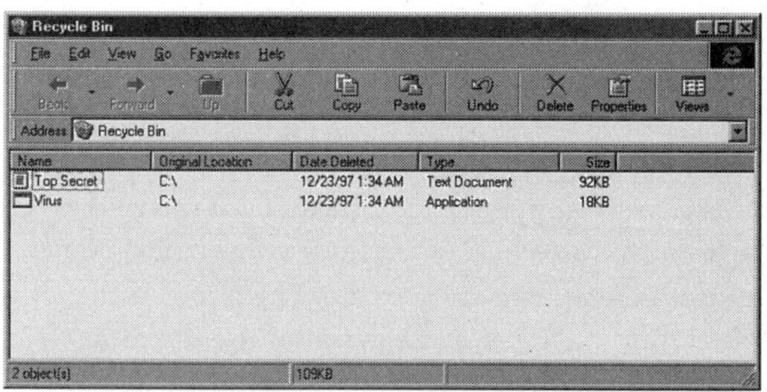

Figure 5.13.
The Recycle Bin lists deleted files that you can recover.

3. If you've deleted at least one file, you should have one or two files already in the Recycle Bin. There might be many more, depending on what has taken place on your system. You will recognize the format of the Recycle Bin's column headings; you can adjust the width of the columns by dragging the column separators with your mouse.

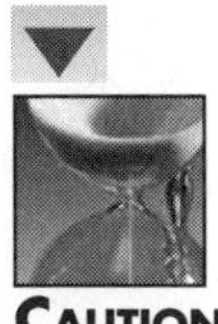

CAUTION

The Recycle Bin dialog box contains all deleted files on your system—not just the deleted files on one of your disk drives. You can change the disks that the Recycle Bin uses for its storage of deleted files, but unless you change your Windows 98 default values, all files that you delete through Windows 98 go to the Recycle Bin.

4. Most of the Recycle Bin dialog box's menu bar commands are identical to the commands in Explorer. When you select an item (or more than one item by using Ctrl+click), the menu commands apply to that selected item.
5. Double-click one of the Recycle Bin's items to display a Properties dialog box for that item. It tells you additional information about the deleted item, such as the date you created and deleted the item.
6. Perhaps the most important menu command is File | Empty Recycle Bin. This command empties the entire Recycle Bin. You can select this command now, if there is nothing in your Recycle Bin that you think you will need later.
7. Select File | Close to close the Recycle Bin dialog box.

TIME SAVER

Double-click (or single-click if you've selected a Web-style desktop) a Recycle Bin icon to look at a document to verify the contents before deleting the document.

JUST A MINUTE

Using a dialog box, Windows 98 asks once more if you want to empty the Recycle Bin. This precaution ensures that you don't inadvertently erase files that you might really need.

Step 3: Review

The Recycle Bin enables you to delete files without really removing those files from your disk. All deleted files go to the Recycle Bin. Those files are not truly deleted from your disk until you empty the file from the Recycle Bin. You can empty a single selected file, several selected files, or the entire Recycle Bin.

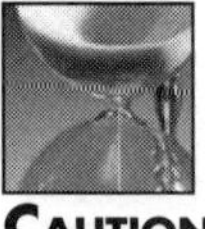

CAUTION

Remember that the Recycle Bin does not hold files you delete from the MS-DOS prompt. When you use MS-DOS to delete a file, Windows 98 erases the file as soon as you issue the command. Unlike earlier MS-DOS versions, the Windows 98 MS-DOS does not include an UNDELETE command. Make sure you want to delete a file when you issue the MS-DOS DEL or ERASE commands.

TIME SAVER

Although the Recycle Bin adds a level of safety to your work so that you have a second chance to recover files that you delete, if you hold the Shift key when you highlight a file and press Delete (from Explorer or any of the My Computer windows), Windows 98 bypasses the Recycle Bin and deletes the files from your system immediately.

Making Windows 98 Easier

There are numerous ways to make Windows 98 easier for your day-to-day work. Three time-saving techniques are as follows:

- Changing the Start menu
- Adding single-key access to programs
- Shortcuts

After you create single-key access to a program or a shortcut or you change the Start menu, those time-savers stay in effect, making work inside Windows 98 much more efficient.

Task 5.7: Adding Time-Savers

Step 1: Description

The time-savers described in this task might not be for everyone, but they often help users of Windows 98. You have to experiment with the techniques until you find the ones that help you the most.

Step 2: Action

1. You can add programs to the top of the Start menu by dragging a program from Explorer or My Computer to the Start button. Open the Explorer window if Explorer is not still running.
2. Click the Windows folder. The folder's contents appear in the right window.

CAUTION

Before adding programs to the Start menu, you must know the command and location of the program you are adding. If you do not know the path to the program, you can use the Find commands described in Hour 10.

3. Scroll down the window to locate a game called Freecell (the extension is .exe). Freecell is a solitare card game.
4. Drag the Freecell icon to your Start button. The icon stays in place, but an outline of the icon moves with your dragged mouse cursor.
5. Release the icon over the Start button. You've just added the Freecell game to the top of your Start menu.
6. Close Explorer and click your Start button. Your Start menu now includes the Freecell game, as shown in Figure 5.14. You can now start Freecell without traversing several Start menu layers for those times when the boss is away for a short while. (Depending on the programs already at the top of your Start menu, you might see additional entries.)

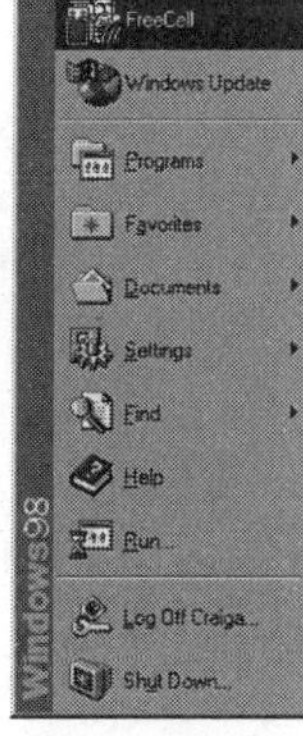

Figure 5.14.
Your Start menu now includes the Freecell game.

JUST A MINUTE

Your Start menu hides extensions for all files you add to the Start menu if you've chosen the Hide file extensions for known file types option in Explorer's View, Options dialog box. If you check this option, all extensions disappear from the Start menu, as well as from other windows where filenames appear.

Time Saver

Windows 98 offers a great way to rearrange and modify your Start menu without going through the windows and buttons of the Settings, Taskbar & Start Menu option. Any time you want to move one of the Start menu's entries from one location to another, display that item on the Start menu and drag that item to another location on the menu. (Don't click the item and release the mouse; be sure that you click and hold your mouse button.) If you right-click over any Start menu item, a pop-up menu appears, enabling you to rename and delete that item.

Caution

Don't change the Start menu too dramatically until you are comfortable with Windows 98. The Start menu is probably best left alone in its current helpful state until you become more acquainted with Windows 98. If you share a computer with others, you could confuse your coworkers if you change the Start menu too much.

7. Delete the Freecell game from the Start menu (you can add it later if you really want it there) by selecting Settings | Taskbar & Start Menu from the Start menu, selecting the Start Menu Programs tab, and clicking the Remove command button. Scroll to the Freecell game and select the Freecell entry.
8. Click the Remove command button to remove the game from the Start menu.
9. Click the Close button but do not close the Start menu dialog box. Instead, click Advanced so that Windows 98 starts Explorer. You can see that mastering Explorer is critical because Explorer windows appear throughout Windows 98.
10. If you click the Programs folder, Explorer displays the items in the Start menu's first set of cascaded menus.
11. Open the Accessories folder to view the contents of the Accessories group. Remember that you're viewing contents of the Accessories menu that cascades from the Start menu. The Calculator program's icon appears in this folder group.
12. Right-click the Calculator icon to display a menu.
13. Select Properties to display the Calculator program's Properties tabbed dialog box (see Figure 5.15).
14. Press Alt+K to move the cursor to the Shortcut key text prompt. Type **C** at the prompt. Windows 98 changes the C to Ctrl + Alt + C on the screen. Ctrl+Alt+C is now the shortcut for the Calculator program. If you run a program that uses a shortcut key you've added to Windows 98, the program's shortcut key takes precedence over the Windows 98 shortcut key.
15. Click OK to close the dialog box.

Figure 5.15.
You can now add a single-key shortcut that will start the calculator program.

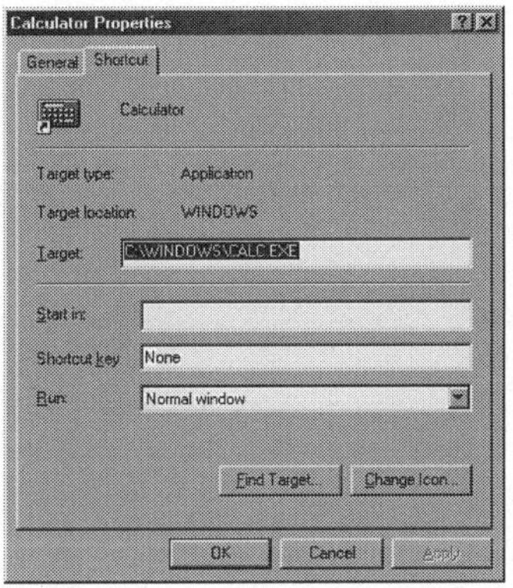

16. Select File | Close to exit Explorer and then close the taskbar Properties dialog box.

    Whenever you now press Ctrl+Alt+C, Windows 98 starts its Calculator program. This single-key shortcut (actually a simultaneous three-key shortcut) enables you to start programs instantly, from virtually anywhere in the Windows 98 system, without having to locate the program's menu or icon.

Windows Minute

Shortcuts

A subfolder resides in your Windows folder called Start Menu. The Start Menu's folder contains all the items that appear on your Start menu, including the items you drag to the Start menu as you did in the previous task. If you display the contents of the Start menu in Explorer, you see small arrows at the bottom of the icons there, as shown in Figure 5.16. The arrows indicate *shortcuts* to the file.

The name *shortcut* has a double meaning in Windows 98—one of the reasons that this task's timesavers can become confusing.

A shortcut is actually better termed an *alias file*. When you create a shortcut, such as on the Start menu, Windows 98 does not make a copy of the program in every location where you place the icon. Windows 98 actually creates a link to that program, called a shortcut, that points to the program on your disk wherever its location might be.

If you right-click a document or folder in Explorer's right window, you see the Create Shortcut command that creates a shortcut to the document or folder to which you are pointing. Windows 98 creates a new icon and title (the title begins with Shortcut to) but does not actually create a copy of the item. Instead, Windows 98 creates a link to that item. The link reduces disk space taken up by multiple copies of the same files. You can even create a shortcut to a networked item that resides on a different computer altogether, as well as to Internet sites; the shortcut appears to exist on your own computer's desktop or menu, while it actually resides on the other machine. The shortcut pointer takes much less space than a copy of the actual file would. Therefore, Freecell still exists only in your Windows folder but the shortcut tells the Start menu where to go to start the game.

Figure 5.16.
Start menu items are actually shortcuts to files.

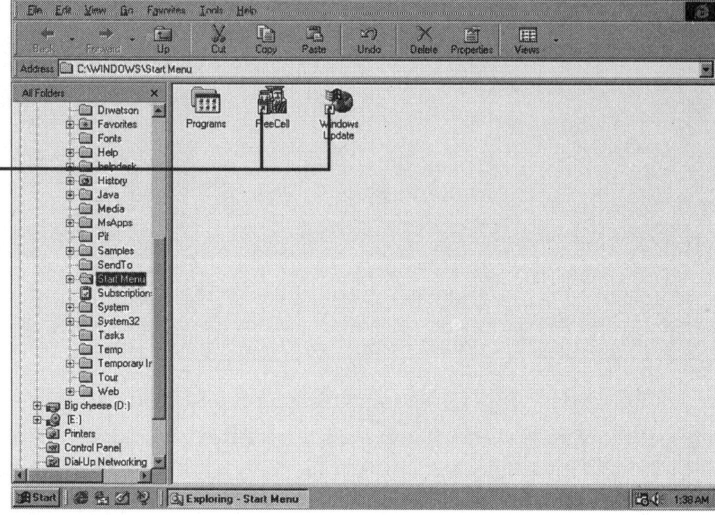

Step 3: Review

You can now add a shortcut to your Start menu by dragging Explorer icons to the Start button. Actually, you can add program shortcuts to any location, including your desktop, so you can start programs by clicking their icons just as you open the My Computer icon's window. Adding shortcuts that make program location faster and shortcut keystrokes that enable you to start a program from anywhere simply by pressing a set of keys enables you to get started faster with the programs that you want to run.

Hour 9, "Giving Windows 98 Your Own Programs," explains how to install new programs on your Windows 98-based PC. Most installation programs automatically add their program icons to your Start menu, but you will learn in Hour 9 how to manage your complete Start menu so that you can add and remove programs from anywhere on the cascaded set of menus.

Summary

This hour showed you how to use the Explorer to search your computer system for documents and folders, as well as how to manage the computer system by using a uniform interface for all your storage devices. Copying and moving among folders and documents are painless functions when you use Explorer. You can display the item to be moved in the right window and drag that item to any device listed in the left window. It is also inside Explorer that you associate file types to programs so that you can click a document and run the appropriate program that works with that of document.

There are three shortcuts that help you access your programs. You can add a shortcut to the desktop, to the Start menu system, and even to the keyboard to start programs quickly.

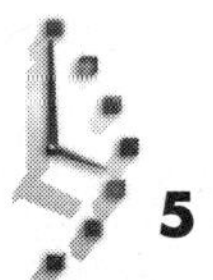

Q&A

Q Why does it seem as though many Explorer functions are available elsewhere, such as in the My Computer window and in Open dialog boxes?

A You can find many of Explorer's capabilities elsewhere. Windows 98 is known for giving you the tools you need where you need them. You don't have to hunt for the tools you need.

Q Do files that I delete but have yet to empty from the Recycle Bin still consume disk space?

A Certainly. The Recycle Bin must keep the entire file intact, or you would not be able to recover it from the Recycle Bin if you needed the file again. Although files in the Recycle Bin consume disk space, they are retrievable until you empty the Recycle Bin. Only after emptying the Recycle Bin does Windows 98 physically delete the file from your disk.

Q I'm confused; are there three kinds of shortcuts?

A There are three versions of shortcuts in Windows 98. You can add a single-key shortcut key to any program. When you press Ctrl+Alt and that key at the same time, Windows 98 starts that program. You can be working in Explorer, at the desktop, or in virtually any other program, but when you press that shortcut keystroke, Windows 98 starts the program you've assigned to that shortcut key.

When you right-click a document or folder and select the Create Shortcut command, Windows 98 creates a shortcut to the item, which is really an alias name that knows the location of the original document or folder but which acts like a copy of the item.

When you add items to the Start menu (or any menu cascading out from the Start menu), you must create a shortcut to that item because you don't want a copy of the same program all over your disk drive. Therefore, the menu command will be a shortcut to the program that, after you select that menu item, finds the program on the disk drive and starts the program.

Workshop

Key Terms

Review the following list of terms:

- ☐ *byte* One character of storage.
- ☐ *Explorer* A powerful file-listing application that gives you both high-level and detailed descriptions of your computer system and the files on the system.
- ☐ *registered* A file is registered when you've associated an application with that file's extension.

- *shortcut* A link (the shortcut) to a file item that takes the place of a copy and saves disk storage.
- *Status bar* A message area at the bottom of a window that updates to show you what is happening at any given moment.

Part II

Hour 6

A Call for Help

This hour shows you how to help yourself! That is—how to help yourself find help when using Windows 98. Although this book is *really* all you'll ever need to use Windows 98 effectively (self-promotion was never one of the author's weak points), when you get confused, Windows 98 offers a good set of online tools that you can access to find out how to accomplish a specific task.

If you've used previous versions of Windows, you will notice that Microsoft has revamped the entire help system. The help system takes on the analogy of a help desk.

The highlights of this hour include:

- ☐ Why Windows 98 includes online help
- ☐ How to access the help system
- ☐ When to search the Internet for answers
- ☐ How to access Windows 98 application help

Introducing the Help System

Even Windows 98 experts need help now and then with Windows 98. Windows 98 is simply too vast, despite its simple appearance and clean desktop, for users to know everything about the system. Windows 98 includes a powerful built-in Help system. The Help system is online, meaning, in this case, that the help is on your disk and available from anywhere within the Windows 98 environment. The Help system is available whenever you need it. For example, if you are working with Explorer and forget how to send a document to the disk, you can search the online help system for the words *send to*, and Windows 98 gives you advice on how to locate and use the Send To command.

There are a number of ways you can request help while working in Windows 98. There are also a tremendous number of places from which you can get help. This hour focuses on the most common ways that you can use online help and also offers tips along the way. The next task explains how to access the top-level online help features.

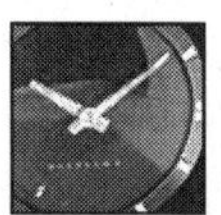

Just a Minute

To use every help feature available to you in Windows 98, you need Internet access. Microsoft keeps up-to-date advice on the Web, such as bug reports and add-on programs to Windows 98 that you can download to improve your use of Windows 98.

Task 6.1: Accessing Help from the Start Menu

Step 1: Description

The taskbar is always available to you no matter what else you are doing in Windows 98. Even if you've hidden the taskbar behind a running program, the taskbar is available as soon as you point the mouse to the bottom of the screen. You can find a Help command on the taskbar's Start menu. Help displays the online help's opening screen by using a Web browser format.

Step 2: Action

1. Click the Start button to display the Start menu.
2. Select Help to request online help. After a brief pause, you see the Windows Help screen shown in Figure 6.1.

The Help window offers two kinds of help: local help that searches your PC's Windows 98 help files for answers to your questions and Web help resources that connect to your Internet provider and accesses Microsoft's huge online help resource.

Time Saver

The Help window contains a complete Web-browsing toolbar.

Step 3: Review

When you need help, you aren't limited to your own system help files. Although you can get many answers from your PC's local help files, Microsoft's online Help window makes it easy for you to contact the large online help databases Microsoft stores on the Web.

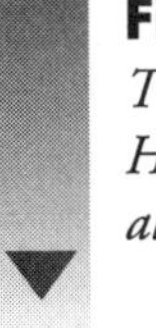

Figure 6.1.
The Windows Help screen offers all kinds of help.

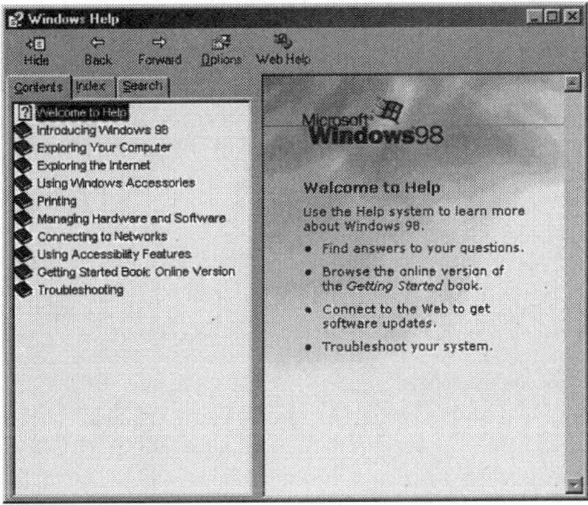

JUST A MINUTE

The Help window resides on your disk as an HTML file, which is the format behind all Web pages. Web pages can be local or on the Internet—your PC reacts to both in the same manner. Therefore, Help window acts like a Web page. When you rest your mouse cursor over a *hot spot* (a link to another location), the mouse cursor changes to a pointing hand to let you know that if you click that hot spot, another page will appear. As with all help pages, you can traverse backward through your help screen travels by clicking the toolbar's Back button.

Task 6.2: Getting Local Help

Step 1: Description

If you have a question about Windows 98 or about a certain utility program that comes with Windows 98, try the local help first. You will find many common Windows 98 answers there, and searching your local disk is generally quicker than waiting on a Web search.

Step 2: Action

1. Open the Help window if you closed the window after the previous task.
2. After a brief pause, the help screen appears that you saw in Figure 6.1.

   The Contents section offers a summary of the help items available to you in an Explorer-like format. The local help system uses a book analogy and each item in the summary represents a different "book" that contains help on that topic. If you click to open one of the book icons, the book's contents open to show book chapters or pages within the books.
3. Open the book labeled `Using Windows Accessories` to open the Windows Accessories book of help. Book chapter titles fall open from the book's icon.
4. Click the Multimedia book icon to see the pages related to multimedia within your help system. You can distinguish between a book or chapter and a page with specific help by the page-like icon that appears next to a page topic.
5. Click the CD Player page to see its detail in the right window, as shown in Figure 6.2.

Figure 6.2.
The right window displays the help topic's page.

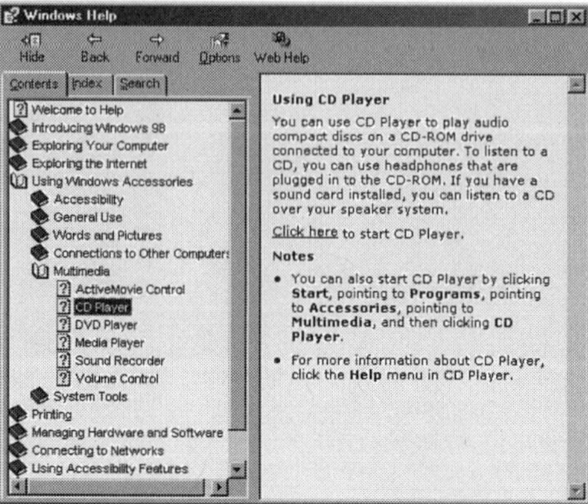

TIME SAVER

If you click the toolbar's Hide button, the book list goes away, and you gain the entire window for the Detail page. Some help pages contain a lot of text, so you might need the extra room. A help page can continue over several Detail pages, as well. Click the Show toolbar button to show the books once again.

6. Press the Back button to see the help screen before you display the detail. As with any Web page, you can click the Back button to return to the previous help screen. If you view several topics in succession, you sometimes want to return to a previous topic. Return to the CD Player's detail by clicking the CD Player page again in the Contents window.

   Don't close the help screen, as Task 6.3 starts with the screen you're currently viewing.

TIME SAVER

If the Help window contains detail you want to save without looking it up again, you can print it by right-clicking the detail and selecting Print.

Step 3: Review

The local help's Contents page contains an Explorer-like view of the entire Windows 98 Help system on your disk. The Contents window summarizes the help topics and the right window displays the detail that you need.

6

Task 6.3: Searching the Index

Step 1: Description

The local help's Contents page groups your Windows 98 help topics into sections that you can traverse like books in a reference library, as you saw in the task 6.2. The Contents page helps you gather all the help available on general topics such as multimedia and printing. The local help window also offers an index search that helps you zero in to a more specific item for which you need help.

Step 2: Action

1. Click the Index tab in the Help window. An alphabetical list of all items within the help system appears in a scrollable window pane, as Figure 6.3 shows. If you know exactly which Windows 98 element with which you need help, you might prefer the Index page over the Contents page.

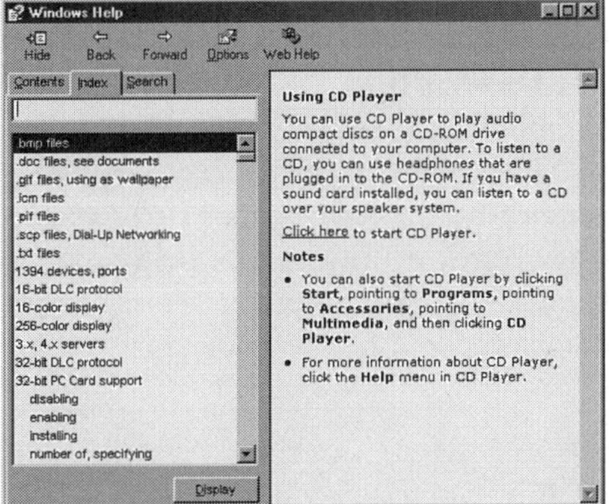

Figure 6.3.
The Index tab enables you to find details quickly.

2. To find an index item, scroll the indexed list to the item you want to find. You can quickly move to an item by clicking the textbox beneath the Index tab and typing your requested entry. As you type, the index item that matches your typed letters begins to appear.
3. Scroll through the entries, looking at the various index items.
4. Read the page indexed by Direct Cable Connection overview. A hot spot appears in the right window labeled `Click Here`. The help pages are often cross-referenced to other related help pages, so you can read all the information related to the topic in which you are interested. As you move to these hot spots, the Back button always returns you to the previous help page, so you can always get back from where you came in the Help system.
5. Every once in a while an indexed topic requires additional information. Sometimes the Help system narrows a search to a more specific item. For example, if you click the indexed item labeled `pasting information`, the Topics Found dialog box appears like the one in Figure 6.4. When you click Display, that topic's Detail page appears.

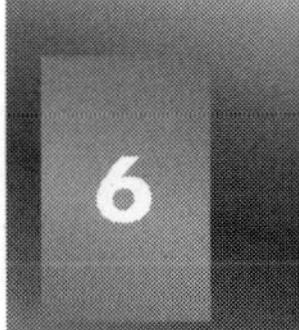

Figure 6.4.
Help needs you to be more specific.

6. Close the help window to return to the main Help window.

Step 3: Review

If you know with which specific Windows 98 element you need help, you can often locate the help quicker by selecting from the Index page instead of the more general Contents page on the local help screen.

Task 6.4: Searching the Internet

Step 1: Description

As new information becomes available, Microsoft adds help sites, set up for you, to the Internet. You cannot update your version of Windows 98 as fast as Microsoft can update its Internet site, so it makes sense for Microsoft to extend the Help system to the online world. When you search the Internet for help topics, you're certain to get the latest information available on Windows 98 topics, including bug fixes, suggested system file replacements, and the latest news about new technology.

CAUTION

You must have Internet access to use the Help system's Web area. You will learn all about Internet access in Hour 13, "Internet Explorer 4.0."

Step 2: Action

1. From the opening Help screen, select any topic and click the toolbar's Web Help button. After another confirmation dialog box, the Help window then connects to the Internet to search for more information on that topic. If you are not currently signed onto the Internet from another window, your sign-in dialog box appears. If the sign-in screen appears, enter your ID and password as usual.
2. After the sign-in completes, Microsoft's technical support page appears, as shown in Figure 6.5, where you can perform extensive detailed searching of the site for information you need.

JUST A MINUTE

You might get a Security Warning dialog box asking if you want to work with Microsoft's interactive site. Although nothing is guaranteed, software that Microsoft's site sends to your PC is generally as secure and virus-free, so if you want to take advantage of the site's full features, you should accept the certification security warning.

Figure 6.5.
The Web Help button takes you to the Web to locate in-depth answers you cannot find locally on your disk.

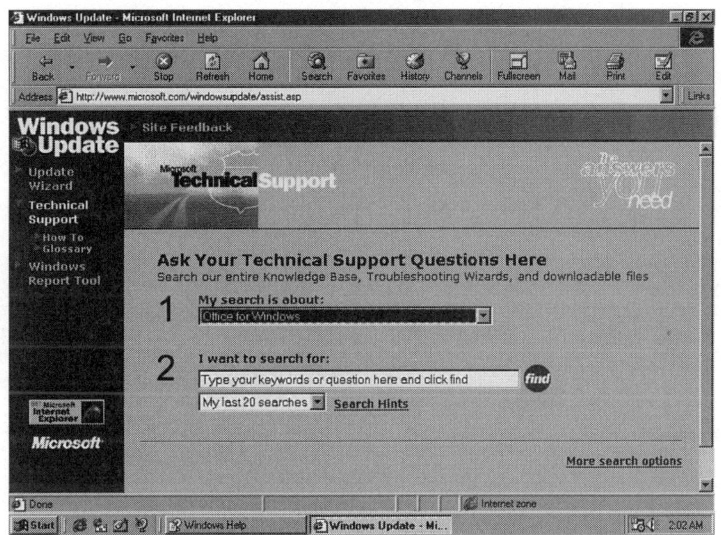

3. After you find the answer you need, you can click the Back button to return to the window you were viewing before clicking the Web Help button.

Step 3: Review

If you cannot find the answer you need in your local Help files, search the Internet. Microsoft's staff constantly updates online sites to provide the latest support information Windows 98 users need.

TIME SAVER

If you locate an Internet help page to which you will want to return, click the Favorites button to open the Favorites menu and select Add to Favorites. Windows 98 adds the page address to your favorites list. You then can return to that page quickly by selecting Favorites from any window menu bar or from the Start menu.

6

Other Forms of Help

When you use a Windows 98 program, you often need help with the program rather than Windows 98. Almost every Windows 98 application's menu bar includes a Help option you can click for help with that program.

For example, if you select Help from the Calculator program, a Help dialog box appears with three tabs: Contents, Index, and Search. You're already familiar with the Contents and Index pages because those mimic the same pages in the Help window. Figure 6.6 shows the Calculator's Index page.

JUST A MINUTE

Some Windows 98 applications do not yet support the Web-like browser style that the Windows 98 Help window supports. Therefore, the Web-like, two-window summary and Detail dialog boxes aren't available for all programs that you use. As Windows 98 usage grows, more software firms should begin incorporating the Web-style browser into their help engines.

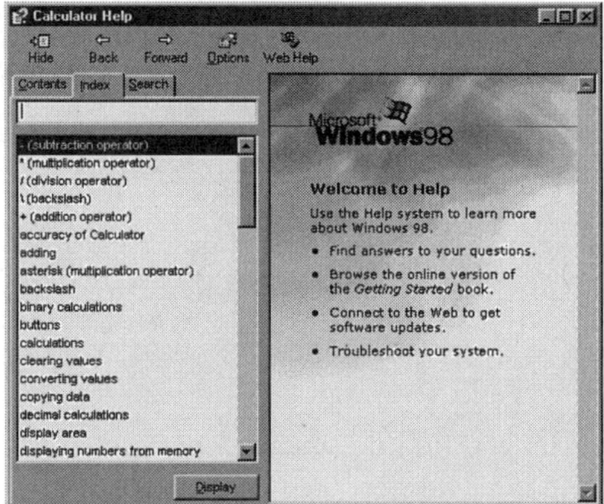

Figure 6.6.
You now will be acquainted with the Index page of Windows 98's programs' help screens.

The Search page makes looking for a particular topic not indexed on the Index tab easier. To search for a topic, click the Search tab look, and then click the command button labeled Just Topics. If the help engine locates your search candidate, a list of all help pages that include your search topic appears, and you can open that help page to view its details in the right pane. Figure 6.7 shows the results of searching for the keyword `view` in the Calculator's Help window.

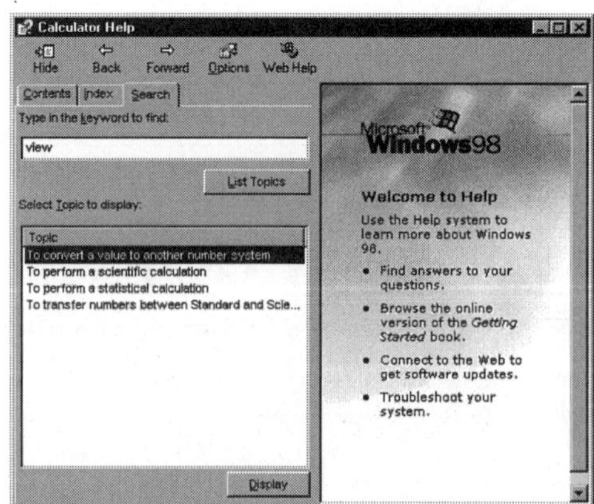

Figure 6.7.
Search using the keywords for which you want help.

For those programs that do not yet support the Windows 98 Web-like help system, you must adjust the way you look for help keywords. Instead of a Search tab, you see a Find tab. (The Contents and Index pages still exist but do not display in the 2-pane Web-style of the Windows 98 help interface.) Many programs will support the pre-Windows 98 Help system interface for years to come, so you need to understand how to use this older interface. (It is interesting to note that even Word 97, a program still being sold at the time of Windows 98's release, does not support the Web-like help system of the Windows 98 interface.)

The tabbed Find page is somewhat clumsy but offers perhaps the most comprehensive search in the help system. Often, its completeness means that you get more information than you can ever wade through easily, and many users ignore the Find page. Nevertheless, the Find page can come in handy when you need help on a program area that you cannot find inside the Contents or Index pages.

To Do

Task 6.6: Using Find

Step 1: Description

The Find page generates a comprehensive database of all the help topics in your program's help file and creates a concordance of all words in the help file. When you access an application that displays a Find tab in its Help window, you can use the Find tab to create your own search keyword index of specific entries.

JUST A MINUTE

If an application supports the Windows 98 Web-like help windows described earlier in this hour, the help window displays a Search tab instead of the Find tab, which makes your keyword searching simpler.

Step 2: Action

1. When you click a help window that does not follow the Windows 98 Web-like interface, such as Word 97, you are presented with a help window with these three tabs: Contents, Index, and Find.
2. Click the Find tab. The Find Setup Wizard screen appears, as shown in Figure 6.8.

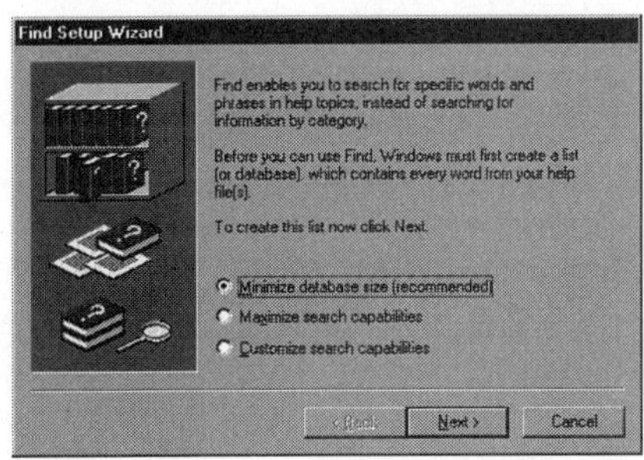

Figure 6.8.
The Find Setup Wizard dialog box builds a word-by-word help concordance.

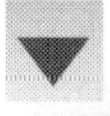

Just a Minute

If anyone has previously generated the Find page's database concordance, you will not see Find Setup Wizard's opening page.

3. When you see the Find Setup Wizard dialog box, you must execute the wizard to create a table of contents for the Find dialog box. Select Maximize Search Capabilities and follow the wizard screens to build the Find contents. After a brief pause, Windows 98 displays the Find page, as shown in Figure 6.9.

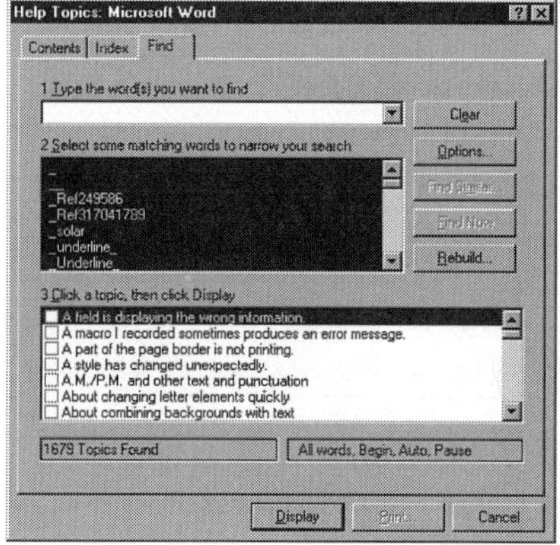

Figure 6.9.
The Find Setup Wizard dialog box locates information from your help database.

Just a Minute

A *wizard* is a Windows 98 routine that guides you through a process of some kind. The wizard that executes when you first select the Find help dialog box builds a table of contents for the Find searches. You can build a large online help database that offers a more complete base of online help but consumes some of your disk space. The minimum help database provides little more than the Index page provides, but the maximum help database that you build, although it takes a few moments, provides a more exhaustive search.

If you do not see the wizard's screens, someone else might have already run the wizard and built the help database for you.

4. At the prompt labeled Type the word(s) that you want to find, type the complete word or phrase for which you want the Help system to search. Basically, the Find dialog box's interface is similar to that of the Index except that Find searches on *all* words, not just those indexed. After you find a topic, you can double-click it and then display its dialog box.

5. Scroll through the list of choices in the bottom window and double-click any of them to display that topic's help dialog box. This dialog box works like the other help dialog boxes described earlier in this hour.
6. Notice the list of command buttons to the right of the Find dialog box. Clear erases all the help topics, so you can look for another. The Options command button displays the Find Options dialog box, as shown in Figure 6.10.

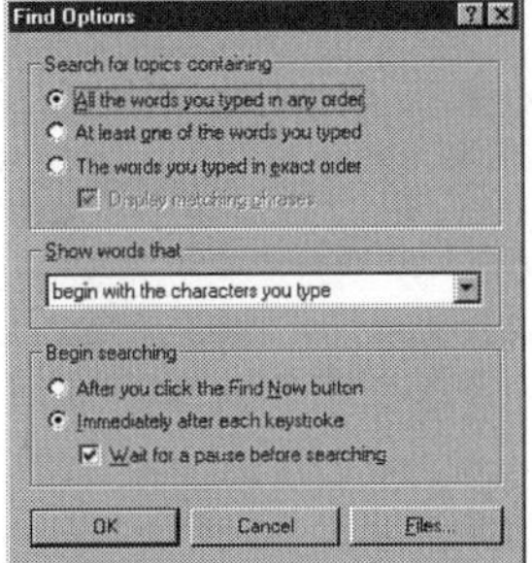

Figure 6.10.
Describe how you want Windows 98 to find your help topics.

The Find Options dialog box describes how you want Windows 98 to find the information, based on your search word or phrase. You can request that Windows 98 search all the words in any order (the default) or at least one word that you type.

There are additional options you can click as you become more acquainted with Windows 98. For now, press Esc or click Cancel to close the Find Options dialog box.

7. After you use the Help system for a while, you might decide that you want more detail when hunting for specific items. You might find that the minimized database that the wizard set up when you first displayed the Find dialog box is not detailed enough. You can rebuild the help database by clicking the Rebuild command button and rerunning the Help Database Build Wizard once again, this time selecting the maximized database size.
8. Click Cancel to close the Find dialog box after you finish getting the help you need.

Step 3: Review

The Find dialog box searches across all your help topic dialog boxes. Whereas the Index dialog box searches strictly through the help topic titles, the Find dialog box searches the body of the help topic text, looking for any and all topics that contain your key search word or phrase.

Summary

This hour showed you how to access the powerful Help features in Windows 98. When you have a question about Windows 98, you can ask Windows 98 for help. There are several ways to access the helpful dialog boxes about a variety of topics. The most common method of getting detailed help is to select the Help command from the Start menu. You can access your local PC's help files or search the Internet for the answers you need.

Most Windows 98 programs contain a Help command that displays a tabbed dialog box containing three different help search screens. The first, the Contents dialog box, displays an overview of Windows 98 in a book-like form that you can read at your leisure.

There are two ways to search for help by using the help tabbed dialog boxes. If you select the Index dialog box, Windows 98 searches the help topic titles for the word or phrase with which you need help. If you display the Find dialog box, Windows 98 searches the help topics themselves for the word or phrase for which you're hunting.

Q&A

Q There are so many kinds of help available; which one should I use?

A The method of help that you access depends on the task you're trying to accomplish. Generally, there are several ways to get help on the same topic. If you want help on a procedure such as moving files, you can probably find related topics grouped together in the Contents dialog box. There, you can find topics, grouped by subject, which you can browse.

If you want to search an application's help system for all topics related to the one you want, such as changing icons on folders and documents, you will probably want to search the Index or Find dialog boxes. The Index dialog box searches topic titles for keywords that you specify. The Find dialog box searches the text for the topic you want to find. The Find dialog box can locate more help topics than the Index dialog box can.

Finally, if you cannot find help on a topic, especially if you want help with the Windows 98 Internet interface, check out Microsoft's Web site for help.

Q When would I want to build a maximized search database?

A If you have plenty of free disk space, you can build a maximized search database so that your Find dialog box searches across much more text than would otherwise be the case for minimized database builds.

Rarely will you search for topics that you cannot find easily with the smaller minimized database. Keep in mind that your searches will be more sluggish if you search across a maximized database of search topics, but the search will be more

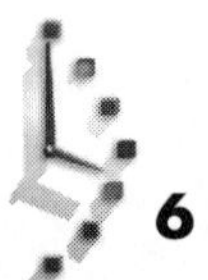

thorough. The index that the wizard builds is an index of key search words and phrases that Windows 98 searches when you subsequently select the Find dialog box.

Workshop

Key Terms

Review the following list of terms:

- *cross-referenced help topic* Green underlined text inside Help dialog boxes that display definitions when you click them.
- *hot spot* A link you can click to see another HTML-based web page.
- *wizard* A step-by-step process that leads you through the execution of a Windows 98 task. Many Windows 98 programs, such as Microsoft Word for Windows, include specific wizards.

Part II

Hour 7

Manage Your Desktop

This hour is a little different from the other hours. Instead of studying a single central aspect of Windows 98, such as Explorer, this hour contains a potpourri of desktop-management tips and procedures that improve the way you use the Windows 98 environment. Previous hours studied topics in depth, but this hour offers advice that you might want to use while you work within Windows 98.

One way to activate your desktop is to use the Windows 98 Active Desktop feature. Place Web pages and other files directly on your desktop to customize your Windows 98 wallpaper. In addition, Windows 98 comes with several screen saver designs, and you can purchase and download additional screen savers. Screen savers not only provide something for your computer to do while it is idle but also offer security features.

This hour also offers a collection of tips that helps you customize Windows 98 to suit your preferences. Start Windows 98 and walk through this hour, trying the shortcuts and advice, to decide which topics best suit your needs. Now that you've mastered the major Windows 98 tools, such as Explorer and the Settings menu, you are ready to streamline the way you use Windows 98.

The highlights of this hour include the following:

- Placing Web pages on your desktop as wallpaper
- Using screen savers to personalize your PC
- Adding security to your PC with screen savers
- Locating the computer's time and date settings
- Changing Windows 98 colors

Activate Your Desktop

Whereas this hour introduces you to the Windows 98 Active Desktop feature, Hour 16, "The Internet's Push and Channel Content," takes the Active Desktop to its next level by describing the *push technology* that you can integrate into your Active Desktop. You will learn how to subscribe to various online services, such as news agencies that send Web content directly to your PC at preset time intervals. You don't have to go as far as push technology, however, to enjoy many benefits of the Active Desktop. The Active Desktop is Windows 98's way of more seamlessly integrating your Windows desktop into the online Internet world.

Web pages are the result of their underlying language, *HTML*, which defines the colors, pictures, embedded *applets* (small programs that activate Web pages by using yet another language called *Java*), and information that appears on those pages. HTML stands for *HyperText Markup Language*.

Why use a Web page on your desktop as wallpaper? Perhaps the page is a support page that you need to tweak Windows 98. Perhaps the page contains a game applet that you want to play in your spare time. Whatever the reason, you easily can change your wallpaper to any HTML file, as the next task demonstrates.

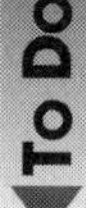

Task 7.1: Making an HTML File Your Wallpaper

Step 1: Description

The Desktop can hold any HTML file as wallpaper. Previous Windows versions enable you to set up graphics files as a wallpapered desktop background, but Windows 98 enables you to place HTML documents there as well. HTML documents end with the .html filename extension and use a Web page icon in Explorer views. Some document names still follow the pre-Windows 95 filename limitations that require a maximum 3-letter extension, so some HTML documents end with a filename extension of .HTM.

Step 2: Action

1. Click the right mouse button over the Windows 98 wallpaper to display the pop-up menu.

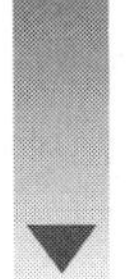

2. Select Active Desktop | Customize my Desktop and click the Background tab if the Background page is not already displayed. The Display Properties dialog box appears, as shown in Figure 7.1. (As with most of Windows 98, you can access the Display Properties dialog box from other locations, such as right-clicking the desktop and selecting Properties.)

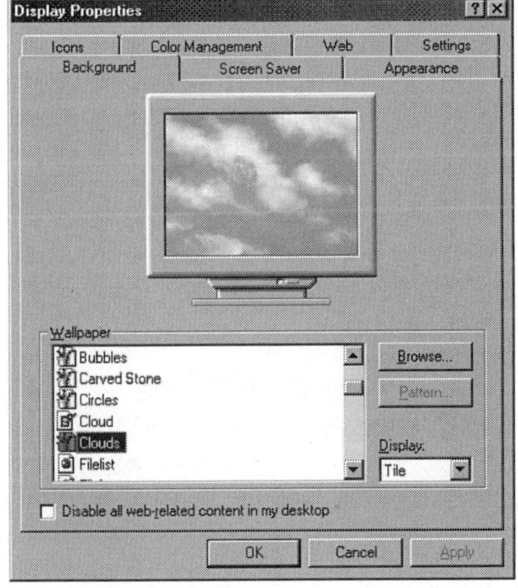

Figure 7.1.
You can set wallpaper to any HTML or graphics file.

3. The Background page enables you to set up a wallpaper file. You can select one of the supplied wallpaper files by scrolling and selecting from the Wallpaper listbox, or you can click the Browse button and search your disk for an HTML file.
4. When you locate the HTML file you want as your wallpaper, click the Open button to select the file. The file and its pathname now appear in the Wallpaper list for subsequent selections.

CAUTION

Your desktop must be set up for active content HTML wallpaper to use. If your desktop is not currently set up for active content when you select the HTML wallpaper file, Windows 98 asks if you want to enable the active desktop option. You must click Yes before Windows 98 can use the HTML file as wallpaper. If you do not enable the active desktop, Windows 98 cannot display the selected HTML file as wallpaper.

5. When you click OK and return to your desktop, the HTML file appears as wallpaper.

Step 3: Review

The wallpaper on your desktop can hold graphics or HTML files. You can easily select HTML files as your desktop wallpaper from the Background page in the Display Properties dialog box.

JUST A MINUTE

You will learn additional ways to activate your desktop in Hour 16. With the help of the Internet Explorer 4 Web browser (you will learn all about IE 4 in Hour 13), you can place Web items on your desktop on-the-fly. The wallpaper you choose in this task consumes your entire desktop, but you can use multiple HTML files on your desktop and watch several Web pages in the background as you work in a word processor. Hour 16 provides the details.

Locating HTML Files

What if there are no HTML files on your system? That's okay because in Windows 98 you can easily store HTML files on your PC. If you browse a Web page, the menu's File | Save command saves the page and its contents to the location you specify in an HTML format.

Virtually *any* file can be an HTML file. Internet Explorer's File | Open can open just about any kind of file, including text and graphics files. Therefore, you can open a file with Internet Explorer and select File | Save from Internet Explorer to save the file as an HTML file and use it as wallpaper.

SOS Save Our Screens!

Want to know an insider's computer industry secret? Here it is: Screen savers really don't save many screens these days. In the past, computer monitors, especially the monochrome green-letters-on-black kind, would *burn in* characters when left on too long without being used. In other words, if you left the monitor on for a long time and did not type anything, the characters on the monitor would begin to leave character trails that stayed on the monitor even after you turned it off.

To combat character burn-in, programmers began to write *screen savers* that blanked the screen or displayed moving characters and pictures. The blank screens had no burn-in problems, and the moving text never stayed in one place long enough to burn into the monitor. The screen savers kicked into effect after a predetermined length of non-use. Therefore, when you left your computer, the screen saver began after a few minutes. Upon returning, you could press any key to restore the computer screen to the state in which you left it.

Almost everybody has heard of screen savers. Computer software stores contain shelf after shelf of screen saver programs that display pictures of your favorite television characters, cartoons, and geometric and 3D designs. Microsoft designed Windows 98 to include several screen savers so you don't have to buy one.

Getting back to that industry secret: Today's monitors don't have the burn-in problem that previous monitors had. Screen savers aren't needed. Why, during an age when they are not needed, are screen savers more popular than ever before? The answer is simple: Screen savers are fun! Screen savers greet you with designs and animated cartoons when you'd otherwise look at a boring screen. It's *cool* to use a screen saver. After you master Hour 16, you will be able to use even live Web pages as your screen saver!

TIME SAVER

If you want to try one of the store-bought screen savers, first try one from Windows 98 to see if you like screen savers. Some people decide they don't like them after they try them.

CAUTION

Screen savers aren't just for fun and games, so don't rule them out before you've looked at them! Even though you might not care for screen savers (as I just mentioned, not everybody does), the Windows 98 screen savers offer an added benefit not found in many other screen savers: The Windows 98 screen saver provides password protection. If you need to walk away from your screen for a while but you want to leave your computer running, you can select a password for the screen saver. After the screen saver begins, a user has to enter the correct password to use your computer. This ensures that payroll and other departments can safely leave their computers without fear of disclosing confidential information. Often, computer stores display their PCs with password-protected screen savers to keep customers from tampering with the systems.

Task 7.2: Setting Up a Screen Saver

Step 1: Description

Windows 98 contains several screen savers from which you can choose. Through the Screen Saver dialog box, you can set up a blanking screen saver or one that moves text and graphics on the screen. You control the length of time the monitor is idle before the screen saver begins.

Step 2: Action

1. Click the right mouse button over the Windows 98 wallpaper. The display menu appears.

JUST A MINUTE

If you are using a word processor or other program, you might not see the wallpaper because the other programs are in the way. Click the taskbar's Show Desktop icon to minimize your open windows to see the wallpaper and right-click over the wallpaper.

2. Select the Properties command. The Display Properties tabbed dialog box appears (shown earlier in Figure 7.1).
3. Click the tab labeled Screen Saver. Windows 98 displays the page shown in Figure 7.2.

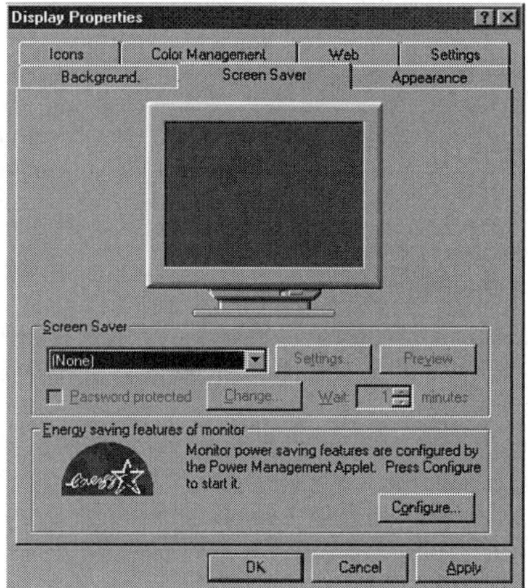

Figure 7.2.
The Screen Saver tab controls the screen saver's timing and selection.

Depending on your attached hardware, the bottom portion of the Screen Saver dialog box might or might not be grayed out. If your monitor is designed to be *Energy Star-compliant*, meaning that your monitor supports energy-efficiency options, the lower dialog box settings will be available to you. You can adjust these options to save electricity costs. The Energy Star controls work independently and override any screen saver settings you might use.

4. The drop-down listbox—directly below the Screen Saver prompt—that you display when you click the down arrow contains a list of Windows 98 screen savers. Click the box now to see the list. When (None) is selected, no screen saver will be active on your system.

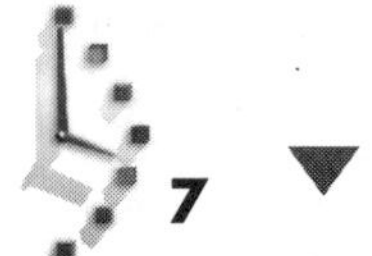

5. If you select Blank Screen, Windows 98 uses a blank screen for the screen saver. When the screen saver activates, the screen goes blank, and a keypress (or password if you set up a password) returns the screen to its previous state.

   The remaining screen savers are more fun than a blank screen saver. If you want to see the other screen savers, click any one of the remaining screen savers in the list (such as 3D Flying Objects or 3D Maze), and Windows 98 will display a preview of it on the little monitor inside the dialog box, as shown in Figure 7.3.

Figure 7.3.
You can preview any of the screen savers.

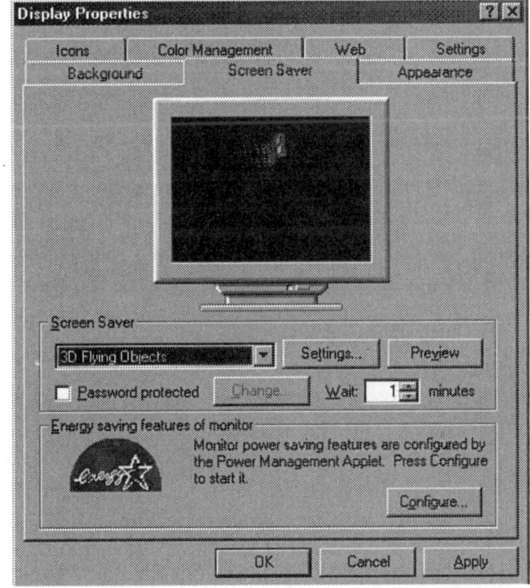

6. The animated screen savers can move fairly fast. To adjust their speed, click the Settings button. In some cases, you also can adjust the number of animated items that appear on the screen saver screen.
7. The Preview button enables you to view, full-screen, the screen saver if you want a better preview than the small screen inside the dialog box provides. Click Preview to see the actual screen saver in action. Press any key or move the mouse to terminate the screen saver preview and return to the dialog box.
8. The Wait prompt determines how many minutes your computer must remain idle for the screen saver to activate itself. By pressing Alt+W (the shortcut key combination for the Wait prompt), you can enter a new minute value or click the up and down arrow keys to change to a new minute value.

Just a Minute

Task 7.3 explains how to use the password option with the screen saver.

9. When you click the OK command button at the bottom of the dialog box, Windows 98 activates the screen saver program. The screen saver remains active in

all future Windows 98 sessions until you change it again by using the Screen Saver dialog box.

10. The screen saver operates in the background but never shows itself, even on the taskbar of program buttons, until your computer sits idle for the specified time value. Don't touch the keyboard or mouse for the waiting time period, and you'll see the screen saver go into action. Press any key (or move the mouse) to return to the desktop.

Step 3: Review

Screen savers are easy to set. Right-clicking your desktop and selecting Properties from the resulting menu activates the Display Properties tabbed dialog box where you can launch a screen saver. Not only can you control which screen saver is used but you can also control the number of idle minutes the screen saver requires before activating. You can control the speed of animated screen savers, as well.

TIME SAVER

> If you don't want a screen saver, select (None) in the screen saver's dialog box.

Task 7.3: Securing Your Screen Saver

Step 1: Description

Using the Display Properties box, you can add a password to any of the Windows 98 screen savers, including the blank screen saver. After the screen saver executes, it requires a password before relinquishing control to you or anyone else who wants to use your computer.

Step 2: Action

1. Display the Display Properties tabbed dialog box once again by right-clicking over your screen's wallpaper and selecting Properties.
2. Click the Screen Saver tab to see the Screen Saver dialog box.
3. Click the Password-protected check mark prompt.
4. Click Change. You must tell Windows 98 the password it requires before releasing a screen saver. The Change Password dialog box opens, as shown in Figure 7.4.

Figure 7.4.
Tell Windows 98 the secret screen saver password.

5. Windows 98 requires you to type the password twice. The password appears on the screen as asterisks so that no one looking over your shoulder can read it. Due to the asterisk protection, Windows 98 asks that you enter the password twice to ensure that you make no mistakes as you type the new password. Type the same password at both prompts.
6. Press the OK command button. Now when Windows 98 starts the screen saver, you must enter the password to use the computer.

CAUTION

> The screen saver password does not guarantee total computer security. Someone can reboot your computer and still use the computer's files. The password-protected screen saver does, however, keep people from looking at the work you were performing before you left the computer idle.

Step 3: Review

The password enables you to protect your computer's screen from being viewed by others. By setting a password, you ensure that people cannot stop the screen saver to look at what you were doing with the computer before the screen saver took effect.

Check the Time

A clock showing the current time appears to the right of your taskbar. (The clock's position might differ depending on where you moved your taskbar.) In addition to the time, your computer and Windows 98 also keeps track of the date.

There are several reasons why you might want to change the computer's time and date settings. Perhaps you've moved to a different part of the world and need to change the computer's clock. Perhaps your computer contains a time and date memory kept current with a battery that has gone bad. Perhaps the person who set up your computer didn't know the right time or date when he or she installed Windows 98. Whatever the reason for setting the time and date, these settings are easy to adjust.

JUST A MINUTE

> Windows 98 uses the international settings, found by double-clicking the Regional Settings icon in the Control Panel, to format all date and time values displayed from within Windows 98. Therefore, the selected country in the Windows 98 international settings determines the appearance of all time and date values.

As you saw in Hour 4, "Understanding the My Computer Window," the Control Panel contains many of your system's hardware and software settings. You can change your computer's date and time settings by double-clicking the Date/Time icon inside the Control Panel. There's a much faster and easier way, though, as Task 7.4 describes.

To Do

Task 7.4: Changing the Time and Date with the Mouse

Step 1: Description

The taskbar gives you access to the time and date settings of your computer. You can double-click the taskbar clock to display the time and date modification dialog box.

Just a Minute

> If you don't see the time on your taskbar, select the Settings | Taskbar & Start Menu command on the Start menu and check the Show Clock option.

Step 2: Action

1. Double-click your taskbar's clock. Windows 98 displays the Date/Time Properties tabbed dialog box shown in Figure 7.5.

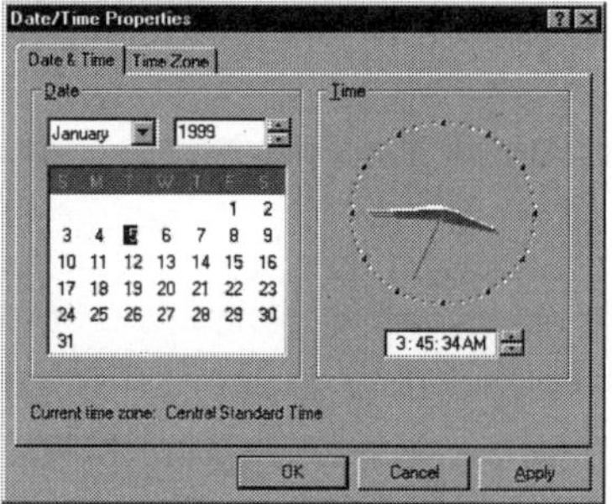

Figure 7.5.
A double-click displays the Date/Time Properties dialog box.

2. This is the easiest clock you will ever set! The up and down controls enable you to change the month or year. If you click a day inside the month, the date instantly changes to that date.
3. Click the hour, minute, or second to change the time. If you highlight the hour (by dragging the mouse cursor over it), minute, or second, click either the up or down arrow next to the time. That highlighted value increases or decreases by one unit. As you change the time value, the analog clock face changes also.
4. When you are done modifying the date or time, click OK to close the dialog box, and the taskbar's time reflects your changes. You can now turn off your computer, and the computer's new settings will still be in effect (up to the second) when you turn on the computer again.

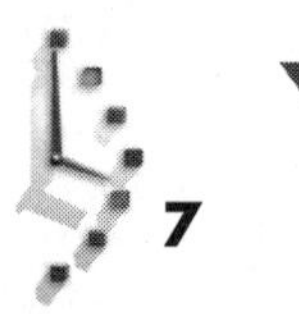

5. Windows 98 is smart and can handle time zones easily. If you display the Date/Time Properties dialog box and click the Time Zone tab, Windows 98 displays the Time Zone page shown in Figure 7.6.

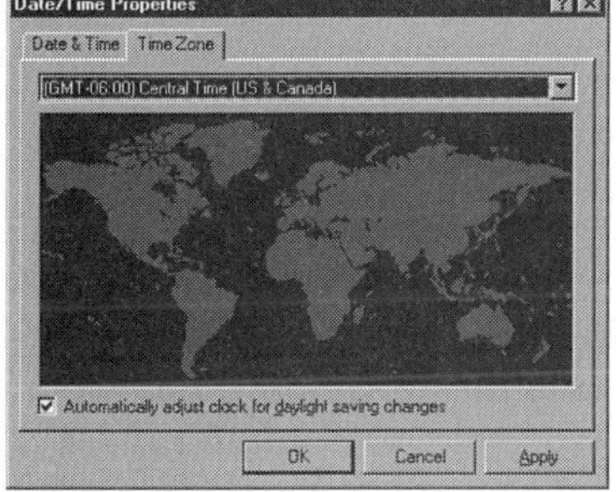

Figure 7.6.
Change the time zone visually or by using a dropdown listbox.

The time zone currently in effect is highlighted on the global world map. If you want to set a different time zone, you either can drag the map's highlighted time zone line left or right or click the dropdown listbox arrow to display the world's time zones. The listbox contains a list of every possible time zone in the world.

Time Saver

Not all time zones respect daylight savings time. For example, people who live in the state of Indiana don't have to change their clocks every six months because they don't follow daylight savings time. For those who don't want Windows 98 to adjust for daylight savings, uncheck the option at the bottom of the screen.

6. After you select the proper time zone and daylight savings time settings, click OK to close the dialog box, and the settings will take effect.

Step 3: Review

Changing the date and time requires double-clicking the time on your taskbar. The tabbed dialog box that appears enables you to change the time, the date, and the time zone. If you want Windows 98 to update the clock every daylight saving time period, you can check an option to have Windows 98 do just that.

Just a Minute

If your computer adjusts the clock due to daylight savings time, Windows 98 lets you know about the change with a dialog box the first time you use Windows 98 after the change.

Paint Windows 98

Windows 98 offers several color schemes that work well together. Depending on your taste, you can choose from conservative to very wild colors.

The color schemes that you can select have nothing to do with the colors of icons, wallpaper, or screen savers on your system. The color schemes determine the color for various system-wide items such as screen title bars, window backgrounds, and dialog box controls.

To Do

Task 7.5: Changing the Color Scheme

Step 1: Description

By selecting from various color schemes, you can determine the colors Windows 98 uses for common items such as window controls, borders, and buttons. The Control Panel contains a Display icon that you use to change the color of your Windows 98 installation.

Step 2: Action

1. Select Control Panel from the Start menu's Settings menu.
2. Double-click the Display icon. The now-familiar Display Properties tabbed dialog box appears. As with most areas of Windows 98, you can access the Windows 98 tools from different places in the system.
3. Click the Appearance tab to display the Appearance dialog box shown in Figure 7.7.

Figure 7.7.
Change system colors by using the Appearance dialog box.

4. If you want to take the time, you can change the colors of every item on the Windows 98 screen including dialog boxes, window borders, and title bars. However, it's much easier to pick a color scheme from the list of the many choices that Microsoft supplies.

   On the Appearance page, the top half contains the currently-selected color scheme. If you select a different color scheme, you see that scheme's color appear at the top

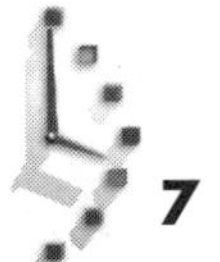

of the dialog box. For example, suppose you're taking your powerful color laptop to Egypt to write with while cruising down the Nile River. Open the dropdown listbox labeled Scheme and select Desert from the list. Instantly, the top half of your dialog box changes colors to a Desert scheme. Now you can compute like a true Egyptian!

5. The color scheme of your Windows 98 installation does not instantly change. You're still in the process of selecting colors at this point. If you don't like the desert color scheme, try another. As a matter of fact, try *all* of them to find one you really like.

TIME SAVER

There are some color schemes that include the additional benefit of large text sizes. As Figure 7.8 illustrates, you can select a color scheme that makes window text easier to see by enlarging the character size of the Windows 98 characters and sharpening the contrast when they appear in dialog boxes and title bars. In addition, high contrast color schemes work well for times when you take your Windows 98 laptop outdoors.

Figure 7.8.
You can change not only system colors but also common Windows 98 character sizes.

6. When you find a color scheme that you really like, click OK to close the dialog box and change the color scheme to your selected colors. You can now begin working with the new color scheme; as soon as you open a window, you see the difference.

Step 3: Review

The Control Panel contains a display icon that enables you to change the color scheme of your Windows 98 installation. After you change the colors and, optionally, the font size, all standard Windows 98 displays, such as windows, borders, and title bars, reflect the new colors.

As you change your color scheme, feel free to change the Windows 98 display font as well. By default, Windows 98 displays icons and window titles and messages in the MS-DOS Sans Serif font. From the Appearance dialog box, you can select a different font for almost every kind of text Windows 98 displays.

Summary

This hour took a brief detour from the style of surrounding hours and gave you some tips and desktop-management tools that can help you work with Windows 98 more effectively. After completing the first part of this book, you should have a good understanding of the tools that are available to you as a Windows 98 user. Now that you've become more comfortable with these aspects of Windows 98, you will appreciate some of this hour's time-saving tips.

In this hour, you learned how to improve your computer's desktop wallpaper by adding your own graphics or HTML-based wallpaper. You will build on the HTML-on-desktop concept as you progress through the remaining 24 hours. Your PC's idle time can be taken up by setting up a screen saver. By password-protecting that screen saver, you can add security to your system so you can safely leave for a few minutes without exiting the program in which you're working.

There are many customization features inside Windows 98. You now know how to change the computer's time, date, and screen colors. These customization tools help both the novice and the advanced user enjoy Windows 98 more fully.

Q&A

Q How does the wallpaper pattern differ from the screen saver pattern? Are they the same thing?

A The wallpaper is your desktop's background. You always see the wallpaper when you first start Windows 98 and when you minimize or close programs you are using within Windows 98. You will never see the screen saver unless you quit working on your computer for a few minutes and the screen saver begins running.

The screen saver must be a moving pattern (or be completely blank) to accomplish the goal of a screen saver. A screen saver is primarily a running program that keeps the screen's characters from getting burned into the screen's phosphorus. The burn-in problem is not too common today, so a secondary goal of a screen saver is to display an animated and often fun screen during your computer's idle times. As mentioned earlier in this hour, you can turn your Web-based wallpaper into a screen saver so that a designated Web page (or HTML document on your disk) appears when the screen saver wakes up.

Q I do serious work. Why would I want a screen saver?

A The screen saver probably will not help your monitor if you have a modern monitor because modern monitors don't have burn-in problems. If you don't like the fancy animated screen saver screens that come with Windows 98 or that are for sale in software stores, you shouldn't activate the screen saver for entertainment purposes.

Depending on the nature of your computing, however, as well as the level of security at which you operate, you might want to activate a password-protected screen saver for precautionary reasons. When you leave your computer, you can activate the screen saver so that, upon returning, you must enter a predetermined password to work with the computer once again. The password-protected screen saver keeps others from snooping into your computer's files.

Q How do I adjust my computer's clock when daylight savings time occurs?

A You don't have to do anything when daylight savings time occurs, as long as you've checked the daylight savings time option in the Date/Time Properties dialog box. When you check this option, Windows 98 monitors the calendar and adjusts your computer's time appropriately. If you live in an area that does not follow daylight savings time, leave the option unchecked so your computer won't change the clock every six months.

Workshop

Key Terms

Review the following list of terms:

- *applets* Small programs, embedded in Web pages that come to your PC, that give life to Web pages by making the pages interactive.
- *burn-in* Characters left on older computer monitors begin to burn into the monitor, leaving their outlines even after the monitor's power is turned off.
- *Energy Star* A name applied to monitors that comply with environmental guidelines that limit the use of continuous power applied to your monitor.
- *HTML* `HyperText Markup Language` is the language behind all Web pages that formats the page to look and respond the way it does.
- *Java* A language that programmers use to create Web page applets.
- *Push technology* Web content sent directly to your PC.
- *screen saver* A program that waits in the background and executes only if you stop using your computer for a while. The screen saver either blanks your screen or displays moving text and graphics. Screen savers have, in the past, helped eliminate burn-in problems.

Part II

Hour 8

Activate DOS-Based Applications

Don't believe the media—MS-DOS is not dead! As a matter of fact, Windows 98 empowers MS-DOS applications more than any version of Windows to date. Not all programs that you run are written for Windows 98 or even for a previous version of Windows. In the past, Windows did not always provide the support that these *MS-DOS programs* required. As a result, sometimes you had to exit Windows completely to run an MS-DOS program.

Virtually every MS-DOS program runs under Windows 98, including many games that were previously off limits to Windows. In addition to handling memory problems that previously plagued MS-DOS programs running inside the Windows environment, Windows 98 provides modern MS-DOS features that will make you think you're running a new version of MS-DOS.

The highlights of this hour include the following:

- When to open more than one MS-DOS session
- How to interpret and use the MS-DOS toolbar
- What copy-and-paste communications Windows 98 and MS-DOS programs use
- Which MS-DOS Command Properties dialog box controls are important

- When to start Windows 98 programs from MS-DOS
- How to run MS-DOS programs from within Windows 98
- How to start the MS-DOS text editor

MS-DOS and Windows 98

If you want to run an MS-DOS program inside Windows 98, you don't have to start MS-DOS first. You can run the program from the Run command on the Start menu (as long as you know the program's path and filename), or you can add the program to one of the Start menu's cascaded menus and click the program description or program icon.

If you want to load the MS-DOS environment, Windows 98 provides an MS-DOS icon on the Start menu's Programs group. If you click the MS-DOS icon, the MS-DOS environment runs in a maximized or minimized window (depending on the settings in the Settings|Taskbar & Start Menu properties dialog box).

TIME SAVER

You can start one or more MS-DOS windows! As a result, you can run several MS-DOS programs at one time, and each will run multitasked inside its own window.

WINDOWS MINUTE

Environment Control

In the Windows 98 Shut Down command's dialog box, there is no command to exit Windows 98. In some early versions of Windows, MS-DOS is the controlling environment for Windows; Windows 98, however, is the controlling environment for MS-DOS.

The Shut Down dialog box does provide an option that enables you to shut down Windows 98 and start a windowless MS-DOS environment. The option is labeled Restart in MS-DOS mode. You want to enter the MS-DOS environment after shutting down Windows 98 and only when you discover one of those rare MS-DOS programs that refuses to run under Windows 98, such as some network interface card utility programs.

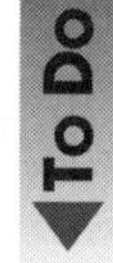

Task 8.1: Starting an MS-DOS Window

Step 1: Description

This task shows you how to enter the MS-DOS environment from Windows 98. MS-DOS is simply another application to Windows 98, so starting MS-DOS requires no special skills. The MS-DOS environment is known as the *MS-DOS prompt* in Windows 98 because the MS-DOS prompt collects keystrokes as you type them in an MS-DOS window.

8

JUST A MINUTE

The MS-DOS window is sometimes called a windowed MS-DOS *VM*, which stands for *Virtual Machine*. Each MS-DOS window acts as if that window contains a separate PC that does not interfere with other MS-DOS VM windows.

Step 2: Action

1. Open the Start menu.
2. Select Programs.
3. Click the MS-DOS Prompt icon. The MS-DOS window opens, as shown in Figure 8.1. Notice that the MS-DOS window contains a toolbar of icon buttons at the top of the window.

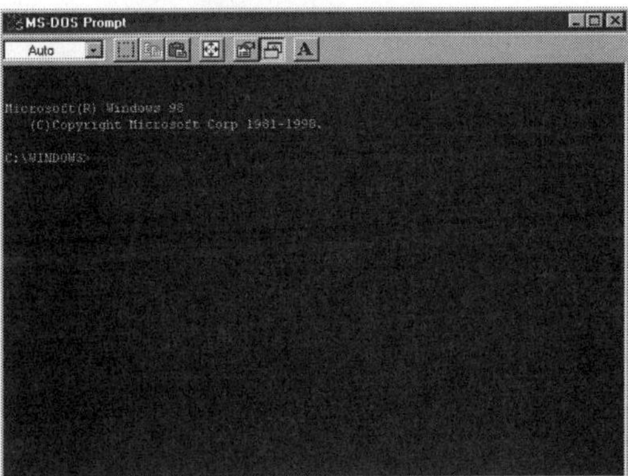

Figure 8.1.
The MS-DOS window acts like any other window in Windows 98.

JUST A MINUTE

Your MS-DOS window might appear fully maximized or resized differently from the MS-DOS window in Figure 8.1.

4. You can maximize MS-DOS windows. Click the maximize button (or double-click the title bar) to produce the maximized MS-DOS window.

JUST A MINUTE

Although the keystroke is not obvious, you can increase the MS-DOS window to full-screen size by pressing Alt+Enter.

When you increase the MS-DOS window size to full-screen by double-clicking the title bar (or by pressing the Ctrl+Enter shortcut key), the MS-DOS window toolbar disappears.

5. Press Alt+Enter to resize the MS-DOS window.
6. Start another MS-DOS window by clicking the MS-DOS prompt's icon on the Programs menu.
7. Start one more MS-DOS window. Previous versions of Windows produced several problems when you opened multiple windows, and you could not properly multitask the MS-DOS windows. Figure 8.2 shows three MS-DOS windows open at one time.

Figure 8.2.
Multiple MS-DOS windows can be open at one time.

8. To close an MS-DOS window, click the close button in the upper-right corner (unless the MS-DOS window is maximized, in which case you won't see any sizing buttons). You also can type **EXIT** at the MS-DOS command prompt, using either upper- or lowercase letters. Close two of the open MS-DOS windows now.

Step 3: Review

The MS-DOS command prompt icon on the Programs menu opens the windowed MS-DOS environment. From the MS-DOS command prompt, you can start MS-DOS programs or issue MS-DOS commands. This task left your Windows 98 environment with one open MS-DOS window. Task 8.2 enables you to practice using the MS-DOS toolbar at the top of that window.

Task8.2. The MS-DOS Toolbar

Step 1: Description

This task describes how to use the toolbar that appears on MS-DOS windows. Figure 8.3 shows the toolbar. Previous versions of Windows contained no toolbar. Remember that the toolbar appears only on non-maximized MS-DOS windows. The toolbar is optional, so you can remove it if you do not want to see it at the top of MS-DOS windows.

8

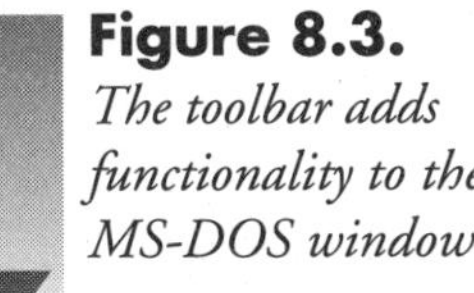

Figure 8.3. *The toolbar adds functionality to the MS-DOS window.*

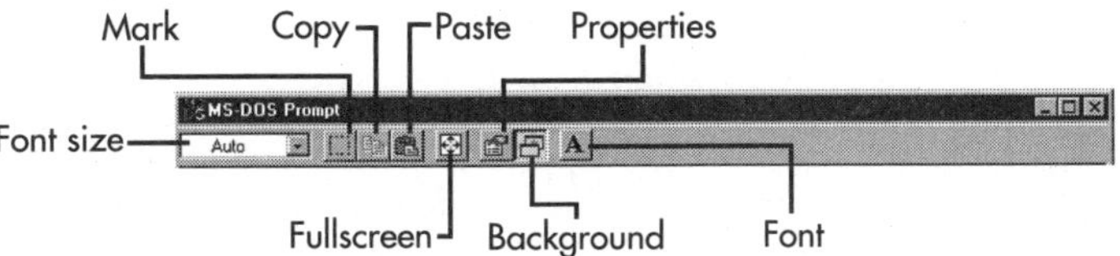

8

Step 2: Action

1. Click the Font size drop-down listbox button (at the far left of the toolbar) to display a scrollable list of font sizes. The values determine the size, in points, of the text characters on the MS-DOS window. The Auto size enables Windows 98 to determine the best size of the characters and MS-DOS window. If you select a different font size, the characters inside the window, as well as the window itself, resize to display the new character point size. If the text inside the MS-DOS window is too small to read, you might want to select a larger point size. When you change the font size, Windows 98 resizes the MS-DOS window to show that font more accurately. You can resize MS-DOS windows, but Windows 98 limits the MS-DOS window size to 1–3 sizes, depending on the font size you select.

Just a Minute

> The double letter T next to a font size indicates that the font is a *True Type* font. True Type fonts are generally more readable than non-True Type fonts.

2. The Mark tool enables you to mark a section of the MS-DOS window to copy to the Windows 98 Clipboard.

   Type the **DIR** command (for *directory*) at the MS-DOS command prompt to display a directory listing. After you see the directory listing, click the Mark toolbar button. With your mouse, drag from a point on the MS-DOS window down to a second point to create a highlighted inverted square, as shown in Figure 8.4.

Figure 8.4. *The highlighted portion of the MS-DOS window is marked for copying.*

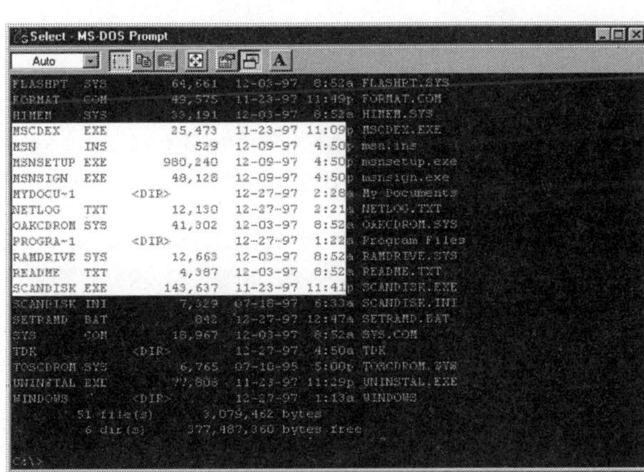

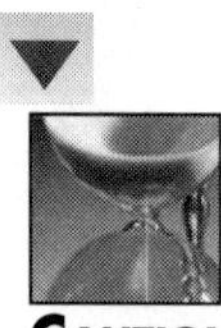

CAUTION

You can copy MS-DOS data to the Clipboard or paste from the Clipboard. You cannot cut data directly from the MS-DOS window with the mouse without using the toolbar or System menu.

Windows 98 uses the same internal file structure as previous versions of Windows; when you create a long filename, Windows 98 automatically converts that filename to a unique name that fits within the older naming convention of eight characters with a three-character extension. The `DIR` command enables you to see both the real internal filename and the long filename that you see in Windows 98 dialog boxes.

Another MS-DOS command that you might want to use with long filenames is the `COPY` command. The following `COPY` command would never have worked with previous versions of Windows due to the long filenames:

```
COPY "My August sales report" "Old report"
```

(The quotation marks are required when using long filenames that contain embedded spaces.) This command copies the file named `My August sales report` to a file named `Old report` so that, at the completion of the copy, two identical files will exist on your computer.

3. Click the Copy toolbar button to send the highlighted MS-DOS data to the Windows 98 Clipboard. As soon as Windows 98 copies the data to the Clipboard, the highlight goes away.
4. To prove that you copied the data to the Clipboard, start WordPad, a small word processor located on your Start menu's Programs | Accessories menu. Select Edit | Paste. The text you highlighted inside the MS-DOS window now appears inside the WordPad window. Terminate WordPad without saving the file by clicking the Close window button and answering No when prompted to save the data file.

JUST A MINUTE

The font used inside the default MS-DOS window is a non-proportional font. Therefore, all character columns in the MS-DOS window consume the same width, and all align properly into columns of data. Your WordPad's default font might be set up as a proportional font so the data, when pasted into WordPad, cannot align in perfect columns as the data does when shown in the MS-DOS window. If you paste MS-DOS data into a word processor and the data does not align correctly, change the font of the pasted data to a non-proportional font such as Courier.

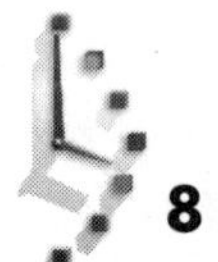

5. Although you pasted the marked text into WordPad and closed the WordPad application, the data still resides on the Windows 98 Clipboard. To see that, click

the Paste toolbar button. Windows 98 pastes the text into the MS-DOS window at the cursor's location.

The MS-DOS command prompt requires specific commands, and the data you are pasting probably does not fit within the normal MS-DOS command requirements. Therefore, MS-DOS might issue error messages as the data is pasted back into the window, but you can safely ignore these messages.

6. Click the Full screen toolbar button to maximize the MS-DOS window to full screen. Issue the `DIR` command again. A maximized MS-DOS window produces readable text, although the toolbar and Windows 98 taskbar go away until you resize the MS-DOS window once again.

   Press Alt+Enter to resize the MS-DOS window to a non-maximized size.

7. Click the Properties toolbar button to display the MS-DOS Prompt Properties tabbed dialog box shown in Figure 8.5.

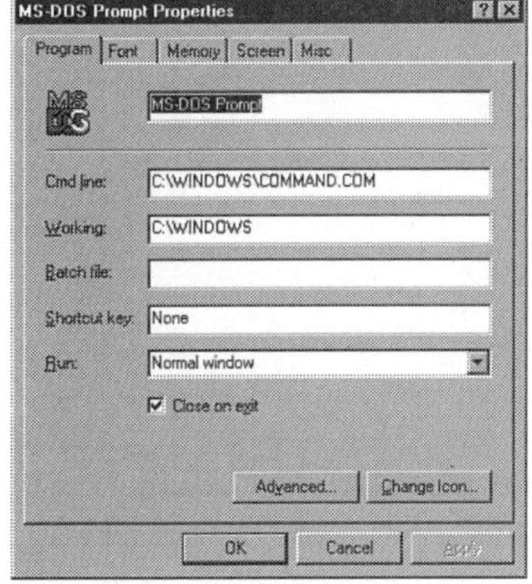

Figure 8.5.
The MS-DOS Prompt Properties dialog box controls the way MS-DOS starts and performs.

The MS-DOS Prompt Properties tabbed dialog box contains several settings that control the way your MS-DOS windows appear and perform. For example, if you press a shortcut key, such as D, at the Shortcut key prompt, you can start the MS-DOS window by pressing Ctrl+Alt+D from almost anywhere within the Windows 98 environment.

The Run prompt determines how you want the MS-DOS window to appear when you run programs within the window. The drop-down listbox contains these three window size prompts: Normal window, Minimized, and Maximized.

If you want the MS-DOS window to close when an MS-DOS application finishes, make sure that the Close on exit option is checked. Most of the time, you will want to leave this option checked.

TIME SAVER

> Actually, most of the time you will want to leave the majority of the MS-DOS Prompt Properties tabbed dialog box settings alone. The default settings almost always make MS-DOS windows perform the way you want them to.

8. Clicking the Change Icon command button produces the interesting horizontally scrolling dialog box shown in Figure 8.6. If you want a different icon to appear next to the MS-DOS taskbar when running MS-DOS programs, select a different icon from the scrolling list of icons and click OK.

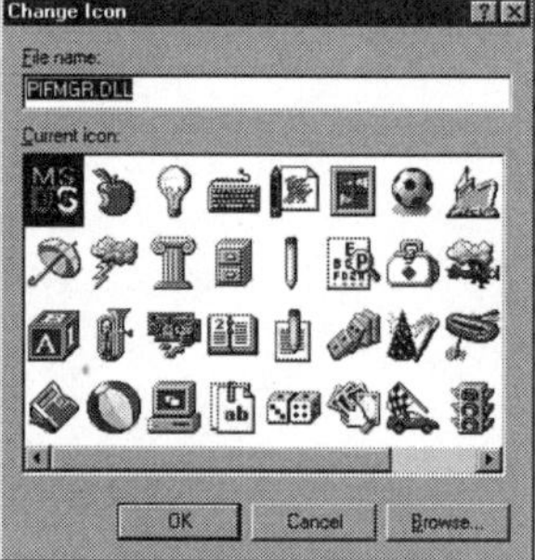

Figure 8.6.
You can change the icon that appears on the taskbar for an MS-DOS window.

9. The remaining tabbed dialog box options are fairly advanced and are usually set to appropriate values. There are a couple you should know about now, however.

   Click the Screen tab to display a dialog box that controls the way the MS-DOS screen appears to the user. Figure 8.7 shows this dialog box.

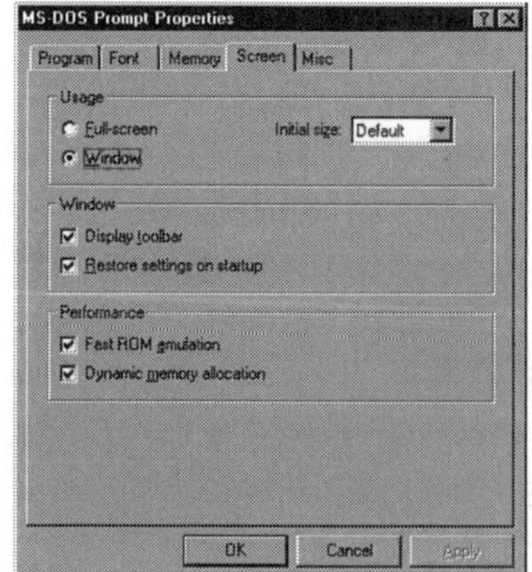

Figure 8.7.
The screen options determine how Windows 98 displays the MS-DOS window.

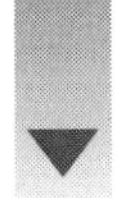

If you uncheck the Display toolbar option, Windows 98 does not display the toolbar in the MS-DOS window. If you want the MS-DOS window to appear maximized when Windows 98 first displays the window (you can still resize the maximized window by pressing Alt+Enter), select the Full-screen option.

Just a Minute

Although you lose some MS-DOS functionality when you remove the toolbar, you gain extra MS-DOS window space that would otherwise be taken up by the toolbar.

10. Click the Misc tab to see another dialog box that controls several miscellaneous MS-DOS window options. You can control whether or not the Windows 98 screen saver is active during the MS-DOS session. Some MS-DOS programs make the Windows 98 screen saver program think that no keyboard action has taken place and will trigger the Windows 98 screen saver, even when you are actively working inside MS-DOS mode.

    You can see how to determine which Windows 98 shortcut keys are active inside MS-DOS. By default, all Windows 98 shortcut keys are active inside the MS-DOS window, and you should not change these without good reason.

    Close the tabbed dialog box now that you've reviewed the highlights of the MS-DOS properties.

11. The Background toolbar button, when clicked, makes your MS-DOS window run in the background, and when clicked again makes your MS-DOS program run in the foreground. When in the foreground, the MS-DOS program maintains complete control of the computer, and other windows do not multitask at the same time that MS-DOS is running. You would click the background toolbar button only if you had a clock-sensitive MS-DOS application that required heavy system resources.

    Click the Font toolbar button to display the Font page from the MS-DOS Command Prompt. Figure 8.8 shows the dialog box that appears. The Font dialog box enables you to control the size and format of the font used inside the MS-DOS window. (The Font size drop-down listbox discussed earlier controls only the font size but not the format.)

    Click OK to get rid of the dialog box. Leave the MS-DOS window open for the next section.

Step 3: Review

The MS-DOS toolbar gives you one-button access to common MS-DOS tasks. You can mark, copy, and paste to and from the Windows 98 Clipboard. You can adjust the screen size and the MS-DOS mode properties so that the MS-DOS session behaves differently. In addition, if you want to use a different font size inside the MS-DOS session, look no further than the help you need to adjust the display font.

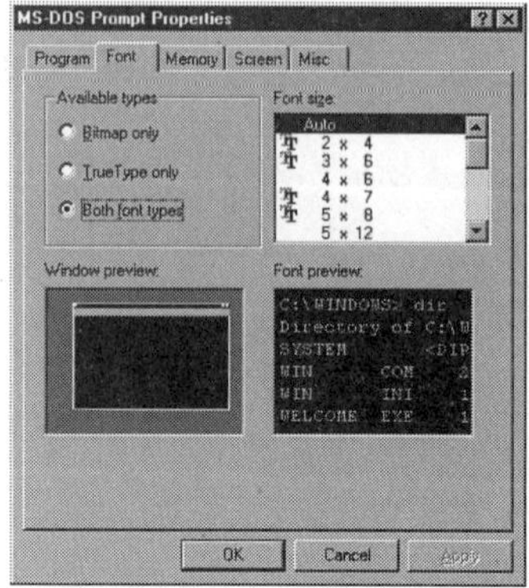

Figure 8.8.
The Font page enables you to control the way characters appear inside the MS-DOS window.

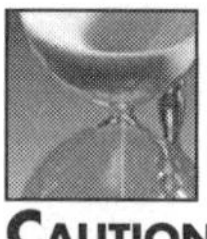

CAUTION

Although you will only rarely find such programs, some older MS-DOS programs and very advanced MS-DOS-based games refuse to run if the program detects Windows 98 running. You can fool these programs into running anyway by right-clicking over their Explorer icon, selecting Properties from the pop-up menu, clicking the Program tab, and clicking the option labeled Suggest MS-DOS mode as necessary. Although the program might still refuse to run because of a memory conflict, most problems will clear up, and the program will execute even though Windows 98 is also running.

Wrapping Up the MS-DOS Window

Over time, you will run across several interesting items in the MS-DOS window. Here's something fun you can try: Open the Windows 98 Explorer program and resize the window so that you can see both the Explorer window and the MS-DOS window. Find a filename in the Explorer's right window and drag that filename to the MS-DOS prompt. As soon as you release the mouse button, the filename, including its complete drive and pathname, appears at the MS-DOS prompt.

When managing files in the MS-DOS environment, you can drag filenames from Explorer and other Windows 98 Open dialog boxes instead of typing the complete disk name, pathname and filename. When working inside MS-DOS windows, you can drag the file from the Windows 98 environment, and Windows 98 substitutes the filename at the cursor. Therefore, if you are in the middle of a `COPY` command, you can drag filenames from Explorer to complete the `COPY` command instead of typing the names.

In addition, Windows 98 has changed the `CD` command (*Change Directory*). As you might know, the following command moves you up one parent directory level:

```
cd ..
```

8

If you are buried deep within several levels of directories while in an MS-DOS session, you can add an extra period to the `CD` command for each directory you want to return to. The following command returns you to three previous parent directory levels:

```
CD ....
```

As always, the following command takes you to the root directory no matter how many directory levels you are buried in:

```
cd \
```

Windows Minute

Starting Programs in MS-DOS

The MS-DOS window is so fully integrated into Windows 98 that you can execute Windows 98 programs *from the MS-DOS prompt.* Therefore, if you know the filename of a Windows 98 program, you will not have to return to Windows 98, if you're working inside a MS-DOS window, to execute a Windows 98 program.

Although Notepad makes an MS-DOS editor redundant and unnecessary, MS-DOS has supplied a text editor since version 1.0 of MS-DOS. There are many MS-DOS die-hards who still want to edit text files from within the MS-DOS environment.

When the Microsoft programmers wrote Windows 98, they decided to update an old standby program, the MS-DOS text editor, to implement the long filenames and to modernize the performance of the program. If you have used an MS-DOS text editor such as EDIT, you'll feel right at home with the updated version of EDIT (its screen is shown in Figure 8.9).

Figure 8.9.

The Windows 98 text editor, EDIT, supports long filenames and an improved keyboard interface.

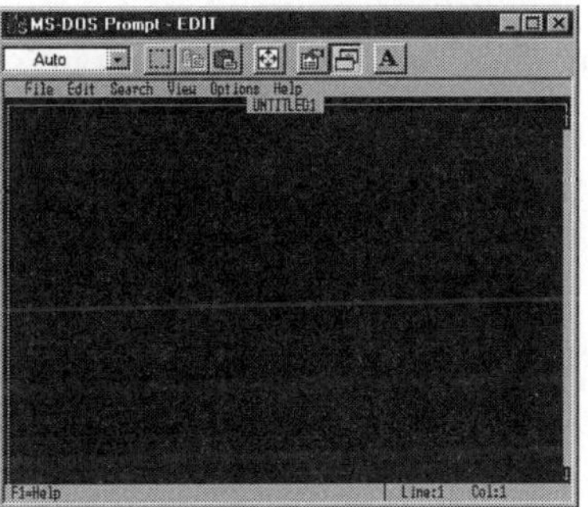

Just a Minute

This hour does not explain EDIT because the Windows 98 Notepad program replaces EDIT. Notepad, which is explained in Hour 11, "Desktop Accessories," is a Windows 98 program that makes the MS-DOS editor obsolete, except to those who already prefer the older editor.

If you want to start MS-DOS in a specific directory, display the MS-DOS Properties dialog box (by clicking the Properties MS-DOS toolbar button); then type the directory's pathname at the option labeled `Working`.

In some cases, an MS-DOS program will refuse to run if you are running a Windows 98 screen saver. Follow these steps to enable the screen saver to work along with such a program:

1. Select Start | Settings | Taskbar & Start Menu.
2. Locate the MS-DOS program's icon in the Programs folder.
3. Right-click over the icon.
4. Select Properties from the icon's menu.
5. Click the Misc tab to display the Misc page shown in Figure 8.10.

Figure 8.10.
Enable a screen saver to work with an MS-DOS program.

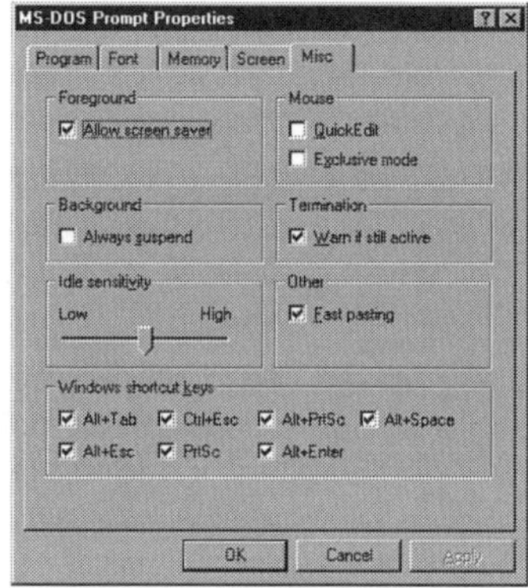

6. Click the option labeled Allow screen saver.
7. Close the dialog box. The program should now enable the screen saver to work in conjunction with the MS-DOS program.

CAUTION

> If the screen saver messes things up, uncheck the option described in the previous steps so that the screen saver goes idle whenever that particular MS-DOS program runs.

Summary

This hour focused on the MS-DOS environment inside Windows 98. Although Windows 98 users often work far from the MS-DOS text-based environment of olden days, the MS-DOS environment is still alive and well due to the many programs still in use today that are written for MS-DOS.

Windows 98 supports MS-DOS programs better than any version of Windows has so far. Windows 98 provides more memory for programs and enables you to open several multitasking MS-DOS programs at one time. In addition, Windows 98 adds a toolbar to MS-DOS windows that makes the management of your MS-DOS windows and programs much easier to work with.

There are people who will work many hours a day with Windows 98 and never need to start the MS-DOS environment. Others still use older MS-DOS programs and current-day games that run only under MS-DOS. Because of the extra memory and runtime support provided by Windows 98, these MS-DOS programs ought to work comfortably inside Windows 98.

Q&A

Q Why would I want to shut Windows 98 down in the MS-DOS environment?

A There are still a handful of rare programs written for the MS-DOS environment that will not run under Windows 98. Microsoft wrote Windows 98 to run most MS-DOS programs, even the ones that previous versions of Windows could not handle. Although the majority of MS-DOS programs work well under Windows 98, the few that do not will run as long as you shut down Windows 98 and restart (via the Shut Down menu command) your computer in MS-DOS mode.

Q When would I want to start more than one MS-DOS window?

A If you want to run two or more MS-DOS programs at once (such as two games) whether or not you are also running Windows 98 programs, the multiple MS-DOS windows enable both of the MS-DOS programs to work in a multitasking mode. Each window works independently of the other(s).

Q Why would I execute a Windows 98 program from the MS-DOS prompt?

A Users of previous Windows versions found that they often wanted to execute a Windows program from the MS-DOS prompt but, until Windows 98, they were unable to do that. Perhaps you like to use an MS-DOS bookkeeping system and you suddenly want to use a calculator. If you know the Windows 98 calculator's filename, CALC (with the extension .EXE), you can type that filename (precede the filename with the file's disk name and pathname), such as typing `c:\windows\calc`, and the program starts immediately (your MS-DOS window still remains open as well).

Q If I like the Windows 98 Notepad program, is there any need to learn the MS-DOS editor?

A Not really. The MS-DOS editor might be good to use if you're already familiar with previous versions of MS-DOS editors such as MS-DOS 5 and 6's EDIT program. You will find that Microsoft implemented needed changes to EDIT without changing the fundamental purpose of the MS-DOS text editor.

Workshop

Key Terms

Review the following list of terms:

- *default drive and directory* When you start MS-DOS, the MS-DOS command prompt always contains a disk drive and directory. The disk drive is normally C:, and the directory is the root directory called \ (backslash). You can change the default disk or directory by entering a new one at the command prompt.
- *MS-DOS command prompt* When you open an MS-DOS window, you must issue a command to the MS-DOS environment. The command prompt, usually shown on the screen as `C:\>` indicating the current default drive and directory, accepts your MS-DOS commands as you type the commands.
- *MS-DOS program* A program written specifically for the MS-DOS environment. MS-DOS programs do not take advantage of the graphical nature of Windows 98.
- *non-proportional font* A font that contains characters that each consume the same width on the screen or printer.
- *proportional font* A font that generally makes for a more natural appearance of text. The letters within the text do not all consume the same screen width. For example, the lowercase letter i consumes less space than the uppercase M.
- *True Type font* A readable font that appears the same on both the screen and printer.
- *VM* Stands for virtual memory and refers to the concept that each MS-DOS window acts like a separate PC that has access to full memory and other system resources.

Part III

Windows 98 Accessories in the Afternoon

Hour

PART III

Hour 9

Giving Windows 98 Your Own Programs

By itself, Windows 98 doesn't do work for you. Your application programs do your work. You use application programs to write documents, create graphics, explore the Internet, manage database files, and play games. Somehow you've got to get application programs onto your PC. Programs come on CD-ROMs (or, less commonly, on disks), and you must run those programs through an *installation routine* so that Windows 98 properly recognizes them.

Although every application program requires a unique, one-of-a-kind installation routine, you'll install most of today's programs the same way. This hour looks at Windows 98's support for adding programs, discusses unique installation problems you may encounter, and reviews how to remove programs that you've installed and no longer need.

The highlights of this hour include the following:

- ☐ Why proper installation is critical
- ☐ How to use the Add/Remove Programs dialog box effectively
- ☐ Where to go when you need to add or remove a Windows 98 component
- ☐ How to properly uninstall programs
- ☐ What to do when no adequate uninstall procedure exists

The Add/Remove Programs Icon

Before Windows, you could add a program to your computer simply by copying a file from the disk you purchased to your hard disk. To remove the program, you only had to delete the file. Things get messier with Windows 98, however, because Windows 98 requires a lot from application programs. Those programs are no longer simple to add or remove, so you must familiarize yourself with the proper techniques.

CAUTION

> If you don't follow the proper program-installation techniques, your application probably won't run correctly. Even worse, with Windows 98's integrated set of files, a program you add to your PC incorrectly might make other programs fail.

The Windows 98 Control Panel contains an entry that you'll frequently visit to manage the programs on your PC. This icon is labeled Add/Remove Programs. When you open this icon, the tabbed dialog box shown in Figure 9.1 appears. Depending on the number of your PC's installed applications, you'll probably see more applications listed in the lower half of the window.

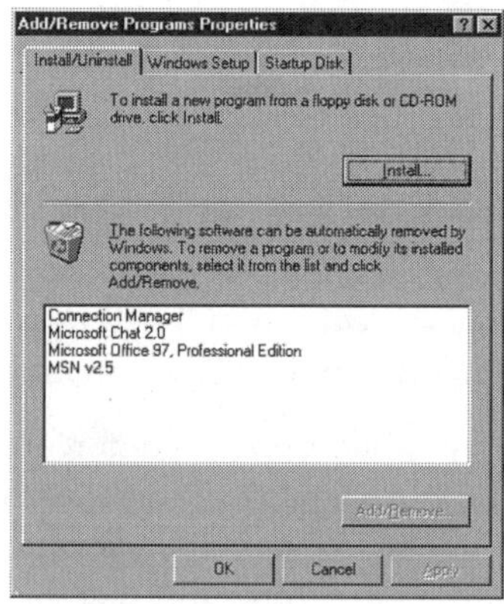

Figure 9.1.
You manage your installed programs from the Add/Remove Program Properties dialog box.

The dialog box's top half contains an Install button that you can click to install new software. Surprisingly, you'll rarely, if ever, use this button when installing Windows 98 programs because most programs install somewhat automatically, as explained later in this hour. The lower half contains a list of application programs on your PC. Not every program on your PC appears in the list. The list contains programs that you can *uninstall* from your system. If you uninstall using the Add/Remove Programs Properties dialog box, you can be assured that the application will completely go away. (The term *deinstall* is sometimes used instead of *uninstall*.)

9

Although you can uninstall most Windows 98 applications, occasionally an application will share a support or system file with another application. Even more common, sometimes the uninstallation routine detects *incorrectly* that the file is shared by another program. Therefore, during some uninstallation routines, you might see a dialog box message asking if you want the routine to remove one of the shared files. Generally, it's difficult to know what to do. The safest advice is to keep the file by responding as such to the dialog box if it appears. Although in many cases retaining the file simply wastes disk space, you'll avoid possible trouble with other applications that might use that file.

If you make a system backup before uninstalling an application (see Hour 22, "Manage Your Hard Drive"), you can safely remove the file and then keep the backup handy until you're convinced that the system is stable. Again, it's often simpler just to keep the file in question when the uninstallation program prompts you about it. These orphaned files often make for heated discussions among the PC community—and rightly so. Windows 98 and uninstallation routines should be written so that they work together more accurately without requiring the user to make such ambiguous file-deletion decisions.

Windows Minute

Shortcuts to Files

Most icons on your Start menu and desktop represent programs and windows that you open. These icons are often shortcuts to your applications, represented by a small arrow in the lower-left corner of the icon that points to the icon's image. If you delete a program's icon from the Start menu or from your desktop, you will not properly remove the program from Windows 98. In most cases, you will remove nothing about the program except the shortcut file that points to the actual file.

Sometimes an icon is not a shortcut pointer but represents the file, so if you delete the icon in that case, the file goes away as well. Nevertheless, Windows 98 programs most often require multiple files. Some reside in the Windows 98 folder, and others reside in the application's folder. Therefore, removing one of these files doesn't erase all of the application from your disk. In some cases, those extra files can cause problems—and those files always consume disk space that you'd probably like to recapture.

Therefore, always perform a proper uninstallation when you want to remove a Windows 98 program. This hour's next-to-last section discusses uninstallation procedures.

The Windows Setup Page

Once you've opened the Control Panel's Add/Remove Programs dialog box, click the Windows Setup tab to display the page shown in Figure 9.2. Unlike applications, you'll never remove Windows 98, because you would be removing the operating system that controls your PC. (You wouldn't sit on the same tree branch you're sawing off, would you?) When you update to a new version of Windows, the new version will remove Windows 98, but you've got plenty of time to worry about that later. For now, the Windows Setup page lets you add and remove various Windows 98 options.

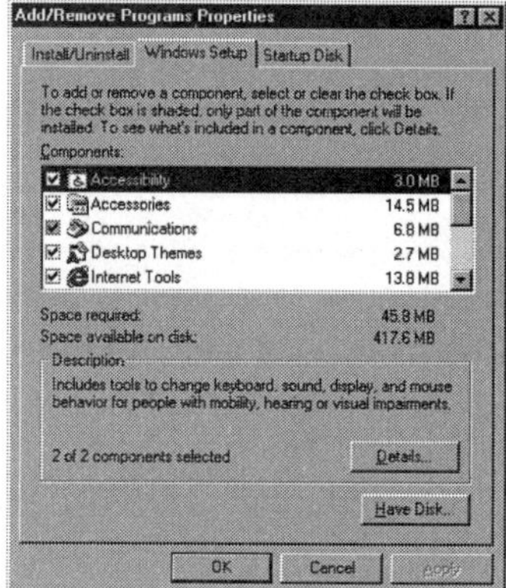

Figure 9.2.
Change Windows 98 options from the Windows Setup tab.

Sometimes you'll rerun an application program's installation routine to change installation settings, just as you change Windows 98 options from the Windows Setup page. Program installations are sometimes the only place where you can modify the program's installed options. This is true for Microsoft Office as well as some other major software titles. When you need to change such a program, you will have to run its install procedure once again (perhaps by clicking the Install button on the Install/Uninstall page), but the program won't really install a second time. Instead, the program will prompt you for changes you want to make to the installation.

Time Saver

If a program stops working properly, you might have to reinstall it completely. Although you can rerun the installation again in some cases, you're probably better off uninstalling the program first to remove all traces of it and then running the installation from scratch again. (Be sure to back up your data files before you do that so you'll have them intact when you reinstall the program.)

When you make a change to a Windows 98 setting, that setting might not show until you restart Windows 98.

9

To Do

Task 9.1: Changing Windows 98 Settings

Step 1: Description

This task shows you how to change Windows 98 installation settings. Although the various Properties menu options you find throughout Windows 98 let you change settings that affect

Windows 98's performance, appearance, and operation, the Windows Setup page in the Add/Remove Programs Properties dialog box lets you add or remove parts of Windows 98 properly.

CAUTION

You'll need your Windows 98 CD-ROM in order to change Windows 98 options, so place it in your CD-ROM drive. If the Windows 98 banner automatically appears, close the window.

Step 2: Action

1. Display the Windows Setup page. The Components scrolling listbox shows which groups of Windows 98 options you've installed. An empty checkbox means that none of those options are installed to run. A grayed-out checkmark means that some of the programs in the group are installed. A regular checkmark means that the entire group is installed. If you didn't install Windows 98, or if you installed Windows 98 using all the default options, you might not be completely familiar with all the groups that appear. As you work through this 24-hour tutorial, you'll learn more about the various options available for Windows 98.

   The checked options indicate that every program in that group is installed. For example, rarely will all of Windows 98's Accessories group be installed, so you'll see a grayed-out checkmark there.
2. Click the title for Accessories (if you click the checkmark, you'll change the setting) and then click the Details button. You'll see a scrollable list of Accessories programs (these are the programs that appear when you select the Start menu's Programs | Accessories option) like the one shown in Figure 9.3.

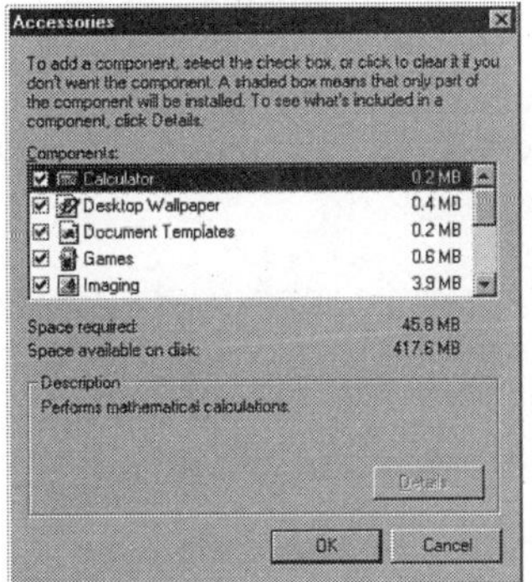

Figure 9.3.
See which Accessories options are installed.

3. Scroll down to the System Monitor entry. Rarely will Windows 98 users have this option checked. If you do, uncheck it to remove it from your Windows 98. (You can repeat this task afterwards to put it back.) If your System Monitor is not installed, check it.

JUST A MINUTE

When you check or uncheck options, Windows 98 will not completely reinstall. Instead, Windows 98 adds or removes the programs necessary to make the changes you request on the Windows Setup page. Whether you install or remove the System Monitor, you'll see the same procedure occur when you begin the update process in the next step.

4. Click OK to close the Accessories window.
5. In the Windows Setup page, click OK once again to start the Windows 98 setup modification. A dialog box appears, telling you the status of the update. The update can take a while if you add or remove several Windows 98 components.
6. Close the Control Panel. When you restart Windows 98, you'll see System Monitor on the Start menu's Programs | Accessories | System Tools menu.

Step 3: Review

This task showed you how to change Windows 98 options installed on your system. Use the Control Panel's Add/Remove Programs dialog box and click the Windows Setup page to make the Windows 98 changes you require.

The System Monitor appears in an Accessories menu group called System Tools. System Monitor is called a *utility program* because it works in the background, enabling you to analyze Windows 98's performance. If your PC ever begins to act sluggishly, run the System Monitor to see which Windows resources you need.

Installed Applications

Almost every time you purchase a new application program to install on your PC, you'll insert its CD-ROM into the drive, close the drive door, and see a message such as the one shown in Figure 9.4.

In most cases, such an application checks your PC to see if the program is already installed. If it isn't, the program gives you a prompt like the one shown in Figure 9.4. The software authors know that you probably wouldn't be inserting the CD-ROM in the drive if you didn't want to install the program.

JUST A MINUTE

If the program is already installed, the program often begins executing (without the installation prompt) after you close the CD-ROM drive door.

Figure 9.4.
An application program is about to install.

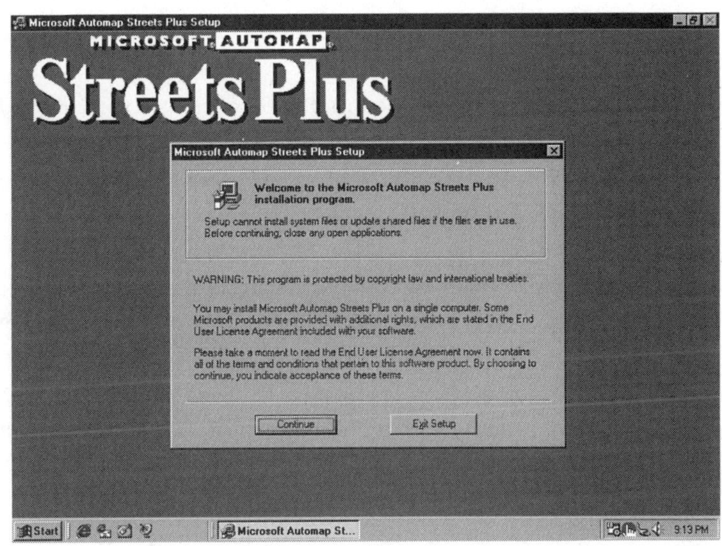

CAUTION

If you insert the CD-ROM and nothing happens, your CD-ROM's *AutoPlay* feature might be turned off, so Windows 98 doesn't recognize that you've inserted a new CD-ROM. See Hour 23, "Multimedia and Sound," for AutoPlay setup information.

If the CD-ROM doesn't start, or if you have AutoPlay disabled and you want to leave it that way, you can choose Run from the Start menu and type `d:\Setup`. (Replace the `d` with the letter of your CD-ROM drive.)

JUST A MINUTE

If you're installing from disks, you'll have to insert the first installation disk into the disk drive, choose Run from the Start menu, and type `a:\Setup`.

If you get an error message, choose Start | Run once again to make sure you've entered the drive, backslash, and Setup command properly. If you get an error message again, your program might require a different command. Replace `Setup` with `Install` to see what happens. If the Run command still fails, you must check the program's owner's manual to locate the correct command.

Each application's setup is different! Therefore, unless every reader had identical software to install, this book could not describe every scenario that occurs past the original installation window. Nevertheless, the following list provides guidelines that almost every installation follows:

- You can often read installation notes (often called a *Readme* file) by clicking the appropriate selection in the installation window.
- Sometimes multiple installation options are available. Check the manual, if one comes with the program, for the installation that suits you if you can't determine from the opening window which one to use.
- Once you start the installation, a wizard usually guides you step-by-step through the process.
- You can often accept all installation defaults if you're unsure whether to install an option during the wizard's performance. The wizard asks questions such as which disk drive and folder you want to install to.
- If you don't have adequate disk space, the installation program will tell you. You'll have to remove other files, get more disk space, reduce the installation options, or do without the program if you don't have the space for it.
- At the end of the installation, you will probably have to restart Windows 98 in order for all the installation options to go into effect. If you're asked whether you want to restart Windows 98, you can answer No, but don't run the installed program until you do restart Windows 98.

Uninstallation Procedures

Most application programs written for Windows 98 include a standard uninstallation routine that removes the application from Windows 98 and from your PC. Remember that an application program is often made up of several files. The program's installation routine stores those files in several different locations. Therefore, without an uninstallation routine, removing the application is a tedious task.

Before displaying the Control Panel's Add/Remove Programs window to uninstall a program you've installed, check the menu group the program resides in. Sometimes, in a program's menu group, the installation routine sets up the uninstallation routine that you can run from that group. For example, if you installed a game called Side-to-Side, you might start the game by selecting from a series of menus that might look like this: Programs | Side Game | Play Side-to-Side. Look on the same menu and see if there's an uninstall option that you would select, such as Programs | Side Game | Uninstall Side-to-Side. Once you begin the uninstallation process, a wizard begins that steps you through the program's removal.

If there isn't a menu option for the uninstallation, you should again look to the Control Panel's Add/Remove Programs dialog box. Scroll through the list of items in the lower part of the dialog box to see if the program you want to remove appears in the list. If so, select that entry and click the Add/Remove button to begin the uninstall wizard.

If no entry appears, you are running out of options! Insert the program's CD-ROM once again and see if the opening window contains an uninstall option. If not, look through the

Readme file to see if you can get help. Also, look in the program's owner's manual. Lacking any uninstall routine at all, you should try one more place if you have access: the Web. See if you can find the company's Web page somewhere in the Readme file or owner's manual. If you can't find it, try going to the Web address `www.companyname.com` and see if something comes up. (If you have no idea how to get on the Web, you'll learn how in Hour 13, "Internet Explorer 4.0.")

A Last Resort

If your search for an uninstall procedure comes up empty, you are forced to do one of two things:

- Leave the program on your system if you have ample disk space
- Manually remove as much of the program as you can

That last option can get messy. You'll need to search for the program files (perhaps you remember the folder where you installed them). In the next hour you'll learn how to search for files, so you might want to browse Hour 10 before attempting to manually remove the application. After you've removed the program's files and the folder where the application resides (just ignore any related program files that might be scattered across your disk because they're almost impossible to find), you need to remove the menu entry as well. Follow these steps to remove the application from the Start menu:

1. From the Start menu, select Settings | Taskbar & Start Menu.
2. Click the Start Menu Programs tab.
3. Click the Remove button to open the Remove Shortcuts/Folders dialog box, shown in Figure 9.5.

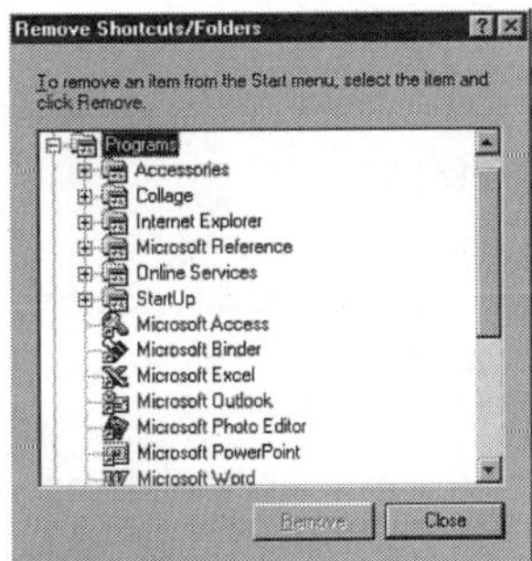

Figure 9.5.
You can remove menu items and menu groups from the Remove Shortcuts/Folders dialog box.

4. Locate the program group that the application resides in. You might have to click one or more of the plus signs to expand a group to get to the one you need. If you only want to remove one or more entries within the group, open the group to display those entries using the Explorer-like techniques you now know.

5. Highlight the group and click the Remove button to remove the group from the Start menu. When you close the dialog box, the entry will be gone from the Start menu.

Time Saver

Several software companies offer uninstallation utility programs that you can purchase. These programs attempt to remove all traces of unwanted programs from your disk. If you purchase one, the program should be able to remove most programs known about before the uninstall product was released. As new programs appear on the market, these software companies update their uninstallation utility programs, so upgrade the utility to ensure that you've got the latest when you need it. (Often you can download updates from the company's web site.)

Summary

This hour described how you install application programs on your PC and also how you remove them. Before Windows came along, program installation and removal was simple because rarely did a program reside in more than one file on your disk. Today's Windows 98 programs, however, install with multiple files in multiple locations, and their removal can get tedious.

The next hour describes how you use Windows 98's file-searching capabilities to locate files on your computer. You might need to search for a file if you manually need to remove a program from Windows 98, as described in the last section.

Q&A

Q Why don't I ever use the Add/Remove Programs dialog box's Install button to install programs?

A Nobody seems to have a good answer for that! It seems as if software companies don't want to access this already-supplied installation resource. If they did, all program installations would basically require the same steps, and, one would think, users would be happier. Nevertheless, companies seem to prefer that the installation routine begin automatically when the user inserts the CD-ROM.

The drawback of this approach is that many times such an installation won't work as expected. Either the AutoPlay feature is turned off, or the user bought the program on disks. (Disk drives don't support the AutoPlay feature.)

Q How do I turn on AutoPlay so my CDs install automatically?

A As you learned in this hour, even users who have AutoPlay turned on don't always see a proper installation. If your AutoPlay is turned off, keep in mind that some

Windows 98 users prefer to keep AutoPlay turned off. These users can insert a CD-ROM at any time without having to wait for a startup or installation window to appear. When they want to see the window or start the program that requires the CD-ROM, they can do so by selecting the CD-ROM from the My Computer window.

Although Hour 20, "Multimedia and Sound," explains how to use AutoPlay, here are some quick instructions if you need AutoPlay for an installation now:

1. From the Start menu, select Settings | Control Panel.
2. Double-click the System icon.
3. Click the Device Manager tab.
4. Click the plus sign next to your CD-ROM drive. The CD-ROM drive's description appears.
5. Select the description.
6. Click Properties.
7. Click the Settings tab. Windows 95 displays a Settings dialog box.
8. Uncheck the option labeled `Auto insert notification` to turn off AutoPlay. (If you subsequently check this option again, AutoPlay will return.)
9. Click OK to close the Settings dialog box.
10. Click OK to close the System dialog box.
11. Close the Control Panel window. When you next insert a CD-ROM, Windows 98 will start the installation, program (if installed), or music (if you insert an audio CD in the drive).

Workshop

Key Terms

Review the following list of terms:

- *installation routine* The steps needed to add programs to your PC so that they interact properly with the Windows 98 environment.
- *Readme file* A file with last-minute changes, notes, tips, and warnings about the software you're about to install. Often a software vendor puts notes in the Readme file that didn't make it into the printed owner's manual.
- *uninstallation* The process of removing installed programs from the Windows 98 environment.
- *utility program* A program that helps you interact with Windows 98 more efficiently or effectively, as opposed to application programs that you run to do your work.

Part III

Hour 10

Looking in All the Right Places

Hard disks are getting bigger, more information appears on the Internet by the minute, and you've got to find things fast! Fortunately, Windows 98 comes to your rescue with powerful searching tools. Windows 98 can quickly find files and folders that you need. You can search by filename, date, and location. In addition, Windows 98 includes several Internet searching tools that enable you to find people and Web sites that match the exact specifications you want to match.

The highlights of this hour include the following:

- How to master the Start menu's Find command
- When to specify wildcard searches
- Which search options help you find information the fastest
- How the Internet search tools help you wade through huge mounds of data
- How to locate people in other parts of the world

Introducing Find

Click the Start menu to see the Find menu, shown in Figure 10.1. Table 10.1 explains each of Find's search targets.

Figure 10.1.
Use the Find command when you want to locate files or information.

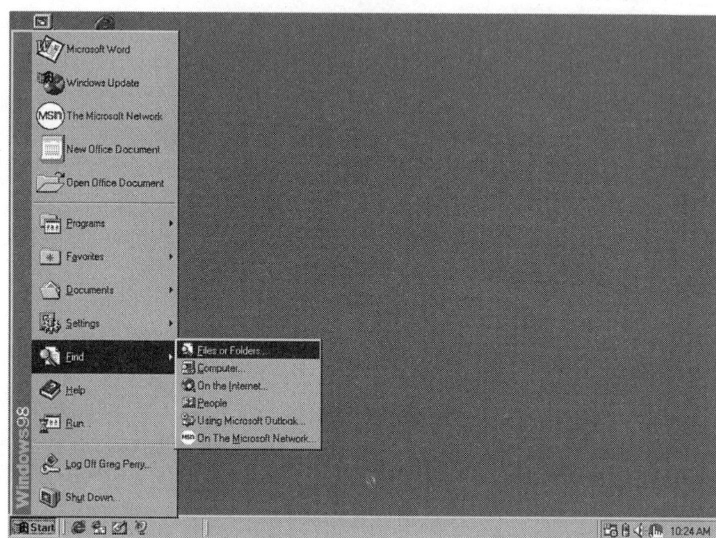

Table 10.1. Using Find to locate information.

Target	Description
Files or Folders	Locates a file or folder on your PC system, including networked drives if you have them.
Computer	Searches for a specific PC located on a networked set of computers.
On the Internet	Searches the Internet for information.
People	Searches across several locations for people.
Using Microsoft Outlook	Searches through the Microsoft Office program named Microsoft Outlook (if you have Outlook installed) for information.
On the Microsoft Network	Searches the Microsoft Network online service for information. (You'll have this entry only if you've set up the Microsoft Network online service.)

Just a Minute

This book doesn't cover searching with Microsoft Outlook or on the Microsoft Network because you must have the Microsoft Office software in order to use Microsoft Outlook, and you must subscribe to the Microsoft Network (MSN) in order to search MSN for information. Hour 15, "Online Services," describes MSN and its relation to other online services that you might subscribe to using Windows 98.

Caution

Microsoft Outlook differs from Outlook Express. Outlook Express is Windows 98's internal email management system. You'll learn about it starting in Hour 17, "Outlook Express: For Mail and Newsgroups."

You should master the Start menu's Find command so that your computer can look for files and folders. You won't have to wade through disks, folders, and subfolders looking for a document you created in the past. Let Windows 98 do the work for you.

Time Saver

Explorer's Tools | Find menu option contains the same searching capabilities as the Start menu's Find command. Therefore, once you master the Find command, you'll also know how to look for information from inside Explorer. By the way, you can quickly display the Find window by right-clicking the Start menu and selecting the Find option.

Windows Minute

Improving Your Searches

You'll often use *wildcard characters* when performing searches. A wildcard character stands for one or more groups of characters, just as a joker often functions as a wildcard in card games. Find supports two wildcard characters: * and ?.

* acts as a wildcard for zero, one, or more characters. For example, if you wanted to see all files that end with the .txt extension, you could specify `*.txt` as your search *criteria* (search instructions). The asterisk wildcard tells Find to locate every file that ends in .txt, no matter what appears before the file extension. The criteria `ABC*.*` represents all files that begin with the letters ABC, no matter what follows the letters and no matter what extension the file has. (`ABC*.*` even locates files that begin with ABC and have no extension.)

The question mark wildcard replaces single characters within a criteria. Therefore, ACCT??.DAT finds all files that begin with ACCT, have two more characters, and end in the .DAT extension. The following files would successfully match that criteria: ACCT97.DAT, ACCT98.DAT, and ACCT99.DAT. However, neither ACCT.DAT nor ACCTjun98.DAT would match, because the two question marks specify that only two characters must replace the wildcards in those positions.

Time Saver

Want to search for a document you began working on yesterday? Display the Start menu's Documents list to see a list of recently created and recently edited data documents you can return to with a click of the mouse. If your Documents list gets too large, select Start | Settings | Taskbar & Start Menu, and then click the Clear button on the Start Menu Programs page to erase the contents of the taskbar's Documents list.

Searching Files and Folders

You'll probably use the Start menu's Find command to search for files and folders on your PC. Find gives you access to many different search criteria. You can search for files in a specific folder, on a disk, or on your entire computer system, including networked drives if you have any.

Task 10.1: Using Find

Step 1: Description

Find locates files that meet a search criteria. You can search an entire disk for a specific file or for a document that contains a certain word or phrase.

If you know a partial filename, you can find all files that contain that partial filename. If you want to search for a file you changed two days ago, you can find all files with modification dates that fall on that day. You can even save searches that you perform often so that you don't have to create the search criteria each time you need to search, as discussed in Task 10.2.

This task searches your Windows folder for a specific filename.

Step 2: Action

1. Display the Start menu and select Find.
2. When the next menu appears, select Files or Folders. The Find dialog box appears, as shown in Figure 10.2.

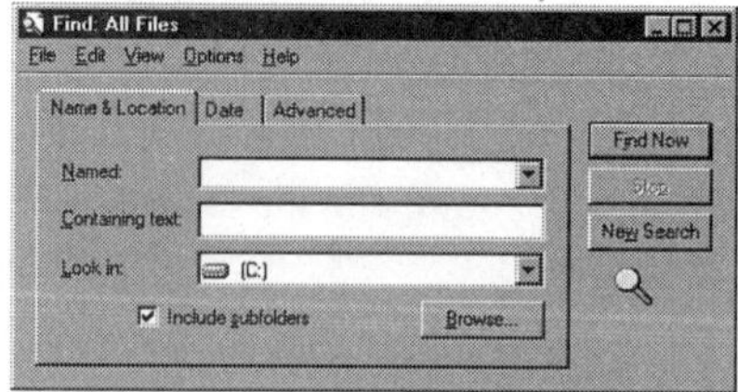

Figure 10.2. *The Find dialog box searches across drives for specific documents and folders.*

3. Type `winmine.*` at the Named prompt. This wildcard specification looks for all files and folders that begin with the letters winmine.

   You will accept the defaults in the other fields. Find defaults to your C drive, which is where Windows 98 is almost always stored. (If you know that your version of

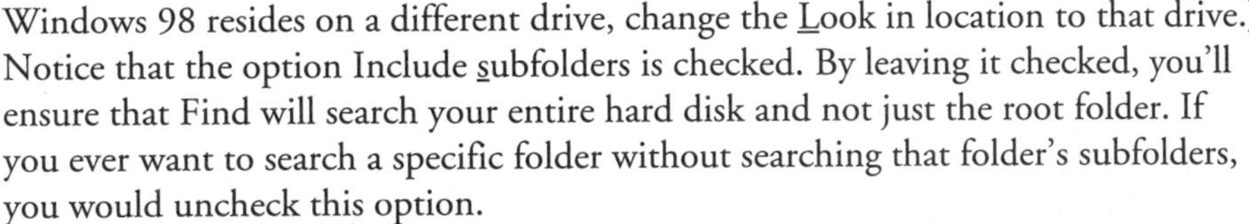

Windows 98 resides on a different drive, change the Look in location to that drive.) Notice that the option Include subfolders is checked. By leaving it checked, you'll ensure that Find will search your entire hard disk and not just the root folder. If you ever want to search a specific folder without searching that folder's subfolders, you would uncheck this option.

4. Click the Find Now button to start the search. (If you press Enter, Find clicks the Find Now button for you, because Find Now is the default button.) After a brief pause, your Find dialog box should resemble the one shown in Figure 10.3. The list contains not only the document's filename, but also the folder that the document resides in, the size of the document, the type of file, and the date and time that the file was last modified.

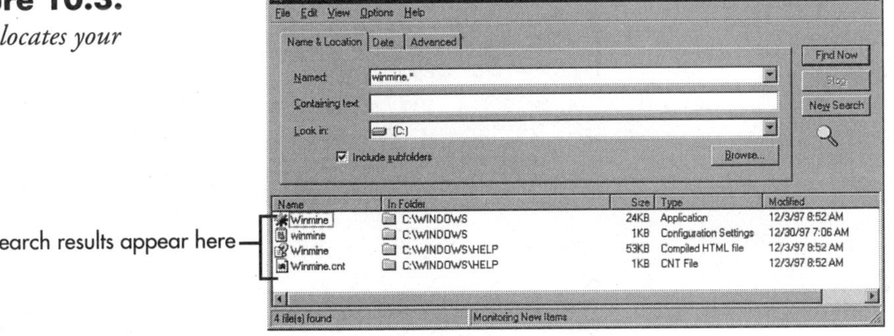

Figure 10.3.
Find locates your files.

JUST A MINUTE

If you don't see filename extensions but you want to, from the Start menu select Settings | Folder Options View | Display the full path in the title bar. (Hour 3, "Take Windows 98 to Task," explains other folder options you can set.)

TIME SAVER

Maximize the Find dialog box window to more fully view the search results.

Your search results always appear in the lower portion of the Find dialog box. You can drag the edge of any column title left or right to expand or shrink the width of that column. If you click a column title, Find sorts the found information in alphabetical, numerical, or date and time order.

At least four files should appear, and they'll all appear in your Windows folder. One of these files has an .exe extension, meaning that you can run (execute) that file.

If you turned off your filename extension display from Explorer, the executable file is the file with the land mine icon to the left of its Name entry. Now that Windows 98 has located the executable file, you can run the program directly from the Find dialog box.

5. Double-click the winmine.exe entry, and a Windows 98 game named Minesweeper (shown in Figure 10.4) appears. Start clicking away on the squares, but be very careful!

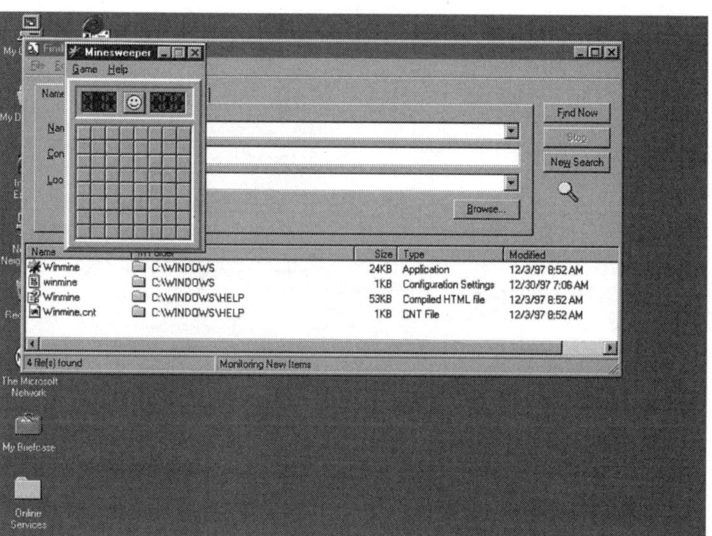

Figure 10.4.
You can start programs directly from Find's search results.

Windows 98 is smart. If the file you click isn't an executable file, Windows 98 attempts to open the file using other resources. For example, if you click a Microsoft Word document, Windows 98 automatically looks for the Microsoft Word program on your PC and opens the document using Word (assuming that you have Word). If you select a help file, Find opens a help window with that file displayed. If you select an email message file, Find locates your email reader and displays the message there. As long as the file is registered (as explained in Hour 5, "Explore the Windows 98 System"), Windows 98 can associate the file's parent program and display the file.

6. After you've played Minesweeper for a while, close its window and then close the Find dialog box.

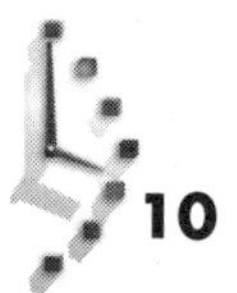

Step 3: Review

The searching capability of Windows 98 finds documents and folders on your system that match certain criteria that you provide. You can search for documents by name or by a search string. Once Find locates the file, you can open it or execute a found program file by selecting it from the list of found entries.

TIME SAVER

> You can leave found results displayed and start additional searches.

Task 10.2: Using Find to Locate Types of Files

Step 1: Description

Not only will Find locate files if you know a partial or complete filename, but you can also search for a file that you modified two days ago or find all files of a specific type. You can even save searches that you perform often so that you don't have to create the search criteria each time you need to search. This task describes the other options available from the Find dialog box.

Step 2: Action

1. Display the Start menu and select Find.
2. Select Files or Folders. Leave the Named prompt empty for this search.
3. Type `C:\WINDOWS` in the Look in prompt. You will scan drive C's Windows folder, looking for specific files.

CAUTION

> If your Windows folder is located on a different drive, type that drive's letter instead of C, or open the Look in dropdown listbox and select the drive and folder.

4. Leave the checkmark next to the Include subfolders option. Find searches the Windows folder as well as all subfolders within the Windows folder.
5. Click the Date tab to display the Date page, as shown in Figure 10.5. Leave the All files option marked. If you want to limit your search to specific dates, the Find all files option enables you to search only for files modified, created, or last accessed between a beginning and ending date or within the last few days or months.
6. Click the Advanced tab to display the Advanced page, as shown in Figure 10.6.
7. Open the Of type drop-down listbox to display a list of file types. These file types are all the file types that are currently registered. If you want to search for files of a certain type, such as Microsoft Word documents only, you can select that file type from the list, and Find ignores all the files that don't match that selected type. You can also search for files that meet a specific size criteria by selecting from the Size is fields.

Figure 10.5.
You can narrow the search to specific dates.

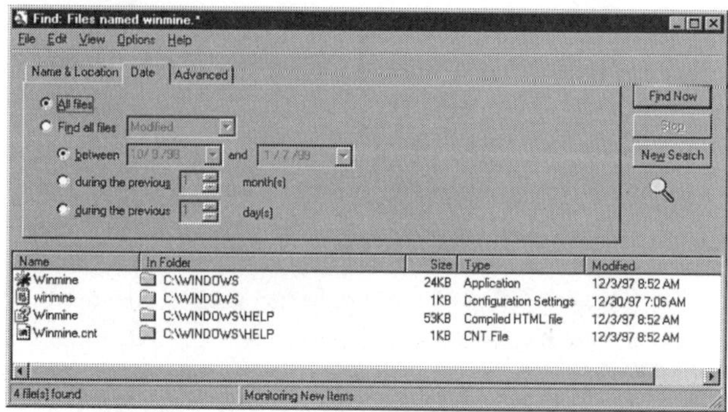

Figure 10.6.
Search through specific file types with the Advanced dialog box.

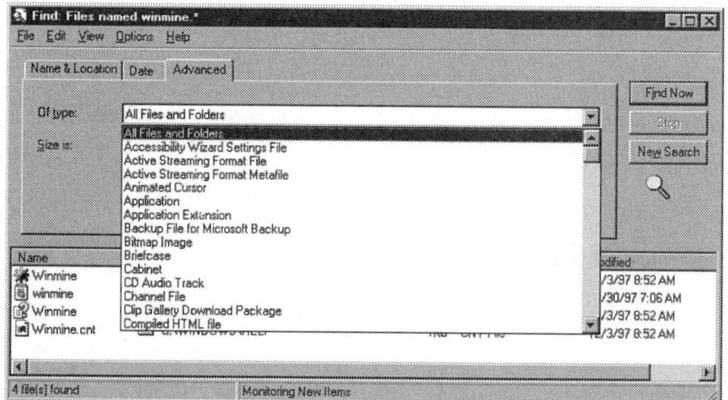

8. Select Cursor from the Of type listbox. You are directing Find to find all mouse cursor files within the Windows folders.
9. Click the Find Now button and wait a bit while Windows 98 scans your disk drive. The search might take a while, depending on the speed of your computer and the number of files in your Windows folder.

TIME SAVER

During a long search, you can click any button on the taskbar to start or switch to another program. The file search can continue in the background while you write a letter or play a game.

10. When the search is complete, the Find dialog box lists the files that meet your search criteria in the bottom portion of the dialog box. If there are several cursor files in the Windows folder (as there should be), Windows 98 displays vertical scroll bars so that you can scroll through the list of choices.

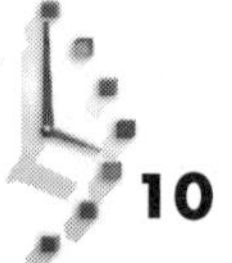

11. If you select File | Save Search | Windows 98 sends the find results and search criteria to an icon located on the desktop, where the search is available for you as a desktop icon at a later time. If you later click this icon after closing the Find dialog box, Find begins once again with all of the search's criteria entered automatically.
12. Select File | Close to close the dialog box.

Step 3: Review

This task showed you additional ways you can use Find to search for documents that meet a file type or date criteria. Depending on how you work, you might need to find a file you worked on around a specific date, or you might want to locate a file whose file type you remember but whose name you forgot. Either way, Find will do the searching for you.

To Do

Task 10.3: Finding Internet Information

Step 1: Description

The Internet provides a wealth of information, but with that richness often comes *information overload.* A lot of material appears on the Internet, and you must wade through stuff you don't want in order to get to the stuff you *do* want. The Start menu's Find command helps you make sense out of Internet searching by providing you with an interactive desktop tool that you can use to look for information.

Step 2: Action

1. Open the Start menu. Suppose you want to search the Internet for information on *Mardi,* a Herman Melville work.
2. Select Find | On the Internet. If you aren't already connected to the Internet, your Internet sign-in dialog box appears so that you can enter your ID and password. (Depending on your Internet connection, you might have to initiate the dial-in sequence to connect to your Internet provider.)

   Once you've signed into your Internet account, the Internet Explorer window opens so that you can select the type of search you want to perform, as shown in Figure 10.7.

CAUTION

If you use a non-Microsoft Web browser, such as Netscape Navigator, your screen's controls will differ slightly from the ones shown in Figure 10.7.

Figure 10.7.
Search the Internet for the information you need.

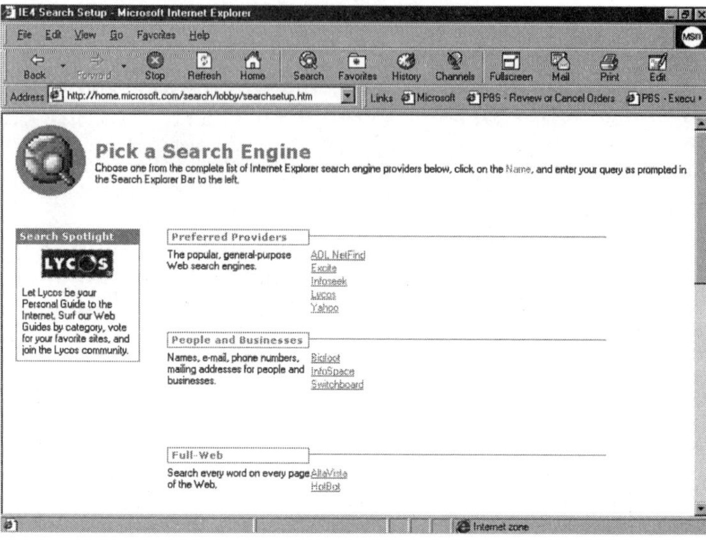

Windows Minute

Using Internet Search Engines

The Internet search screen enables you to use one of several Internet *search engines* to locate your information. A search engine is a web-based program that searches the Internet. Search engines have names such as Infoseek, AOL NetFind, Lycos, Excite, and Yahoo!. Different search engines offer different options and searching abilities, and some are better than others for different topics. Which are the best? That's hard to say these days because competition between them makes most of them equally powerful.

Once you've selected your preferred search engine, that search engine becomes the default for subsequent searches until you select another from the drop-down list. After you select a search engine, the left window pane displays that search engine's search text box so that you can enter the criteria for your search.

3. After you've selected a search engine, type `Mardi` (the text cursor always appears in the search text location) and click the seek button (sometimes called `Search` or `Find`, depending on your selected search engine). You might see the security warning shown in Figure 10.8. This warning informs you that you are sending information over the Internet and that some smartie might somehow look at the information you send. Nevertheless, unless you search for classified information, search criteria is rarely secret information, so click Yes to see the search results.

Figure 10.8.
Your browser might warn you that you are sending information over the Internet.

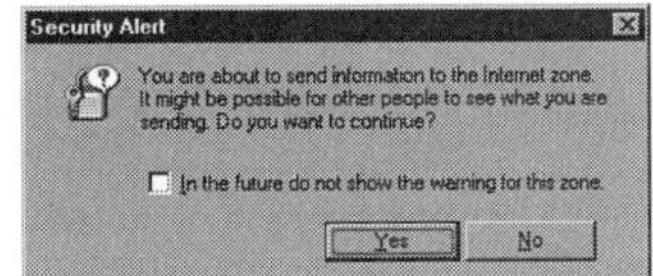

When the search is finished, the left window shows the results. Often, unless you search for very specific information, you'll get several resulting Web locations where your search engine found the information. Most search engines give you the choice of scrolling through a summary list of 10 or 20 sites at a time, looking for the sites you want to view. Figure 10.9 shows how such a listing from the Infoseek search engine looks after the width of the left window was increased to show the search results.

Just a Minute

Expect to find lots of advertising on the search engine pages. This advertising means revenue for the search engine to fund the service that's free to you.

Figure 10.9.
Many times, too much information is found, and you'll be overloaded!

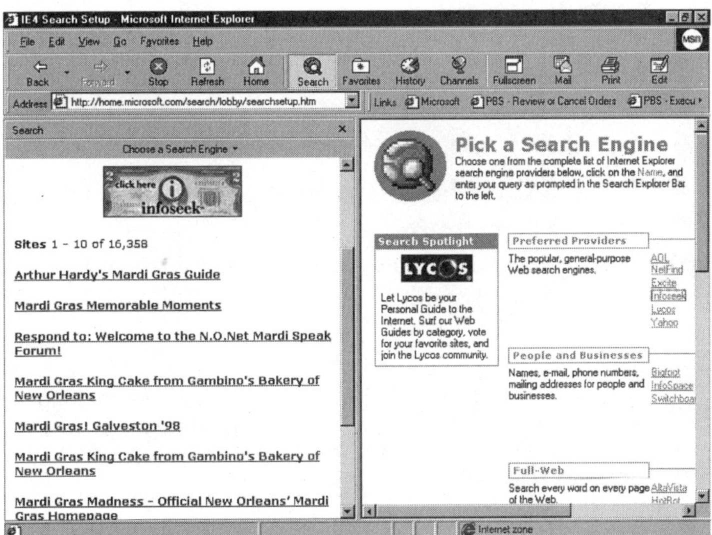

4. By now, you've figured out that searching for `Mardi` turns up more information about Mardi Gras celebrations than about a literary classic! Therefore, you've got to narrow the search a bit. Type `+Melville +Mardi` and click the seek button to ensure

that you get only web sites that list Melville's name as well as the word `Mardi`. The plus signs in front of each word ensure that the resulting Web page will contain both words. (The words don't have to appear together or in order, as they would in a phrase.) When you click any of the found links that contain your search topic, the corresponding Web page appears in the left window. (You can close the left search engine window when you've found the Web information you want in order to give the Web page more screen room.)

As you become more familiar with search engines and their options, you'll learn ways to narrow your Internet searches. Most search engines support the same options, and most have an options button you can click to get help on the options available. If you enclose a phrase in quotation marks, you're telling the search engine to look for Web pages that contain your exact search phrase. Use lowercase letters unless you are searching for a proper name. As you've seen, a plus sign in front of a word forces that word to appear in the resulting Web page. A minus sign would require that the word be absent before a successful search is determined.

When you narrow your search, you'll find fewer Web pages and a more meaningful result. You can scroll through the results and click any entry that describes Melville's book.

5. When you finish reading about *Mardi,* you can close your Web browser (don't sign off just yet) and return to the Windows desktop.

Step 3: Review

Windows 98's Internet search takes you to the Web and offers a selection of search engines. As you use different ones, you'll learn which respond to your searches better than others. You'll also begin to explore more of each engine's options, such as the capability to search through newsgroups and foreign-language sites.

Task 10.4: Finding People

Step 1: Description

You can search for an old pal or a long-lost love using the Find menu. Windows 98 uses a collection of people-finding search engines to look for people you want to find.

JUST A MINUTE

Windows 98 uses a new people-searching standard called *Lightweight Directory Access Protocol* (LDAP) to locate people by looking both on your local PC's address books as well as on the Internet.

Step 2: Action

1. Open the Start menu and select Find | People. You see a dialog box similar to the one shown in Figure 10.10.

Figure 10.10.
Search locally or on the Internet.

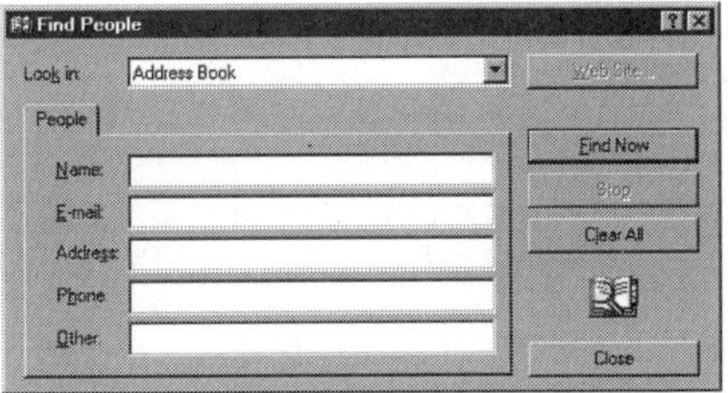

2. The people-search engines that Windows 98 uses are subject to change. Microsoft could add or remove one or more as you receive Windows 98 updates. The Address Book entry resides on your local PC and contains the repository of address information on your PC. If you choose one of the other people-search engines from the Searc<u>h</u> listbox, you can use a Web-based search engine. For example, to search for your favorite movie star's email address, type the star's name in the <u>N</u>ame field, select a search engine, and then click <u>F</u>ind Now.

   You can enter a name, email address, or other known information to help narrow your search. Some searches come up with addresses and phone numbers, and other searches come up empty.
3. If you aren't successful, you might want to go to one of the people-search engine's Web pages by selecting the engine name and clicking <u>w</u>eb Site. The page should offer hints that will help you find the person.
4. When you find the person you want, click <u>A</u>dd to Address Book to add that person's information to your local PC's address book. You won't have to perform an Internet search to find that person in the future, because the information will be on your own PC.
5. Close the Find People dialog box and sign off your Internet account to return to your Windows 98 desktop.

Step 3: Review

When you want to locate a friend or a famous person's Web site, email address, or perhaps their phone number if it's available within the search engine databases on the Internet, select the Start menu's <u>F</u>ind | <u>P</u>eople option. You'll be able to update your Windows Address Book easily with the information you find.

JUST A MINUTE

> Most people-search engines enable you to edit or remove your own data from the files. The search engine's companies get the information from phone books around the world.

Summary

This hour helped you find information you need on both your own PC and the Internet. Get in the habit of using Find for your PC files when you need them. You can search for the file you want to find and then select the file to open it and begin working with it.

The Internet search engines help convert the Internet's information overload to a manageable repository of information. You can search Web sites that fit your exact criteria, as well as look for people's names and addresses.

The next hour's material really gets fun. You'll learn how to use Windows 98's Accessories programs. Even if you haven't yet purchased a word processor or a paint program, you can use the ones supplied with Windows 98 to generate virtually any material you want to publish.

Q&A

Q I just bought my PC, and I don't have many files yet. Why will I need to search for anything?

A Sometimes you save a file in an unexpected folder, forget an exact filename, or save multiple copies of the same file on a disk across different folders. Even though you don't yet have many files, you could easily forget what you recently named a file or where you saved it.

Q I don't yet have Internet access. Can I still access the Internet searching tools?

A Sadly, no. You must sign up with an Internet service provider to gain Internet access before you can use Find's full potential. You will need to subscribe to an Internet service before you can search the Internet for information or people's addresses and phone numbers.

Workshop

Key Terms

Review the following list of terms:

- *criteria* Search instructions that help you target information you need.
- *information overload* Confusion that occurs when too much information passes by you, as with the Internet, without proper search tools to filter out unwanted material.
- *lightweight directory access protocol (LDAP)* A people-searching standard for locating people's data on local and remote computer address books.

- *Microsoft Outlook* A program that comes with Microsoft Office that keeps track of contacts, to-do lists, phone calls, messages, faxes, and your appointment calendar.
- *Outlook Express* A Windows 98 integrated address book and email system that handles email messages and gives you access to Internet newsgroups.
- *search engine* A Web-based program that looks for Internet information for you.
- *wildcard character* A character that represents one or more characters in file and folder names.

Part III

Hour 11

Desktop Accessories

Windows 98 comes with several application programs you can use right away to do work. These programs—Calculator, WordPad, and Paint—all appear on your Start menu's Accessories menu list. As their names suggest, you can perform calculations, create text documents, and paint pictures by using these three accessory programs.

The Calculator program comes in handy when you want to perform quick calculations without the need of a more powerful program such as an electronic spreadsheet. WordPad does not offer the power of Microsoft Word, but you can create formatted word-processed documents quickly with WordPad, which is simple to learn. Paint is a simple but effective drawing program that you can use to create colorful pictures. If you're a good artist, you might want to paste one of your creations on your Windows 98 desktop as wallpaper!

The highlights of this hour include the following:

- How to use the Windows 98 Calculator program
- What differences exist between the scientific and standard calculator views
- How to use WordPad to create word-processed documents
- How to use Paint to create colorful graphics
- Which of Paint's advanced editing tools professionally manipulate your images

Calculate Results

The Calculator program performs both simple mathematical and advanced scientific calculations. You will find the calculator program in the Programs | Accessories menu.

The Calculator program provides you with all kinds of computing benefits. Throughout a working day, you use your computer constantly, writing letters, printing bills, and building presentations. As you work, you often need to make a quick calculation and, if you're anything like computer book authors, your calculator is probably covered up beneath papers stacked a foot high. As soon as you start the Windows 98 Calculator program, it is never farther away than the taskbar.

TIME SAVER

The Calculator program actually contains *two* calculators, a *standard calculator* and a *scientific calculator*. Most people need the standard calculator that provides all the common mathematical operations required for day-to-day business affairs. The scientific calculator contains additional operations, such as statistical and trigonometric operations.

Tasks 11.1 and 11.2 walk you through the use of the two calculator versions.

Task 11.1: Using the Standard Calculator

Step 1: Description

The Windows 98 standard calculator provides full-featured calculator functions. When you use the Calculator program, you can sell your own desktop calculator at your next yard sale. Windows 98 even enables you to copy and paste the calculator results directly into your own applications.

Step 2: Action

1. Start the Windows 98 Calculator program, as shown in Figure 11.1. If you see a calculator window with many more buttons than the figure's, select View | Standard to work with the non-scientific calculator.

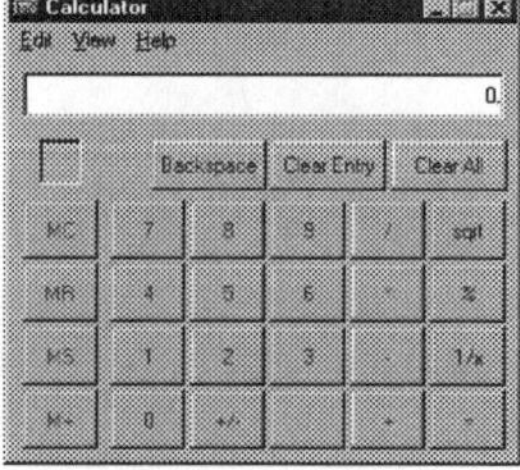

Figure 11.1.
The Windows 98 Calculator program goes beyond a pocket calculator.

CAUTION

You cannot resize the calculator window. You can only minimize the Calculator program to a taskbar button and move the window.

2. To steal from an old cliché—it doesn't take a rocket scientist to use the calculator. The calculator performs standard addition, subtraction, multiplication, and division. In addition, the standard calculator includes memory clear, recall, store, and memory add.

JUST A MINUTE

All of the calculator operations produce *running totals*, meaning that you can continuously apply operations, such as addition to the running total in the calculator's display.

CAUTION

The calculator has keyboard-equivalent keys. Instead of clicking with your mouse to enter 2 + 2 for example, you can type **2 + 2 =** (the equal sign requests the answer). Not all keys have obvious keyboard equivalents, however. For example, the C key does not clear the total (Esc does). Therefore, you might need to combine your mouse and keyboard to use the calculator.

3. Click the numbers 1, then 2, then 3. (You can use your keyboard if you like, but make sure that your Num Lock key is turned on first.) As you click, the numbers appear inside the display.
4. Click the multiplication sign (the asterisk).
5. Click the 2.
6. Click the equals sign, and the calculator displays the result of 246.
7. Click C or press Esc to clear the display.

TIME SAVER

The Backspace key erases any character that you type incorrectly.

8. The percent key produces a percentage only as a result of multiplication. Therefore, you can compute a percentage of a number by multiplying it by the percent figure. Suppose that you want to know how much 35 percent of 4000 is.

Type **4000** and then press the asterisk. Type **35** followed by the percent key (Shift+5 on the keyboard). The value `1400` appears. The result: 1400 is 35 percent of 4000. (The word *of* in a math problem is a sure sign that you must multiply by a percentage. Calculating 35 percent of 4000 implies that you need to multiply 4000 by 35 percent.)

9. When you want to negate the number in the display, click the +/– key. Suppose that you want to subtract the display's current value, 1400, from 5000. Although you can clear the display and perform the subtraction, it's faster to negate the 1400 by clicking the +/– key, press the plus sign, type **5000,** and press the equal sign to produce –3600.

Just a Minute

The calculator displays a letter `M` above the four memory keys when you store a value in the memory.

10. To store a value in memory, click MS. Whenever you want the memory value to appear in the display, click MR. MC clears the memory and M+ adds the display to the total in memory. If you want to store a running total, click the M+ button every time you want to add the display's value to the memory. The `M` disappears from the memory indicator box when you clear the memory.

Time Saver

When you want to switch from your application to the calculator to perform a calculation and then enter the result of that calculation elsewhere (such as in your word processor), select Edit | Copy (Ctrl+C) to copy the value to the Clipboard. When you switch back to the other Windows 98 application, you will be able to paste the value into that application.

11. Leave the calculator window open for the next task.

Step 3: Review

The standard calculator performs all the operations that most Windows 98 users need most of the time. The interface is simple and enables the use of a mouse or keyboard to enter the values. Perhaps most people will find that the keypad offers the easiest interface to the calculator as long as the Num Lock key is active.

Task 11.2: Using the Scientific Calculator

Step 1: Description

The second Windows 98 Calculator program, the scientific calculator, supports many more advanced mathematical operations. Despite its added power, the scientific calculator operates almost identically to the standard calculator. The standard keys and memory are identical in both calculators.

Step 2: Action

1. To see the scientific calculator, select View | Scientific. Windows 98 displays the scientific calculator shown in Figure 11.2. The scientific calculator offers more keys, operators, and indicators than the standard calculator.

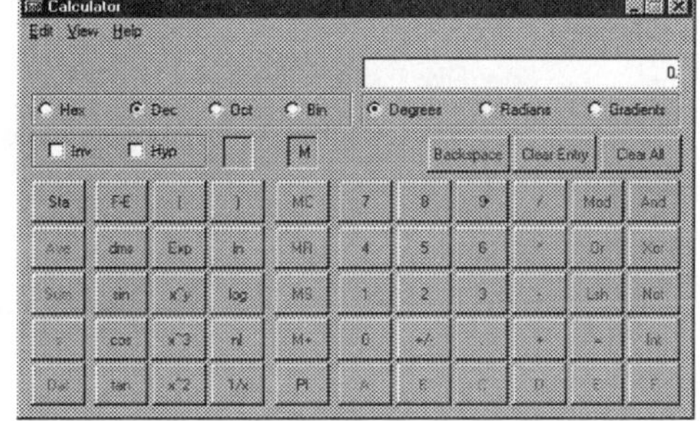

Figure 11.2.
The Windows 98 scientific calculator provides advanced operations.

2. This task does not explain how to understand each of the scientific operations. Actually, if you need these operations, you probably already understand their use. The only new interface that you need to master to use these advanced operations is the statistical interface. To compute a mean or standard deviation, you must work with several values at a time (a *series*). The Statistics Box contains the series of values as you enter them because the calculator's display shows only a single line at a time.

   Enter `15`. Click Sta, and the calculator displays the statistics display. The box is empty right now, but you'll fill it up as you go. Click the Dat key to add the value of 15 to the Statistics Box and return to the calculator so you can enter more values.

3. Enter `45`, click Sta, and then Dat.
4. Enter `65`, click Sta, and then Dat.
5. Enter `20`, click Sta, and then Dat. Your Statistics Box should look like the one in Figure 11.3. As you can see, Sta simply shows the Statistics Box dialog box, and Dat adds the current value to the Statistics Box.
6. Click Sta and then Ave to see the average mean.
7. Click Sum to display the sum of the Statistics Box. You don't have to show the Statistics Box before clicking the four statistical buttons, as long as you've entered a series of values.
8. Click Inv and then s to see the standard deviation with a population parameter of n–1.
9. Close the calculator's window.

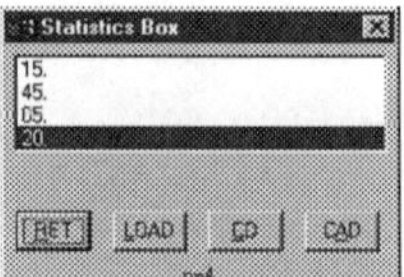

Figure 11.3.
The Statistics Box keeps track of your series of values.

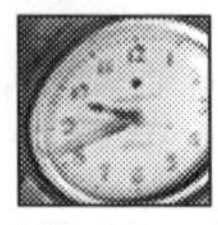
Windows Minute

The Statistics Box

The Statistics Box contains four command buttons labeled RET, LOAD, CD, and CAD. The RET button returns you to the calculator's screen by minimizing the Statistics Box. The LOAD button sends the selected value from the series to the calculator's display. CD removes the selected value from the series. CAD removes all values from the series.

In addition, the calculator always displays the number in the current series (the value of n) at the bottom of the Statistics Box. If you already entered the value of 20, your screen shows `[]= 4`.

Step 3: Review

The scientific calculator requires more mathematical knowledge to use. The calculator itself is not difficult to use, but understanding some of the math can be. To use the calculator fully, you must master the Statistics Box. The Statistics Box contains a series of values on which you can calculate statistical results.

Write with Flair

Windows 98 contains a word processor called *WordPad*, which appears on your Programs | Accessories menu. Although WordPad does not contain all the features of a major word processor, such as Microsoft Word, WordPad does contain many formatting features and can accept documents created in several word processing programs. This section introduces you to WordPad.

Just a Minute

NotePad also appears in your Accessories menu group, but NotePad is a scaled-down version of WordPad and offers very few of the formatting capabilities that WordPad offers.

WordPad edits, loads, and saves documents in all the following formats: Word for Windows, Windows Write (the word processor available in Windows 3.1), text documents, and RTF (*Rich Text Format*) documents. As a result, when you open an RTF or Write or Word for Windows 6 document that contains formatting, such as underlining and boldfaced characters, WordPad retains those special formatting features in the document.

WordPad contains a toolbar that you can display to help you access common commands more easily. WordPad also supports the uses of a Ruler and format bar that help you work with WordPad's advanced editing features. When you type text into WordPad, you won't have to worry about pressing Enter at the end of every line. WordPad wraps your text to the next line when you run out of room on the current line. Press Enter only when you get to the end of a paragraph or a short line such as a title that you don't want combined with the subsequent line. (Two Enter presses in a row adds a blank line to your text.)

To Do

Task 11.3: Working with WordPad

Step 1: Description

WordPad contains features for the novice as well as for advanced writers. If you have no other word processor on your system, you can use WordPad to produce virtually any kind of document that you need. This task leads you through the basic steps for using WordPad and its features.

Step 2: Action

1. Start the WordPad program from the Accessories menu. You'll see the WordPad screen shown in Figure 11.4.

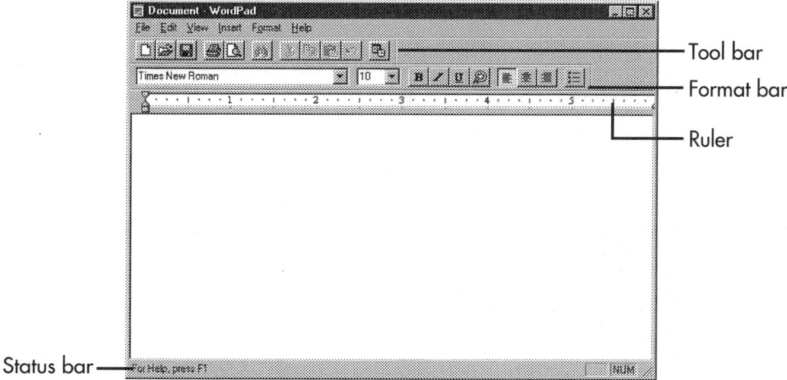

Figure 11.4.
WordPad offers many word-processing features.

11

JUST A MINUTE

If your WordPad screen does not look exactly like the one in Figure 11.4, you can use the View menu to add a check mark to each of the first four commands—Toolbar, Format Bar, Ruler, and Status Bar—so that you display each of these four optional tools.

2. For this task, you'll practice entering and formatting text. Type the following text: **A large line**.
3. Select all three words by highlighting them with the mouse or keyboard. With the mouse, select by pointing to the first character and dragging the mouse to the last character. With the keyboard, you can select by moving the text cursor to the first letter and pressing Shift+Right Arrow until you select the entire line.

4. Click the format bar button with the letter B. The text stays selected but something changes—the text becomes boldfaced. Press any arrow key to get rid of the highlighted text and see the boldfaced text.
5. Select the three words once again. Click the second format bar button with the letter I. WordPad italicizes the text. Now click the third format bar button with the letter U. WordPad instantly underlines the selected text. Keep the text highlighted for the next step.
6. By default WordPad selects a *font* (a typestyle) named Times New Roman. You can see the font name directly below the format bar. The font's size, in *points* (a point is 1/72 inch), appears to the right of the font name (the default font size is 10 points).

   You can change both the font and the font size by clicking the drop-down lists in which each appears. When you select text, select a font name, WordPad changes the font of the selected text to the new font name style. After selecting the text, display the font name list by clicking the drop-down listbox's arrow and select a font name. If you have the Comic Sans MS, use that font to correspond to the next figure in this book. If you do not have that font name, select another font name that sounds interesting.

   Open the point size drop-down listbox and select 36 (you can type this number directly into the listbox if you want to). As soon as you do, you can see the results of your boldfaced, underlined, italicized, large-sized text displayed using the font name you selected. Press the left or right arrow key to remove the selection. Figure 11.5 shows what your WordPad window should look like.

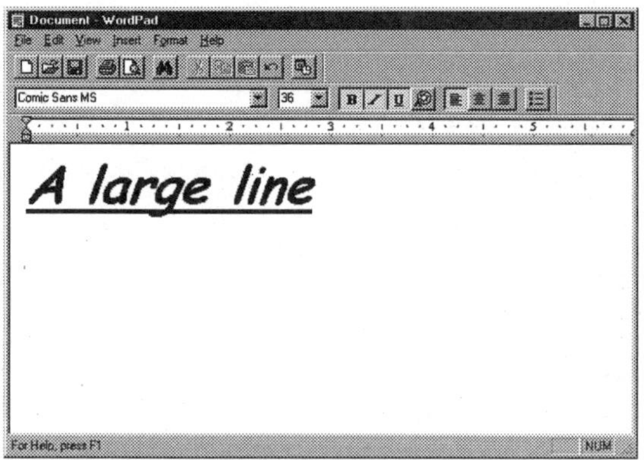

Figure 11.5.
The text is formatted to your exact specifications.

WordPad applied all of the previous formatting on the three words because you selected those words before you changed the formatting. If you select only a single word or character, WordPad formats only that selected text and leaves all the other text alone.

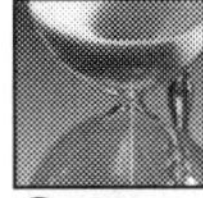

CAUTION

Don't overdo the formatting of text! If you make text too fancy, it becomes cluttered, and your words will lose their meaning amidst all the italics, underlines, and font styles. Use italics, boldfacing, and underlining only for emphasis when needed for certain words and titles.

7. Press Enter. Click the B, I, and U format bar buttons and return the font name to Times New Roman. Lower the font size to 10. Type the following: **Windows 98 is fun** and press the Spacebar. If you do not like the font size, click the down arrow to the right of the font name list and select a different size.
8. Suppose you want to italicize your name. If you now click the format bar for italics, all subsequent text that you type will be italicized. Click the italics format bar button now and type your first name. The name will be italicized, but the other text is not italicized.
9. Click the italics format bar button once again and continue typing on the same line. Type this: **and I like to use WordPad**.
10. As you can see, you don't have to select text to apply special formatting to text. Before you type text that you want to format, select the proper format command and then type the text. WordPad then formats the text, using the format styles you've selected, as you type that text. When you want to revert to the previous unformatted style (such as when you no longer want italics) change the style and keep typing.

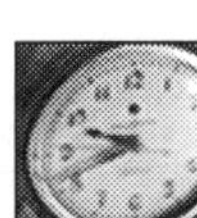

WINDOWS MINUTE

Font Controls

Ctrl+B, Ctrl+I, and Ctrl+U are the shortcut keys for clicking the B, I, and U format bar buttons. You can also change the formatting of text characters by selecting Format | Font. WordPad displays a Font dialog box, as shown in Figure 11.6, on which you can apply several formatting styles.

As you change the style, the Font dialog box's Sample area shows you a sample of text formatted to the specifications you provide. When you close the Font dialog box, WordPad formats subsequent text according to the Font dialog box settings.

11. Select File | Print Preview to see a *thumbnail sketch* of how your document will look if you were to print it. By looking at a preview before you print your document, you can tell if the overall appearance is acceptable and if the margins and text styles look good. You can quit the preview and return to your editing session by pressing Esc.
12. Close WordPad for now. Don't save your work when prompted to do so.

Figure 11.6.
The Font dialog box provides all formatting specifications in a single place.

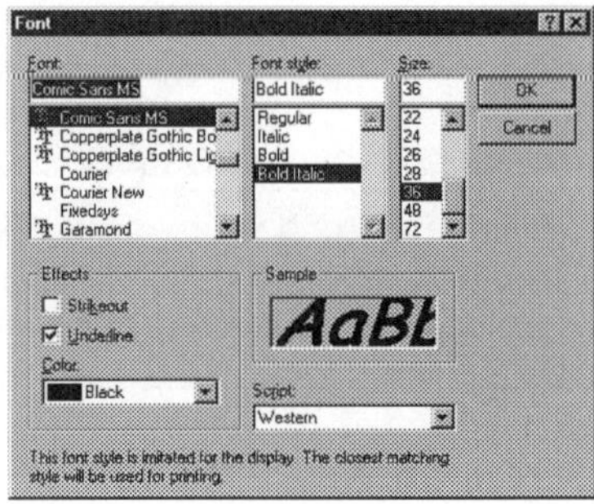

Step 3: Review

You've only seen a taste of the text-formatting capabilities available, but there's just enough time left in this hour to discuss one final accessory program called *Paint*. Before moving to Paint, however, browse some of the following word-processing features list that WordPad supports:

- The Ruler indicates where your text appears on the printed page when you print the document. Each number on the Ruler represents an inch (or a centimeter if your computer is set up for a metric setting in the View | Options dialog box). As you type, you can watch the Ruler to see where the text appears as you print the document. If you select the Format | Paragraph command, WordPad displays the Paragraph dialog box in which you can set left and right indentations for individual paragraphs as well as tab stops.

TIME SAVER

> You can place tab stops quickly by double-clicking the Ruler at the exact location of the tab stop you want.

- The toolbar's Align Left, Center, and Align Right toolbar buttons left-justifies, centers, and right-justifies text so that you can align your text in columns as a newspaper does. The center alignment format bar button is useful for centering titles at the top of documents.
- If you have a color printer, consider adding color to your text by clicking the toolbar's color-selection tool.
- The far-right format bar button adds bullets to lists you enter. Before you start the list, click the Bullets button to format the list as a bulleted list.

Paint a Pretty Picture

Paint provides many colorful drawing tools. Before you can use Paint effectively, you must learn how to interact with Paint, and you also must know what each of Paint's tools does. The Paint screen contains five major areas, listed in Figure 11.7. Table 11.1 describes each area.

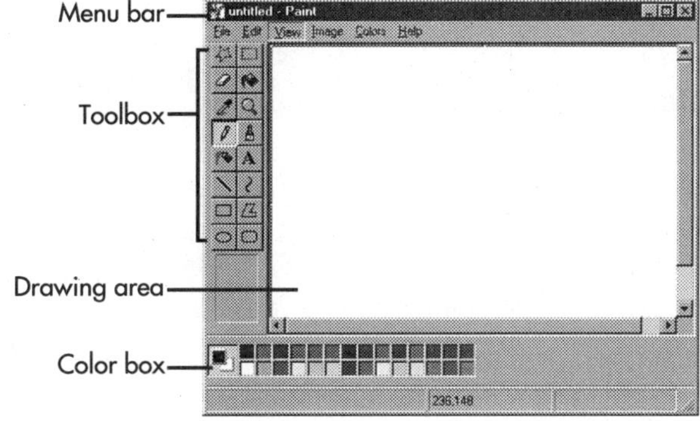

Figure 11.7.
The five major areas of the Paint screen enable you to create and edit your graphic images.

JUST A MINUTE

Paint does not contain a toolbar with buttons as do WordPad and other Windows 98 programs. Paint contains a tool box that is the most important area of Paint. It is from the tool box that you select and use drawing tools.

Table 11.1. Paint's five areas help you draw better.

Area	Description
Drawing area	Your drawing appears in the drawing area. When you want to create or modify a drawing, you work within this area.
Color box	A list of possible colors you can choose to add color to your artwork.
Menu bar	The commands that control Paint's operation.
Status bar	Displays important messages and measurements as you use Paint.
Tool box	The vital drawing, painting, and coloring tools with which you create and modify artwork.

The two scroll bars on the drawing area enable you to scroll to other parts of your drawing. The drawing area is actually as large as a maximized window. If, however, Paint initially displays the drawing area maximized, you can not access the menu bar or the tool box or read the status bar. Therefore, Paint adds the scroll bars to its drawing area so that you can create drawings that will, when displayed, fill the entire screen.

To Do

Task 11.4: Getting to Know Paint

Step 1: Description

This task enables you to start Paint and navigate around the screen a bit. Practice using Paint and learn Paint's features as you use the program.

Step 2: Action

1. Start Paint. Paint is located on the Programs | Accessories menu.
2. Maximize the Paint program to full size. Paint is one of the few programs in which you'll almost always want to work in a maximized window. By maximizing the window, you gain the largest drawing area possible.
3. If you do not see the tool box, the status bar, or the color box, display the View menu and check each of these three important screen areas to ensure that all five areas show as you follow along in this hour.
4. Take a look at Figure 11.8. This figure labels each of the tool box tools. Each tool contains an icon that illustrates the tool's function. The tools on the tool box comprise your collection of drawing, painting, and coloring tools. When you want to add or modify a picture, you have to pick the appropriate tool. As you work with Paint in subsequent tasks, refer to Figure 11.8 to find the tool named in the task.

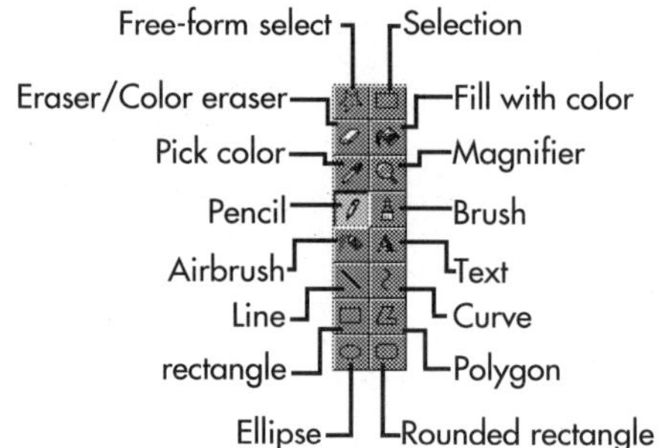

Figure 11.8.
The tools on the tool box.

5. Click the Pencil tool.
6. Move the mouse cursor over the drawing area, and the cursor changes to a pencil (the same icon that's on the pencil tool).
7. Hold down the mouse button and move your mouse all around the drawing area. Make all sorts of curves with the mouse. Notice that Paint keeps the pencil within the borders of the drawing area. Figure 11.9 shows what you can do when you really go crazy with the Pencil tool.
8. The default color for the pencil drawing is black. Click a different color on the color bar, such as red or green, and draw some more. The new lines appear in the new color. Select additional colors and draw more lines to beautify the picture even more.

Figure 11.9.
The Pencil tool enables you to doodle.

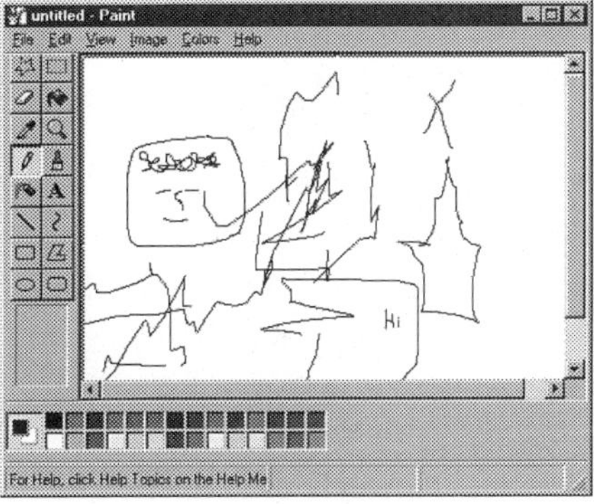

TIME SAVER

Every time you change a tool or color or draw a separate line, Paint saves the next group of changes to the drawing area. As with most Windows 98 accessory programs, Paint supports an Edit | Undo feature (Ctrl+Z or Alt+Backspace). You can undo up to three previous edit groups. Therefore, if you've just drawn three separate lines, you can remove each of those lines by selecting the Undo command three times.

9. Erase your drawing by selecting File | New. Don't save your current drawing. Paint clears the drawing area so that you can start a new document image.
10. Click the Line tool. Use the Line tool to draw straight lines.

    A straight line is defined by two coordinates: the starting coordinate position and the end coordinate position. To draw a line, you must anchor the line's starting position and extend the line to its ending position. Paint automatically draws a straight line from the starting position to the end position. You can draw lines, using the Line tool, in any direction.
11. Get used to reading *coordinate pair* numbers in the status bar. The numbers tell you the number of drawing points from the left and top of your window. Move the mouse around the drawing area (do not press a mouse button yet) and watch the pair of numbers at the right of the status bar change.
12. Select a different color and draw another line. Paint draws that line in the new color.

TIME SAVER

Now that you've selected the Line tool, look at the area below the tool box. You'll see five lines, with each line growing thicker than the one before. By clicking a thick line, the next line you draw with the Line tool appears on the drawing area in the new thickness. You can change the thickness, using this line size list, for any of the geometric shapes.

13. Click the thickest line in the list of line sizes. Draw a couple of lines to see the thicker lines. If you change colors before drawing, the thicker lines appear in the new color.
14. The rest of the geometric shapes are as easy to draw as the lines are. Select File | New to clear the drawing area. Don't save any changes.
15. Click the Line tool to change the line thickness size to the middle line thickness (the third thickness size). Always change the Line tool's thickness before selecting one of the geometric drawing tools. The Line tool's line size determines the line thickness for all the geometric tools.
16. Select the Rectangle tool. Rectangles, like lines, are determined by their starting *anchor position* and the rectangle's opposite corner's position. Begin drawing a rectangle at coordinates 190,75. After anchoring the rectangle with the mouse button, drag the mouse until it rests at 385,270. The status line indicator will show 200,200, meaning that the rectangle is 200 by 200 drawing points. When you release the mouse, you will have drawn a perfect square.

TIME SAVER

> Drawing a perfect square is not always easy because you have to pay close attention to the coordinates. Paint offers a better way to draw perfect squares. Hold down the Shift key while dragging the mouse, and the rectangle always appears as a square. Shift also draws perfect circles when you use the Ellipse tool.

The three rectangles below the tool box do not represent the line thickness of the rectangles. They determine how Paint draws rectangles. When you click the top rectangle (the default), all of the drawing area that appears beneath the next rectangle that you draw shows through. Therefore, if you draw a rectangle over other pictures, you see the other pictures coming through the inside of the new rectangle. If you click the second rectangle below the tool box, the rectangle's center overwrites any existing art. As a result, all rectangles you draw have a blank center, no matter what art the rectangle overwrites. If you select the third rectangle, Paint does not draw a rectangular outline but does draw the interior of the rectangle in the same color you've set for the interior (the default interior color is white).

17. Now that you understand the rectangle, you also understand the other geometric tools. Click the Ellipse tool to draw ovals (remember that Shift enables you to draw perfect circles). Click the Rounded Rectangle tool to draw rounded rectangles (or rounded squares if you press Shift while dragging).

Click the top rectangle selection (to draw see-through shapes) and click the Ellipse to draw circles. Click the Rounded Rectangle tool and draw rounded rectangles. Fill your drawing area with all kinds of shapes to get the feel of the tools.

18. A blank drawing area will help you learn how to use the Polygon and Curve tools, so select File | New (don't save) to clear your drawing area.
19. Select the Polygon tool. The Polygon is a tool that draws an enclosed figure with as many sides as you want to give the figure. After you anchor the polygon with the mouse, drag the mouse left or right and click the mouse. Drag the mouse once again to continue the polygon. Every time you want to change directions, click the mouse once more. When you finish, double-click the mouse, and Paint completes the polygon for you by connecting your final line with the first point you drew.
20. Clear your drawing area once again. The Curve tool is one of the neatest but strangest tools in the tool box. Click the Curve tool (after adjusting the line thickness and color if you wish to do so).

    Draw a straight line by dragging the mouse. After you release the line, click the mouse button somewhere just outside the line and drag the mouse around in circles. As you drag the mouse, Paint adjusts the curve to follow the mouse. When you see the curve that you want, release the mouse so that Paint can stabilize the curve.
21. The Eraser/Color Eraser tool erases whatever appears on the drawing area. The Eraser/Color Eraser tool comes in four sizes—a small eraser that erases small areas up to larger erasers that erase larger areas at one time. When you select the Eraser/Color Eraser tool, you can also select an eraser thickness. (The color you choose has no bearing on the eraser's use.) Select the Eraser/Color Eraser tool now and drag it over parts of your drawing to erase lines you've drawn.
22. Clear your drawing area and exit Paint.

11

Step 3: Review

The geometric tools generally require you to select a line width, a drawing style (such as rectangles that hide or don't hide their backgrounds), and an exterior and interior color and then draw the shape. You draw most of the shapes by anchoring their initial position and then by dragging the mouse to extend the shape across the screen. If you make a mistake, you can use the Eraser/Color Eraser tool to correct the problem.

Just a Minute

Although Paint can only create bitmap files with the .BMP filename extension, the Paint program can read both bitmap and PC Paintbrush files. PC Paintbrush filenames end with the PCX filename extension. If you read a PCX file and save the file, Paint saves the file in the bitmap file format.

TIME SAVER

Want to create your own desktop wallpaper? Use Paint! All desktop wallpaper images must appear in the bitmap format with the .BMP, extension and those are exactly the kinds of files that Paint creates. Therefore, you can create a bitmap image with your company's logo and use the image for your desktop's wallpaper.

In addition to the desktop wallpaper, you can also create your own startup logo. The startup logo is the logo you see while Windows 98 starts. Create a Paint image and save the image under the name LOGOS.SYS in the Windows directory. Windows 98 will subsequently use this file when you start Windows 98 in the future. You can also display a shutdown graphic image that appears when you shut down Windows 98. Name the shutdown Paint image LOGOW.SYS, and you will see your image when you shut down Windows 98 before you turn off your computer.

JUST A MINUTE

Drawings often have titles. Graphs often have explanations. Maps often have legends. Pictures that you draw often need text in addition to the graphics that you draw. The Text tool enables you to add text by using any font and font size available within Windows 98. You can control how the text covers or exposes any art beneath the text. After clicking the Text tool, drag the text's outline box (text always resides inside this text box that appears). When you release your mouse, select the font and style and type your text. When you click another tool, your text becomes part of the drawing area.

The Paint Pros Modify Their Art

There are many advanced editing features available inside Paint that you will want to study after you've mastered the basic drawing tools described in the previous tasks. You already know enough to draw virtually anything you will ever want to draw; the Image menu, however, contains additional commands that go far beyond the fundamental drawing capabilities offered by the tool box.

The Image | Flip/Rotate command enables you to rotate the drawing area. The Flip and Rotate dialog box, shown in Figure 11.10, enables you to determine whether or not you want to completely reverse the image horizontally, vertically, or by a specific number of degrees.

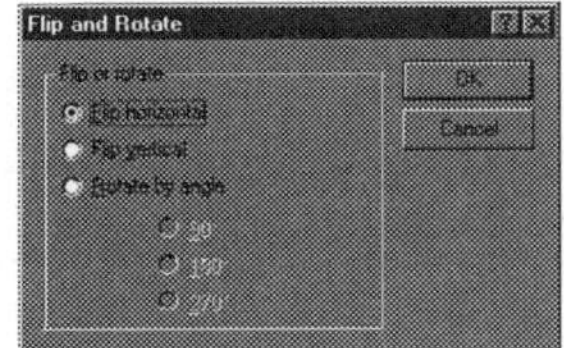

Figure 11.10.
The Flip and Rotate dialog box controls the direction and amount of rotation.

The Image | Stretch/Skew command produces a dialog box that enables you to stretch the entire drawing area (or the selected area) by a certain number of degrees. By skewing or stretching an image, you can add snowy and wavy special effects to your artwork.

Artists understand better than computer book authors what color inversion is all about. All colors have complementary colors. (The red compliments the blue by telling blue how nice he looks, or something like that!) A complementary color is an offsetting color that is a color's opposite in the color spectrum; white's complement is black, for example. Artists and designers use color charts and color wheels to determine complementary colors when they need to produce offsetting colors in a painting or a room. Paint complements all colors in the drawing area or within the selected area if you select Image | Invert Colors.

The Image | Attributes menu command enables you to change the size of a drawing area. Image | Attributes displays the Attributes dialog box that determines how large (you specify either in inches, centimeters, or *pixels* (drawing points), depending on the option you select) you want the drawing area to be. In effect, the Attributes dialog box determines the size of your drawing paper. If you want to draw in shades of black and white (as you would do if you are going to print the image on a black and white printer) you want to create the drawing in black and white and shades of gray, so you will know on the screen what the drawing will look like when printed.

Summary

This hour showed you three desktop accessory programs. The Calculator program offers advantages over its real-world desktop equivalent because the calculator always is available on your Windows 98 desktop as you work with other programs.

WordPad gives you introductory word-processing features that enable you to create documents that contain special formatting. WordPad is limited compared to the word processors sold today. For example, WordPad contains no spell checker. Nevertheless, WordPad offers simple introductory word-processing features and supports several file formats so that any WordPad documents you create will be available in other word processors you eventually purchase.

The Paint accessory program enables you to draw. Paint's drawing tools rival many of the drawing tools supplied in art programs that sell for several hundred dollars. Paint includes geometric tools that help you draw perfect shapes. You can color the shape outlines, as well as their interiors with Paint's coloring tools. The menu bar provides commands that resize, reshape, invert, and stretch your drawn images. If you want precision editing, you can have it by zeroing in on the fine details of your drawing by using the Magnifier tool.

TIME SAVER

> If you work with photographic art files, you might benefit from the program named Imaging (located on the Accessories menu). The Imaging program enables you to manage and view photographic image files, such as those you receive as faxes and scan.

Q&A

Q Why can't I read all the text on the Print Preview?

A The Print Preview feature was not designed to let you read text necessarily. The Print Preview feature simply draws a representation of your document when you print the document on the printer. Instead of printing the document and discovering there is a margin or formatting error, you can often find the errors on the Print Preview screen, so you can correct the problem before printing the document.

Q I'm no artist, so why should I learn Paint?

A As just stated, there are many applications that combine text and graphics. In the world of communications, which ranges from business to politics, pictures can convey the same meaning as thousands of words can. Graphics catch people's attention more quickly than text. When you combine the details that text provides with the attention-grabbing effect of graphics, you're sure to have an audience.

There are many other graphic reasons to master Paint, as well. You might want to use Paint to produce these graphic publications:

- Flyers for volunteer or professional organizations
- Holiday greetings
- Letters that include drawings by the kids
- Sale notices for posting on bulletin boards

Perhaps the best reason to learn to use Paint: It's fun!

Workshop

Key Terms

Review the following list of terms:

- ☐ *anchor position* The starting coordinate pair of lines and other geometric shapes.
- ☐ *coordinate* A point position on the screen defined by a coordinate pair.
- ☐ *coordinate pair* A pair of numbers in which the first represents the number of drawing points from the left edge of the drawing area of an image, and the second represents the number of drawing points from the top edge of the drawing area. In Paint, the coordinates appear on the status bar.
- ☐ *font* A specific typestyle. Fonts have names that distinguish them from one another. Some fonts are fancy, and others are plain.
- ☐ *imaging* The Windows 98 accessory program that enables you to view and manage photographic image files.
- ☐ *pixel* Stands for *picture element*. A pixel is the smallest addressable dot on your screen.
- ☐ *point* A measurement of 1/72 of an inch (72 points equals one inch). Most computer onscreen and printed text measures from 9–12 points in size.
- ☐ *Print Preview* A full-screen representation of how your document will look when you print the document.
- ☐ *running total* The calculator maintains a constant display. For example, if the display contains the value 87 and you press the plus sign and then press 5, the calculator adds the 5 to the 87 and produces the sum of 92.
- ☐ *scientific calculator* A Windows 98 calculator that supports trigonometric, scientific, and number-conversion operations.
- ☐ *series* A set of values on which you perform statistical operations.
- ☐ *standard calculator* A Windows 98 calculator that performs common mathematical operations.
- ☐ *Startup logo* The image you see when Windows 98 loads.
- ☐ *Statistics Box* A box that holds your entered series of statistical values. (The calculator's display can hold only a single value at a time.)
- ☐ *tool box* Paint's collection of drawing, coloring, and painting tools.
- ☐ *thumbnail sketch* A small representation that shows the overall layout without showing a lot of detail.

Part III

Hour 12

Aid via the Accessibility Options

This hour describes all the Windows 98 tools that provide help for users with special needs. Previous operating environments did not support the full set of user accessibility options that Windows 98 provides. The Windows 98 accessibility options change the behavior of the keyboard, screen, and speakers so that they operate differently from their default behaviors. Microsoft designed Windows 98 so that everybody can take advantage of the new operating environment.

The highlights of this chapter include the following:

- How to run the Accessibility Settings Wizard
- How to magnify your screen
- Which accessibility options might benefit you
- How to change the keyboard's response so that combination keystrokes are easier to type
- Why visual clues can replace audible signals and alarms
- Where to set the screen's display so that you can read enlarged letters, icons, title bars, and high-contrasting screen colors
- How to make the keyboard respond as if you were moving and clicking the mouse

The Accessibility Settings Wizard

Windows 98 includes an Accessibility menu on the Programs, Accessories menu that contains the following options:

- Accessibility Settings Wizard
- Microsoft Magnifier

The Accessibility Settings Wizard is a front-end question-and-answer wizard that guides you through various *accessibility options* available in Windows 98. The accessibility options provide different approaches to various Windows 98 activities that you will perform. For example, you might be unable to distinguish between certain screen colors or you might be limited in what you can do with a mouse. The Windows 98 accessibility options provide alternative methods for triggering and responding to various Windows 98 tasks.

The Microsoft Magnifier is a program that magnifies part of your Windows 98 screen. As you move your mouse around the screen, the magnified viewer updates to show you a magnified view of your mouse cursor's area.

Task 12.1: Running the Accessibility Settings Wizard

Step 1: Description

This task looks at the Accessibility Settings Wizard so that you will know what Windows 98 might be able to help you with. Although you can set any of the accessibility options without the wizard, as explained in the sections that appear later in this hour, the wizard is simpler to use when setting the options you require.

Step 2: Action

1. Select the Start menu's Programs | Accessories | Accessibility | Accessibility Wizard option. The dialog box in Figure 12.1 appears.

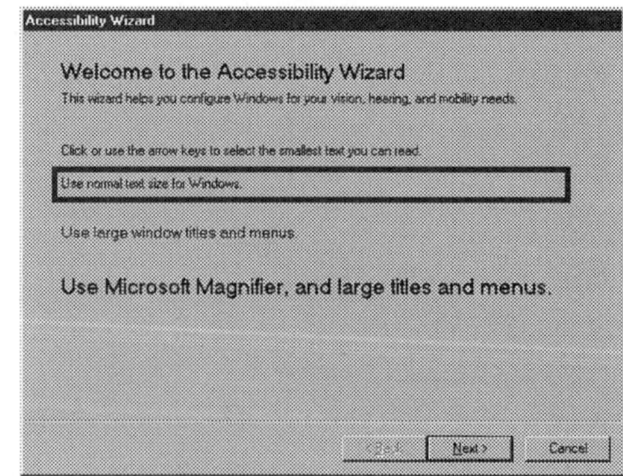

Figure 12.1.
The Accessibility Wizard helps you designate special Windows 98 options.

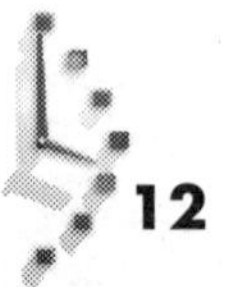

2. Click the various options that you want help with (each option has a hot key, so you can use your keyboard to add a check mark next to any option). The options you select determine the screens that next appear.
3. Click the Next button to move to the next wizard screen. The screen offers help on one of the options you selected. For example, if items are too small for you to read in Windows 98, a wizard screen enables you to adjust the size of common window elements, such as window titles and menu options. If you cannot hear response sounds that Windows provides at various times (such as occurs when an error dialog box appears), a screen appears that enables you to substitute flashing warnings when a sound would otherwise occur. Other screens might appear, such as the one in Figure 12.2, that show a mouse cursor selection window where you can choose a more readable mouse cursor.

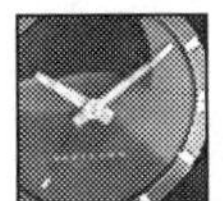

JUST A MINUTE

> Throughout the wizard screens, you will see some strange new terms like *StickyKeys* and *SoundSentry*. These refer to various accessibility option names located throughout Windows 98. The next section explains each of these options.

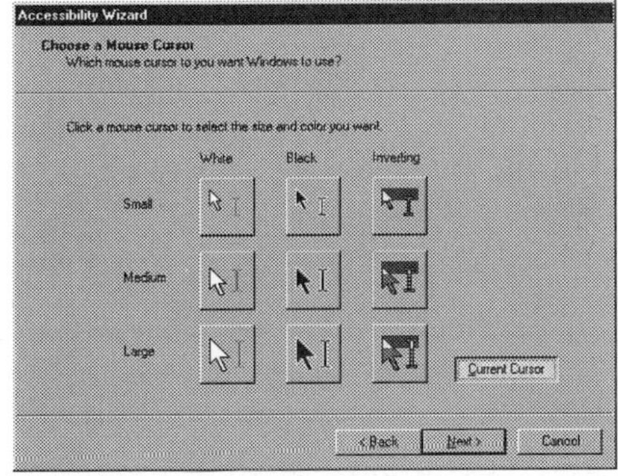

Figure 12.2.
Select a mouse cursor that you can best see.

12

4. After you complete the wizard, setting the options you prefer, Windows 98 takes on the accessibility attributes you selected. At any point, you can run the wizard to adjust, change, or remove any settings. In addition, you can adjust the settings from your Control Panel, as described throughout the sections that follow.
5. If you have trouble reading text on your screen, you might want to try to Microsoft Magnifier. Although the Microsoft Magnifier program consumes some of your screen space to show a magnified area, text is much more readable than on the standard Windows 98 screen. Select the Start menu's Programs | Accessories | Accessibility | Microsoft Magnifier option to start the Microsoft Magnifier program. Figure 12.3 shows the resulting screen.

Figure 12.3.
As you move your cursor around the lower half of your screen, the magnified upper half gives you a better view of the details.

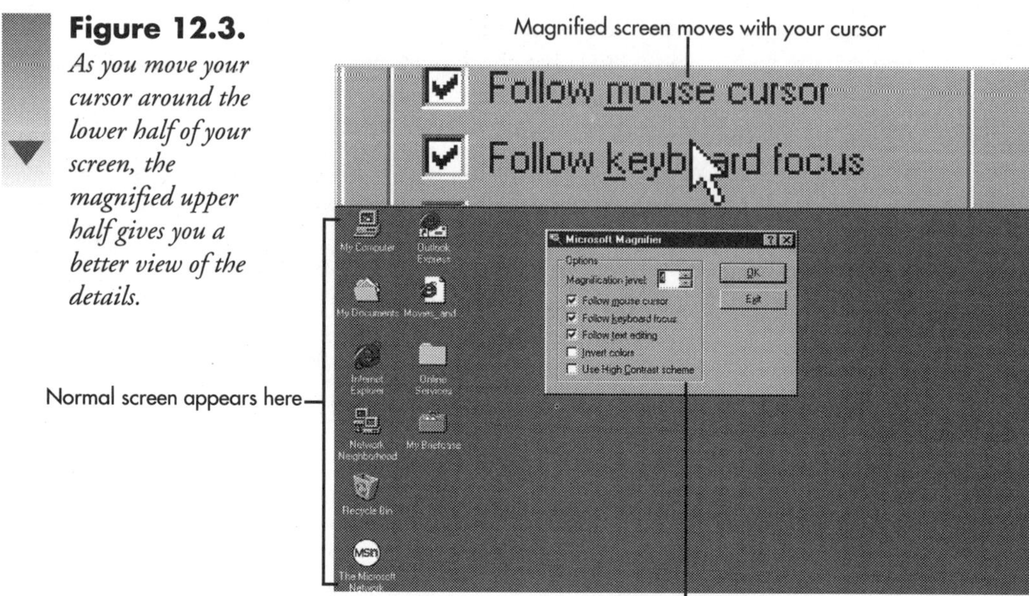

6. Adjust the options in the settings box to control the elements Windows 98 magnifies. Perhaps you just want to magnify the area of the screen where the mouse cursor moves. Perhaps you want to magnify areas where you enter text. You soon will find the appropriate settings that give you the view you need to more effectively use Windows 98.

TIME SAVER

You can adjust the magnified and unmagnified portions of the screen by dragging the dividing line up or down.

7. Click the Exit button to terminate Microsoft Magnifier. You regain the full screen, and the screen elements return to their normal size.

Step 3: Review

The Accessibility menu option gives you access to the Windows 98 accessibility options by using the Accessibility Settings Wizard. The Accessibility Settings Wizard guides you through a series of wizard screens to which you respond to set Windows 98 accessibility settings. In addition, the Microsoft Magnifier program enlarges elements of your screen as you move the mouse cursor to make viewing easier.

All of the Accessibility Settings Wizard's screens control the Windows 98 accessibility options. You have more control over these options if you access them through the Control Panel, as described in the following sections. Although the Accessibility Settings Wizard is simpler to use when making accessibility option settings, you can control the settings in more detail via the Control Panel, as explained next.

The Accessibility Options

The Accessibility Options tabbed dialog box contains settings for the accessibility options that you might want to set up for your Windows 98 environment. All of the accessibility options are available from this dialog box. You can set any or all of the accessibility options from the Accessibility Options tabbed dialog box.

When you double-click the Accessibility Options icon on the Control Panel you will see the Accessibility Properties tabbed dialog box shown in Figure 12.4.

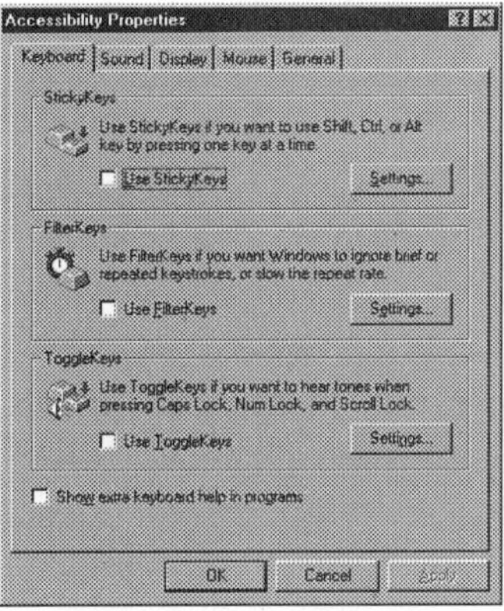

Figure 12.4.
Set one or more accessibility options from this tabbed dialog box.

12

Table 12.1 contains a list of every accessibility option available in Windows 98. Using the task approach, the rest of the chapter describes how to access and use each of these accessibility options.

Table 12.1. The accessibility options.

Option	Description
Accessibility reset	When the computer sits idle for a preset period of time, the accessibility options revert to their default state. (The accessibility options, such as BounceKeys, will no longer be in effect.)

continues

Table 12.1. continued

Option	Description
Accessibility status	A graphical display of icons that describes which accessibility indicator options are turned on at any given time.
BounceKeys	Keeps users from producing double keystrokes if they accidentally bounce keys several times in succession.
Customizable	You can change the mouse pointer to make the mouse cursor pointer easier to see.
FilterKeys	The group of keystroke aids that include RepeatKeys and BounceKeys.
High-contrast	By changing the Windows 98 color scheme to a different color scheme set, you can make the screen's color contrast more obvious and discernible for people with impaired vision.
High-contrast mode	In addition to offering adjustable high-contrast color schemes, Windows 98 can also ensure that applications adjust themselves to display the highest possible contrast so that visually impaired users can distinguish between background and foreground screen elements.
MouseKeys	Enables you to simulate mouse movements and clicks by using the keyboard.
RepeatKeys	Users can turn on or off the repetition of keys so that holding down a key does not necessarily repeat that keystroke.
SerialKeys	Enables the user to use a non-keyboard input device.
ShowSounds	Provides visual feedback on the screen when applications produce sounds.
SlowKeys	Windows 98 can disregard keystrokes that are not held down for a preset time period. This aids users who often accidentally press keys.
SoundSentry	Sends a visual clue when Windows 98 beeps the speaker (in the case of warning and error message dialog boxes).
StickyKeys	Enables the user to press the *modifier* keys (the Shift, Ctrl, or Alt keys) individually instead of having to

Option	Description
	press them by using combined keystrokes. Therefore, the user can press Alt, let up on Alt, and then press C instead of combining the two for Alt+C.
ToggleKeys	Sounds a noise on the speaker when the user presses the CapsLock, NumLock, or ScrollLock keys to make them active.

To Do

Task 12.2: Controlling the StickyKey Actions

Step 1: Description

Users who need help with the keyboard can set the keyboard options to take advantage of the StickyKeys, FilterKeys, and ToggleKeys options. After you request the keyboard help, you can use the modified keyboard to set the other options. This task explains how to set up and use the StickyKeys feature.

Step 2: Action

1. Display the Accessibility Properties tabbed dialog box by opening the Control Panel and double-clicking the Accessibility Options icon.
2. Make sure the tab marked Keyboard is selected.
3. Click the Settings button at the top of the dialog box. You see the dialog box shown in Figure 12.5.

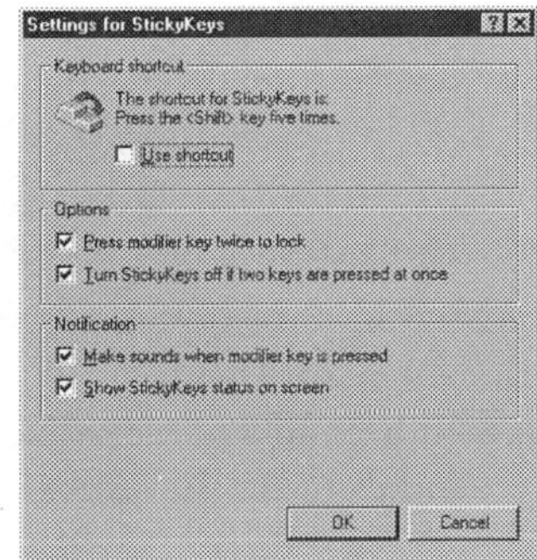

Figure 12.5.
The settings available for StickyKeys.

12

4. Click the top option to turn on the shortcut key for StickyKeys. After you set this option, you are able to turn on and off the StickyKeys by pressing the Shift key five times.

If you share your computer with other users, both you and others can quickly turn on and off the StickyKeys feature by pressing the Shift key five times without having to return to the Control Panel again.

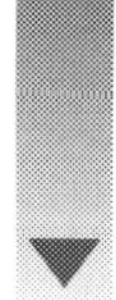

5. If you check Press modifier key twice to lock, Windows 98 activates the modifier keys if you press any of them twice in a row. For example, instead of having to press the Ctrl key and then P while still holding Ctrl, you will be able to press Ctrl twice to lock the Ctrl key in place, and then press P by itself to simulate the Ctrl+P keystroke. This keystroke-locking feature enables users who can type only one keystroke at a time to issue combination keystrokes. (Some users must type by pressing the keys with a pencil.)

   After turning on StickyKeys, you need to decide how you want the StickyKeys feature turned off. As just mentioned, you can toggle the StickyKeys on and off by using a multi-Shift keypress, but there's an even better way. If you check Turn StickyKeys off if two keys are pressed at once, the StickyKeys feature stays active as long as you press the modifier keys individually without combining them and their matching keys. In other words, the StickyKeys feature stays on as long as you keep pressing the modifier keys by themselves. If you (or someone else who comes along) press Ctrl+P (or any other modifier keystroke combination) at the same time by using a single keypress, Windows 98 turns off the StickyKeys feature.

   There are two final options: Make sounds when modifier key is pressed and Show StickyKeys status on screen. These options determine whether or not Windows 98 sounds a beep on the speaker when you press a modifier key and whether or not Windows 98 displays a StickyKeys icon next to the taskbar clock when StickyKeys is active. These signals aid users who want audible or visual StickyKeys feedback. The taskbar icon changes when you press a modifier key.

   For this task, check every option on the Settings screen so you can practice using the StickyKeys feature. Click OK to return to the Accessibility Options tabbed dialog box. Don't check the Use StickyKeys option now, but click OK. If you check the Use StickyKeys option, Windows 98 immediately turns on StickyKeys, but you're going to turn on the feature differently in the next step.

6. Press the Shift key five times. When you do, see a dialog box appear that reminds you of the StickyKeys feature. Click OK to finish activating StickyKeys. Not only will you then hear an audible sound that indicates StickyKeys is active but you also will see an indicator on the taskbar.

TIME SAVER

If you right-click the taskbar's icon, Windows 98 displays a pop-up menu from which you can adjust the StickyKeys settings. If you select Show Status Wndow, Windows 98 displays a pop-up dialog box on the screen that displays the accessibility options icons using a larger icon size than what appears on the taskbar.

7. Start WordPad by clicking the WordPad icon on the Programs | Accessories menu.
8. Press the Shift key (either the left or right Shift) and release the key. You hear an audible signal. You've locked the Shift key for the next keystroke. Press the **A** key. An uppercase A appears at the cursor's location. You have not locked the Shift key, however. Press the **A** key again, and a lowercase a appears. Press Shift once again, release Shift, and press **B** to see the uppercase B appear. Press **B** once again to see a lowercase b appear.

   You can keep pressing any modifier key, Alt, Ctrl, or Shift, to lock that modifier key before pressing the next key.
9. Now press Shift+A by using a normal, single, combination keystroke. Not only will an uppercase A appear, *but you also will turn off the StickyKeys feature.* Remember that earlier you checked the option labeled Turn StickyKeys off if two keys are pressed at once. Therefore, when you press a normal combination keystroke by using one of the modifier keys, Windows 98 turns off StickyKeys.

   Two users can now share the StickyKeys feature. One can turn on StickyKeys by pressing Shift five times. A second user who does not need StickyKeys does not have to worry about turning off the feature; as soon as the second user presses a combined modifier keystroke as usual, Windows 98 automatically turns off StickyKeys.

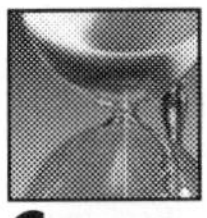

CAUTION

If you find yourself needing to use StickyKeys only occasionally, *don't* check Turn StickyKeys off if two keys are pressed at once. Force yourself to turn on and off StickyKeys consciously by pressing Shift five times. If you don't, you will find yourself inadvertently turning off StickyKeys the first time you combine a modifier key with another key.

Step 3: Review

StickyKeys determines how you want Windows 98 to recognize modifier keys. For users who can only type one keystroke at a time, the StickyKeys feature enables them to press and release Alt, Ctrl, or Shift *before* their counterpart keystrokes. Therefore, these users can press Shift, release the Shift, and then press the letter that needs to be capitalized.

JUST A MINUTE

You will use Task 12.2's basic steps to set most of the accessibility options. When an accessibility option provides a Settings button, you can click that button to adjust that particular accessibility option's specific settings.

Task 12.3: Controlling FilterKey and ToggleKey Actions

Step 1: Description

Inadvertent errors can occur when users hold keys down too long or press keys by using a bouncing motion that often doubles or triples keystrokes. Windows 98 supports the use of FilterKeys to control some of the extra keystrokes that result from certain unintended actions. This task explains how to set up and control FilterKeys.

Step 2: Action

1. Display the Accessibility Properties tabbed dialog box by opening the Control Panel and double-clicking the Accessibility Options icon.
2. Make sure the tab marked Keyboard is selected.
3. Click the Settings command button inside the FilterKeys section of the dialog box. You see the dialog box shown in Figure 12.6.

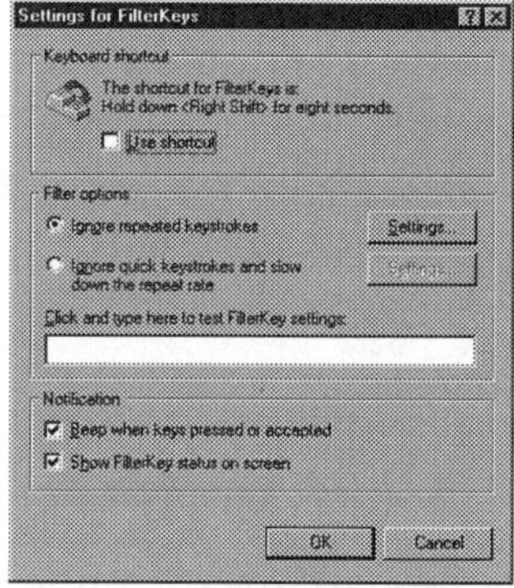

Figure 12.6.
The settings available for FilterKeys.

4. Check <u>U</u>se shortcut so that you can turn on and off the FilterKeys aid by pressing and holding down the right Shift key for eight seconds.
5. The Ignore repeated keystrokes option requests that Windows 98 ignore bounced keys that sometimes result in two or three repeated letters appearing on a line, such as in *theese wooordss*. This option controls the Windows 98 BounceKey feature. Certainly, you don't want Windows 98 to prevent you from typing double letters, because many words, such as *book* and *puppy*, require double-letter combinations. Windows 98 initially sets a fairly long pause rate between letters. Therefore, you might want to decrease the time between double keystrokes that Windows 98 recognizes as an error. You can press the Settings command button to change the delay between accidental double keystrokes.
6. The option labeled "Ignore quick keystrokes and slow down the repeat rate" controls the RepeatKeys and SlowKeys features. There might be some users who accidentally press keystrokes from time to time. By checking this option, you can

keep Windows 98 from receiving these accidental keystrokes as actual keystrokes; if a key is accidentally held down too long, you minimize the repeated keystrokes that would occur.

JUST A MINUTE

The two options described in steps 5 and 6 are *mutually exclusive*, meaning that you can set either one option or the other. Therefore, you can activate either the BounceKeys feature, or you can activate the RepeatKeys and SlowKeys features.

7. If you check Beep when keys are pressed or selected, Windows 98 beeps whenever it recognizes a valid keystroke. If you select Show FilterKey status on screen, Windows 98 displays a stopwatch icon on the taskbar when the FilterKey option is active. Click OK to close the window.

TIME SAVER

If you right-click the taskbar's icon when you've turned on FilterKeys, Windows 98 displays a pop-up menu from which you can adjust the FilterKeys settings.

8. If you select the ToggleKeys feature, Windows 98 sounds a high beep when you activate the CapsLock, NumLock, or ScrollLock keys and sounds a low beep when you press these keys once again to turn them off. Select the ToggleKeys feature now from the Accessibility Options dialog box. Press CapsLock once to turn on the CapsLock key, and you hear a high beep. Press CapsLock again to hear the low beep, meaning that the second CapsLock keypress deactivated CapsLock.
9. Some Windows 98 programs contain their own accessibility options keyboard features and display onscreen help related to their special keys. If you want to see this help in such programs, check Show extra keyboard help in programs. Windows 98 informs all Windows 98 programs you run that you've selected this option, and those programs respond with appropriate help when available.

12

Step 3: Review

The keyboard accessibility options change the behavior and functionality of keystrokes. The three modifier keys receive the most attention because they often require a double keypress that some users are not able to perform. The other keyboard accessibility options control accidental keystrokes to keep Windows 98 from recognizing bad keystrokes as valid.

Task 12.4: Controlling the Sound Accessibility Options

Step 1: Description

The Accessibility Options icon's Sound dialog box controls the features of the SoundSentry and ShowSounds accessibility options. These options provide visual feedback that some users require to let them know that certain audible sounds occurred. For instance, if a user cannot always hear the usual warning sounds an application makes when the wrong key is pressed, the user can request that Windows 98 display a visual clue that a sound was made.

Step 2: Action

1. Display the Accessibility Properties tabbed dialog box by opening the Control Panel and double-clicking the Accessibility Options icon.
2. Select the Sound tab. You see the dialog box shown in Figure 12.7.

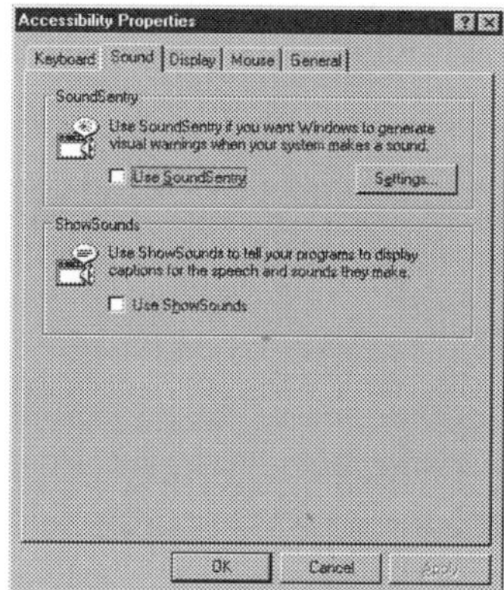

Figure 12.7.
The Sound accessibility options page provides visual sound clues.

After you activate the SoundSentry feature, Windows 98 flashes a title bar or another part of the screen when an application makes a sound.

TIME SAVER

Control which visual clue Windows 98 uses for sounds by clicking the Sound dialog box's Settings command button to display the SoundSentry dialog box.

3. If you click the ShowSounds check box, Windows 98 turns on the ShowSounds option, which displays a visual response to audio sounds (programs must be written specifically to support ShowSounds).

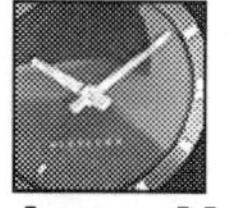

JUST A MINUTE

The SoundSentry and ShowSounds features can help you if you are hearing impaired, work in a quiet environment in which sounds might disrupt others, or work in a noisy environment in which you cannot always hear your computer's sounds.

Many applications produce sounds, such as music and speech, that some users cannot hear. By turning on the ShowSounds option, you request that Windows 98 produce visual clues whenever an application sounds from the speaker.

If you want to turn on the ShowSounds feature, now you can. Click OK to close the dialog box, and, if you have some kind of playback device such as a sound card, double-click the Sounds icon inside the Control Panel. Select a sound and click the playback button to hear an audible sound, as well as see a visual representation of that sound.

Step 3: Review

Use the ShowSounds and SoundSentry options when you need visual clues for the sounds that applications produce. This task explained how to turn on and control these features.

Task 12.5: Controlling the Display

Step 1: Description

This task explains how to change the display to increase the contrast Windows 98 uses so that people with vision impairments can see the screen more easily. Windows 98 can change the contrast and letter size, using the high-contrast mode.

Step 2: Action

1. Display the Accessiblity Properties tabbed dialog box by opening the Control Panel and double-clicking the Accessibility Options icon.
2. Select the tab marked Display. You see the dialog box shown in Figure 12.7.

Figure 12.8.
The Display accessibility option page provides high-contrast viewing of the screen.

3. Click the Use High Contrast option to turn on the high-contrast feature. Windows 98 displays all dialog boxes, menus, and screen colors using a readable and legible display. Although you can click the Settings button to change the high-contrast settings, the default often suffices nicely. Windows 98 also turns on the scalable user interface elements to make icons, title bars, and text easier to read.

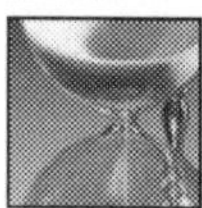

CAUTION

> When you use the high-contrast option, Windows 98 increases the size of icons, menus, and screen elements. Although these elements are easier to read by the descriptions beneath icons and on title bars, the terms are often abbreviated because of their large size.

4. Click the OK command button. Windows 98 instantly changes the display to a high-contrast screen that displays more readable text.

Step 3: Review

If you need extra help reading the screen, you can turn on the accessibility options high-contrast option to increase the size of title bars, menus, and other screen elements, as well as to change the color contrast to distinguish between screen elements more easily.

Task 12.6: Controlling the MouseKeys Feature

Step 1: Description

The MouseKeys feature enables you to simulate mouse movements and mouse clicks by using the numeric keypad on your keyboard. If you have trouble using the mouse, or if you sometimes work with a laptop that has no mouse, you might want to turn on the MouseKeys feature.

Step 2: Action

1. Display the Accessibility Properties tabbed dialog box by opening the Control Panel and double-clicking the Accessibility Options icon.
2. Select the tab marked Mouse. You see the dialog box shown in Figure 12.9.

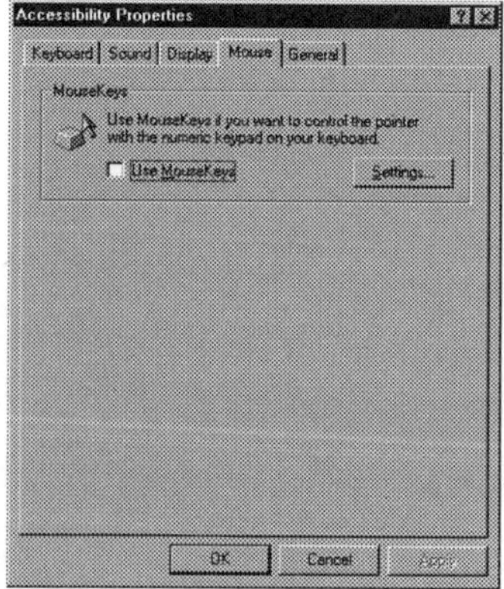

Figure 12.9.
The Mouse accessibility option page enables you to simulate the mouse with keyboard action.

3. If you want to use the keyboard to simulate mouse movements and mouse clicks, click the Use MouseKeys check box, and then click OK. If, before clicking OK, you want to see the setting values for the MouseKeys option, click Settings. The MouseKeys settings, as shown in Figure 12.10, control the way the keyboard intercepts the mouse actions.

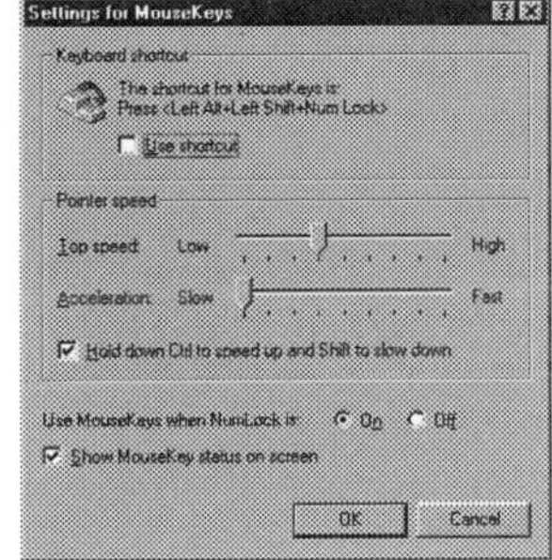

Figure 12.10.
You can change the MouseKeys settings.

Click the Use shortcut option to enable the turning on and off of the MouseKeys feature from the keyboard shortcut (Left Alt+Left Shift+NumLock). Change the mouse's response speed by dragging the two slider controls left or right to adjust the mouse pointer's speed and acceleration from a resting position.

4. Check On to use the MouseKeys when the NumLock is on if you want to use NumLock to control both the numeric keypad and the MouseKeys feature at the same time. When the feature is on, you can switch between using the numeric keypad for normal keyboard cursor navigation and using the numeric keypad for MouseKeys operation at the same time.

5. If you want visual feedback from a taskbar icon that MouseKeys is active, click the Show MouseKey status onscreen option.
6. Click OK to close the Settings dialog box, and then click OK again to close the Accessibility Options dialog box.
7. Press NumLock and then press cursor-movement keys on the numeric keypad to move the mouse cursor. The keypad's number 5 simulates a single mouse click, and the plus sign simulates a double-click of the mouse. All other keys on the keypad move the mouse cursor in various directions.

Step 3: Review

The MouseKeys setting converts your numeric keypad to a mouse-controlling keypad when you press the NumLock key. If you have difficulty using the mouse, or if you don't have a working mouse attached to your computer, you can simulate all mouse movements by setting the various MouseKeys options.

Task 12.7: Controlling the Remaining Accessibility Options Features

Step 1: Description

The tab marked General on the Accessibility Options tabbed dialog box controls the remaining accessibility options. You can control the amount of time the accessibility options remain active and the notification of various accessibility options, and you can determine how Windows 98 recognizes a SerialKeys device that you might have attached.

Step 2: Action

1. Display the Accessibility Properties tabbed dialog box by opening the Control Panel and double-clicking the Accessibility Options icon.
2. Select the tab marked General. You see the dialog box shown in Figure 12.11.

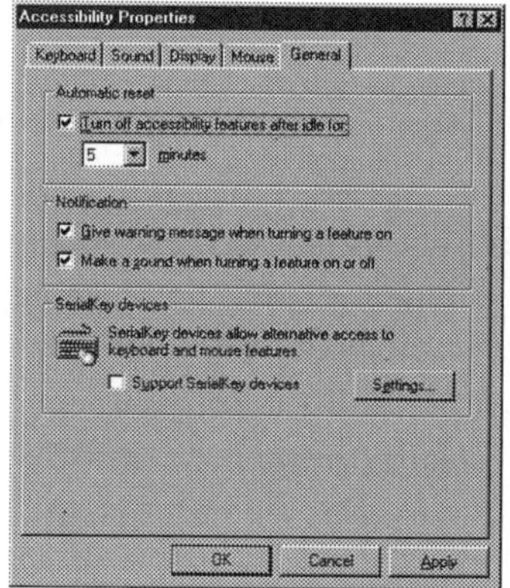

Figure 12.11.
The General accessibility option page provides remaining accessibility option controls.

3. The minutes value determines how long Windows 98 waits before turning off the accessibility options. If you check the option labeled Turn off accessibility features after idle and then enter a minutes value, Windows 98 turns off all accessibility options after the computer has been idle for the specified number of minutes.

   Once the options are set, a user can use the computer's accessibility options and then walk away from the computer to let someone else use the machine. After the specified number of minutes, Windows 98 turns off the accessibility options so that the next person to use the computer (after the time limit passes) will use the computer with no accessibility options in effect.

   Either click off the check mark from this option, or change the minutes value to suit your working environment.

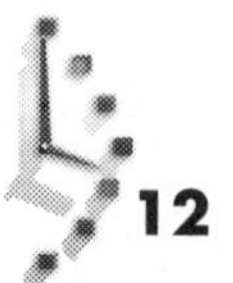

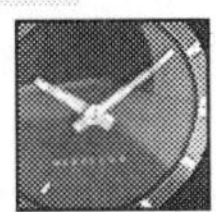

Just a Minute

> If several users share the same PC, you can set up different user profiles, some with accessibility options and some without, and those users whose login names match the appropriate profile will have access to the accessibility options. See the person in charge of networking System Administration in your company for more details.

4. The Notification section determines whether or not Windows 98 should issue the warning dialog box telling you that an accessibility option is turned on when you press the shortcut key for that option. If you want audible feedback when an accessibility option starts, be sure to check the second Notification option.
5. If you use an alternative input device that attaches to a serial port, check the Support SerialKey devices option and click Settings to inform Windows 98 which serial port the device is attached to and the baud rate of the device. The alternative input device should contain instructions for the appropriate values.

Step 3: Review

The General section of the accessibility options determines the final settings for the accessibility options. You can control how long the computer is idle before Windows 98 turns off any accessibility options. Also, Windows 98 can notify you of any accessibility options when you click the proper notification options. Finally, you can tell Windows 98 which alternative input devices you use through the SerialKeys options.

Summary

This hour explained how you can control the accessibility options inside Windows 98. Microsoft designed Windows 98 to be accessible to virtually anyone who needs to use a computer, even if that person requires extra help with the keyboard, video display, or mouse.

The accessibility options contain audible and visual clues that tell you when you set or reset these options. The high-contrast display options help improve the screen's visibility. In addition, you can set up the keyboard to control all mouse movements in case you're missing a mouse or cannot use a mouse.

Q&A

Q How can users who have trouble using the default keyboard interface access the accessibility options?

A The Accessibility Settings Wizard should get most people through the basic accessibility options they need to set. If you need more detail available from the

Control Panel, you only need to get help the first time by having another user display the Control Panel's Accessibility Options tabbed dialog box. Click the option labeled Use StickyKeys. From that point forward, users can activate StickyKeys by pressing either Shift key five times in a row.

Q How can I remember to turn off StickyKeys when my coworker is finished using the StickyKeys feature?

A Make sure the Accessibility Options StickyKeys Settings dialog box has a check next to the option labeled Turn StickyKeys off if two keys are pressed at once. As soon as you press a modifier key in conjunction with any other key, Windows 98 turns off StickyKeys.

Workshop

Term Review

- *FilterKeys* The group of keystroke aids that includes RepeatKeys and BounceKeys.
- *modifier keys* The Alt, Ctrl, and Shift keys.
- *MouseKeys* Enables you to simulate mouse movements and clicks by using the keyboard's numeric keypad.
- *Mutually exclusive* Two or more Windows 98 controls, such as option buttons, are mutually exclusive if you can set only one option at a time.
- *RepeatKeys* Users can turn on or off the repetition of keys so that holding down a key does not necessarily repeat that keystroke.
- *SerialKeys* Enables the user to use a non-keyboard input device.
- *SlowKeys* Windows 98 can disregard keystrokes that are not held down for a preset time period. This aids users who often accidentally press keys.
- *ShowSounds* Provides visual feedback on the screen when applications produce sounds.
- *SoundSentry* Sends a visual clue when Windows 98 beeps the speaker (in the case of warning or error message dialog boxes).
- *StickyKeys* Enables the user to press the Shift, Alt, or Ctrl keys individually instead of having to press them with their combined keystrokes.
- *ToggleKeys* Sounds a high noise on the speaker if the CapsLock, NumLock, or ScrollLock keys are activated and a low noise when these keys are deactivated.

Part IV

Late Afternoon Internet Integration

Hour

PART IV

Hour 13

Internet Explorer 4.0

In today's world, the Internet is a much larger part of computer users' lives than ever before. Windows 98 includes Internet Explorer 4.0, an Internet *browser* that enables you to access the Internet from within Windows 98. In designing Windows 98, Microsoft kept the Internet firmly in mind by providing access to the Internet throughout Windows 98 rather than just from the separate Internet Explorer browser, as in the past. As you will learn throughout this part of the book, the Internet Explorer concept runs throughout Windows 98, and you can access the Internet or your desktop from almost anywhere in Windows 98.

This hour introduces the Internet to you and shows you some of the ways Windows 98 integrates itself with the Internet. You will learn how to access the Internet with Internet Explorer.

The highlights of this hour include the following:

- What makes the Internet such an important online tool
- Why modern Internet access techniques, such as Web pages, make the Internet more manageable
- How to start and use Internet Explorer to surf the Internet
- How you can navigate the Internet and view the multimedia information you find there

- Where you must go to obtain Internet access
- How to specify search criteria so that you can locate the exact Internet information you need

The Internet

The Internet is a world-wide system of interconnected computers. Whereas your desktop computer is a standalone machine, and a network of computers is tied together by wires, the Internet is a world-wide online network of computers connected to standalone computers through modems. Hardly anyone understands all of the Internet because it is not one system but a conglomeration of systems.

The Internet began as a government- and university-linked system of computers, but it has grown to be a business and personal system that contains almost an infinite amount of information. The Internet is so vast that nobody could access all of its information today.

JUST A MINUTE

> There is no central Internet computer anywhere. Instead, Internet is the term given to the entire system of connected computers. The term *Web* is given to the interconnected system of Internet information pages that you can access to read specific information, as described throughout this hour.

The Internet's vastness almost caused its downfall. How does one access or find information on the Internet? Fortunately, Internet technicians began standardizing Internet information when it became apparent that the Internet was growing and becoming a major information provider.

The WWW: World Wide Web

The *WWW*, or *World Wide Web*, or just *Web*, is a collection of Internet pages of information. Web pages can contain text, graphics, sound, and video. Figure 13.1 shows a sample Web page. As you can see, the Web page's graphics and text organize information into a magazine-like, readable and appealing format.

Generally, a Web site might contain more information than will fit easily on a single Web page. Therefore, many Web pages contain links to several additional extended pages, as well as other linked Web pages that might be related to the original topic. The first page you view is called the *home page*, and from the home page you can view other pages of information.

Figure 13.1.
Web pages provide Internet information in a nice format.

JUST A MINUTE

Each Web page has a unique location that includes the source computer and the location on that computer, but such locations would be difficult to keep track of. Therefore, the Internet has standardized Web page locations with a series of addresses called *URLs*, or *uniform resource locator* addresses. You can view any Web page if you know its URL. If you do not know the URL, the Internet provides several *search engines* that find Web pages when you search for topics.

JUST A MINUTE

Surely you've run across computer addresses that look like this: `www.microsoft.com` and `www.mcp.com`; these are URLs that access the Web pages. These two happen to be the URLs for Microsoft Corporation and Macmillan Computer Publishing, respectively.

Introducing the Internet Explorer Web Browser

Before you can access and view Web information, you need a program that can display Web page information, including text, graphics, audio, and video. The program you need is called a *Web browser*—or just a *browser*. Although several companies offer browsers, Windows 98 integrates one of the best Web-browsing programs, called Internet Explorer. Although Internet Explorer has been around for a few years, the Windows 98 release is Internet Explorer version 4.0.

This hour and the next three use Internet Explorer in the figures and descriptions. Some people prefer to use a competing Web browser, such as Netscape Navigator, and you can use that browser from Windows 98 to access Web pages. Internet Explorer 4.0 integrates the best with Windows 98 (because Microsoft wrote both products). Also, the fact that Internet Explorer comes with every copy of Windows 98 makes Internet Explorer the obvious choice to use in a book on Windows 98.

Before you can access the Internet's Web pages, you need to get Internet access through an *ISP*, or *Internet service provider*. Hour 15, "Online Services," describes how to connect to the Internet through one of several services available to Windows 98 users from the Windows 98 desktop. If you want Internet access through another ISP, such as a local Internet provider in your town, your provider will tell you how to use Internet Explorer or another Web browser to access the ISP's Internet system.

To Do

Task 13.1: Starting Internet Explorer

Step 1: Description

Internet Explorer is easy to start. You literally can access the Internet with one or two clicks by running Internet Explorer. This task explains how to start Internet Explorer. You must already have Internet access through the Microsoft Network or another provider, and you must know the phone number to that provider. (Your provider will have to give you the specific access and setup details.)

Step 2: Action

1. Double-click the Windows 98 desktop icon labeled The Internet. If you get an Internet Connection Wizard dialog box, you must contact your service provider to learn how to hook up Internet Explorer to the Internet.

Time Saver

> You can also click the taskbar's Internet Explorer button if you've installed the Quick Launch toolbar on your taskbar.

2. If you access the Internet through the Microsoft Network provider, you will see Figure 13.2's dialog box. If you use a different provider, you will see a different dialog box. Some providers, including some versions of Microsoft Network, don't require that you wait for such a dialog box when you indicate you want access to the Internet. Some providers sign you in to the Internet automatically if you've already entered sign-in information.

   If required, enter your Internet ID and password and click Connect to dial up the Internet.

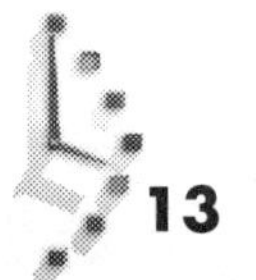

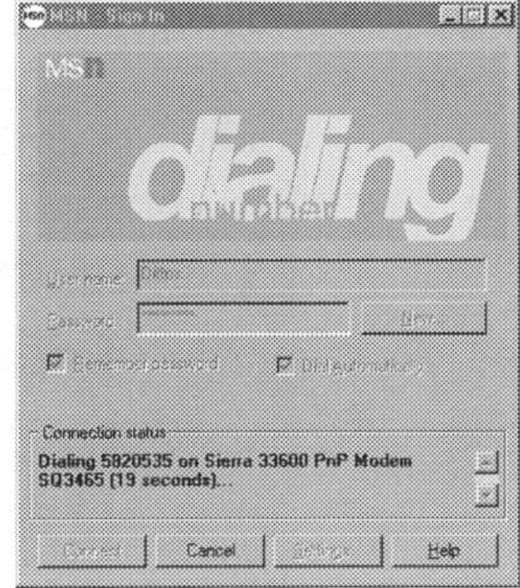

Figure 13.2.
You might need to log in to your Internet provider to use Internet Explorer.

3. Assuming that you have Internet access and you are set up with a provider, Internet Explorer dials your provider and displays the page set up to be your initial browser's *home page*. Depending on the amount of information and graphics on the page, the display might take a few moments or might display right away.

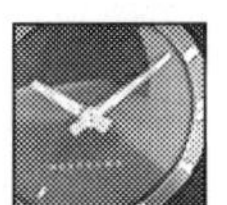

JUST A MINUTE

> Internet Explorer's Home toolbar button displays your browser's opening home page. At any time during your Internet browsing, you can return to Internet Explorer's home page by clicking this Home button. You can change your browser's home page address by entering a new home page address within the View | Options dialog box's General page. When you enter a new home page address, Internet Explorer returns to that page whenever you click the Home toolbar button or when you start Internet Explorer in a subsequent session.

Step 3: Review

Using Internet Explorer to access the Internet and Web pages requires just one or two clicks. Internet Explorer automatically displays an initial start Web page from which you then can access additional Web pages and surf the Internet!

Task 13.2: Managing the Internet Explorer Screen

Step 1: Description

Internet Explorer makes it easy to navigate Web pages. Before looking at a lot of Internet information, take a few minutes to familiarize yourself with the Internet Explorer screen.

Step 2: Action

1. Study Figure 13.3 to learn the parts of the Internet Explorer screen. Internet Explorer displays your home page and lists the home page's address in the address area.

Figure 13.3.
Learn the Internet Explorer screen so that you can maximize the Internet Explorer browser.

JUST A MINUTE

You probably recognize Internet Explorer's toolbar. Windows 98 intentionally puts similar buttons throughout all its windows so you can navigate the Web from Windows 98 Explorer, My Computer, and other locations.

2. Some Web site addresses are lengthy. Drag the Address text box left or right (giving more or less room to the link buttons) to adjust the address display width. The more room you give the Address text box, the less room there is for the other toolbar buttons. You can maximize and minimize the Address text box by double-clicking its slider control.
3. Click the down arrow at the right of the address entry to open a list of recently traversed site addresses. If this is the first time you or anyone has used your computer's Internet Explorer, you might not see sites other than the current start page sites. The toolbar's History button opens the left window pane shown in Figure 13.4, enabling you to return to sites you've gone to in past Internet visits. If you click any of the sites (you might click other day names to open that day's sites), the display area (now at the right of the screen) updates to show that site. You can return to a single-page view by clicking the left window pane's Close button.
4. Click the scroll bar to see more of the page. Most Web pages take more room than will fit on one screen.

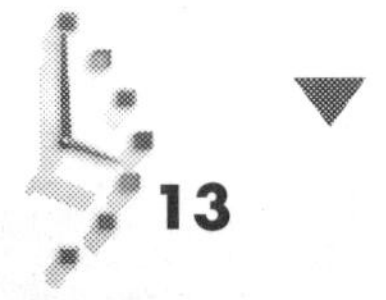

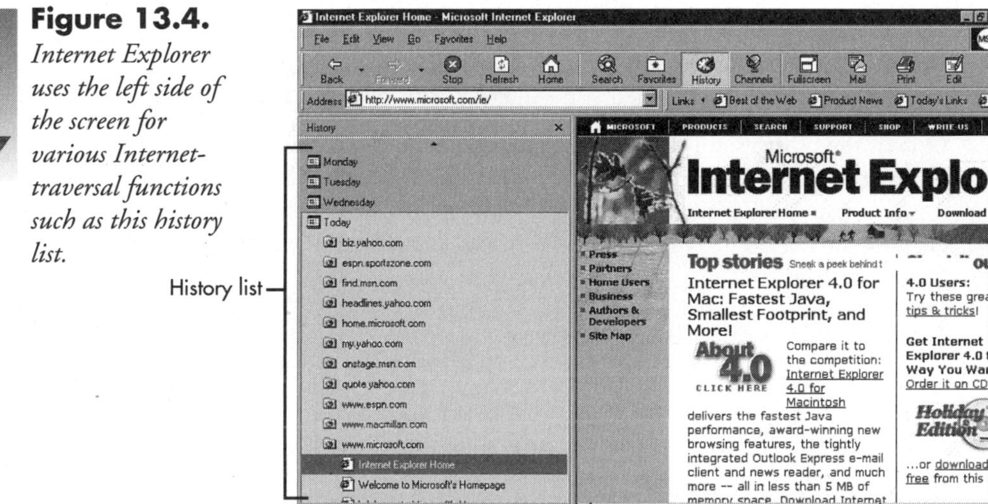

Figure 13.4.
Internet Explorer uses the left side of the screen for various Internet-traversal functions such as this history list.

5. Select View | Full Screen to dedicate all of your screen to the Web page except for a part of your toolbar at the top of the screen.
6. When viewing a full screen view, your menus still work so you can once again change the view by clicking Alt+V to display the View menu.

Step 3: Review

Familiarize yourself with Internet Explorer's screen elements. As you traverse the Internet, Internet Explorer will aid you—as you see throughout the rest of this chapter. By adjusting the screen's elements, you can see more or less of the large Web pages you encounter.

Surfing the Internet

Remember that theWeb is a collection of inter-connected Web pages. Almost every Web page contains links to other sites. These links (often called *hot links* or *hypertext links*) are often underlined. You can locate these links by moving your mouse cursor over the underlined description. If the mouse cursor changes to a hand, you can click the hand to move to that page. After a brief pause, your Web browser displays the page.

TIME SAVER

A link is nothing more than a URL address to another Web site. The link often displays a description and not a technical URL address. (As you move your mouse cursor over a link, your Web browser's status bar displays the actual URL address to the link.) Therefore, you can traverse related Web pages without worrying about addresses; just click link descriptions to move to those sites. In the next hour, you will learn that if you change the display properties of the Windows 98 desktop, you can make your desktop act like hot links and view areas on your own PC inside Internet Explorer's Web page.

Suppose you view the home page of your financial broker. The page might include links to other related pages, such as stock quotation pages, company financial informational pages, and order-entry pages in which you can enter your own stock purchase requests.

One of the most useful features of Internet Explorer and every other Web browser is the browser's capability to return to sites you've visited, both in the current session and in former sessions. The toolbar's Back button returns you to a site you just visited, and you can keep clicking the Back button to return to pages you've visited this session. The Forward toolbar button returns you to pages from where you've backed up.

Keep in mind that you can click the Address drop-down listbox to see a list of URL addresses you've visited. In the History pane, you'll find addresses from the current as well as previous Internet Explorer Web sessions.

If you know the address of a Web site you want to view, you can type the site's address directly in the Address textbox. When you press Enter, Internet Explorer takes you to that site and displays the Web page. In addition, you can select File | Open to display a URL dialog box and enter an address in the dialog box. When you click OK, Internet Explorer displays the page associated with that address. From the Start menu, you can even enter a URL the Run dialog box to see any page on the Web.

JUST A MINUTE

> As discussed previously, Internet Explorer 4.0 more fully integrates into Windows 98 and Windows 98 applications than any previous Windows version. Most of the Office 97 products, for example, include an Internet Explorer-like interface in many areas, and they link directly to Internet Explorer when you perform certain Internet-related tasks from within an Office 97 product. In some cases, you can bypass Explorer when you want a file listing or when you want to view a file while surfing the Internet. From Internet Explorer's own Address textbox or the File | Open dialog box, instead of entering a URL address, type a disk, pathname, and filename. If Internet Explorer recognizes the file's registered type (see Hour 4, "Understanding the My Computer Window"), you see the file's contents.

If you find a location you really like, save that location in Internet Explorer's Favorites list. (This is the same Favorites list found on your Start menu.) For example, if you run across a site that discusses your favorite television show and you want to return to that site again quickly, click the Favorites toolbar button and the site is added to your Favorites list. The Address history does not keep track of a lot of recently visited addresses; you can, however, store your favorite sites in the Favorites folders so that you can quickly access them during another Internet session.

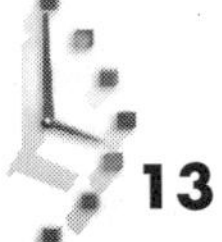

TIME SAVER

Many non-browser products, such as Microsoft Office 97, let you add Web links to non-Internet documents such as Word documents. When you type a URL address in Word, Word underlines the address. If you—or someone who reads your document from within Word—clicks on the URL link, Word automatically starts Internet Explorer (or whatever browser you use); as soon as Internet Explorer locates the page, it appears onscreen.

Task 13.3: Moving Between Pages

Step 1: Description

This task enables you to practice moving among Web pages by using the Internet Explorer browser. After you visit a site, you can return to that site very simply.

Step 2: Action

1. If you have not started Internet Explorer, start it and log on to the Internet.
2. Click the Address listbox to highlight your start page's URL address.
3. Type the following Web page address: **http://www.mcp.com**. Macmillan Publishing's home page appears, as shown in Figure 13.5. (Depending on the changes that have been made to the site recently, the site might not match Figure 13.5 exactly.)

Figure 13.5. *Macmillan Publishing's home page.*

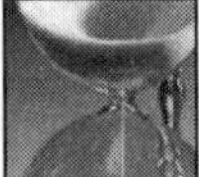

CAUTION

Often, you see Web addresses prefaced with the text http://. This prefix enables you and your browser to both know that the address to the right of the second slash is a Web page's URL address. Internet Explorer does not require the http:// prefix before URLs. Be sure to type forward slashes and not the MS-DOS backslashes you might be used to typing on PCs.

TIME SAVER

Most Web addresses begin with *www* and end with *com*. Knowing this, Microsoft added a time-saving feature to the Address listbox: Type the *middle* portion of any Web site that follows the general format `http://www.sitename.com`, such as `mcp`, and then press Ctrl+Enter. Internet Explorer surrounds your entry with the needed *www* and *com* to complete the address.

4. Click any link on the page (indicated by a hand mouse pointer or a text color change when you move the mouse over a link's hot spot). After a brief pause, you see the linked Web page.
5. Click the toolbar's Back button. Almost instantly, the first page appears.

JUST A MINUTE

Internet Explorer (as well as most browsers) keeps a history of Web page content in memory and on your disk. Therefore, if you revisit a Web site that you've recently viewed, your browser will most likely still have that site in its storage buffer. Instead of waiting for a long download once again, the page appears quickly because your browser actually reloads the page from memory and not from the original site. While waiting on non-buffered sites, the Internet Explorer status bar shows you the progress of the page's loading.

6. Once back at Macmillan Publishing's home page, practice building a favorite site list by clicking the Favorites toolbar button.
7. Select the Favorites | Add to Favorites menu option. Internet Explorer displays the Add to Favorites dialog box.
8. Enter a description for the page (such as `Macmillan Computer Book Publishing`).

9. Click OK.
10. Click the Favorites toolbar button once again. You see the new entry. When you select the favorite entry, Internet Explorer looks up that entry's stored URL address and goes to that Web page.

Step 3: Review

The toolbar makes it easy to visit and revisit Web sites that interest you. You can return to previous sites and move forward once again. The Favorites toolbar button enables you to add descriptions to your favorite Web sites so that you can return to those sites by clicking your mouse over the site's description in the Favorites list.

JUST A MINUTE

If you add too many favorites, your Favorites list might become unmanageable. You can create folders from the Add to Favorites dialog box's Create In button. By setting up a series of folders named by subjects, you can group your favorite Web sites by subject.

TIME SAVER

Visit Microsoft's site often. Microsoft will give you advanced information on Windows 98 and Internet Explorer. To make locating Internet Explorer updates easier for you, Microsoft added a Help | Product Updates option.

Speeding Web Displays

You'll find that some Web pages take a long time to display. Often, Web pages contain a lot of text and graphics, and that data takes time to arrive on your computer. Therefore, you might click to a favorite Web site but have to wait a minute or longer to see the entire site.

To speed things, Internet Explorer will attempt to show as much of the page as possible, especially the text on the page, before downloading the graphic images. Internet Explorer puts placeholders where the graphic images will appear. For example, Figure 13.6 shows a Web page with placeholders. This page appears quickly. If you view this page for a few moments, the placeholders' images begin to appear until the final page displays in its entirety, as in Figure 13.7.

13

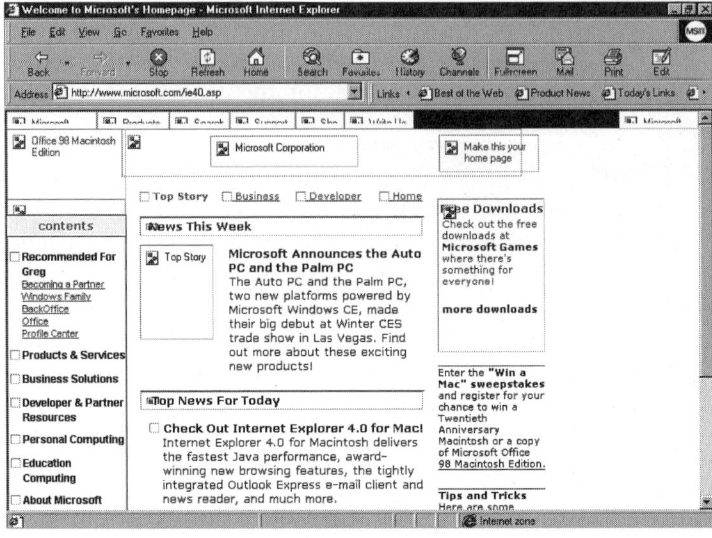

Figure 13.6.
Placeholders let you see the overall Web page design and text.

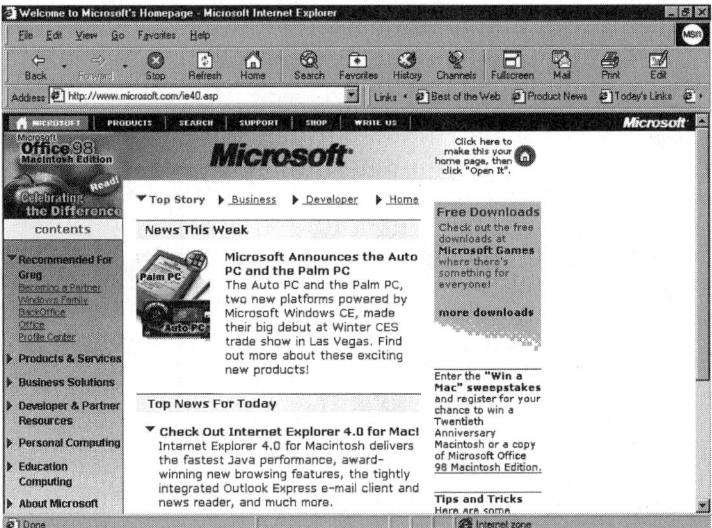

Figure 13.7.
After the images all arrive, the placeholders turn into graphic images.

To Do

Task 13.4: Refreshing and Stopping the Display

Step 1: Description

As you saw in the previous task, Internet Explorer saves recent Web page contents in a memory buffer. Therefore, even if a Web page contains lots of information and requires a minute or longer to load, if you return to that page in a subsequent session, your browser will

often display the in-memory Web page. Although the memory buffer speeds things up, you might not want to see the buffer's Web page. You might, instead, want to see the original page in case the site has changed since your last visit.

Step 2: Action

1. Return to Macmillan Publishing's Web site (`http://www.mcp.com`, in case you did not save the site).
2. Click a link from that site.
3. Click the Back button to go right back. The site should appear almost instantly because you are actually viewing the site from your stored memory buffer.
4. Suppose you suspect that data has changed on the site and you want to see the real address's site once again. Click the toolbar's Refresh button. Internet Explorer reloads the Web page from its original location. After the page loads, you see the page once again with any updates that might have been applied since your last visit.
5. Click the Refresh button once again to redisplay the page, but then immediately click the toolbar's Stop button. Instantly, Internet Explorer stops refreshing the page. Any graphic images not yet loaded remain as placeholders and do not appear no matter how long you view the page. The Stop button is useful for stopping the loading of a slow-loading Web page. If you have no need to see the images, but you're only interested in the text that quickly appears, you can reduce the Internet traffic by stopping the page before it completely loads. Obviously, you will not want to stop the loading process unless you are familiar with the page's contents. Some Web pages contain videos and sound files that can take a while to load.
6. If you want to limit the type of content sent from the Internet to Internet Explorer, to speed your Web page surfing, select View | Internet Options and click the Advanced tab. Uncheck the options under the Multimedia entry to limit pictures, animations, videos, or sounds from entering your browser when you reach a Web page.

Step 3: Review

Use the Stop and Refresh buttons to control the loading of Web pages. The Stop button keeps Web pages from fully loading. You can click Stop as soon as you see as much of the page as you want to see. Click Refresh if you view a Web page from your memory buffer but want to reload the page from its URL address. If you suspect that a Web page has been updated since you last visited the page, click Refresh so that you can be assured you've seen the most recent version. In addition to controlling individual pages with Stop and Refresh, you can set options that prevent certain time-consuming Web page elements, such as videos and sounds, from arriving at your browser along with the Web page text.

Search for the Information You Need

How can you expect to find any information on a vast network of networks such as the Internet? Web pages offer linked sites in an appealing format that enables you to comfortably view information and see related pages, but you must know the location of one of the site's pages before the links can help.

Fortunately, Internet Explorer (as well as most Internet Web browsers) offers a searching mechanism that helps you locate information on the Web. By clicking the Search toolbar button, you select one of several search engines and enter your search value.

TIME SAVER

For a review of Internet searching, refer to Task 10.3 in Hour 10, "Looking in All the Right Places." Hour 10 describes how you can start an Internet search from the Start menu without first running Internet Explorer.

The search Web page offers the benefit of multiple *search engines*. A search engine is a Web program that enables you to enter words and phrases to search for, and then the search engine scans the vast information on the Web to locate sites that contain the phrase. The accuracy of the search depends on the words and phrases you enter, as well as the capability of the search engine. For example, some search engines you can choose from search only Web pages while others search *newsgroups* (discussion areas that hold files and messages related to topics).

After the search page concludes the search, Internet Explorer displays from zero to several address links on which you can click to find information about your topic. For example, Figure 13.8 shows the result of one search after dragging the search window edge to the right to read more of the search results. By scrolling down the page (and by clicking the additional pages of links if your search turns up a lot of sites), you can read the descriptions of the pages (the descriptions often contain the first few lines of the located Web page text). When you click a search result, that result's URL appears in the right window of the Web browser.

Each search engine locates information differently, and each search engine has its own rules for the words and phrases you enter. Keep in mind that the more specific your search phrase is, the more accurately the search engine can find information that will help you.

TIME SAVER

If your search failed to locate information you think is on the Web, or if the search turned up too many sites and you want to narrow the search, you can often click the site list's pages Options or More Information button to read the search criteria rules for that search engine.

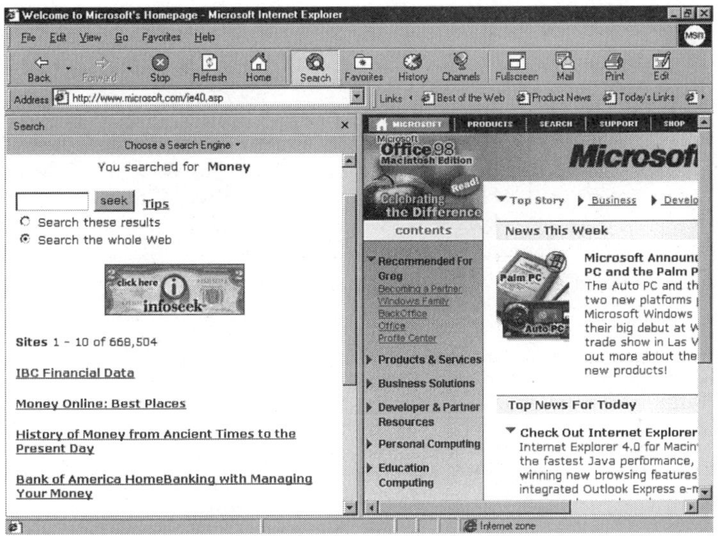

Figure 13.8.
The results of a search might produce several pages of Web sites.

Generally, you can use these guidelines with most search engines:

- Enclose a multiple word phrase in quotation marks if you want the search engine to search for those words in the order you list. For example, if you enter "**Bill Clinton,**" the search engine searches for that specific name. If, however, you enter **Bill Clinton** (without the quotes), most search engines locate every site that contains the word Bill and every site that contains the word Clinton, most of which would have nothing to do with the man you originally wanted to locate.
- Place a plus sign before each word or quoted phrase when you want to search for Web sites that contain every word and phrase in the list. For example, entering **+"Rush Limbaugh" +Congress** would find only those sites that contain the name Rush Limbaugh and the word Congress but would not find sites that listed only one or the other.
- Place the word **OR** between the words or quoted phrases if you want to search for sites that contain one or more of your words and phrases. For example, entering **"Bill Clinton" OR "Rush Limbaugh"** locates any and every site that contains the name Bill Clinton or that contains the name Rush Limbaugh or that contains both names.

Remember that these search criteria rules are only guidelines. Some of the search engines follow slightly different rules, so you'll have to look up that search engine page's help references for specific information if the previous rules do not seem to work the way you expect.

JUST A MINUTE

Most of the search engines are case-sensitive; that is, you need to type words and phrases exactly as you expect them to appear if you want the search to match your search case exactly. Otherwise, if you enter a search criteria in all lowercase letters, the search engines generally do not base the match on case. Therefore, if you want to locate the city named Flint (in Michigan), enter **Flint**. Otherwise, if you enter the name in all lowercase letters, the search engine will probably search both for the city name as well as the rock.

Summary

This hour introduced you to the Internet, a vast collection of inter-related computers all around the world. You can access the Internet as long as you have access through an Internet Service Provider. Although Internet information appears in many forms, the most useful information often appears on Web pages that contain text, graphics, sound, and video.

Windows 98 supports the Internet Explorer Web browser with which you can view Web pages. Internet Explorer includes searching tools as well as a history system that keeps track of recent web pages. Not only can you view Web pages with Internet Explorer, but you also can view other kinds of files on your computer. As the Internet becomes more organized and as Internet access gets faster and cheaper, you will make the Web browser a greater part of your daily computing routine. One day, you might find that you do most of your work with Web browsing software such as Internet Explorer.

Workshop

Key Terms

Review the following list of terms:

- *browser* Software that searches for, loads, and displays Web pages. Browsers display the text, graphics, sound, and even video that appear on modern Web pages.
- *home page* A Web site's foundational page from which all other pages connect. Often, your browser's starting page will be the home page of a Web site such as Microsoft's home page.
- *hot links* (Also called links and hypertext links) Web page items with descriptions that you can click to display other Web pages. Often, a Web page will contain several links to other sites that contain related information.

- *Internet* A collection of networked computer systems that you can dial in to by using a modem that contains a vast assortment of information.
- *Internet Explorer* The Web-browsing software that Microsoft provides with Windows 98.
- *search engine* A program that locates information on the Web.
- *site* The location of a Web page or set of related Web pages.
- *URL address* (Stands for Uniform Resource Locator) The technical address of a Web page's location. When you enter the URL address in your browser's Address textbox, the browser locates that address's Web page and displays the Web page's contents.
- *Web* A system for formatting Internet information into readable and manageable pages of text, graphics, video, and sound.
- *WWW* (Stands for Wide World Web) See Web.

Q&A

Q I've clicked the Internet icon, but I don't see Web pages. What do I have to do to get on the Internet?

A Do you have Internet access from Microsoft Network or from another Internet service provider? Generally, unless you work for a company that offers Internet access to its employees, you must sign up for Internet access, get the access phone number, pay a monthly fee (most Internet service providers offer unlimited access for a flat monthly rate), and set up your browser, such as Internet Explorer, to access that provider.

If you want to use one of the services inside the desktop's Online Services folder, Hour 15, "Online Services," tells you how to access the services by following wizards that sign you up for a subscription.

Q How do I know whether I'm viewing a Web page from the memory buffer or from the actual site?

A If the page appears almost instantly after you enter the address, the chances are great that you are looking at the page from your browser's memory. In most cases, the memory's page will match the actual Web site. Nevertheless, if you want to make sure you're viewing the latest and greatest version of the Web page, click the Refresh toolbar button. Refresh forces Internet Explorer to reload the page from the actual site's address.

PART IV

Hour 14

Windows 98's Tight Web Connection

The biggest differences between Windows 98 and its predecessor, Windows 95, are not the snazzy, easy-to-use interface, new menu structure, or new hardware support; The greatest advancement of Windows 98 is its tight Web connection. If you aren't connected to the Web, you probably soon will be, and Windows 98 makes that connection simple.

Actually, Windows 98 blurs the line between online and desktop computing. In parts of Windows 98, it's difficult to tell if you're working on the Internet, on a local disk file, or a combination of both. You will find Web-related features throughout all areas of Windows 98. Even the Windows desktop, for years the local PC's wholly-owned area, now might contain live content, sent there from the Internet.

The highlights of this hour include the following:

- Why the web-like Windows 98 interface eliminates desktop and Internet access differences
- Why an Internet connection can sometimes hamper your Web usage
- How your taskbar gives simple access to the Internet
- How to set up a Web-page element as wallpaper

- Why any HTML file works as a desktop component
- How to apply any Web page as a desktop component

Your Desktop and the Web

In Hour 2, "Tour Windows 98 Now," you learned how to add Web-like selection and execution to your desktop icons. On the Web, when you click an icon that links you to another spot, the single-click takes you to that remote spot. In Windows 98 a single-click selects (highlights) an icon, but a double-click normally opens the program window beneath the icon. By underlining icon titles and offering single-click program execution, your desktop becomes more Web-like, blurring the distinction between your desktop and the online world. Figure 14.1 shows a desktop using the Web style as opposed to the classic Windows style.

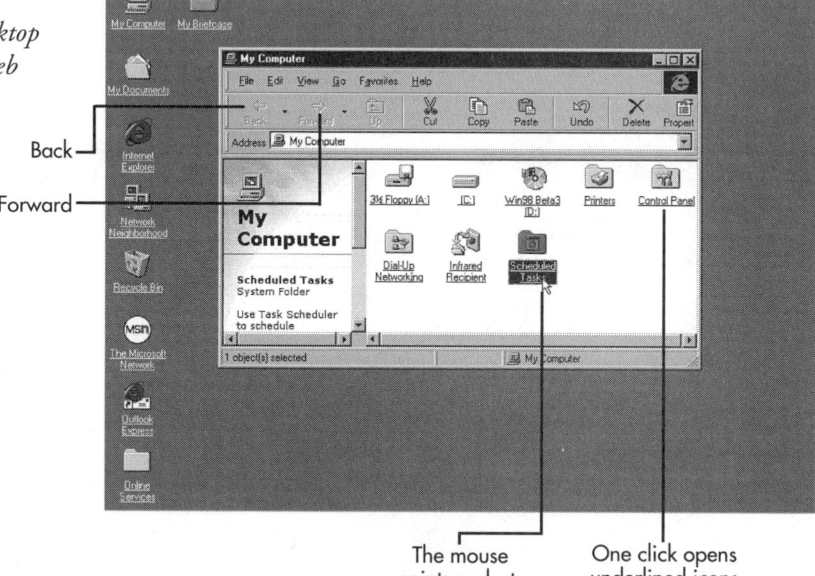

Figure 14.1.
The Windows 98 desktop can respond as the Web responds.

Microsoft is pushing the desktop/Web integration for good reason: The Internet is part of today's computing environment. Although millions of PC users don't use the Internet, the Internet's growth has outpaced all expectations, and the sheer number of current users plus the expected growth in the next five years makes the Internet the most important component in the computing world.

If you've used the Internet to search various online sites with a browser (the previous hour explained all about browsers and the requirements you need to go online), you know how to move from site to site. Unlike a book that you read from beginning to end, the Internet

has no sequential nature. When you traverse the Internet, you move from site to site by clicking the hot spots that you find on the Internet pages. Rarely will you read an entire page before you click a link to take you to a different page. The Back and Forward buttons enable you to move back and forth between Web pages that you already read. By the time you've spent an hour or more on the Web, you have looked at Web sites that are related and often unrelated.

When you work at your desktop PC without being on the Web, you also work in a seemingly random fashion. For example, you might open a document that you've been working on for an annual report. During your lunch break, you might write a letter to your aunt. Your boss might knock on your door and request that you update sales figures in the spreadsheets for which you are responsible. You might continue editing the annual report before you finish the spreadsheets. In other words, you move back and forth between data documents, spreadsheets, word-processed reports, and other kinds of data such as email, databases, and setting windows as you use your PC. The Back and Forward buttons found in Windows 98 windows enable you to traverse the typical data tree you've traveled during your work sessions.

Why should the desktop be distinct from the online world? You access files on your disk drives, perhaps on networked drives, and also on the Internet. Shouldn't you use the same browser to access all of them? Shouldn't your interface for any file, no matter where that file resides, be the same so that you don't have to learn two separate programs to manage your data?

Just a Minute

Online via Modems and T1 Connections

The tight Web and desktop combination does fall apart in one respect—at least for the time being. If you access the Internet through a company's *T1 connection* (a high-speed wired Internet connection that gives you constant Web access) you will more likely understand how the desktop and Web can work together. If, however, you use a modem to access the Internet, as millions do each day, the desktop and Web distinction blur as much as possible, but you still face two real walls: *speed* and *connection*.

If you have a quick Internet connection such as a T1, and if you don't have to fight busy signals to log in, moving from a one-PC desktop to a connected desktop is not a leap. Your own files as well as those on the Internet are available when you want them. A Web page that you traverse appears almost as quickly as a word processor file you stored yesterday on your hard disk. If, however, you must fight busy signals, log in, and use a fairly slow connection (as you have to do even with the fastest of today's modems), you are painfully aware that even though the Windows 98 desktop provides access to a seamless Internet connection, the reality is that you always must make some effort to get onto the Internet.

Perhaps you can be reassured that such Internet connections are probably not going to last forever. Wireless (satellite-based) Internet connections are here and getting less costly every day. The Internet's slow modem speeds are being worked on. Although more and more people use the Internet each day, your speed should never get *worse* than today's speed, and many companies are working on making the Internet faster for all. Therefore, the seamless Web-style desktop is worth the trouble even if you still use a modem for Internet access. Although you still face the modem connection woes that often arise, your Windows 98 desktop is prepared for the arrival of that fast Internet connection.

Taskbar Web Access

If you've set up the taskbar's Quick Launch toolbar, you can go to your Internet browser's start-up home page by clicking one of the Internet Explorer icons on your taskbar. In addition, if you add the Address toolbar to your taskbar, you can type Web addresses directly on your taskbar and explore Web sites.

Task 14.1: Setting Up the Taskbar for the Web

Step 1: Description

This task shows you how to set up your taskbar for Web exploration. Your taskbar is always present (although possibly hidden if you've selected AutoHide from the Start, Settings, Taskbar & Start Menu option), so if you make your taskbar Web-accessible, it is possible to get to the Web whenever you want.

Just a Minute

If you use a dial-up Internet service provider (ISP) and you are not signed into the Internet when you use a Web-based taskbar component, your Internet sign-in window will appear temporarily while you sign into the Internet. After you sign in, your task will complete.

Step 2: Action

1. Right-click your taskbar and select the Toolbars menu.
2. If Address has no check mark next to it, select Address to add the address text box to your taskbar.
3. If Quick Launch has no check mark next to it, select Quick Launch to add the Quick Launch toolbar to your taskbar, as shown in Figure 14.2. As always, you can drag the taskbar's slider controls left or right to give more room to any of the elements there. The Internet Explorer icon launches Internet Explorer and takes you to your browser's home page. The Show Desktop icon minimizes all open windows. The View Channels button gives you access to your push content, as explained in Hour 16, "The Internet's Push and Channel Content."

Figure 14.2.
Your taskbar is now ready for the Web.

Just a Minute

Depending on your hardware and Windows options, you might see a different set of icons next to your taskbar's clock from those in Figure 14.2.

4. Click the Internet Explorer icon (the blue letter *e*) to sign on to the Internet (if you're not already signed on) and to view your browser's home page.
5. Although you can use your browser to enter a URL, click your taskbar's Address field, and enter a Web address such as `www.microsoft.com` to see its page. Even if you are not on the Internet and even if you do not have your browser running from step 4, the page appears when you enter its address in the taskbar's Address textbox.

Step 3: Review

The taskbar provides easy access to the Web when you work within Windows 98.

Just a Minute

You do not have to set up your active Windows 98 desktop in the Web style before using the Web-related icons on the taskbar.

Active Desktop

One of the newest desktop features is the active desktop. The active desktop is so simple, you might not realize the power behind it right at the beginning. You can use *anything* that appears in your Web browser on your desktop as wallpaper. If you access a Web page with a graphic, a link to another page, an *ActiveX* or *Java applet* (ActiveX and Java applets are miniature programs that arrive in your browser with a Web page), or straight text, you can place that Web page element on your desktop for later reference. Check out `www.msnbc.com` or `www.ESPN.com` sites for common examples of sites with ActiveX and Java components.

Task 14.2: Sending Web Page Information to Your Desktop

Step 1: Description

This task shows you how to send Web page information to your desktop as wallpaper.

Step 2: Action

1. Display a Web page from your browser.
2. Right-click a graphic or title on the Web page.
3. Select Set as Wallpaper. After a brief pause, click your taskbar's Show Desktop button to see your new wallpaper. Depending on your Display Properties settings, your wallpaper might be centered, *tiled* (repeated to cover your entire desktop), or stretched to fill your whole screen.

JUST A MINUTE

If you open your Display Properties dialog box (by right-clicking the desktop area), you see your new wallpaper listed in the Background page's Wallpaper list.

4. Display your Web browser again.
5. Locate a link to another site.
6. Drag that link to your desktop. After a brief pause, your desktop holds a shortcut to that page. You can subsequently go to that link simply by clicking the new desktop icon.

Step 3: Review

You can set any Web element, such as a graphic or active applet, as wallpaper by right-clicking that element on a Web page. Your new wallpaper either fills your entire screen (if you've set up a properly tiled or stretched display property) or sits in the middle of your desktop.

CAUTION

If your wallpaper element changes on its original Web site, your wallpaper might not reflect the change until you right-click the wallpaper element and select Refresh. If, however, the Web site contains an ActiveX or Java component (such as you can find at www.ESPN.com), you can drag that active component (such as a news or stock ticker) to your desktop, and the component will continue to change just as it does on the Web page. Of course, if you close your Internet connection (by logging off the Internet), the active component cannot update from its live data.

Add Desktop Components

You can add *components* to your desktop. A component is any Web-based document. A Web document generally has the filename extension *.html* after the *HyperText Markup Language* used for Web page layout. You can create your own HTML files and place them on your desktop or use Web pages as a component.

JUST A MINUTE

> The difference between a component and wallpaper is that you can place as many components on your desktop as you have room for and resize them. You can activate one and only one element to be used as your desktop's wallpaper background at any one time.

The desktop components form the basis of the *push technology* that you will learn about in Hour 16, "The Internet's Push and Channel Content."

Task 14.3: Adding Desktop Components

Step 1: Description

Almost any program written recently for Windows 98 enables you to save the data as an HTML file. These files can serve as desktop components, as you will see in this task. If you have wallpaper, the components do not replace the wallpaper but sit atop the desktop wallpaper. This task teaches you how to create your own HTML file and use that file on your desktop as a component.

Step 2: Action

1. Select your Start menu's Programs | Accessories | Notepad program. Notepad, a text editor, appears on your screen.
2. Type **I want to activate my desktop**.
3. Select File | Save As to open the Save As dialog box.
4. Click the Up One Level button until the Save in field shows only your C: drive without a pathname after it.
5. Type **Trial.html** in the File name field.
6. Exit the Notepad application.
7. Right-click your desktop.
8. Select Active Desktop | Customize my Desktop.
9. Click the Web tab to display Figure 14.3's dialog box page. (Your dialog box might differ slightly due to items you might see in the listbox.)
10. Click New to create a new component. If a dialog box asks you if you want to visit a Web site, click No. (You will visit this site in Hour 16.)
11. Click the Browse button. You now must locate the HTML file you created.
12. Click the Up One Level folder button until you get to your C: drive's root folder (the location where you stored Trial.html).
13. Double-click the Trial.html file (the filename extension might not show), and then click OK. Windows 98 adds that file to the list of components you can place on your active desktop. A check mark should appear next to the Trial.html file, but if one does not, click the check box to add the check mark.

Figure 14.3.
Set up active desktop items from the Web page.

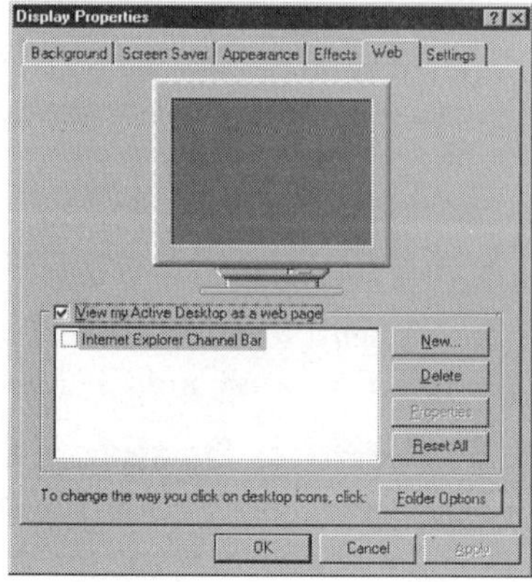

14. Click OK. After a brief pause, a new box with your Notepad file appears on your desktop, as shown in Figure 14.4. If you move your mouse over the new component, the note turns into a window with resizing handles and a Close button, enabling you to treat the window just like any other window.

Figure 14.4.
Your Notepad file now appears as a desktop component.

Step 3: Review

You can set any HTML file on your desktop as a component and turn any document into a component.

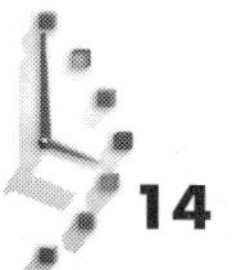

To Do

Task 14.4: Adding Active Components

Step 1: Description

If all Web pages are created as HTML files (and they are) and if you can use any HTML file as a desktop component (and you can), why not create a more active desktop by placing a complete Web page or two on your desktop? This task shows how you can make a component out of any Web page due to the Web's adherence to HTML files.

Step 2: Action

1. Right-click your desktop.
2. Select Active Desktop, Customize my Desktop.
3. Click the Web tab. You see the Trial.html file you created in the previous task in the list. (Delete removes any items you no longer want to use as a component.)
4. Click New to create a new component. If a dialog box asks you whether you want to visit a Web site, click No. (You will visit this site in Hour 16.)
5. Type **http://** followed by the Web address you want to use, such as **http://www.microsoft.com**.
6. Click OK. Windows 98 logs you on to the Internet if you are not already logged on. Windows 98 displays the Add item to Active Desktop dialog box.
7. If the site you entered requires a password (most public sites require no password) click Customize Subscription and enter the password information. Otherwise, click OK. The Web page address appears in the Active Desktop list with a check mark next to the Web page's address (if one does not, click the filename to add the check mark). (Uncheck the Trial.html checkbox if the check mark is still there.) You might see a "Downloading Subscription" dialog box appear as Windows 98 downloads the Web page information to your computer.
8. Click OK. After a brief pause, your desktop shows a new box with the Web-page component in it, as shown in Figure 14.5. When you rest your mouse over the top edge of the Web-page component, the component turns into a typical window with resizing handles, enabling you to resize or close the component if you want to change it.

Step 3: Review

You can now place Web pages on your desktop as components. Resize and move the components as needed. The components act like regular windows with one exception: When you click the Show Desktop taskbar icon, all open windows minimize, but the components stay open. Therefore, live Web pages remain on your desktop. Keep up with the latest scores or stock ticker if you access Web sites with such information.

14

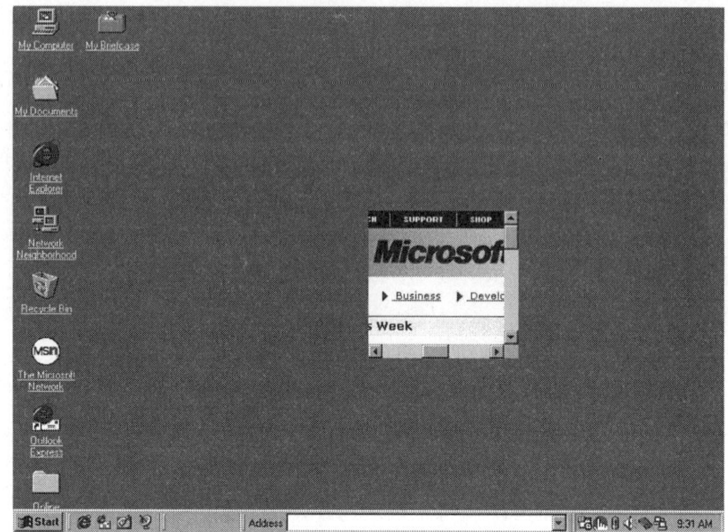

Figure 14.5.
Your desktop now contains an active Web component, and you can add others as well.

For Web Pros Only

If you have worked with HTML source code (the language behind Web pages), you might be interested in knowing about the Windows 98 window customization feature. Windows 98 includes an HTML editor called *FrontPage Express*. Each window on your desktop can have a corresponding HTML document that describes that window's look. When someone opens that window, the window opens to look just like its HTML description. In other words, you can make any window look and act (with controls such as command buttons and check boxes) just like a Web page.

Open any window, such as the My Documents window. When you select View | Customize this Folder, Figure 14.6's opening wizard window appears. If you choose to create or edit an HTML document and click Next twice, Windows 98 opens the window's HTML description page inside the FrontPage Express editor, as shown in Figure 14.7. After you edit the window's HTML page, click Finish, and open the window, the window takes on a new look. By using this technique, you can customize every window in Windows 98.

CAUTION

If you do not see the View | Customize this Folder option, you need to add FrontPage Express to Windows 98 from the Control Panel's Add New Programs dialog box. Select the Windows Setup tab and add FrontPage Express in the Internet Tools detail area. Not all windows, such as the system's My Computer window, enable you to customize the window even if you have loaded FrontPage Express.

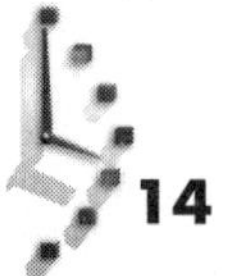

14

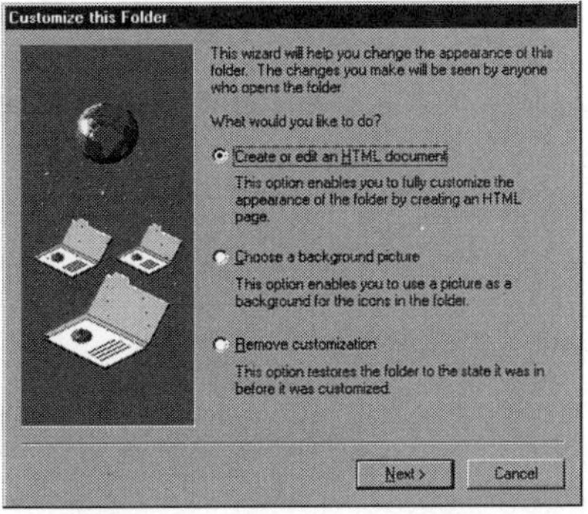

Figure 14.6.
Customize your desktop windows.

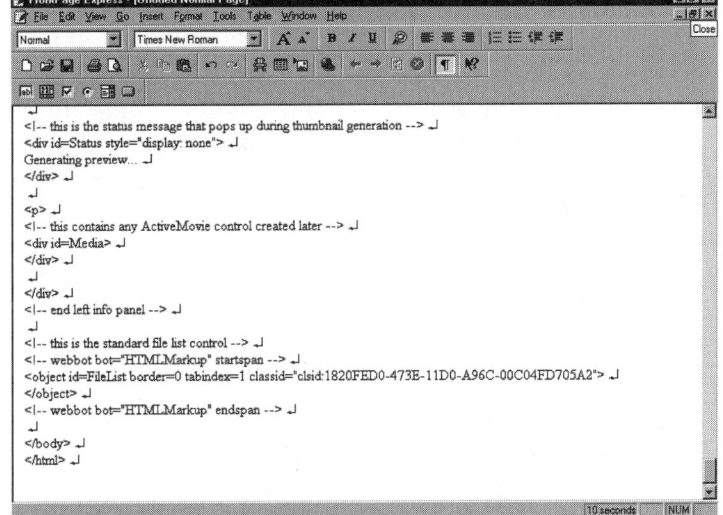

Figure 14.7.
With Windows 98 FrontPage Express, you can change the way your desktop windows look.

JUST A MINUTE

If you don't want to go into HTML editing but just want to add a graphic background to your window, select the wizard's second option and place a graphic image on the window's background.

Summary

This hour shows how Windows 98 integrates with the Internet. Although your Internet connection might hamper the true invisible marriage between Windows 98 and the Internet, the Windows 98 desktop does open itself up to full Internet integration so that you can access the Internet as easily as you access files on your own disk. As you saw in this hour, you can even place live Web pages on your desktop as wallpaper elements or as components so that you can view information when you need it.

Q&A

Q I use the Internet for email but for nothing else. Can the active desktop help me?

A Perhaps not right now. Nevertheless, you probably will be using the Web before long. As the Web becomes faster, and as more content is put on the Web, it should become more of a staple for all PC users. At that time, your desktop and Internet relationship will be critical.

Q I've added a Web page to my desktop, and its small window now appears on the desktop. Why, however, when I click Show Desktop, does that Web page window stay open when my other application windows minimize?

A You must remember that when you add a Web page to your desktop, that Web page might act like a window just as your other open windows act, but the window is actually a part of your desktop. As long as you are logged on to the Internet, that window remains open and current.

Q I've added a Web page as a desktop component. Everything works fine, but why does Internet Explorer open when I click a desktop component's link?

A Although a Web-page component looks and acts like a Web page inside your Web browser, the component is not a browser. You can only keep the Web page on your desktop that you added to the desktop. Nevertheless, you can click a component's hyperlink and Internet Explorer automatically opens Internet Explorer and displays that link's Web site.

Workshop

Key Terms

Review the following list of terms:

- *ActiveX* A replacement for OLE controls that enables Web page designers to place small active programs in a Web page that show a video or interact with the Web page user.
- *Applet* A miniature program often found on a Web page.
- *FrontPage* An HTML file editor that enables you customize your desktop windows.
- *HTML* Stands for *HyperText Markup Language* and refers to the language that programmers use for Web pages.
- *Java* A language that Web page designers use to place small applet programs on Web pages.
- *T1 connection* A high-speed constant Internet connection available to people who work in companies that install T1 lines.
- *Tiled wallpaper* Desktop wallpaper that repeats until your entire desktop is covered.

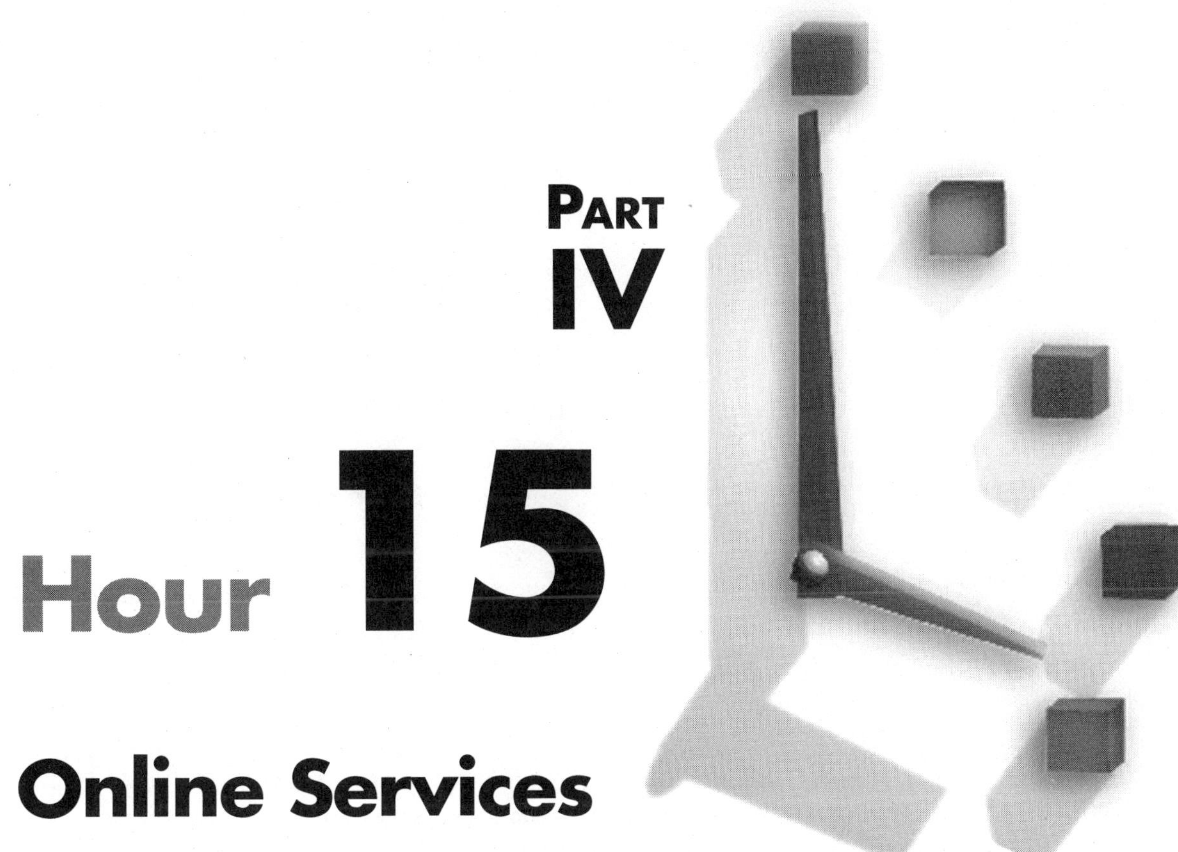

Part IV

Hour 15

Online Services

This hour helps you locate an Internet service provider (ISP) by using one of the services available in the Windows 98 Online Services desktop folder. Although you can sign up for Internet service through a local ISP, Windows 98 provides you with the software needed to try out several popular online services that provide Internet capabilities, as well as other kinds of online benefits.

The highlights of this hour include the following:

- Why you should use an online service as your Internet service provider
- What advantages a service gives you over a straight ISP
- How to sign up for online service
- Why you should sign up for trial memberships

Introduction to Online Services

When you open the Online Services desktop folder, you see the set of icons shown in Figure 15.1. Each of the services, with the exception of AT&T WorldNet, are more than just Internet providers; the services offer unique advantages for the Internet user who wants more than straight Internet Web access. (WorldNet provides only an Internet connection.) If your Online Services window does not contain all of the icons in Figure 15.1, run Windows Setup from the Control Panel's Add/Remove Programs dialog box.

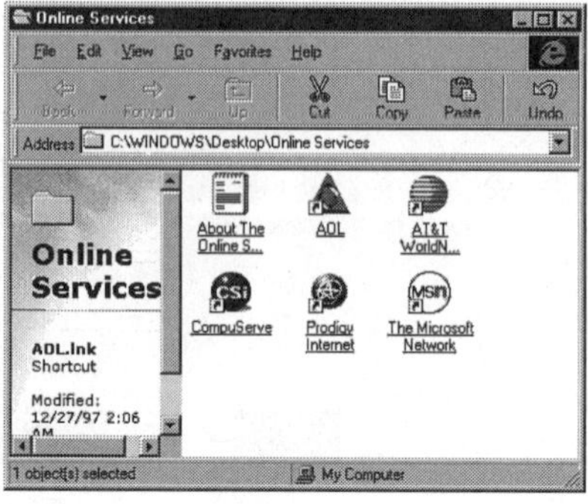

Figure 15.1.
You can sign up with any of these service providers.

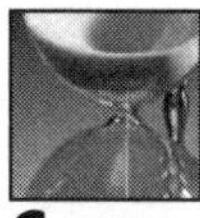

CAUTION

If you do not see the Online Services on your desktop, you might need to run the Control Panel's Add/Remove programs and add the online services from the Windows Setup dialog box page.

All the services charge a fee for their access. Although they all offer somewhat different pricing plans, most services compete with one another, so you must decide which is right for you based on your needs, the reliability of the service, the capabilities each provides, and recommendations from others. If, for example, you have a new 56Kbps modem, you will probably want to use a service that supports your modem standard (two 56Kbps standards exist—*56Kflex* and *56K*—and neither works with the other). You'll find that some services, such as AT&T WorldNet, don't offer ISDN lines for ISDN modem users at the time of this writing, so if you use an ISDN modem, check out the service ahead of time.

Don't discount recommendations; if most of your coworkers and friends subscribe to a service, such as Prodigy, you should consider Prodigy because you will communicate with the others without problem, and they can help you get started quickly.

JUST A MINUTE

All the online services offer *flat-rate pricing plans*. With a flat-rate plan, you pay one monthly fee no matter how much (or how little) you use the service each month. In addition, the services provide local numbers, so you don't have to pay long distance charges in most areas.

The primary difference between using one of the Windows 98-supplied online services for your Internet connection and a local ISP that provides more of a generic Internet connection is that the online services offer unique content available only to their subscribers. In addition, many of the online services offer their own interface to the Internet and its content. The drawback to online services is that they offer abundant advertisement at virtually every turn.

These ads, as well as the extra graphics and menus they provide on their home pages, mean somewhat slower access in some cases than you can get from a standalone Internet service provider.

CAUTION

The companies that provide the online services want the services made available to as many users as possible. Therefore, they try to make these services simple to install. The very nature of online communications requires fiddling, even with the best of installation routines, but these services generally install without a lot of intervention on your part. If, however, you use a local ISP and opt not to use one of the online services, you often face somewhat-difficult setup routines, and depending on the quality (or lack) of support through your ISP, you might not get much help. These setup risks might not outweigh the lower cost of a local ISP, but you should consider the risks when shopping for a provider.

The growth of the Internet, with its millions of Web sites, takes much of the uniqueness out of the *unique content* provided by online services. For example, CompuServe might offer movie reviews, but so does a plethora of Web sites, many of which offer as many or more movie reviews as CompuServe. Most daily newspapers, magazines, and entertainment services now offer Web sites. If you're willing to search the Internet for a specific reviewer's take on a new movie, you can often find as good a review or better outside your particular service provider's unique content.

However, one reason online services, such as The Microsoft Network, are successful is that they offer more than just unique content. The online services generally utilize a proprietary interface. Although you can often use the service in conjunction with Internet Explorer, for example, to access the Web, you can also use the online service's customized interface to access information. For example, Figure 15.2 shows CompuServe's opening screen. From this screen you can access one of several categories easily, whereas with a more generic Internet service provider you would need to know the Web locations to find such information using Internet Explorer.

CAUTION

Prodigy is the only Windows 98-supplied online service that does not offer its own Web-browsing interface. You use Internet Explorer or another Web browser to get to Prodigy's online features.

Figure 15.2.
Online service providers offer their own managed interface to the Internet and its information.

JUST A MINUTE

Here's some industry news that surprised a few million online users: American Online (AOL) purchased CompuServe towards the end of 1997. AOL promises to keep CompuServe a separate online service and business entity with its own personality.

Newcomers to online technology often prefer the organized content available through an online service. Setting up Internet Explorer or another browser is not always a trivial task with generic ISPs. In addition, the dedicated toolbar buttons and menu structure of the online services get the newcomer (as well as the pros in many cases) to their information destinations faster.

One of the benefits of using the supplied online service if you don't have an Internet provider or if you want to make a change is that all the software for the service setup comes with Windows 98. You've got everything you need to set up America Online, CompuServe, and the others shown in your Online Services folder, so you don't have to wait to get started.

JUST A MINUTE

You must have a credit card handy when signing up for a service.

One of the benefits of using Windows 98 to set up an online service is that you can try a service free for a month before deciding if you want to keep it. The services compete heavily with one another and you, the user, benefit from that competition. Try all the services free for a month and explore their benefits before you decide which one is right for you. (The section that follows this task compares and contrasts all the services.)

When you choose which online service you want to try, you'll need to set up that service in Windows 98 and subscribe to it. All of the online services require that you set up the service before you can use it. Each service is compressed to save disk space until you are ready to use it. This task shows you how to set up CompuServe, but you'll follow the same general setup guidelines to set up any of the services.

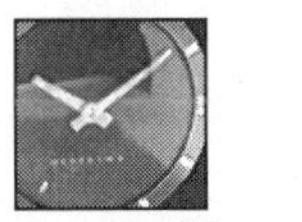

JUST A MINUTE

Once you set up a service, if you need a new software update, most services will automatically download the update to your PC and update the software for you.

To Do

Task 15.1: Setting Up CompuServe

Step 1: Description

Each Online Services folder icon starts a wizard that sets up one of the services. The wizard walks you through the CompuServe setup instructions and adds the appropriate service icons to your Start menu.

Step 2: Action

1. Open your desktop's Online Services window.
2. Open the CompuServe icon. A dialog box makes sure that you want to continue by asking if you want to install CompuServe.
3. Click Yes to begin the wizard. After a brief pause the CompuServe setup wizard begins.
4. Select your country and click the Next button. The online services are international, so the wizard needs to know your country to set up the appropriate service.
5. If you are setting your first online service, select the Express install from the window shown in Figure 15.3. If you already have an ISP and want to access CompuServe from your existing connection, select Custom. (You will need to contact your ISP to determine which settings CompuServe needs before you can connect to CompuServe with this option.)

Figure 15.3.
Select the kind of CompuServe service connection that you desire.

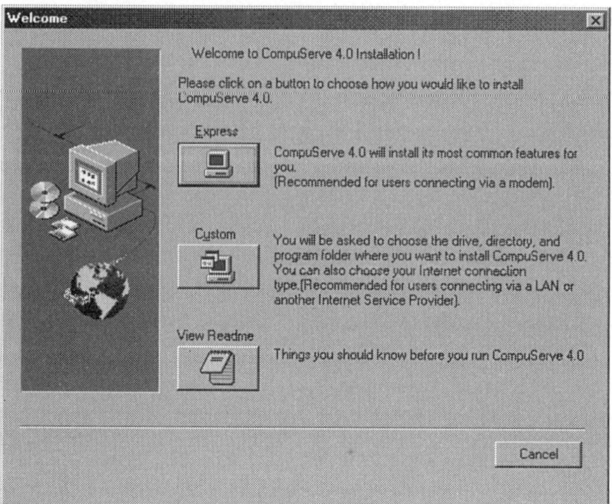

Consider Online Security

All the online services provide fairly adequate levels of security. Although no online service can ensure that your every keystroke's privacy is guarded, online services do provide more security than regular voice calls, credit card purchases in stores, and purchases you make by mail. The stories you may have heard about online privacy issues are generally overblown.

Use common sense when you provide information over an online service or over the Internet. If you order products from a reputable dealer, the odds are vastly in your favor that you'll have no security troubles. Almost every financial transaction made today over an online service uses a *secure connection*, meaning that information you supply is encrypted on your end before being sent and then decrypted on the receiving end.

6. CompuServe displays the Create a Keyword dialog box shown in Figure 15.4.

Figure 15.4.
Your keyword provides security during your online sessions.

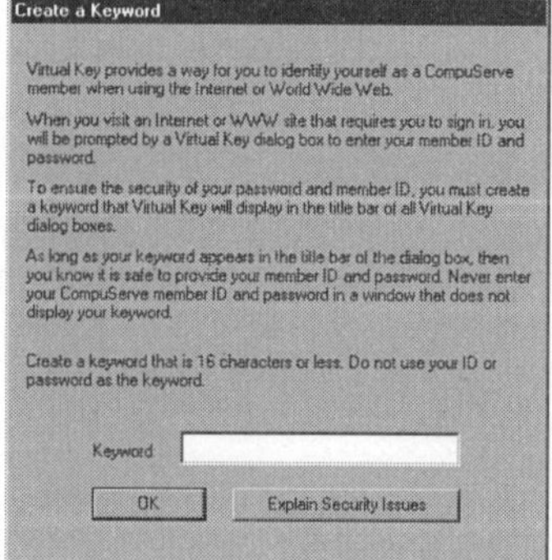

Enter a keyword, up to 16 characters, that acts as your security password. Although you'll need a password to sign in to CompuServe, the keyword offers yet another level of security for those times when you must provide information, such as a credit card number. Any time an online CompuServe screen asks you for secure information, you will be prompted to enter this keyword to help encrypt the information so it gets to CompuServe without any security violation along the way. Select a keyword you can remember, such as your Mother's maiden name.

7. CompuServe requires that you restart your PC after you set up the CompuServe files. Click the Restart button.
8. After your PC restarts, you can select your Start menu's Programs | Online Services menu to see a new submenu called `CompuServe`. Select the entry named `CompuServe 4.0` to complete your set up.
9. At the opening CompuServe screen, click Signup to sign up for a new CompuServe account. CompuServe requires a sign in name, password (one that differs from your security keyword), personal information such as your name and address, as well as credit card information. Unless you cancel the service, CompuServe will bill your credit card monthly for the service.
10. When you first sign in, CompuServe enables you to select the phone number you want to use. If you've elected to use CompuServe in conjunction with an existing provider, you won't need to enter phone number information. When you select any service, CompuServe dials the Internet using your existing dial-up provider.

Step 3: Review

This task walked you through the preliminary steps needed to set up and access CompuServe, one of the online service providers available through Windows 98. After you set up a service, you can access that service's specialized areas as well as surf the Internet using the service's Internet browser. Some of the services let you use your own Web browser, such as Internet Explorer, if you don't want to use the proprietary browser that comes with the service.

Comparing the Online Services

Which online service is right for you? Only you can answer that question, but the following sections briefly explain advantages of each of Windows 98's online services so you can better choose between them.

In comparing the services, keep in mind that competition makes all of them worthwhile contenders and they each provide some advantages over the others. All the services provide the typical Internet-based online service features described in Table 15.1. Each online service, however, goes about implementing the features in different ways.

Table 15.1. Look for these features in your online service provider.

Feature	Description
Chat	Lets you interactively communicate with others who are signed on at the same time you are. All online services, including a straight Internet connection, provide text-based chats where you type messages back and forth to others who have joined your *chat room.* Chat rooms are areas of interest sorted by topic, such as *PC Support, Teen TV, Religious Talk, Windows Troubleshooting, Politics,* and *Movies.*
Email	Stands for *electronic mail* and describes the service with which you can transfer messages and files to other users on your online service and across the Internet. The receiving user does not have to be signed in to receive mail you send.
FTP	Stands for *File Transfer Protocol* and lets you transfer files to and from other Internet-based computers. Online services almost always provide their own FTP alternative when you want to retrieve files from the service. Generally, a service will offer a file-search section where you can search for files of particular interest and download those files by clicking a button.
Internet Phone	If you have a multimedia PC (and who doesn't these days?) with a microphone and speaker, you can speak to others anywhere in the world. You are not charged the long distance connect rates, but you are charged for your regular online service (some exceptions apply). Internet Phone is not all peachy, however, because the quality is low and both you and the other party must be signed on at exactly the same time, and you both must know which Internet location the other will be at to connect. Internet Phone holds promise, but for now not too many people use it despite its initial appeal.
Mailing Lists	Free (usually) subscription-based Internet services that sends you any and all new messages and files posted to the mailing lists you choose via email.
Newsgroups	An area of the Internet accessed through your online service, that contains files and messages, organized by topic that you can read, download, and send to. (Newsgroups have nothing to do with Web pages that contain world headline news.)
Web	Web pages you browse from your Windows 98 desktop using Internet Explorer and your online service.

Keep in mind that you get the standard Internet service explained in Table 15.1 no matter which online service provider you subscribe to. In addition, if you prefer to subscribe to a local ISP that offers nothing but an Internet connection, you can access any of the services listed in Table 15.1. Remember, however, that most online services put a friendly interface in front of these Internet services that make the them much simpler to use. In addition, the online services provide you with support, news and current events, and entertainment areas that are more complete than you'll find with a straight Internet connection.

CAUTION

> Most online services provide nice, friendly interface layers between you and the Internet. In addition to the interface, each service provides unique content such as online magazines that you cannot get elsewhere. Generally, an online service costs more than an Internet-only connection you can get locally, but you'll see a cost in another area as well: disk drive space. Most of the online services require between 30 and 50 megabytes of disk space. The unique content and interface requires a presence on your hard disk.

America Online (AOL)

AOL is the number one online service in use today. Its sheer number of users makes AOL a mixed blessing sometimes. Although AOL's content is some of the most complete and its service offers perhaps the largest selection of specialized benefits, some users have a difficult time getting onto the service during peak hours. In addition, AOL throws a lot of advertising at you while you use the service. This advertising keeps your costs down and the content massive.

JUST A MINUTE

> AOL is considered to be one of the easiest online services to use.

AOL's opening page, shown in Figure 15.5, offers a push-button topic selection throughout its entire interface. When you want to access the Internet, you must use AOL's provided browser that does not support the active desktop features that Internet Explorer supports (see Hour 14).

AOL provides a wide variety of daily news, periodicals (newspapers and magazines), local weather, movie reviews and preview, and health forums.

Figure 15.5.
AOL is one of the easiest online services to use.

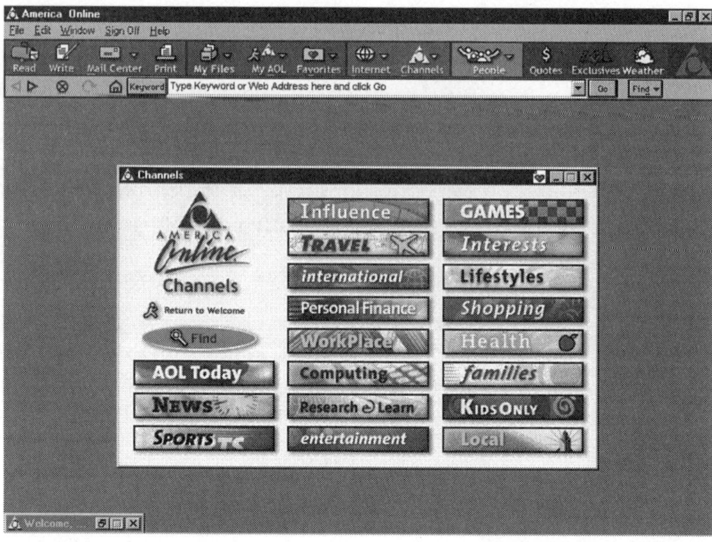

TIME SAVER

AOL lets you sign on up to five members in your household. Each member can have her or his own distinct account and can send and receive email separately from the primary account holder. You don't pay extra for the extra users, but only one user can be signed into AOL at a time.

AOL lets you send and receive email between AOL and every other service and Internet user. The email area is simple to user and you are nicely reminded, verbally through your speakers, when you have new email (you can turn this off). Another AOL service that should weigh into your online selection is that AOL offers you up to 2MB of storage for your own personal home page. You'll have your own URL address and be registered so others on the Internet (both AOL and non-AOL users) can access your Web page.

AT&T WorldNet Service

AT&T WorldNet service is not a true online service with unique content but an Internet Service Provider available from within Windows 98. Billing is simple for most customers because AT&T WorldNet Service bills through the AT&T long-distance service if you use AT&T. (If you have a credit card that offers extras such as airline miles, you may opt not to bill through your AT&T long-distance carrier but select a credit card billing option to rack up those miles.)

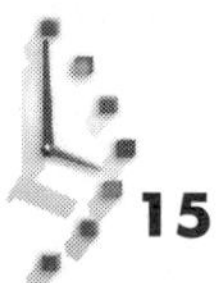

AT&T WorldNet offers nothing fancy. You'll use Internet Explorer or another Web browser to surf the Internet and the Microsoft Outlook email and newsgroup reader works fine for the AT&T WorldNet access. AT&T WorldNet charges extra for 2- to 5MB of Web page storage if you want a Web page.

CompuServe

CompuServe has been around the longest of all the online services listed in Windows 98's Online Services window. Due to its maturity, CompuServe offers more depth of information and a wider selection of forums than any other service. Want information on travel to Jakarta? CompuServe probably has more information than the other services. Do you need help locating a replacement disk drive door for your 1983 IBM-PC? CompuServe's hardware forums probably have the address where you can buy one.

As Figure 15.6 shows, you can easily access CompuServe's areas of interest by selecting services similar to the way you traverse AOL's push-button interface.

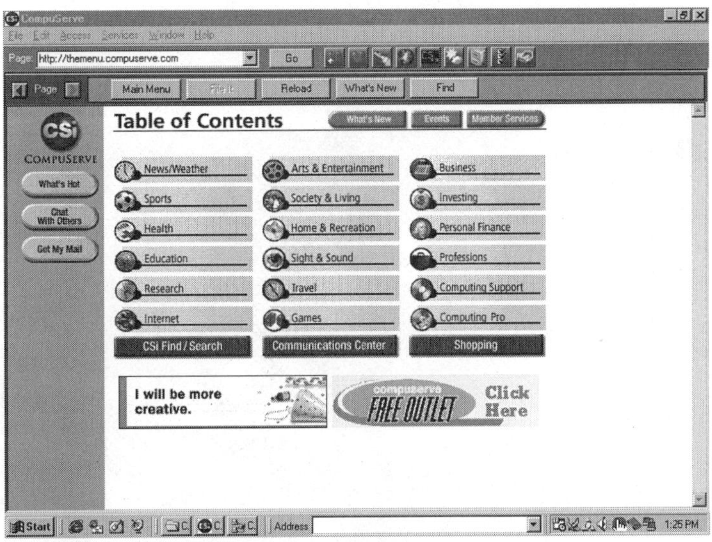

Figure 15.6.
Access CompuServe's primary services through a selection interface not unlike that of AOL.

CompuServe uses a proprietary email service, meaning that you cannot always send and receive email to others who use different online services. You can send and receive regular Internet-ready email so you can communicate with anyone else whose service also provides for pure Internet email.

Despite its email limitation, you can subscribe to various email services through CompuServe that let you access your email with a pager or listen to your CompuServe messages over a voice phone. Such services are vital if you travel without a laptop and need your messages. Although a CompuServe sign-in name and email address is often cryptic (such as *420120,23433*) you can request a customized name such as *Casper* and people can get email to you by sending your email to *Casper@compuserve.com*.

If you want a Web page, CompuServe gives you 5MB, more than twice AOL's 2MB storage limit, for the Web page you desire. For those who prefer Internet Explorer 4.0's active desktop features, CompuServe lets you use Internet Explorer in place of the proprietary Web browser in CompuServe.

The Microsoft Network (MSN)

The Microsoft Network offers the largest assortment of Microsoft-related sites and tools and seems to integrate more fully into Windows 98 than the other online services. (One might expect this because both Windows 98 and MSN are Microsoft products.)

MSN is known for its attempt to be *hip. MSN* sounds out jazz music and a video when you install it. MSN's black background adds an effectual interface that doesn't take itself too seriously but seems more laid back than the other services. The Microsoft programmers seemed to create a service that they wanted and the results are fairly good. Figure 15.7 shows MSN's opening screen.

Figure 15.7.
The Microsoft Network screen offers a television-like 6-channel interface for its topics.

MSN's Web browser interface acts a lot like Internet Explorer 4, although you cannot directly send active content to your desktop unless you use Internet Explorer to access the Web after you've signed onto MSN. If you use the proprietary Web interface, you can select or enter URLs from the MSN screens and surf the Web with a surprisingly powerful (for a proprietary service) browser.

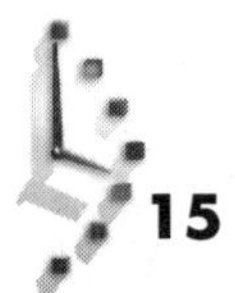

You can use Windows 98's Outlook Express for newsgroups and email. When you search a newsgroup of check your email from within MSN, MSN starts Outlook Express for you.

MSN takes advantage of the Windows environment and places an MSN icon on your taskbar when you install the MSN software. As Figure 15.8 shows, you can click on the taskbar to display an MSN menu at any point during your MSN session or even when you aren't signed in.

Figure 15.8.
The Microsoft Network provides a taskbar icon you can click to display a menu.

As you use MSN, a timer pops up from the taskbar every few minutes to let you know how long you've been using MSN in that particular session. If you routinely chat with others, you can designate a list of online friends and the taskbar icon pops up to let you know which of your friends sign on during your MSN session so you can contact them through a service to let them know you are signed on as well.

Prodigy

Prodigy's online service, now called *Prodigy Internet*, provides unique content over what you'll find on just the Internet. However, Prodigy's interface takes place entirely within Internet Explorer 4, so you don't have to learn new commands to access the content Prodigy provides. Prodigy is more seamless than the other services, and you can switch back and forth between Prodigy and the Internet's Web pages without as much distinction as you might feel in the other services.

Just a Minute

Prodigy adds a Prodigy-based toolbar to Internet Explorer, giving you quick access to its unique content.

Figure 15.9 shows the opening screen that appears when you sign in to Prodigy for the first time. (The screen changes, so yours will be different.) An icon is added to your taskbar while you access Prodigy that, although not as full-featured as MSN's taskbar icon, helps give you control when you work with other applications.

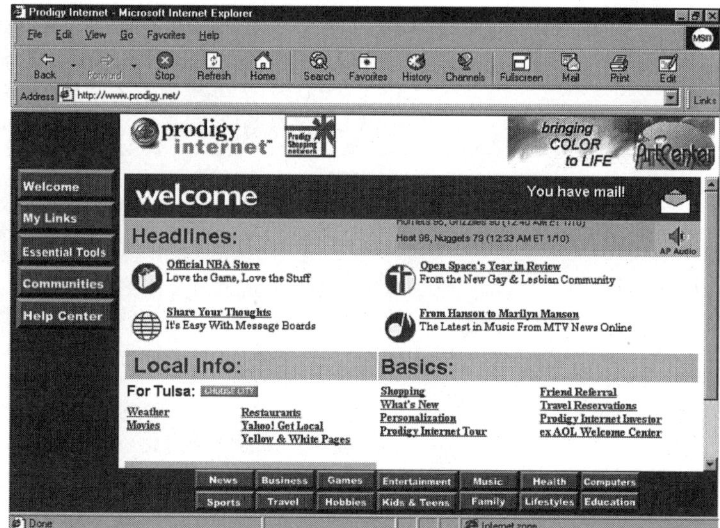

Figure 15.9.
Prodigy uses the familiar Internet Explorer as its interface environment.

Prodigy gives you 2MB of storage for your own Web site, but you must use tools that you find elsewhere to create your Web page. Prodigy supplies no Web site-creation programs. However, you can use the Windows 98 Web page-creation program, FrontPage Express, which is covered in Hour 14, to create a Web page. You can also use Word 97 or any number of Web page-development programs on the market to create Web pages.

Prodigy's Internet Explorer interface enables you to use Microsoft Outlook, the Windows 98 Newsreader and Internet Mail program, so you don't have to learn new commands to access newsgroups and email. Hour 17 explains how to use Microsoft Outlook to access email and newsgroups from the Internet.

Summary

This hour explains how you can use one of the Windows 98 online services to access the Web, newsgroups, and email if you don't already have access to a service. The online services, with the exception of AT&T WorldNet, provide unique content that you cannot get from a Web ISP alone. You will have access to forums, news, entertainment, and other links that offer more structured content than an Internet-only ISP. In addition, the online services offer a simpler interface to Web services than an ISP and a Web browser.

Q&A

Q Should I subscribe to more than one service?

A Probably not, although you might want to sign up for multiple services for a trial month. The services compete with one another greatly and, although they differ, every one of them offers vast content as well as standard Web capabilities such as email and newsgroup access.

If your service is frequently busy when you dial in, a secondary service offers a backup number so that you can get to the Web when you need access. Too many busy signals for a certain service might make you decide against that service provider because you want to be able to access it when you need it. Nevertheless, a few dial-in attempts usually gets you through if you're patient.

Q Do I have to provide my credit card number if I want to try the service for a trial period?

A Unless you use AT&T WorldNet and bill your AT&T long-distance carrier, you must provide a credit card number even if you sign up for a trial, one-month period. The online service wants your business, and at the end of the trial period, they want your money. By requesting a credit card number when you first sign up, the service ensures that you will pay for each month you stay with the service. All the services offer email customer support, so you can let them know if you want to cancel the service.

Workshop

Key Terms

- *chat* An online keyboard-based conversation you have with others in the chat room you've selected.
- *chat room* An area of interest where people can meet to discuss a particular topic.

Different online services offer a different assortment of chat room topics.

- *email* Electronic mail service that enables you to transfer files and messages to others who have an online account.
- *flat-rate pricing plan* An ISP payment plan where you get unlimited usage for the same monthly rate.
- *Internet Phone* A program that enables you and another to speak to each other over your Internet connection.
- *mailing lists* Services organized by topic that you can subscribe to and receive free (usually) messages and files for the topics that interest you.
- *newsgroups* Areas of the Internet, organized by topic, that contain files and messages you can read and send.
- *secure connection* An online connection with controls in place to protect the current transaction.

PART
IV

Hour 16

The Internet's Push and Channel Content

The Internet is a vast collection of data, much of it random. When you want something, you have to locate it. Even when you know the location of a Web site or the information that you need, you must traverse the Web to get to that information. All that is changing, however. Instead of searching for Internet data, you can now have that data sent to you.

This hour explains how to use Windows 98's new *push technology* to receive Internet data on your desktop. Push technology refers to information that comes to your desktop from the Internet without your having to first locate the data. Push technology involves much more than receiving email (although some push technology-based sites incorporate email), as you will learn in this hour.

The highlights of this hour include the following:

- What push technology is all about
- Why push technology delivers what you want
- How to place push content on your desktop
- Why channel technology gives you more specific information than push technology
- How to subscribe to the channels you want

Introduction to Push Technology

When you receive push technology, information comes from the Web to your desktop or Web browser. Several forms of push technology exist. In its simplest form, you can receive regular email, such as the morning news, so that when you start your PC, the information is waiting for you.

Windows 98 offers more advanced push technology than regular email, however. As you learned in Hour 14, "Windows 98's Tight Web Connection," Windows 98 enables you to place Web components right on your desktop. You can have Web pages and specific content sent to your desktop or your Web browser automatically. In addition, you can view only the information that has changed since the last time you visited a Web site. The push information might appear on your taskbar (such as a scrolling stock ticker with your personalized stock quotes) or in a screen saver during your PC's lull times. Internet Explorer contains special window panes in which you can view push technology information.

Push Is a Development Nightmare

You, the user, benefit from push technology. The Web site developer, however, faces some challenges to offer push content. For one thing, Microsoft's implementation of push technology differs somewhat from other vendors such as Netscape (the makers of Netscape Navigator, Internet Explorer's primary competitor). Microsoft has proposed a new standard for push technology content called *Channel Definition Format* (*CDF*) that enables existing Web pages to incorporate push content. (In addition to CDF, Microsoft promotes a new version HTML the Web page language, called *Dynamic HTML* that better supports modern push technology than current HTML.)

CDF is based on a service that enables you to subscribe to channels of push content. The channels enable you to design exactly the content you want. Instead of receiving an entire newspaper, you can subscribe to your own channel that sends you the sports and weather.

All of the various push technologies require some Web site developers to supply the same Web page in a variety of formats, depending on the user's tools. Microsoft Internet Explorer users might need a page that differs somewhat from Navigator users. As with most new technologies, the push technology is evolving, and a *de facto* standard will surely take over. Microsoft has a big headstart, considering that most Windows 98 users have access to Microsoft's push technology.

Active Desktop Push

In Hour 14, you previewed how to send push content directly to your desktop. By using push technology to place Web page content on your desktop, you can incorporate images and

other Web controls such as stock tickers on your desktop as wallpaper or as a component. Windows 98 updates the active desktop components while you are signed on to the Internet.

Task 16.1: Placing Active Desktop Content

Step 1: Description

This task reviews active desktop content as it relates to push technology. Microsoft provides active content sites that you can access to place Web topics on your desktop. The desktop links remain active as long as you're signed on to the Internet.

Step 2: Action

1. Right-click over your desktop.
2. Select Active Desktop | Customize my Desktop to display the Desktop Properties window.
3. Click the Web tab.
4. Click the New button. The Display Properties offers to visit Microsoft's Active Desktop gallery, as shown in Figure 16.1.

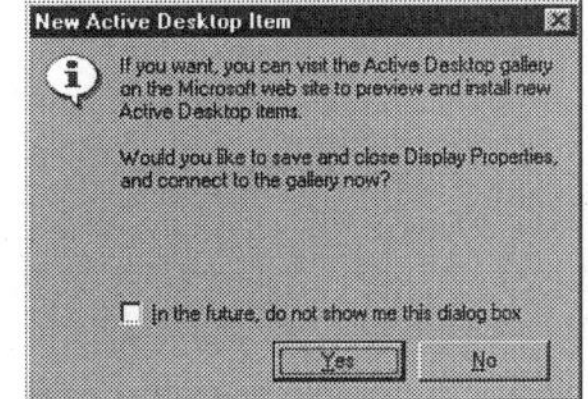

Figure 16.1.
Microsoft enables you to sign on to the Internet to retrieve active desktop content.

5. Click Yes to visit the site. If needed, your Internet sign-in window appears, so you can sign on to the Internet. After a brief pause, the Web page shown in Figure 16.2 appears. The page offers active content that you can place on your desktop.

   The active desktop Web site you see might differ from Figure 16.2 because Microsoft adds to and changes the Web site frequently. Visit the site often to see if new active content that you want appears.
6. Select one of the active components, and the Web site displays a description for you.
7. If you want the content (click your browser's Back button to return to the previous page for a different item), click the Description page's button, labeled `Add to Active Desktop`. If your browser's security options are set to confirm whether or not you want to add the item to your desktop, a Security dialog box will appear.
8. A final dialog box appears, describing the item and its URL address. You can click the Customize Subscription button to select how you want the item updated. The default Scheduled option generally works well, but you also can manually control when the update occurs.

Figure 16.2.
Microsoft gives you a gallery of active desktop choices from which to select.

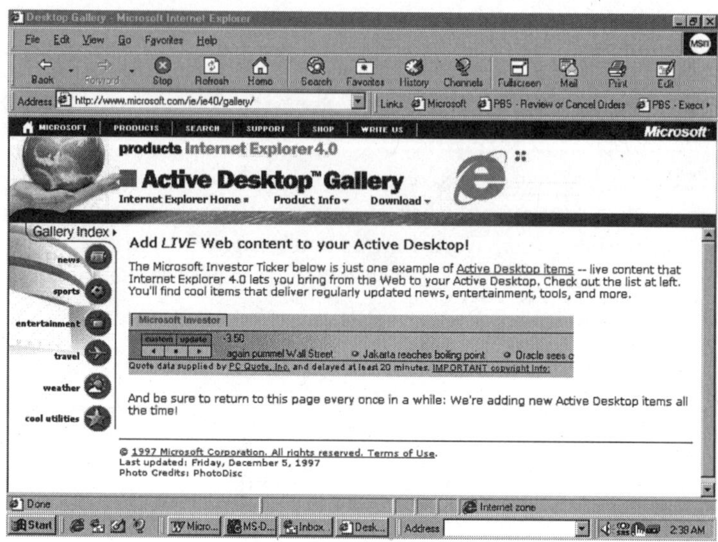

9. Click OK to begin the download to your desktop. You don't have to close any windows to see the new item. Remember to use the Show Desktop icon on your taskbar when you want to see your desktop by minimizing (but not closing) all open windows. (The Quick Launch toolbar must still be on your taskbar). Click the Show Desktop taskbar button to see the active content. Figure 16.3 shows business news headlines running across a window, not unlike a stock ticker. A business news and stock quote ticker is available from Microsoft's site. (The scrolling news and ticker, as with most of the active content, contains buttons that enable you to customize the item to see your favorite stock quotes.)

Step 3: Review

Place active push content on your desktop. You don't have to search the Web every time you want a stock quote or any other piece of information. Instead, direct your Internet Explorer to capture and place the information on your desktop.

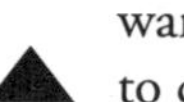

Channels and Windows 98

Perhaps the best way to experience the power of channels is to use them. Before you can access a channel, you must subscribe to that channel's content. As with other Internet activities, Microsoft has designed a series of pre-tuned channels to which you can subscribe.

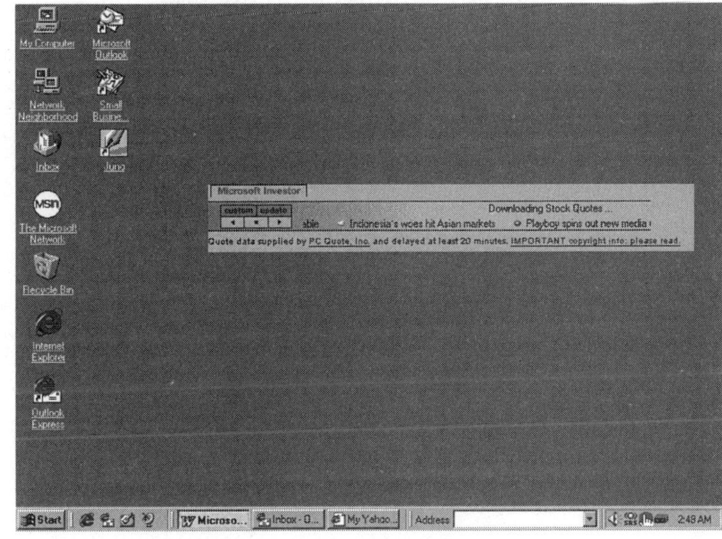

Figure 16.3.
You can view stock quotes and business news headlines.

JUST A MINUTE

Some of the channel content comes to you via audio and even video. You can listen to the channel content and watch moving video when you select such content.

Task 16.2: Using Channels

Step 1: Description

This task explains how to subscribe to and view channels on your desktop. The channels provide push information that you need. The information appears inside your Internet Explorer Web browser and also appears in its own window as a taskbar button.

JUST A MINUTE

If your desktop displays a list of channels, you can access channels without using the Quick Launch toolbar button. Follow along with Task 16.2, however, to practice working with the channels when they are not in view.

Step 2: Action

1. Click your taskbar's View Channels button to view Figure 16.4's screen.

Figure 16.4.
You must designate the channel you want to view.

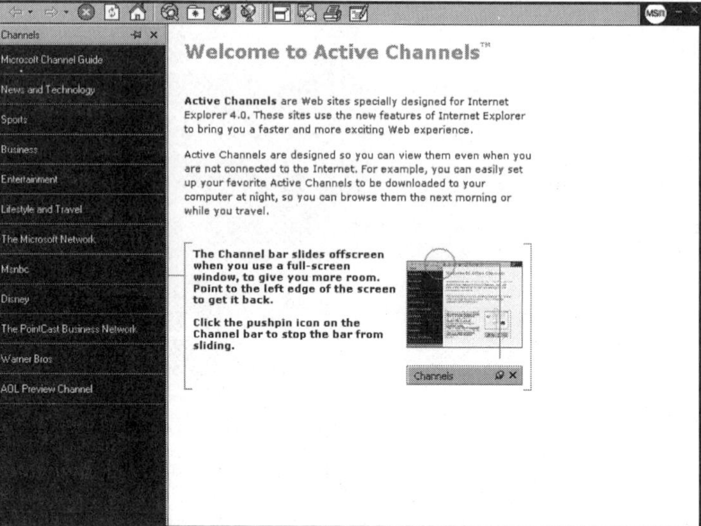

CAUTION

The channels on the left side of your screen might differ from those of Figure 16.4 because Microsoft changes the channel content every once in a while. In addition, your channels will collapse to the left to reveal the instructions underneath. To see the channels again, point to your screen's left edge, and the channels will come into view.

TIME SAVER

Click the channel listing's push-pin in the channels' upper-left window to keep the channel list from moving off to the left.

2. Click any channel to view the content provided. As you can see, each channel opens to display a list of specific choices. In other words, the channel is the general topic from which you select a more specific topic to view. The Entertainment channel, for example, offers details such as Hollywood Online, The AudioNet Channel, and the Comics Channel. More will appear over time.
3. Select the channel with the content that you want to view. The Web page for that content opens, offering even more detail.
4. After you verify that the channel contains something you want on your desktop, click the page's Add Active Control button (sometimes labeled *Subscribe* button). The page offers a specific list of choices that you can add to your desktop. After you

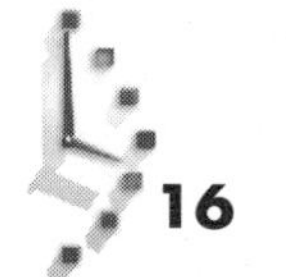

determine the schedule for download, click the OK button to receive that content on your desktop.

JUST A MINUTE

Channel push technology resides inside a browser and never on your desktop unless you place some of the channel content on your desktop. Often, however, a channel gives you the option to place the content on your desktop. Click the channel's Web page to see if you can place the information on your desktop. If you receive the option to place the content on your desktop, right-click the desktop and select Refresh to see the content. As with any desktop component, the content becomes a regular window when you point to an edge of the item, so you can close the window in the usual manner to remove the item from your active desktop space.

Step 3: Review

Activating channel push technology requires a few steps to get exactly the information you want. As soon as you subscribe to the channel, however, the rest comes to your desktop automatically inside Web page views or on your desktop, if you've placed the content there.

Task 16.3: Streamlining Channels

To Do

Step 1: Description

Task 16.2 described how to get to the channel technology and to view instructions under the channels on the page that opens when you click the View Channels taskbar buttons. As with most tasks, Windows 98 offers shortcuts that take you to your channels after you've subscribed to one or more channels.

Step 2: Action

1. Open the Start menu's Favorites option. A list of your favorite Web sites and documents opens. The first option is Channels.
2. Select the Channels option to view a list of channels. The channels open to the specific channel content to which you can subscribe. By viewing channels from the Start menu, you don't have to open the Web page described in Task 16.2. The Web page is good for beginning channel users because the channel guide's instructions appear beneath the channels.

   As Figure 16.5 shows, some channels offer a great deal of material, such as shopping and entertainment activities.
3. Continue adding the channels by using the skills you learned in the previous task. If you opt to view a site only after its content changes, a channel will not appear until its content updates.

Step 3: Review

Activating channel push technology is as simple as selecting from the Start menu's Favorites option.

Figure 16.5.
Windows 98 describes a channel's content fully before you subscribe.

Task 16.4: Monitoring Content

Step 1: Description

You might not always want channel content to consume a taskbar button and reside in its own Internet Explorer window or on your desktop. If you want to see the channel content only when the information within the channel changes, you can request to see the channel only at that time.

Step 2: Action

1. Suppose you subscribe to a specific cartoon or to a news service (such as Microsoft's MSNBC), and you want to view the subscribed channel's contents only when the channel changes. Perhaps you've read the current news and don't want to be bothered until the news changes. Begin by subscribing to the channel in the usual manner, as explained in Task 16.2.
2. When the Channel Subscription Wizard asks whether you want to view the channel at all times or only when the channel changes, indicate your preference in the dialog box that appears.

   In addition to viewing channels only when their content changes, you might want to receive an email notification when the content changes instead of having your PC log on to the Internet regularly to check the page. The Subscription Wizard enables you to do this whenever the email option is available.

When you finish with the Subscription Wizard, your channel will be set up the way you requested.

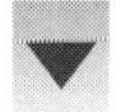

Step 3: Review

You do not have to receive your channel content through an active browser. Instead, you can receive content only when the site changes. If you prefer to receive email when a subscribed Web site changes, instead of getting the site itself, you can request such email.

Turn Push Technology into a Screen Saver

Some channel content can be made into screen savers. When you subscribe to the content's channel guide, you learn if a screen saver is available. You can then request that push technology only appear when your screen saver activates. Not all channel sites are available as screen savers, so you have to check with the specific channel content provider to see if a screen saver option is there.

Summary

This hour described how to access push technology. Why should you search the Internet every time you want information? To let the Internet come to you!

You can request that Web information be sent directly to your desktop at the times you schedule. You might want to be notified by email if something changes, or you might want certain Internet information to always appear on your screen when you click your taskbar's Show Desktop button.

The channel subscription service that Internet Explorer offers provides you with specific content and a rich assortment of sites that place information in a minimized taskbar window or even on your active desktop. Many channel sites provide services that send active content to your PC as a screen saver to view when your PC is idle.

Q&A

Q Do I have to pay for push content that I subscribe to?

A At this time push content is free. Many sites do throw in advertisements to defray the costs of the push material. Keep in mind that as push content grows and more and more material is available, however, you might have to pay for some premium push content. If, however, you don't have to pay to access a Web page, you don't have to pay to retrieve push content from that site.

Workshop

Key Terms

Review the following list of terms:

- *Channels* Specific areas of Web content you can subscribe to.
- *Channel Definition Format (CDF)* Enables existing HTML-based Web pages to incorporate push content.
- *Push technology* Receiving information automatically from the Internet without having to traverse the Web. Push technology data comes to you.

PART V

An Evening with Extended Windows 98

PART

V

Hour 17

Outlook Express: For Mail and Newsgroups

The Internet Explorer 4 portion of Windows 98 includes a new program called *Outlook Express* that manages both email and newsgroup information. Outlook Express replaces older Windows messaging programs called *Windows Messaging* and *Windows Exchange*. By combining a newsgroup reader with email capabilities, you can manage more information easier than before.

Email plays as big or bigger role in today's communications than regular mail. Email's paperless aspect keeps your desk less cluttered, and email generally arrives at its destination within a few minutes to a few hours. Newsgroups offer a different kind of messaging center for messages you want to communicate publicly on a topic. You can post newsgroup topics, answers, and questions, as well as read responses from others interested in the same subject.

The highlights of this hour include the following:

- How Outlook Express enables you to view and send email messages
- When to attach files to email messages you send
- How to post and read newsgroup messages
- How to set up Outlook Express for multiple accounts

The Email World

It is common for computer users to access more than one online service. Perhaps you work on the Internet as well as on CompuServe. Each morning you might log on to the Internet to get incoming messages and send your outgoing Internet messages. When finished, you might log on to CompuServe to send and receive those messages. The burden of managing email grows as more people sign up for more online services.

Just a Minute

Are we living in a *paperless society*, as promised by the Management Information System gurus of the early 1970s? Not a chance. Computers help us use more paper and at a *faster* rate than ever before. It's often said in the computer industry that, despite the prevalence of electronic mail, we'll have paperless bathrooms before we'll have a paperless society!

Wouldn't it be nice to tell your computer to send and receive all your email without any intervention on your part? The computer could store all received mail in a central location; you could then manage, sort, print, respond to, or delete from there. Outlook Express provides the one-stop answer.

Caution

Don't confuse Outlook Express with Outlook 97. Outlook Express is not the same program as Outlook 97, which comes with Office 97. It looks as if Outlook Express, or some form of Outlook Express, will replace Office 97's Outlook soon, perhaps by the time you read this.

Managing Email with Outlook Express

Outlook Express offers benefits over previous email programs because Outlook Express supports several formats within an email message. Although you could send text data, *binary data* (compressed data such as programs and graphics), sound files, and video as email in previous programs, Outlook Express enables you to store HTML code inside your message so that you can customize the look of your message. A message you send might look like a Web page. You can even send complete Web pages as email inside Outlook Express. If you embed a URL inside an email message, your message's recipient can click that URL and go straight to that site on the Web (as long as the recipient uses Outlook Express or some other email package that converts URLs to hyperlinks automatically).

Here are some of the additional features of Outlook Express's email capabilities:

- Send or receive email in plain, unformatted text to speed performance at the loss of seeing formatted messages.
- Attach files to your messages.
- Check spelling before you send a message.
- Reply to messages and forward messages to other recipients.
- Connect to Web-based email address search engines, such as Four11, to find people's addresses (see Hour 10, "Looking in All the Right Places," for more information on Web searching).
- Connect to the Windows Address Book program. Address Book is compatible with several other address programs, such as Office 97's Outlook.
- Send and receive mail to and from multiple Internet accounts.

17

JUST A MINUTE

> Outlook Express is a part of Internet Explorer 4 as well as Windows 98. You can start Outlook Express from Internet Explorer (as this hour generally suggests) or open the desktop's Mail icon to start Outlook Express.

Task 17.1: Setting Up Outlook Express

Step 1: Description

This task explains how to set up Outlook Express for use within Internet Explorer.

JUST A MINUTE

> If the wizard begins when you start Outlook Express the first time, you need to answer the wwizard's prompts to set up your email account. Most of the online services, such as Prodigy, automatically set up Outlook Express, but if you see the wizard, you may need to contact your ISP to determine which settings are needed for Outlook Express to recognize your ISP-based email account.

Step 2: Action

1. Start Internet Explorer and sign into your Internet account.
2. Select View | Internet Options and click the Programs tab to display the Options dialog box, as shown in Figure 17.1.
3. Select Outlook Express from the first two options labeled Mail and News, as Figure 17.1 shows. (Microsoft NetMeeting enables you to contact other Internet users and set up chat and even voice-based meetings.)
4. Click OK to close the Options dialog box. When you send or receive mail, Internet Explorer will now use Outlook Express as your email program.

Figure 17.1.
Make sure Internet Explorer knows about Outlook Express.

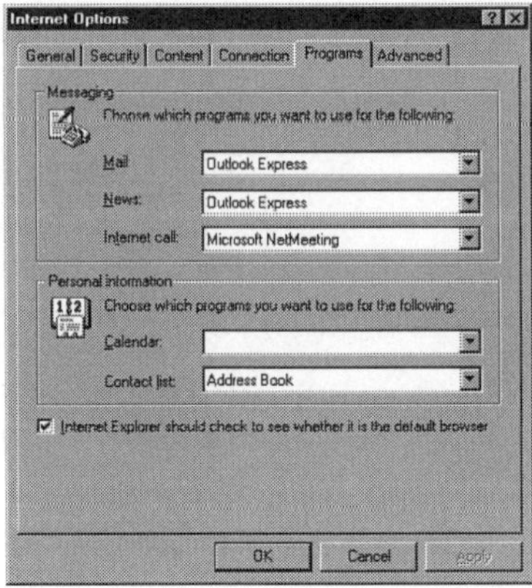

TIME SAVER

Outlook Express is smart and recognizes whether you've already set up another email program before installing Windows 98. If you see the dialog box in Figure 17.2 the first time you use Outlook Express to send or receive a message, Outlook Express offers to use your previous email program's messages and addresses so you don't have to re-enter them. Follow the Wizard to load any or all of your previous program's options.

Figure 17.2.
Outlook Express will import your messages and addresses from your former email program.

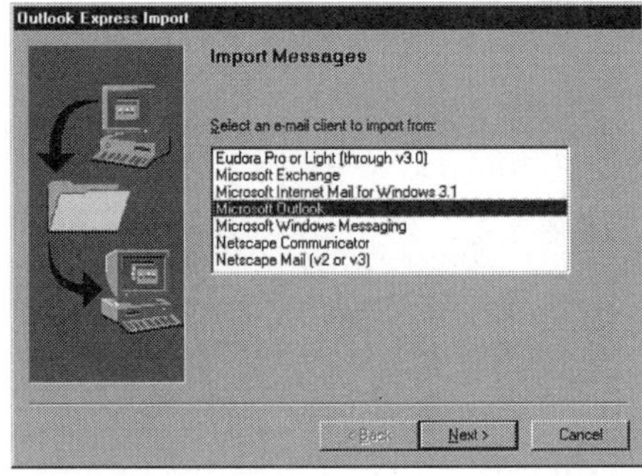

Step 3: Review

After you've told Internet Explorer that you want to use Outlook Express as your email program, Internet Explorer remembers your setup and uses Outlook Express every time you send or receive email.

To Do

Task 17.2: Sending Mail with Outlook Express

Step 1: Description

This task explains how to send various forms of email to recipients. Outlook Express has many options, but you can send email messages and files to others very easily without worrying too much about what else is under Outlook Express's hood.

Step 2: Action

1. Start Internet Explorer and sign into your Internet account.
2. Click the toolbar's Mail button and select New Message from the menu that drops down. (You can also click the Windows 98 Taskbar's Outlook Express icon if you've displayed the Quick Launch toolbar.) The New Message dialog box opens, as shown in Figure 17.3.

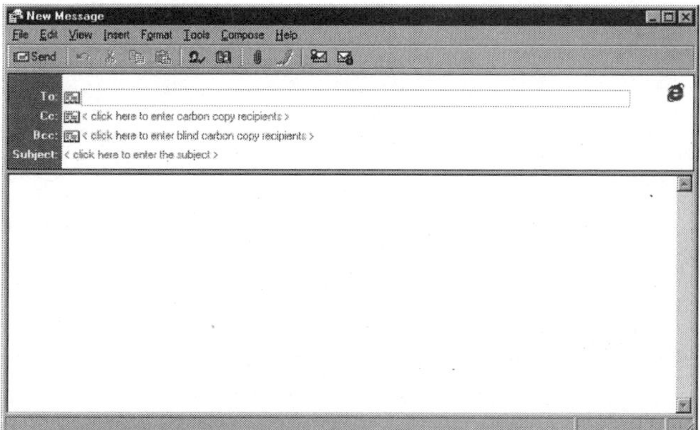

Figure 17.3.
You can now send a message to one or more recipients.

3. Enter your recipient's email address in the To field or click the file card icon next to the To field to select the field. If you know the name under which you stored an email address in the Windows Address Book, you can type the name instead of the email address in the To field.
4. Use the Cc ("Carbon copy") field to send copies of your message to another recipient. The recipient will know that the message was copied to him or her. If you enter an email address in the Bcc ("Blind carbon copy") field, the To and Cc recipients will not know that the Bcc recipients got copies of the message.
5. Enter a subject line. Get in the habit of entering a subject so your recipients can file your messages by subject.
6. Press the Tab or Shift+Tab key to move from field to field. When you type the message in the message area, the scroll bar appears to enable you to scroll through messages that don't fit inside the window completely. Use the formatting toolbar above the message area to apply formatting, color, and even numbered and bulleted

lists to your message. You must be careful, however, to make sure that your recipients have an email program capable of reading all the formatting that Outlook Express can produce; unless you send plain text messages, your recipient may not be able to read your message clearly without Outlook Express or a fully compatible email program.

7. If you want to attach one or more files to your message, click the Attach toolbar button (the one with the paper clip) and select your file from the Insert Attachment dialog box that appears, as shown in Figure 17.4.

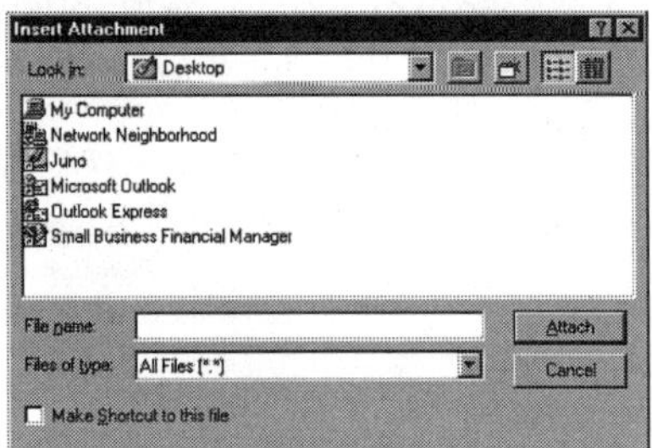

Figure 17.4.
Select the file or files you want to send along with your message.

8. To send the message, click the Send button (the toolbar button with the flying envelope) and the message goes on its way toward the recipients.

Step 3: Review

Sending email messages and files requires only that you know the person's email address or that you've stored the address in your Windows Address book. Attach files of any type to your message and the recipient will receive the message and the files.

Task 17.3: Sending Web Pages as Email

Step 1: Description

This task explains how to send Web pages to email recipients.

Step 2: Action

1. Start Internet Explorer and sign into your Internet account.
2. Display the Web page that you want to send to somebody. (You can send the page to your own email account for a test.)
3. Click the toolbar's Mail button.
4. Select Send Page. If the Web page is complicated, it may be considered a read-only Web page that cannot be edited. If so, Internet Explorer displays a message telling you that your recipient may receive the message as an attached file or as a read-only file. In this case, if you are sending the page to yourself or to someone you know has Internet Explorer, send the page as a read-only page.
5. The email window opens so that you can select a recipient and add copies to others if you like. You can see the Web page at the bottom of the window as shown in Figure 17.5. Now *that's* quite a fancy email message!

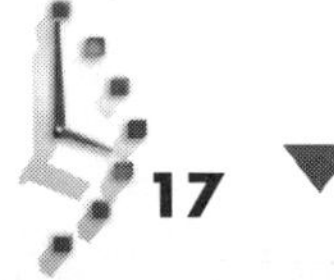

Figure 17.5.
The recipient will see the Web page when viewing this email.

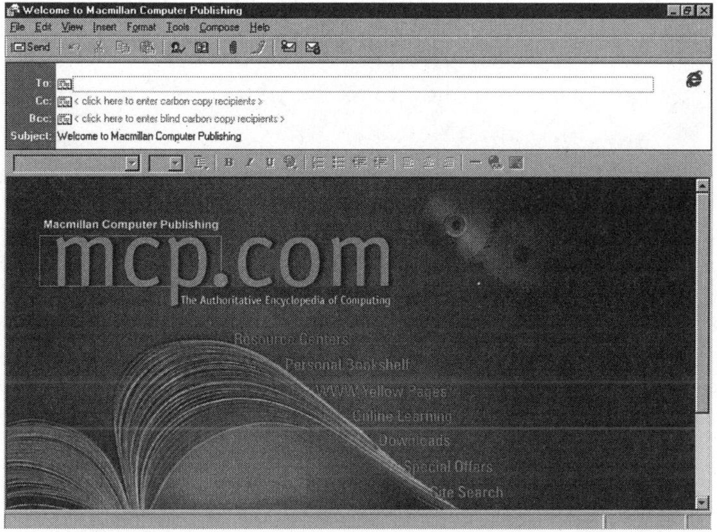

6. Click the Send button to send the Web page.

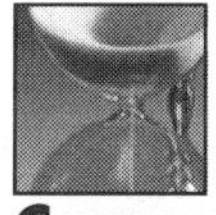

CAUTION

Remember that your recipient must also use an email program, such as Outlook Express, that can display HTML code, or the recipient will get a lot of garbage in the message. Your recipient will still be able to read the mail's text, but the email will be messed up due to all the HTML formatting codes that the recipient will see that are normally hidden. You can convert HTML pages to straight text from the Format menu.

Step 3: Review

If you locate a Web site you want someone else to see, send that site to the person via email. Internet Explorer's Mail toolbar button contains a menu option that makes sending Web pages to others a breeze.

TIME SAVER

One of the reasons that the Internet is slower than it has to be is that people send great amounts of information, sometimes needlessly. Although the transmission of Web pages is a good feature, if you can send just the Web page address, instead of the entire page, your email will arrive more quickly and your recipient can browse that address with an Internet browser program such as Internet Explorer. Some Web page content changes frequently, however, and you may want to send a snapshot of the page to a friend, in which case the ability to send a Web page is useful.

Task 17.4: Receiving Email

Step 1: Description

This task explains how to receive your email that people send to you.

Step 2: Action

1. Start Internet Explorer and sign into your Internet account.
2. Click the toolbar's Mail button.
3. Select Read Mail. The mail center window appears, as shown in Figure 17.6.

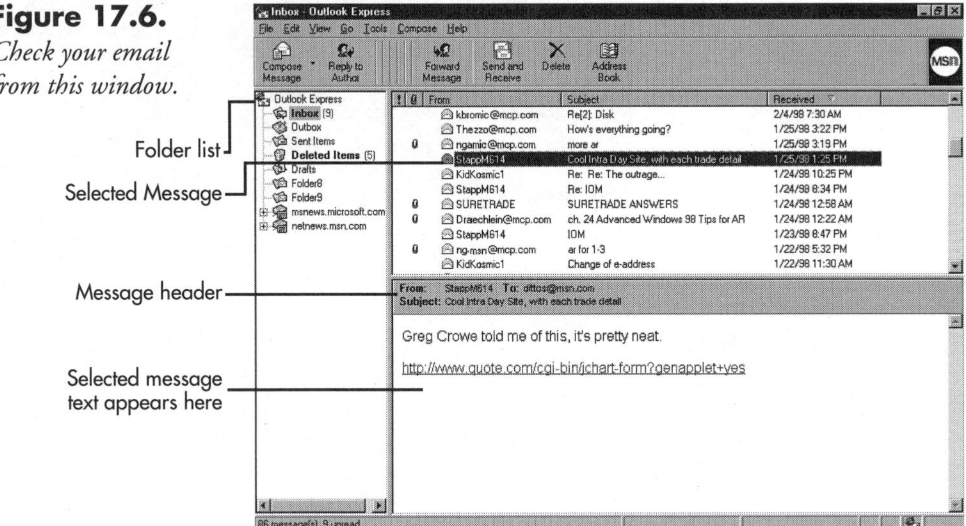

Figure 17.6.
Check your email from this window.

Email comes to your *Inbox* (the preview area) at regular intervals, but Outlook Express does not constantly check for new mail or your Internet connection would slow down due to the mail check. At any time, you can manually check for new mail and send any that has yet to be sent by clicking the toolbar's Send and Receive button. You don't have to be signed onto the Internet to create email.

Time Saver

Select Tools | Options and enter a new time value for the option labeled Check for new messages every *10* minutes if you want Outlook Express to check for incoming email more or less often than the 10-minute default.

The Outbox area (you can click on the Folder list to see your Outbox contents) holds items that you've readied to send but that have not actually gone out yet. When your Outbox contains unsent mail, the icon changes to show mail in the Outbox.

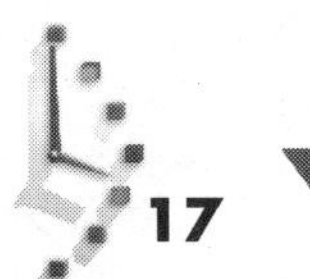

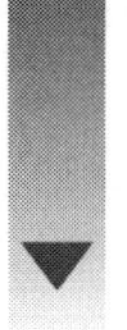

4. As you click on the headers in the Inbox, a preview appears for that message in the lower pane. (Drag the center bar up or down to make more or less room for the headers.) If you double-click on an Inbox item, a window opens so you can view that message from a larger window without the other screen elements getting in the way.
5. Delete mail you do not want by selecting one or more message headers and dragging them to the Deleted Items icon. Deleted Items acts like the Windows 98 Recycle Bin. Mail does not really go away until you delete items from the Deleted Items area by clicking on the Deleted Items icon and removing unwanted mail.
6. You can easily reply to a message's author, or to the entire group if you are one of several who was sent mail, by clicking the Reply to Author or Reply to All toolbar button. In addition, when reading email, you can compose a new message by clicking on the toolbar's Compose Message button.

TIME SAVER

Create new folders in the Folder list column so that you can organize your email the way you want it. Right-click over the bar and select New Folder. For example, you may want to create a new folder that holds business correspondence and one for personal email. You can drag messages to either location to put mail with others that match the same purpose.

Step 3: Review

Receiving email with Outlook Express is easier than going to your front porch mailbox! From Internet Explorer you click the Mail icon and read your Inbox message headers. A *header* is the message's sender ID and subject that you see from the Inbox.

TIME SAVER

When you're in Outlook Express, click the Folder list's icon labeled Outlook Express to see the one-click Outlook Express window shown in Figure 17.7. From this window you can easily read and compose email, modify your Microsoft Address Book entries, locate people, and check newsgroups. (The next section describes newsgroup access.)

Using Newsgroups

In a way, a newsgroup acts like a combination of a slow email program and a community bulletin board. Newsgroups have little or nothing to do with the daily news. Newsgroups are thousands of lists, arranged by subject, that hold messages and files that you and others can post and read.

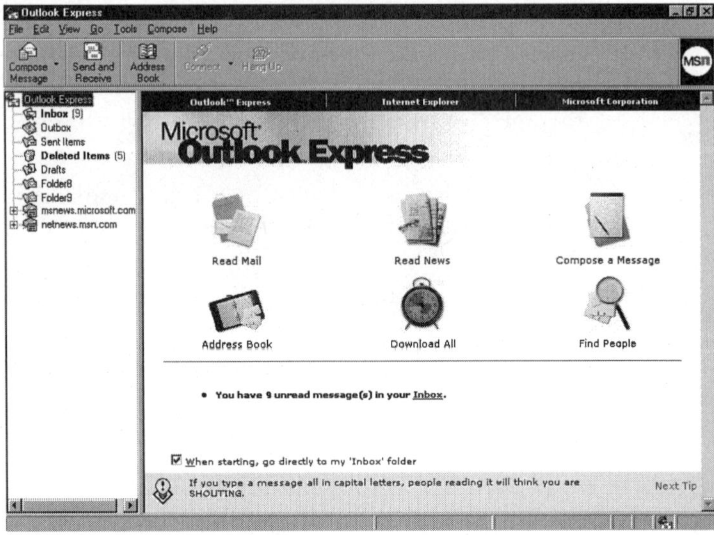

Figure 17.7.
The Outlook Express folder shows this one-step usage screen.

Suppose you are interested in roller-blading and want to trade information you have with others who are interested in the sport. You could find one of the several newsgroups related to roller-blading and read the hundreds of messages and files posted to that newsgroup. Depending on the Internet service you use and the newsgroup filing rules, you may find messages months old or only from the past few days. Often, the larger newsgroups can keep only a limited number of days' worth of messages and files in the newsgroup.

This is how newsgroups act like slow email services: If someone has posted a question you know the answer to, you can post a reply. Your reply will be seen by all in the newsgroup who want to read the reply. There is no guarantee that the person who submitted the question will ever go back to the newsgroup to read the answer, but the postings are for anybody and everybody who is interested.

Each Internet ISP provides access to a different number of the thousands and thousands of newsgroups in existence. To see newsgroups available to your service, click Internet Explorer's Mail button and select Read News. Although your ISP may give you access to thousands of newsgroups, subscribe just to those that interest you. Click Outlook Express' Newsgroups button to display the Newsgroups listing dialog box, as shown in Figure 17.8.

You may see one or more news servers in the left column. Each news server contains a different set of newsgroups. Your ISP determines the number of servers that appear in the news server column. When you click on a server, the list of newsgroups that reside on that server appears in the center of the window.

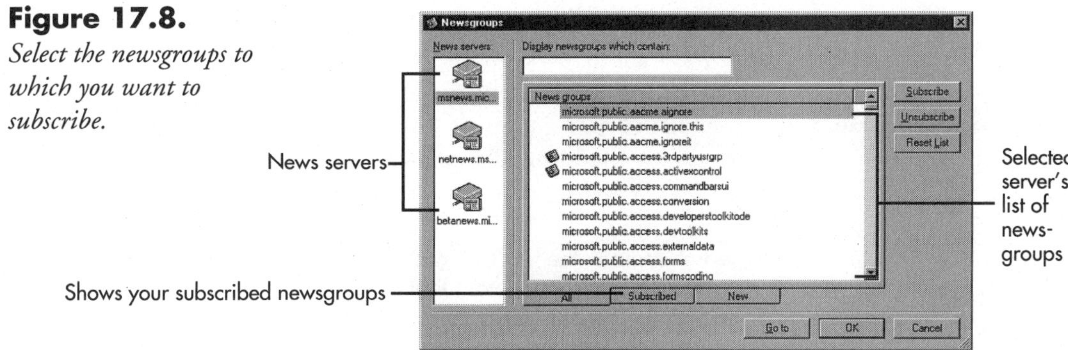

Figure 17.8.
Select the newsgroups to which you want to subscribe.

CAUTION

> Bear in mind that some servers contain thousands of newsgroups, and the first time you access a news server, that list downloads from the server to your PC, so you can quickly scroll through the list in subsequent sessions. This download process may take a few minutes, as indicated by the dialog box that appears during the download.

The newsgroups have strange names, such as `rec.pets.dogs` and `alt.algebra.help`. Table 17.1 describes what the more common newsgroup prefixes, the first part of the name, stand for. Somewhere else in the newsgroup name you can often glean more information about the newsgroup's primary topic; for example, a newsgroup named `rec.sport.skating.roller` would probably contain skating news, and `alt.autos.italian` would contain files and messages pertaining to Italian cars (*i macchina l'italiani!*).

Table 17.1. Common newsgroup prefixes describe the nature of the newsgroup.

Prefix	Description
`alt`	Groups that allow for informal content and are not necessarily as widely distributed as the other newsgroups
`biz`	Business-related newsgroups
`comp`	Computer-related newsgroups
`misc`	Random newsgroups
`rec`	Recreational and sporting newsgroups
`sci`	Scientific newsgroups
`soc`	Social issue–related newsgroups
`talk`	Debate newsgroups

Scroll through the newsgroup list to find the newsgroups you want to see. When you find one or more newsgroups you want to see, subscribe to those newsgroups by double-clicking on the newsgroup name (or highlight the name and click Subscribe). If you click the Subscribe tab, you see the list of newsgroups to which you've subscribed. Click the OK button to close the Newsgroups window and prepare to read the news.

TIME SAVER

> Enter a search topic in the text box at the top of the Newsgroups window to display newsgroups that contain that topic. As you type more of the topic to search for, the list below the textbox shrinks to include only those newsgroups that include the text you enter.

Task 17.5: Reading and Posting Newsgroup News

Step 1: Description

This task explains how to read newsgroup messages and post messages to the newsgroups. Keep in mind that a message might be a short note or an entire file. As with email, if a news posting contains a file, the file will come as an attachment to the message.

Step 2: Action

1. Start Internet Explorer and sign into your Internet account.
2. Click the toolbar's Mail button.
3. Select Read News. A list of your subscribed newsgroups appears, as shown in Figure 17.9.

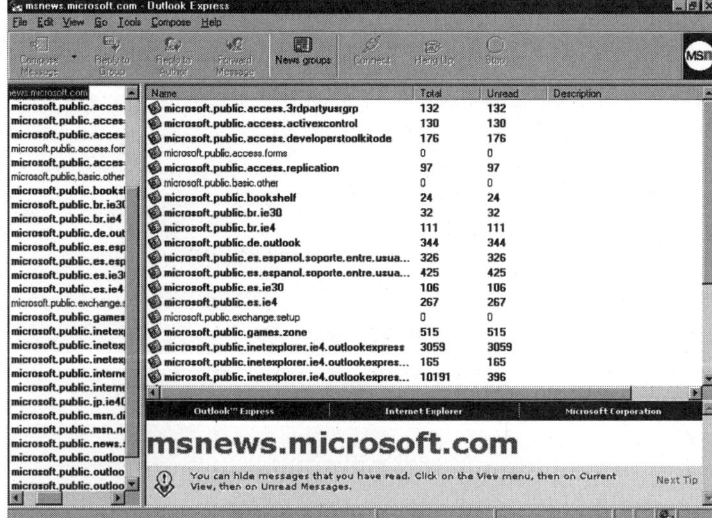

Figure 17.9.
Your subscribed newsgroup messages appear when you first request newsgroup access.

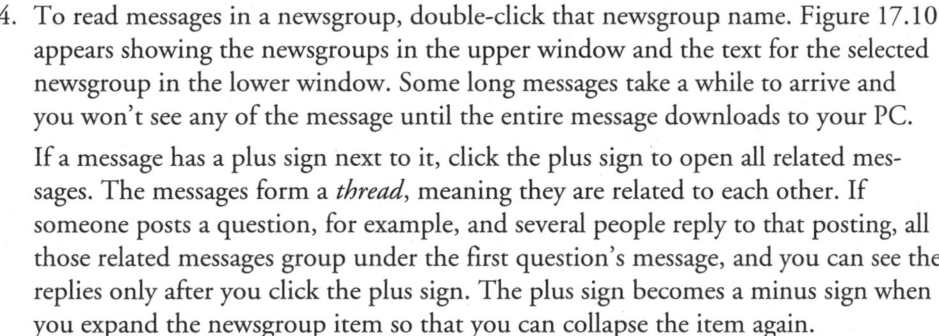

4. To read messages in a newsgroup, double-click that newsgroup name. Figure 17.10 appears showing the newsgroups in the upper window and the text for the selected newsgroup in the lower window. Some long messages take a while to arrive and you won't see any of the message until the entire message downloads to your PC.

   If a message has a plus sign next to it, click the plus sign to open all related messages. The messages form a *thread*, meaning they are related to each other. If someone posts a question, for example, and several people reply to that posting, all those related messages group under the first question's message, and you can see the replies only after you click the plus sign. The plus sign becomes a minus sign when you expand the newsgroup item so that you can collapse the item again.

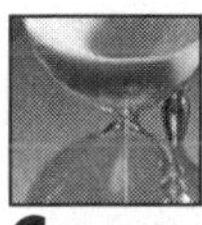

CAUTION

> Some newsgroups are moderated better than others. You'll often find unrelated messages throughout all newsgroups that don't belong within that newsgroup.

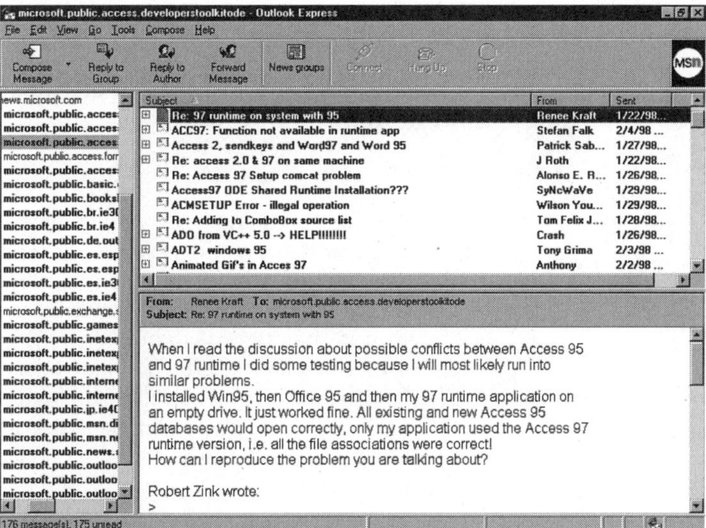

Figure 17.10.
Scroll through the news message headers and see detail in the lower window.

5. Check the Size column to determine whether you can read the message in the lower window or whether you should open up a new window to view the message. If a message is over 2 or 3 kilobytes, you should probably double-click the message header to view the message inside a scrollable window. The window contains a menu that enables you to save the message in a file on your disk for later retrieval. If a message has an attachment, you must open the message in a separate window to save the attachment as a file on your disk.

After you read a message inside the preview pane, you can click another message header to view another message. If you view a message in a separate window, you can close the window to view a different message.

6. If you want to reply to a message, you have two options: reply to the group, in which case everybody who subscribes to the newsgroup can read your reply (which is the general idea of newsgroups), or reply to the author privately via email. The Reply to Group and Reply to Author toolbar buttons accomplish these purposes. Each copies the original message at the bottom of your reply.

   You don't have to reply to existing messages. You can also start a new message *thread* (related postings) by clicking the Compose Message button and typing a new message. Your message appears in the newsgroup as a new post and not part of a chain of previous postings.

Step 3: Review

Probably the biggest problem with newsgroups is the time you waste in them! You may hop over to a newsgroup to see whether the group contains an answer you need, and two hours later you're still reading the postings there. Newsgroups can provide a wealth of information on thousands and thousands of topics. Although the Web is great for organizing information into collections of pages, newsgroups are useful for the straight messages and files that people want to share with each other.

CAUTION

Given that people can post newsgroup messages anonymously, you'll find all kinds of comments on the newsgroups, and not all will pertain to the topic. Some will contain some surprising subject matter, comments, and complaints as well. You may want to visit a newsgroup and read several of its messages before posting any of your own. Some newsgroups, especially those with *moderated* in their titles, have some posting rules that you'll want to familiarize yourself with. If you see a newsgroup message with the word *FAQ* in its title, that message probably contains *Frequently Asked Questions* about the newsgroup and about the kinds of postings that are accepted.

Summary

This hour explained how to use Outlook Express, Internet Explorer's email program and newsgroup manager. Email is a major part of the Internet user's life these days and you'll appreciate Outlook Express's advanced support and email management simplicity.

If you want detailed information on a subject, you can search the Web for all kinds of data, but remember to look for related newsgroups as well. Whereas some Web sites are often

consumer-related collections of merchandise and hype, newsgroups often contain thousands of messages from people such as you who have questions and answers for others with the same interest.

Q&A

Q How can I get email from my multiple Internet accounts?

A If you subscribe to multiple online services or to multiple ISPs, you can set up Outlook Express to send and retrieve email from all your Internet accounts. Select Tools | Accounts to display the Internet Accounts dialog box. Select Add | Mail and follow the Wizard to add your accounts to the email. You will almost surely have to contact your ISP to get the Wizard's requested information. After you set up the accounts, Outlook Express will check each one when you request new mail.

Q I read a newsgroup message last month that I can no longer find in the newsgroup. How can I see old messages?

A Often you cannot. Each news server holds a limited number of messages (your news server has only so much disk space!). Often, Outlook Express downloads, at most, 300 messages at any one time. Sometimes the server will have more than 300 messages available. To request that Outlook Express retrieve additional messages, select Tools | Get Next 300 Headers. If more than 300 messages are available, Outlook Express will download up to 300 more. By the way, you can change the number of messages that Outlook Express downloads, from 1 to 1,000, by changing the number from the Tools | Options menu item on the Read dialog box page.

Workshop

Term Review

binary data Compressed data, such as programs and graphics, as opposed to text files.

header The Inbox's one-line display that shows incoming messages' sender, subject, and date received.

Inbox The Outlook Express folder that holds your incoming email.

Outbox The Outlook Express folder that holds your outgoing email that has yet to be sent. After Outlook Express sends the message, the Sent items folder holds a copy of the message.

Outlook Express A Windows 98 program that manages both your email and newsgroup access.

read-only Web page A Web page that contains frames and other advanced HTML code that cannot be changed.

Sent items folder The Outlook Express folder that holds all messages that have been sent over the Internet from you.

thread A set of postings that go together, such as a question and the answer replies.

`Windows Exchange` A pre–Windows Messaging program used by earlier versions of Windows to manage email.

`Windows Messaging` A program used by earlier Windows versions to manage email.

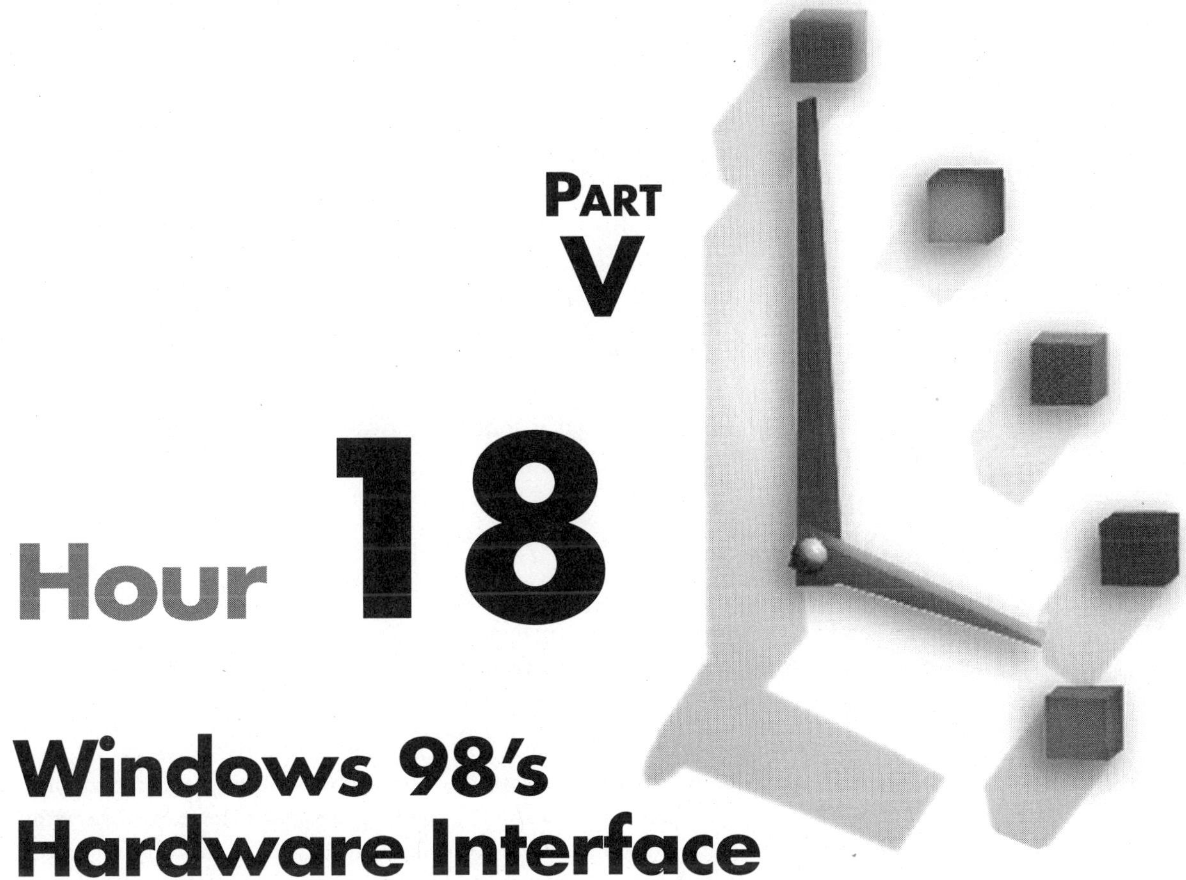

Part V

Hour 18

Windows 98's Hardware Interface

This hour shows how the Windows 98 interface supports your hardware. Windows 98 supports *Plug and Play*, a term that describes automatic installation of new hardware you add to your PC. Before Windows, you had to set jumper switches and make operating system settings. Often, hardware and software conflicts would occur, creating many hours of debugging headaches. With Plug and Play, you simply plug new hardware components (memory, disk drives, CD-ROM drives, and expansion boards) into your computer, and Windows 98 immediately recognizes the change and sets everything up properly.

Plug and Play requires almost no thought when installing new hardware to your system. At least that's the theory. In reality, you may still encounter problems, as this hour explains. If Plug and Play does not perform as expected, Windows 98 provides a hardware setup wizard that you can use to walk you through the new hardware's proper installation.

Windows 98 has not only made it easier to change hardware on one system, but it also contains a program that aids you in changing entire machines! Many people work on multiple PCs. Perhaps you have a laptop and also a desktop computer. Perhaps you work both at home and at the office. Whatever your situation, the Windows 98 *Briefcase* will help you synchronize your document files so they remain as current as possible.

The highlights of this hour include the following:

- What Plug and Play is all about
- Which components must be in place for Plug and Play to work
- How Plug and Play benefits both you and hardware companies
- How to use the Hardware Wizard to add special hardware that requires more than Plug and Play
- How direct cable connection makes connecting two computers virtually trouble-free

Plug and Play

Some computer users actually refer to Plug and Play as *Plug and Pray*; these users are actually making a good point. Despite the industry hype over Plug and Play, it does not always work. If you attempt to install an older board into your computer, Windows 98 might not recognize the board, and you could have all kinds of hardware problems that take time to correct.

Things do not always go right when installing non–Plug and Play hardware. (New hardware that supports Plug and Play often has a seal with *PnP* on the box indicating its compatibility.) You often have to set certain hardware switches correctly. You may also have to move certain jumpers so that electrical lines on your new hardware flow properly to work with your specific computer. The new hardware can conflict with existing hardware in your machine. Most hardware devices, such as video and sound boards, often require new software support contained in small files called drivers that you must install and test.

JUST A MINUTE

Hardware designed before the invention of Plug and Play specifications is called *legacy hardware.*

Before Plug and Play can work in Windows 98, these two Plug and Play items must be in place:

- A Basic Input Output System (called the *BIOS*) in your computer's system unit that is compatible with Plug and Play. The computer manual's technical specifications or technical support should tell you whether the BIOS is compatible with Plug and Play. Fortunately, virtually all PCs sold since early 1996 have supported Plug and Play.
- A device to install that is compatible with Plug and Play

You are running Windows 98, which is compatible with Plug and Play. If you do not have the Plug and Play BIOS inside your computer (most computers made before 1994 have no

form of Plug and Play compatibility at all), you have to help Windows 98 with the installation process by answering some questions posed by a new hardware setup wizard. When you purchase new hardware in the future, try to purchase only hardware rated for Plug and Play compatibility.

Time Saver

One key in knowing whether the hardware is designed for Plug and Play is to make sure the Windows 98 logo appears on the new hardware's box or instructions. Before a hardware vendor can sell a product with the Windows 98 logo, that product must offer some level of Plug and Play compatibility. If you have older hardware already installed under a version of Windows when you install Windows 98, you will not have to reinstall this hardware.

If you run Windows 98, own a computer with a Plug and Play BIOS, and purchase only Plug and Play hardware, the most you usually have to do is turn off the computer, install the hardware, and turn the computer back on. Everything should work fine after that.

18

Just a Minute

Although most hardware sold today supports Plug and Play, some notable exceptions do not. For example, the Iomega Jaz and Zip high-capacity drives require several non–Plug and Play steps that you must go through to install these devices (the parallel port versions are simpler but are slower in their operation).

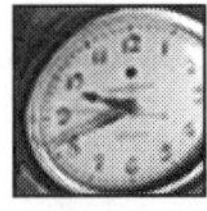

Windows Minute

Moving from Plug and Play to Play and Play!

The Plug and Play standard should help both you and computer companies. Think of these benefits, if Plug and Play delivers as designed:

- Installing new hardware will no longer be troublesome.
- You will have less computer downtime and will be able to get back to work faster. (Hey, wait a minute... Perhaps we should rethink this Plug and Play business!)
- Hardware companies will have to staff fewer technical support people.
- Hardware companies will not have to buy as many support phone lines.
- Hardware companies will be able to cut costs.
- Hardware products will come down in price, due to the decrease in the support costs just mentioned.
- You will have more money in your pocket to vacation in Italy!

Plug and Play works both for newly installed hardware and for removed hardware. If you remove a sound card that you no longer want, or remove memory and replace that memory with a higher capacity memory, Plug and Play ought to recognize the removal and reconfigure the computer and operating system automatically. Again, Plug and Play is not always perfect and does not always operate as expected, but as long as you run a Plug-and-Play BIOS and install Plug and Play hardware, there should be little installation trouble ahead for you.

JUST A MINUTE

> Plug and Play does not make legacy hardware obsolete. If you install Windows 98 in a computer that has older non–Plug and Play legacy hardware, Windows 98 and the hardware should work fine together, although sometimes you may have to change your PC's BIOS setup as described in your hardware's installation instructions.

Windows 98 Offers Hardware Help

If you install hardware and find that Windows 98 does not properly recognize the change, double-click the Add New Hardware icon in the Control Panel window. Windows 98 starts the Add New Hardware Wizard, shown in Figure 18.1, which helps walk you through the installation process.

Figure 18.1.
The Add New Hardware Wizard helps you install non–Plug and Play hardware.

The Wizard goes through a series of tests and attempts to detect the newly added hardware. Remember that Windows 98 recognizes most Plug and Play hardware; that is, when you install a new graphics card, for example, then restart Windows 98, Windows 98 recognizes the graphics card and configures itself for use with your new card. Nevertheless, Windows 98 cannot automatically recognize all Plug and Play hardware. The Wizard, therefore, first analyzes your system in detail, looking for hardware that is Plug and Play but unrecognized from the second Add New Hardware Wizard dialog box page, shown in Figure 18.2.

Figure 18.2.
The Add New Hardware Wizard helps you install non–Plug and Play hardware.

You can elect to have the Add New Hardware Wizard search for the new Plug and Play hardware, or you can select the hardware from the list of vendors and products Windows 98 offers. Of course, if your hardware is newer than Windows 98, Windows 98 will not list your specific hardware.

CAUTION

> You can let the Add New Hardware Wizard search for the new hardware, and if the Wizard does not recognize the hardware, you can select from the list of devices.

Be sure to read your new hardware's installation documentation thoroughly before you begin the installation. Often the new hardware comes with updated drivers that fix minor bugs and add features to drivers that Windows 98 already includes. Therefore, instead of letting the Wizard search for the new device, and instead of selecting from the list of supported devices (shown in Figure 18.3), you use a disk or CD-ROM that comes with the new hardware to add the latest hardware support for the device to Windows 98. Therefore, you have to click the dialog box's Have Disk button and select the hardware's disk or CD-ROM location to complete the installation.

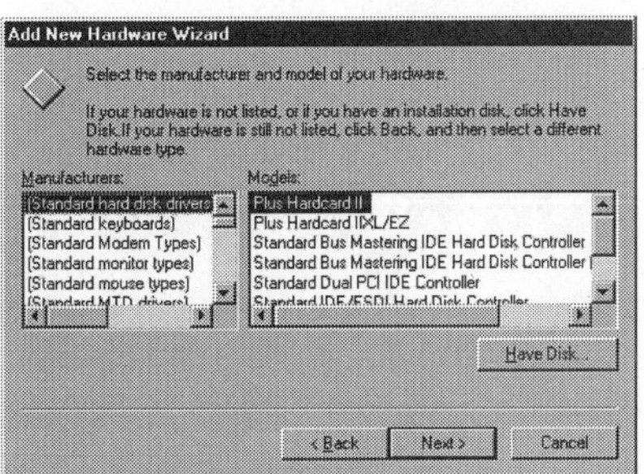

Figure 18.3.
Select from the list of known hardware or use your hardware's own installation disk.

CAUTION

> If you add a new modem to a serial port or a printer to a parallel port, you should not run the Add New Hardware Wizard. The Wizard works only for hardware you physically connect to the system unit, such as a disk drive or graphics card. If you plug a modem into an existing serial port, that serial port will already be installed, so you don't need to run Add New Hardware. You will, however, have to double-click the Control Panel's Modems icon and select your modem from the list of modems displayed.

If you have a laptop or desktop with a PC card (PC cards are sometimes called PCMCIA cards), you can plug PCMCIA cards directly into the laptop, changing a PC card hard disk to a PC card modem, and Windows 98 will adjust itself automatically. Hour 19, "Using Windows 98 on the Road," explains more about mobile computing and the hardware issues you'll encounter.

WINDOWS MINUTE

> **Additional Hardware Support**
>
> Windows 98 uses a Registry and hardware tree to keep track of the current and changeable hardware configuration. The Registry is a central repository of all possible hardware information for your computer. The hardware tree is a collection of hardware configurations, taken from parts or all of the Registry, for your computer. (In addition, your Registry holds software settings.)
>
> Luckily, you don't have to know anything about the Registry, because Windows 98 keeps track of the details for you. If, however, you want to look at the hardware tree currently in place on your computer, you can display the Control Panel, double-click the System icon, and choose the Device Manager page. Windows 98 displays the System Properties tabbed dialog box, shown in Figure 18.4. The hardware tree shows the devices currently in use.

Setting Up a Second PC

When you purchase a second PC, such as a laptop or a second home PC, you'll probably want to transfer files from your current PC to the new one. For example, you may have data files on the current PC that you want to place on the new one. Windows 98 supports a feature called Direct Cable Connection that lets you transfer files between computers without the need of a network and without moving data between the PCs via disk.

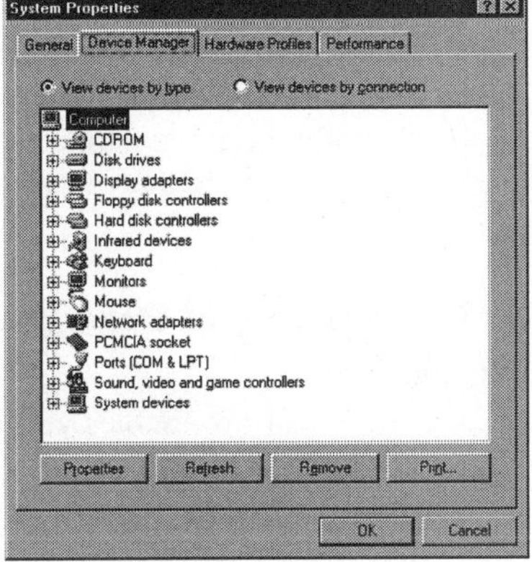

Figure 18.4.
The Device Manager page in the System Properties dialog box.

JUST A MINUTE

Hour 19 describes a wireless method for transferring files via new infrared devices.

If you attach a high-speed parallel or serial cable between two computers, those computers can share files and printer resources with one another. This is a simple replacement for an expensive network if you want only two computers to share resources.

The Direct Cable Connection option should be available in the Accessories menu. (If the Direct Cable Connection option is not installed, run the Windows Setup option from the Control Panel's Add/Remove Programs icon if you need to install Direct Cable Connection.) When you select Direct Cable Connection, Windows 98 initiates the wizard shown in Figure 18.5. After answering the wizard's prompts, your two computers will be linked, as Task 18.1 describes next.

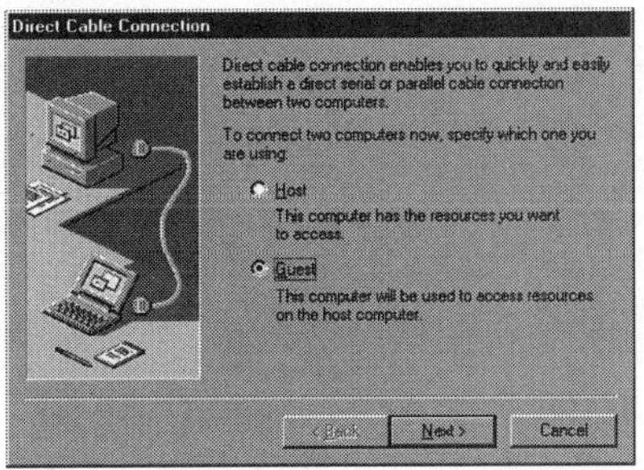

Figure 18.5.
The Accessories menu contains the Direct Cable Connection Wizard.

Just a Minute

> The two computers connected using a direct cable connection must use the same type of port. Therefore, you must connect two parallel ports with a bidirectional parallel cable or two serial ports with a null-modem cable. You cannot connect a parallel port to a serial port.

Task 18.1: Making a Direct Cable Connection

Step 1: Description

The Direct Cable Connection enables you to easily transfer files between two computers using both computers' parallel or serial ports. After you connect the two machines with the cable, you must start the Direct Cable Connection Wizard, select the sending and receiving computer, and select the files you want to send over the cable connection.

Step 2: Action

1. Connect your two computers with the cable.
2. Select the Start menu's Programs | Accessories | Communications | Direct Cable Connection option on both PCs to display the wizard's opening window, shown in Figure 18.5.
3. Select one PC as the host and one as the guest by clicking the appropriate options on the wizard's first page. The host is the PC from which you'll transfer the file (or files), and the guest receives those files. After you designate a host and guest, you cannot send information in the other direction without restarting the wizard.
4. Click the Next button to select the port on which you've connected the computers from the dialog box that appears in Figure 18.6. You'll have to select the port on each PC.

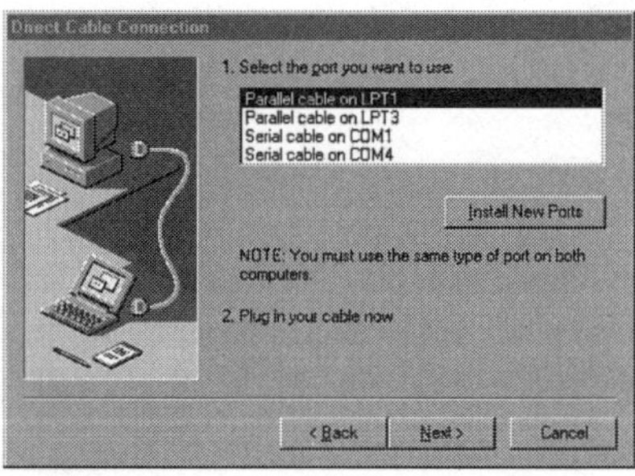

Figure 18.6.
Tell the wizard which port the cable connects to.

5. Click the Next button on both PCs so that the Finish button appears in the guest's window. The host dialog box will display a button labeled File and Print Sharing. Click this button to give access to both your files and printer from any guest PC that connects.

6. Click the host's File and Print Sharing button to specify whether you want to share files, your printer, or both. If you've never specified printer or file sharing, you may find that the host PC's wizard requires a system reboot to work after you've determined the file and printer sharing access. If so, you can restart the host PC's wizard and return to the final dialog box described in the next step without making a change on the waiting guest PC.
7. Click OK to return the host PC to the Direct Cable Connection Wizard.
8. If you want to require a password from the guest PC before allowing file or printer sharing (sometimes this is helpful when more than one person uses a computer connected to another's), click the Use password protection option and click Set Password to enter a password that the guest PC user will type to gain access.
9. Click Finish to make the connection. If the two PCs recognize each other, you've made the connection properly. Otherwise, you may have to check cable connections and rerun the Wizard to ensure that all the options are set (for example, you'll want to make sure that both PCs are not set as host or both as guest).
10. The guest's Windows Explorer or My Computer window now holds an icon for the host PC, and you can transfer files from the host as easily as you can transfer from one of your disks to another. In addition, the guest's application programs can now print to the host printer because the host printer will be available from all File | Print dialog boxes.

Step 3: Review

The Direct Cable Connection provides a way for you to connect two computers to use the files and printer on one (the host) by the other (the guest). The Direct Cable Connection enables the guest computer to share the host's file and printer resources without requiring expensive and more elaborate networking hardware and software.

JUST A MINUTE

After you set up a host or guest PC, your subsequent use of Direct Cable Connection is easier. You then have to specify the dialog box settings only if you change computers or if you decide to change directions and switch between the host and guest when transferring files. Figure 18.7 shows the dialog box that appears when you start the host's Direct Cable Connection Wizard after you initially set up the connection.

Figure 18.7.
Tell the wizard which port the cable connects to. The next time you use the cable connection, you don't have to specify a cable or port.

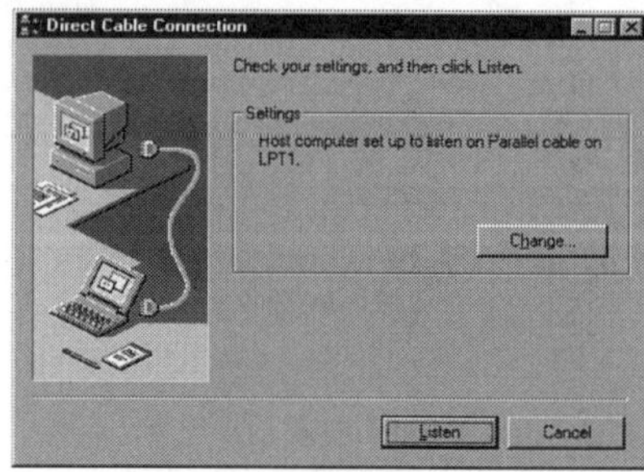

CAUTION

Do not use the Direct Cable Connection to transfer Windows 98 application programs from one PC to another. Windows 98 applications, unfortunately, are spread all over your disk and not located in a single disk folder. If you transfer a folder with a program from one PC to another, the odds are high that you will be unable to run that program on the second PC. As mentioned in the previous section, the system Registry contains important hardware information, but the Registry is also a repository for your applications. The Registry gets its information from your application's installation routine. When you want the same application on both PCs, run the application's installation routine on the second PC just as you did originally. Transfer only data files from one PC to the other.

WINDOWS MINUTE

Keep Your File Dates Organized

Sometimes, especially when you often transfer files between a desktop and laptop, the files can get out of synchronization. You can easily end up with the same filenames but each with different material, based on which PC you've most recently worked on. Generally, you want to work with the latest version of a file, but comparing dates and times yourself is tedious and error-prone. The My Briefcase option described in Hour 19 helps solve that problem by making the time and date comparisons for you and refreshing any set of files that need refreshing to make sure both systems have the latest versions of document files.

Summary

This hour got fairly technical during the discussion of hardware. An operating system must run through several operations before it can recognize and work with new hardware. Fortunately, the Plug and Play process makes such work slightly easier and sometimes trouble-free.

If you do not use 100 percent Plug and Play hardware, the Add New Hardware Wizard will walk you through each installation and help make the hardware easier to install. Suppose, for example, you add an internal modem, but you cannot communicate with it. The Add New Hardware Wizard may realize that you have a new internal modem after running through its series of tests, but may not be able to determine exactly what kind of internal modem you have. You and the wizard together should be able to determine the proper configuration.

The Direct Cable Connection Wizard means that you'll be connecting more computers than ever before. You'll be able to transfer files and share printers easily from one to the other by attaching a cable between the parallel or serial ports of each machine.

Q&A

Q How do I know whether I have Plug and Play?

A You have Windows 98, which means that installing hardware ought to be easier than with previous operating systems and earlier versions of Windows. Perhaps the best way to see whether you have Plug and Play is to plug the next device you get for your computer into the computer, power on your machine, and see what happens. (Of course, you should read the new hardware's installation instructions to learn the correct way to install the device.)

If you turn on your computer and the computer responds to the new device properly, you have, for all intents and purposes, all the Plug and Play compatibility you need. You have Plug and Play, at least, for that one device. Just because Windows 98 and your BIOS are compatible with Plug and Play, however, does not mean that the hardware you install will also be compatible with Plug and Play. Some hardware might be compatible with Plug and Play and some may not.

Q I don't want to buy and install a network in my house, but how do I easily connect my laptop to my desktop to share files between them?

A Use the Windows 98 Direct Cable Connection. Connect a parallel or serial cable to both parallel or serial ports. Your laptop will be able to access the desktop's shared files. As simple as the Direct Cable Connection is, if your laptop contains an infrared port, you'll learn in Hour 19 how to share files between the laptop and another device without the need of wires.

Workshop

Term Review

BIOS Basic Input Output System. The system unit's ROM-based code that handles I/O devices.

direct cable connection The connection between two computers with a cable attached to both parallel or serial ports.

drivers Software files that often accompany hardware to tell the computer how to control the hardware when you install it.

guest The computer that uses files and printer resources, accessed by cable, in the Direct Cable Connection Wizard.

hardware tree A collection of hardware configurations, taken from parts or all of the Registry, that your computer may require.

host The computer that supplies the file and printer resources shared by guest computers in using the Direct Cable Connection.

I/O Input and output.

legacy Older hardware that was designed before engineers invented the Plug and Play specification.

Plug and Play The name Microsoft gives to hardware that you can install without making any hardware or software changes. The Windows 98 Plug and Play feature takes care of setting up things correctly for you.

Registry A central repository of all possible information for your hardware.

Part V

Hour 19

Using Windows 98 on the Road

This hour shows how Windows 98 supports mobile computing environments. If you use a laptop, you'll appreciate the laptop features Microsoft included with Windows 98. Windows 98 recognizes when you change a laptop's configuration using sort of a *Plug and Play on-the-fly* because you don't even have to turn off your laptop when making common hardware changes, such as docking the laptop into a docking bay.

Perhaps you use a laptop while on the road and a desktop computer at the office or at home. If so, you need to transfer files easily between them and, at the same time, keep those files in synchronization so that you always work with the latest file version. Whatever your situation, the Windows 98 *Briefcase* will help you synchronize your document files so they remain as current as possible.

The nature of laptop use is mobile computing. The cables you must plug in when connecting your laptop to a printer or to another PC make the laptop somewhat cumbersome when you want to communicate to another device. Fortunately, most of today's laptops come with infrared ports so that you can access other devices without cables.

The highlights of this hour include the following:

- Why automatic configuration for mobile computing environments is so important
- Why the My Briefcase icon is one of the most important icons on the Windows 98 desktop for users of both portable and desktop computers
- Which common laptop hardware changes Windows 98 detects
- How infrared connections make communicating with peripherals and other computers simpler than using cables

Docking Your Laptop

The Microsoft programmers understood the need for mobile computing environments when they developed Windows 98. Mobile computing environments refer to those environments in which portable computers such as laptops are used. In the past few years, companies have begun developing *docking stations* for computer users who take a laptop with them on the road. Now they can come home and plug the laptop directly into a docking station. The docking station is a device that connects the laptop to a full-size color screen, printer, mouse, and keyboard. Therefore, the computer user uses the laptop on the road and then uses the laptop's system unit at home or in the office, with regular-size peripheral equipment.

Windows Minute

Sitting at the Dock

Many devices known as docking stations are more accurately described as *port replicators* because they extend the laptop's expansion ports, such as the printer and serial port, to the docking station device on your desktop. Leaving all your peripherals plugged into the docking station is simpler than plugging each device into your laptop every time you arrive back at your desk. You only have to slide your laptop into the docking station to access those peripherals plugged into the docking station.

Windows 98 can detect whether a computer is docked and make appropriate adjustments instantly and accordingly. When undocked, Windows 98 can use the laptop's screen, and when docked, Windows 98 can immediately adjust the screen to a larger and higher-resolution monitor.

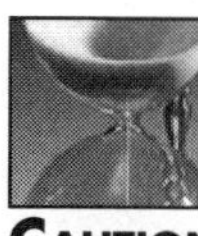

Caution

If your hardware is not compatible with Plug and Play, you have to reboot your computer before Windows 98 can reconfigure itself to the docking. If, however, you have full Plug and Play compliance, as most laptops sold since 1996 do, you don't have to reboot for Windows 98 to recognize the change in docking status.

Windows 98 often can recognize that a computer has been docked, but most hardware does not allow you to undock your PC without Windows 98 knowing about the undocking. If Windows 98 does not recognize the fact that you've undocked, you can select Eject PC from the Start menu, and Windows 98 will know to reconfigure for the undocking and use the laptop's own configuration. For example, if your laptop contains an internal modem, the laptop, when undocked, will no longer be configured to use the docking station's modem.

JUST A MINUTE

> When undocked, the Eject PC option does not appear on your Start menu.

Using PC Cards

For several years, laptops have supported PC Cards (PC Cards are sometimes called *PCMCIA cards*), the small credit card–sized expansion peripherals that plug into the side on your laptops. These cards enable you to add a modem, memory, networking capabilities, and even another hard disk to your laptop.

Three card types exist:

- **Type I** The original card soon replaced with Type II (Type I cards are no longer available)
- **Type II** The most common PC Card you can purchase today, primarily used for modems, memory, and networking
- **Type III** A double-sized card used primarily for disk expansion (yes, you can fit several megabytes into the size of a couple of credit cards)

Most laptops in use today support two Type II (or Type I) cards at once, or one Type III PC Card, due to its double width.

The Control Panel includes an icon labeled PC Card (PCMCIA) that contains the PC Card control you need as you work in Windows 98. When you select this Control Panel item, Windows 98 opens the PC Card Properties dialog box shown in Figure 19.1.

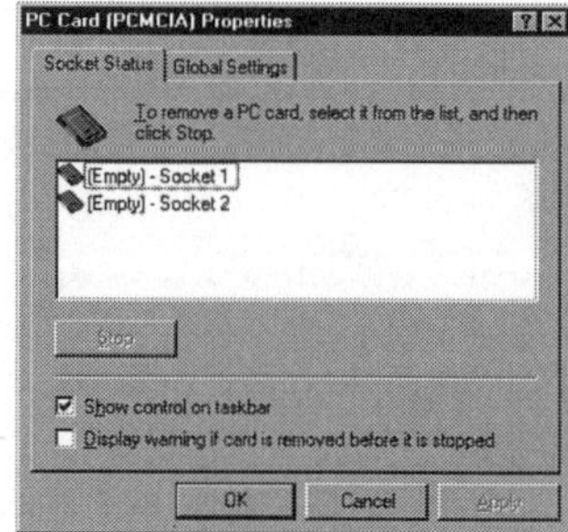

Figure 19.1.
The PC Card Properties dialog box enables you to control your PC Card settings.

Figure 19.1 indicates that the laptop has two PC Card sockets (as most laptops sold today have) and that both are empty. The first option at the bottom of the dialog box determines whether the PC Card icon will appear on your taskbar, as Figure 19.2 shows, giving you quicker access to the PC Card Properties dialog box than going through the Control Panel. If selected, the second option warns you if you remove a PC Card before you stop the card. Although you can insert and remove most PC Cards during the operation of Windows 98 without stopping the card first, if you use a PC Card with a hard disk, you stop the card *before* removing it to ensure that all unwritten data is on the card's disk.

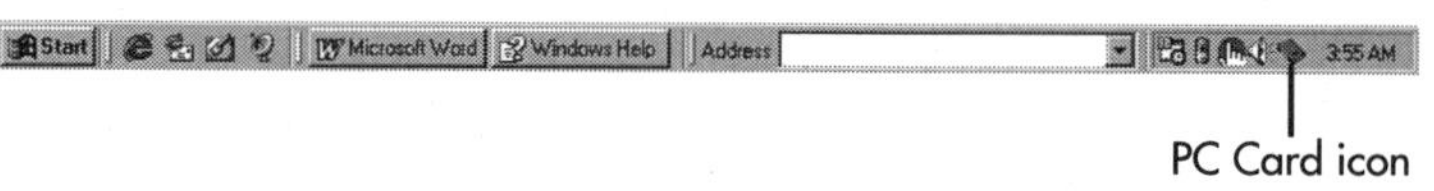

Figure 19.2.
Your taskbar gives you quick access to the PC Card Properties dialog box.

To start any card, simply insert the card into the appropriate PC Card slot. Your PC can be on or off for this operation, one of the only times you can modify PC hardware with the power on. Windows 98 senses the change, installs the modem support through Plug and Play, and adds the card to the list in the PC Card Properties dialog box that will no longer be empty. To remove the card, you eject the PC Card from its slot and Windows 98 reconfigures itself accordingly.

TIME SAVER

> To stop a PC Card before you eject the card, open the Control Panel's PC Card Properties dialog box, click the PC Card you want to stop, and click the Stop button. Windows 98 then displays a dialog box telling you that you can remove the card and removes the PC Card icon from your taskbar.

Clicking the Global Settings tab on the PC Properties dialog box opens the tabbed page shown in Figure 19.3. You should uncheck the Automatic selection option only if your PC

Card manual indicates the need to do so. You then can control the memory used by the PC Card, as specified in your card owner's manual. The second option lets you enable and disable sound effects that occur when you insert and remove a PC Card.

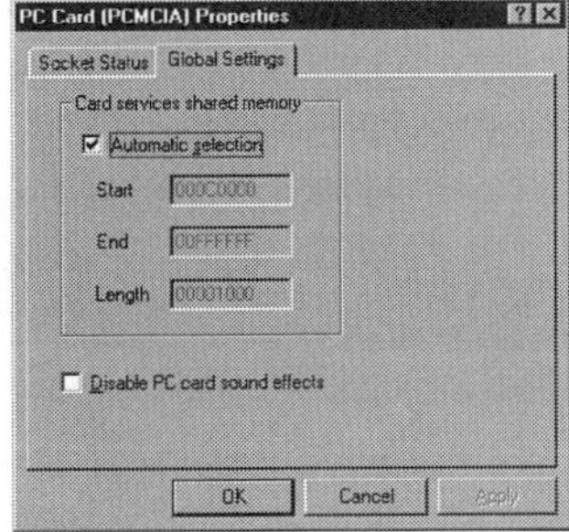

Figure 19.3.
Control PC Card memory and sound effects through the Global Settings.

CAUTION

The PC Card Properties sound effects option has nothing to do with the sounds your modem makes when you initiate a phone call. The option controls a sound that Windows 98 plays when you insert or remove a card.

TIME SAVER

Some PC Cards are easy to eject—almost *too* easy! Therefore, by checking the sound effects option, you hear if you accidentally eject the PC Card from its slot while your PC is in use.

The Windows 98 Briefcase

When on the road, you want to work with the most up-to-date data files possible. Therefore, users often copy the latest files from their desktops to portable PCs before leaving on a trip. The direct cable connection, described at the end of the last section, is a great way to copy those files. (Users also use floppy disks to transfer data between two computers.)

When they return, those users often have to reverse the process and copy their latest laptop data files over the ones on the desktops to refresh the desktop's files so that both computers stay in synchronization with each other. Until Windows, the only way to ensure that you were working with the latest data files was to look at the file date and time values and work with only the latest. At best, trying to maintain the latest files was a hassle and often caused confusion and errors as well.

The Briefcase application does all the nitty-gritty for you and synchronizes two computers that you have connected via a network or by cable. You'll find the Briefcase application on your desktop. When you open the My Briefcase icon, Windows 98 displays the My Briefcase window, shown in Figure 19.4.

Figure 19.4.
My Briefcase is ready for your files.

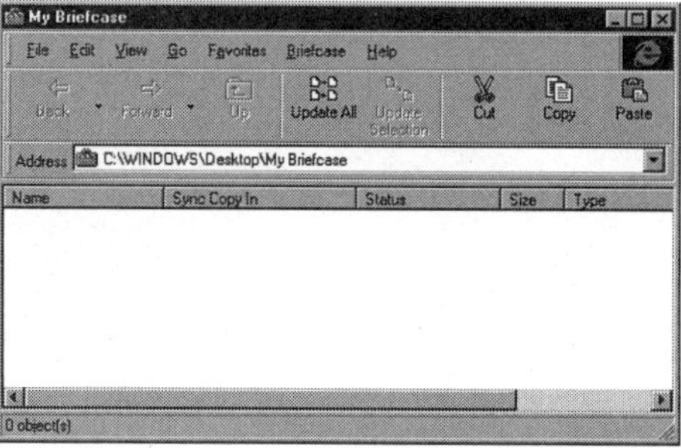

Just a Minute

The Briefcase icon appears on the desktop and not on the Control Panel or within the Start menu so that you can drag files onto the Briefcase from Explorer or from an Open dialog box.

Briefcase acts just like a briefcase that you take between your office and home. Before leaving in the morning, you put important papers in your briefcase. In the Windows 98 environment, before going on the road with your laptop, you should drag all data files that you want to work with to the Briefcase.

Suppose you copy two files to the Briefcase icon by dragging the files from Windows Explorer to the My Briefcase desktop icon. Figure 19.5 shows two files in the Briefcase window ready to be transferred to a laptop computer. Notice that the toolbar changed slightly from the empty Briefcase in Figure 19.4; now the Update All toolbar button is available.

Figure 19.5.
There are two document files in My Briefcase at the moment.

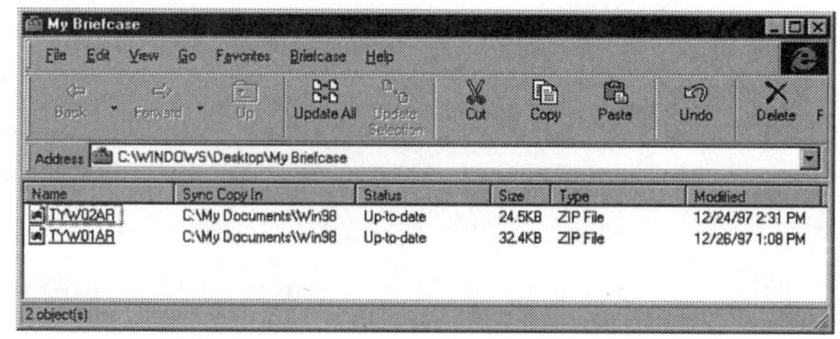

If you are using a floppy disk for the Briefcase intermediary storage media, move the My Briefcase icon to the floppy disk. You can display the floppy disk by displaying the Explorer window, or open the My Computer window and then drag the My Briefcase icon to the floppy disk drive. You must have a formatted disk in the drive before you copy the desktop's My Briefcase icon there.

CAUTION

Insert the floppy disk into your laptop's disk drive. While on the road, you can work with those files in the Briefcase. If you save a Briefcase file to the laptop's hard disk, be sure to return the file to the laptop's Briefcase before you reconcile the files on your primary desktop computer later.

When you get back to the desktop, insert the floppy disk into the desktop's disk drive and double-click the desktop's My Briefcase icon again. Select Briefcase | Update All (or click the toolbar button) or select only those files you want to update, and then select Briefcase | Update Selection (or click the toolbar button). Briefcase synchronizes the desktop's files by doing one of three things:

- If your desktop does not have one or more Briefcase files, the Briefcase application copies those files to the desktop computer.
- If your desktop already has those files on its disk, Briefcase transfers files from the Briefcase *only* if the Briefcase's files are newer than the desktop's.
- If your desktop already has one or more Briefcase files and the files are older than the Briefcase versions, the Briefcase application copies the newer versions over the old ones on the desktop.

19

TIME SAVER

If you want to update files using a direct cable connection, infrared connection (see the next section), or network instead of an intermediary floppy disk, make the physical connection first to the laptop with a direct cable or plug the laptop into your network. Then drag the files from the desktop computer to the laptop's My Briefcase icon. This sends the files to the Briefcase on the laptop. While on the road, work with the files inside the Briefcase icon. When you reconnect to the desktop or network, you can select the Briefcase | Update All menu command to bring the desktop up-to-date.

Going Wireless with Infrared

In the 1980s, IBM introduced the PCJr, a PC designed for home use and one that used an *infrared port* for its keyboard. (You cannot see infrared light, but infrared signals work well in remote control devices such as television remotes.) The user was not encumbered by a wire on the keyboard; the user could lean back in the chair and point the keyboard in the general direction of the PC to use the PCJr.

IBM was years ahead of its time and years behind the market. The computer's sales bombed.

Today, the home computer market has not only grown, it's far surpassed anyone's expectations. With the integration of the television and PC, along with wireless keyboards and other peripherals, we can see that the PCJr's demise was due to bad timing.

JUST A MINUTE

Interestingly, Microsoft got into the home software market with its "Microsoft At Home" applications just as the home market was beginning its tremendous growth. At the end of 1997, the height of home computer and software sales, Microsoft announced that they were pulling most of their At Home software off the shelves due to slow sales. The PC market is always fun to watch but never fun to predict!

Windows 98 fully supports infrared devices. At the time of Windows 98's release, the most common device that uses infrared technology is the laptop PC. Infrared allows the laptop user to transfer files from one PC to another without the use of networks or even cables. As you saw in Hour 18, "Windows 98's Hardware Interface," Windows 98's Direct Cable Connection makes transferring files simple, but you can get even simpler if you use infrared transfer. Just point your laptop at your desktop, and Windows 98 automatically senses the infrared devices and makes the connection you need.

JUST A MINUTE

Many manufacturers are adding infrared ports to peripherals such as printers and networks. Forget about cables—just point your PC in the direction of your printer to begin printing!

TIME SAVER

Although many vendors sell laptops with infrared ports on them, rarely will a desktop PC have an infrared port attached. You can purchase them for your desktop PC to help improve communications with a laptop or other peripheral.

Most infrared devices are truly Plug-and-Play. Turn on your printer and Windows 98 configures itself for the printer, emitting a sound telling you that the infrared ports are communicating.

As with many Windows 98 features, including the PC Card support described in the previous section, an infrared icon appears on your taskbar when your PC or laptop is ready for infrared communications. If you do not see the icon, you can add it to your taskbar.

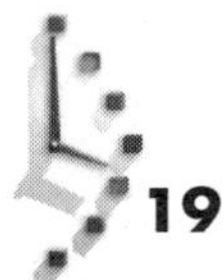

To Do

Task 19.1: Enabling Your Infrared Port

Step 1: Description

You must enable your infrared port before you can use it. This task shows you how to let Windows 98 know that you want the port enabled for use.

Step 2: Action

1. Open the Start Settings | Control Panel dialog box.
2. Open the Infrared icon's window to display the Infrared Monitor dialog box.
3. Click the Options tab.
4. Click the first option to enable infrared communications. Figure 19.6 shows the dialog box. You can determine how often your PC should search for infrared devices within range. The default is a scan that occurs every 3 seconds.

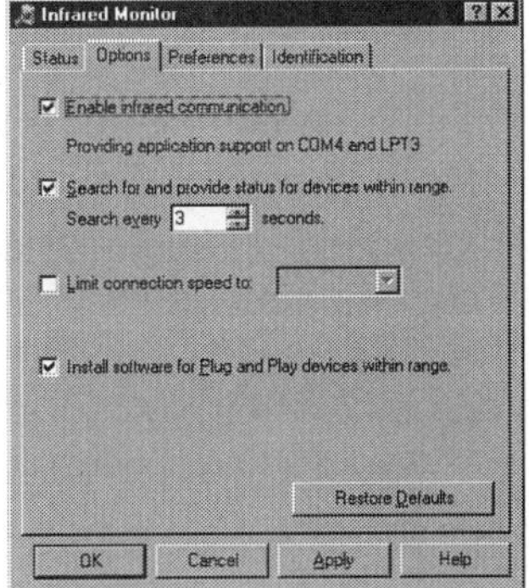

Figure 19.6.
Enable your infrared device from the Infrared Monitor dialog box.

5. Click the Identification tab to locate your PC's name and description (created when you installed Windows 98). If you communicate with another PC with an infrared port, the other PC will recognize your PC and display its name in the recognized device list that you can display.
6. When you click OK, your taskbar will show the infrared icon, as shown in Figure 19.7. The icon shows a blinking infrared indicator. If another infrared device comes within range, your taskbar will show two icons blinking at each other, indicating that another device is within range. (As Figure 19.7 shows, the taskbar can become full.)

Figure 19.7.
The taskbar loaded with icons.

Step 3: Review

When you enable your infrared port, the icon will appear on your taskbar and your PC will be ready to search for another infrared device. Your PC sends out a signal every time interval that you specify in the Infrared Monitor dialog box, and the icon will show a second icon if another device comes within range.

Task 19.2: Finding Infrared Devices

Step 1: Description

As your PC searches for an infrared signal, you can continue to work within Windows 98 as you always have. When you are ready to communicate with an infrared device, such as a printer or another PC with an infrared port, your PC will recognize that device.

Step 2: Action

1. Enable your infrared port, if you have not already, using Task 18.1.
2. Bring the second infrared device within range of your PC. Generally, the devices must be within 3 feet and you should aim their ports in the other's general direction. Windows 98 indicates the recognition of the other device.
3. You can now begin printing or sharing files between the two PCs. If you want to transfer files from your laptop to a desktop infrared port, use the Direct Cable Connector Wizard (see Hour 18) to set up a connection. The infrared port will replace the serial or parallel connection that you initiate.

   If you use an infrared printer, check the printer's manual to see which infrared port to use. Although you have only one physical infrared port on your PC, Windows 98 sets up the port as both a serial and a parallel infrared port to handle both kinds of data transmission and multiple infrared devices at one time. Although the printer might normally be a parallel printer, some printers require a serial infrared port connection.
4. Explorer and the File | Open dialog boxes now will display the other PC if you connect to a PC's infrared device, and the Print dialog boxes will display the infrared printer if you have connected to a printer device.

Step 3: Review

Connecting another infrared device to your laptop is simple. Windows 98 does all the configuration as long as you bring the second device within range. You will have no need to hook cables between two PCs with infrared devices or between a PC and an infrared printer. The infrared port is especially helpful for laptop users who want to use a wireless connection to transfer files between the PCs using the Direct Cable Connection Wizard.

Time Saver

After you make the infrared connection between a laptop and another PC, you can use the infrared transmission to communicate between the two Briefcase windows.

Summary

This hour showed how laptop users can take advantage of Windows 98's special mobile support features. Windows 98 includes support for docked laptop computers, so the configuration changes whenever you dock and undock. In addition, infrared ports make communicating between two infrared devices simple and wire-free.

The easy interconnection possible in Windows 98 means that you'll be connecting more computers than ever before. With those connections comes confusion, however. A desktop and laptop computers' files can get out of synchronization. Generally, you want to work with the latest version of a file, but comparing dates and times yourself is tedious and error-prone. The My Briefcase icon solves that problem by making the time and date comparisons for you and refreshing any laptop or desktop files that need it to make sure both systems have the latest versions of document files.

Q&A

Q I often cross time zones and change my laptop accordingly. Will Briefcase be affected by the time changes?

A It is possible for Briefcase to make incorrect decisions when copying files using different time zones. You can do very little to make Briefcase happy when you move across time zones. The best thing you can do is resist the temptation to change the laptop's clock while on the road. Keep your laptop clock set the same as your desktop computer, so that when you return to the desktop, Briefcase will have no trouble reconciling your files.

Q I don't use a desktop PC, so do I need a docking station for my laptop?

A Actually, those without a desktop are the *best* candidates for a docking station. When on the road you can use your laptop, and when you return to your desk you can use the laptop's processor as your desktop PC. The docking station can connect to a full-screen monitor, keyboard, mouse, modem, and printer. To access these devices and to configure your laptop to use those devices, you only insert (*dock*) your laptop into the docking station, and Windows 98 reconfigures itself for the new devices.

Q Can I add an infrared port to my older laptop that has none?

A Probably, but doing so requires that you purchase a standalone infrared port. You have to plug the port into your laptop when you use the infrared communications. Probably such cabling defeats the purpose and makes infrared communications only slightly better than a wired file or printer connection.

Workshop

Term Review

Briefcase The Windows 98 application that synchronizes the document files from two computers so that you can always have the most up-to-date files.

docking station A device into which you can insert some laptop computers, which instantly connects the laptop to a full-size screen, keyboard, mouse, and printer.

infrared Invisible light that works well for transmitting between digital devices, such as television remote controls and infrared peripherals.

mobile computing environments The computer environment that includes laptop computers and desktop docking stations for the laptops.

PCMCIA Cards Also called *PC Cards*. Small credit card–sized I/O cards that add functionality, such as modems and memory, to laptops and to some desktop systems.

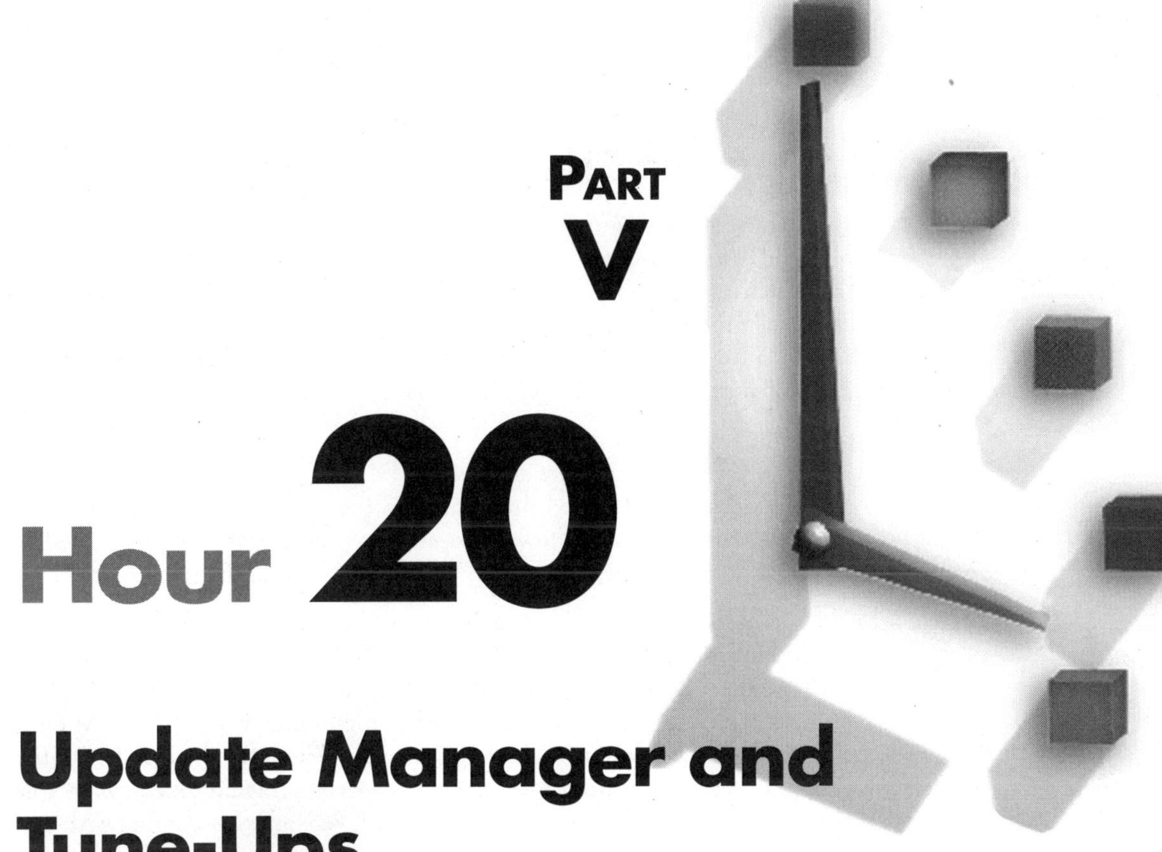

Update Manager and Tune-Ups

This hour shows you how Windows 98 checks and updates itself. If you have Web access, you don't need to wait for a disk mailing or go to the store to get the latest Windows 98 drivers and updates. You only click a menu option and Windows 98 updates itself.

Not only can you be assured that you have the latest Windows 98 support files, you can keep Windows 98 running in tip-top shape. By fine-tuning your system's performance, a task that Windows 98 considerably helps you with, Windows 98 responds to your requests as soon as possible.

The highlights of this hour include the following:

- What DLL files are and how they impact your system
- When the System File Checker corrects file conflicts
- How to update Windows 98 system files
- When to schedule system tune-ups

Checking System Files

A *DLL file* (DLL stands for *dynamic link library*) is a file used by more than one program. A *program* is a collection of many routines. Most Windows applications require several routines to do their work. When a program uses a common routine that other programs might be able to use, programmers store these routines in a special DLL file. (DLL files have the filename extension `.DLL`.) DLL files do not have to reside in memory until the program needs them, so not only can applications share DLL files, the applications take fewer memory resources to execute.

The goal of this section is not to make you an expert at DLL files because you don't have to understand them to use the DLL-based programs. To better understand Windows 98, however, and to better ensure that Windows 98 runs at its peak performance, you need to do everything you can to make sure your system has no DLL file conflicts.

Typical Windows 98 users have somewhat of a dilemma: you needn't understand DLL files to use them, but you must understand DLL files to use Windows 98 *most efficiently*. Before Windows 98, users either ran Windows at less-than-peak performance—sometimes with serious DLL errors of which they were not aware—or a programmer who understood DLL files would help them recover from such errors. Fortunately, Windows 98 takes care of the hard part so you don't have to! Windows 98 includes a special program called *System File Checker* that makes sure you do not run two or more DLL versions that conflict with one another.

Windows Minute

Who Cares?

DLL files are so critical because Windows 98 uses them so much. Windows 98 is really just one huge program and, as such, requires multiple DLL files to do its job. Often, other applications use Windows 98's DLL files also. Therefore, for proper system performance, it's vital that your DLL files don't conflict with one another.

Suppose you update Windows 98 and a new DLL file replaces one used by an earlier Windows 98 release. If an application program relies on something in the original DLL file but the replacement does not have that item, your application will not work.

System File Checker will restore original DLL files from your Windows 98 CD-ROM if an older DLL file replaces a newer one and an application requires the newer version. The System File Checker will be able to restore files only as recent as your Windows 98 CD-ROM. If the System File Checker finds a DLL newer than your Windows 98 CD-ROM version, the System File Checker assumes the file is up-to-date.

System File Checker performs an additional function. Your Windows 98 files are compressed onto the installation CD-ROM. In other words, not all your Windows 98 files will fit on the CD-ROM, so Microsoft compressed the files before making your CD-ROM. System File Checker can extract single files from those compressed files.

To Do

Task 20.1: Using System File Checker

Step 1: Description

This task shows you how to start and use System File Checker to ensure that you have the proper Windows 98 DLL files running.

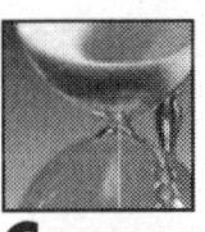

CAUTION

> Be very careful with DLL files! Even with System File Checker you can run into problems because of the technical nature of DLL files. If you don't have a clue what a DLL file means, you should probably keep the file and ignore the System File Checker–generated error; or at least back up your current DLL file (as explained in Step 2) in case you need to restore it later.

Step 2: Action

1. Select the Start menu's Programs | Accessories | System Tools | System File Checker option. The window shown in Figure 20.1 appears.

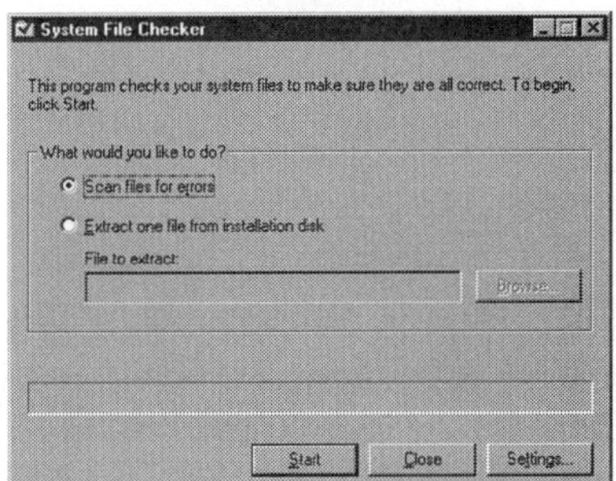

Figure 20.1.
System File Checker checks your system for invalid DLL files.

2. Click the Start button to check your system for DLL file problems. The check can take a while if you have a large disk and several applications.

JUST A MINUTE

> When you install an application, that application registers itself with the Windows 98 Registry database. The Registry keeps track of all DLL files on your system and also notes which applications use those DLL files. Therefore, System File Checker relies heavily on your Registry to locate DLL file conflicts.

3. If System File Checker runs into a possible DLL file error, System File Checker displays a dialog box such as the one shown in Figure 20.2.

Figure 20.2.
System File Checker found a potential problem.

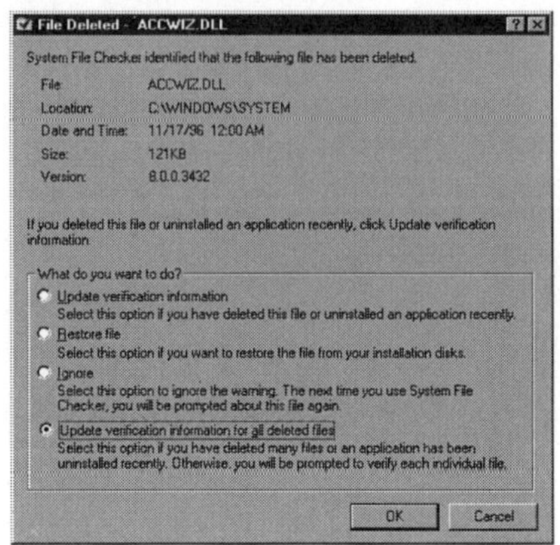

From the window you may be able to determine the problem, but many people will not understand the problem. That's okay. You select the first option if you know that you've installed a program that updated that conflicting DLL file. In other words, a new program overwrote one of Windows 98's DLL files. As long as you've not had problems with the program, you can select the first option and continue with the scan. If you suspect the mismatched DLL file has caused problems, keep the Restore file selected so that System File Checker restores your Windows 98 CD-ROM's original DLL file to your disk. (You may have to guess from the filename and its location what the file does. Even knowing the name and location often does little good if you cannot recognize the file as belonging to a particular application.) If you select Ignore, System File Checker will never flag that DLL file as having an error again.

4. Most of the time you keep the Restore file selected so that Windows 98 loads the original file from the installation CD-ROM. Click OK at this window. System File Checker gives you a chance to back up the file onto a disk or to a backup folder if you suspect you may need the file again.

Time Saver

Whether or not you're a DLL file expert (and few are), you can play sleuth and sometimes determine a DLL file conflict. Suppose you are having trouble playing AVI video files with the Media Player program, and System File Checker indicates that you have an incorrect DLL file named `AVIFILE.DLL`. You certainly should restore the original `AVIFILE.DLL` to see whether the problem goes away. As you can see, the DLL filename often indicates the file's purpose.

5. When System File Checker completes its task, you can click the Details button to see a summary of the work performed. When you click OK, System File Checker returns to its opening dialog box.
6. You can extract any file, not just a DLL file, from the CD-ROM's compressed files by selecting the System File Checker's Extract option and clicking Browse to locate the Windows 98 file you want to replace from the CD-ROM. In other words, if you accidentally delete or overwrite a Windows 98 system file, such as the `Drwatson.exe` program that you'll learn about in Hour 23, "Multimedia and Sound," you can extract the file from the installation CD-ROM. System File Checker replaces your hard disk's file with the original one.
7. Click Close to terminate System File Checker.

Step 3: Review

System File Checker checks your registered DLL files and looks for version conflicts between applications that use Windows 98 DLL files. In addition, System File Checker enables you to extract any Windows 98 file from the original CD-ROM to your hard disk.

JUST A MINUTE

System File Checker offers no information on which application caused the DLL file conflict, and it does not tell you when the conflict took place. Therefore, you should save the replaced DLL file when System File Checker gives you the opportunity, in case the replacement causes more system errors than before the replacement.

TIME SAVER

Back up your system before performing a series of DLL file updates. If you regularly back up your system (Hour 22, "Windows 98 Advanced System Tools," explains how to make backups), you may want to run System File Checker after every backup so you can restore the backup if you cannot determine which System File Checker DLL file replacement triggered the new error.

20

Updating Windows 98

As long as you have Internet access, you can request that Windows 98 check the Microsoft Internet sites and update any Windows 98 files that have changed, added, or that have bugs and have been corrected. The update site gives you full control over the update. You can

- View a list of files that are needed by your system to run the latest versions
- Read a description of each update to help you decide whether you need the update

- ☐ Submit problem reports that you experience
- ☐ Keep track of the updates you apply to your system

Just a Minute

Actually, the Windows 98 update is not a program on your PC but a Web site control that checks, from Microsoft's Web site, your PC's system files to make sure you have the latest Windows 98 files.

Task 20.2: Performing a System File Update

Step 1: Description

This task shows you how to check the Microsoft Web site for system updates you may need. The automatic update manager enables you to read descriptions of the update files and decide whether you want to apply those updates from over the Web site.

Step 2: Action

1. Select the Start menu's Programs | Accessories | System ToolsFiles | Windows Update option. The window shown in Figure 20.3 appears after you receive the Internet connection. (The Windows Update menu option sometimes appears toward the top of the Start menu if you cannot find it on the System Tools menu. Windows Update also appears on the Start menu's Settings option.)

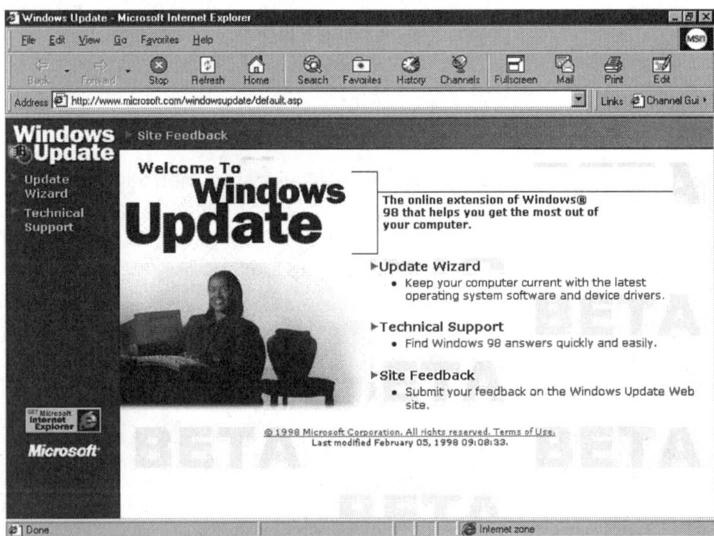

Figure 20.3. *Windows 98 automatically connects to the Update wizard is performing an automatic update.*

Just a Minute

Microsoft revises the Windows Update site often, so your screen may differ from the one in Figure 20.3.

2. To run the Update Wizard, click on the Update Wizard link.
3. If Update Wizard requires that you register your copy of Windows 98, go ahead and do so. After registering or bypassing the registration, you'll see the primary Update Wizard screen shown in Figure 20.4.

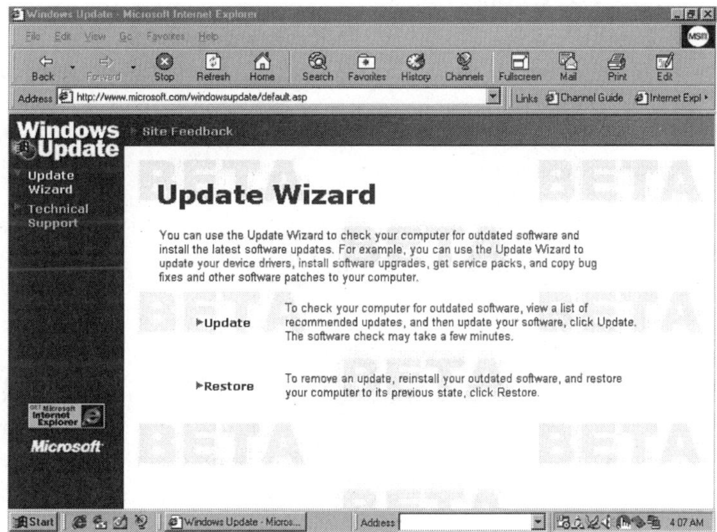

Figure 20.4.
You can update Windows 98 or restore a previous update to its original state.

If a previous update caused problems, the Restore hot link enables you to remove the update. An update may conflict with older software versions (although that's rare), and you can reverse the update if you want.

4. Click the Update hot spot to begin the update. A new Internet Explorer window will open that gives you a list of updates along with descriptions of those updates.

   You may have to wait for the update list to load. The Update Wizard is actually an ActiveX component that downloads from the Web page to your PC and runs on your PC. The Wizard checks your PC's system files and determines which need updating. If you get a note that reads `An ActiveX object on this page may be unsafe. Do you want to allow it to initialize and be accessed by scripts?`, you are given the choice to allow the update or not. Although rare, some ActiveX components can contain viruses. Allow updates if you are certain that the Web site is a reputable, company site.
5. Click an update and read the description to determine whether you want the update. If so, click the Install button and the update will begin.

Just a Minute

> You may have to reboot before some updates go into effect.

6. Continue updating your system until you've applied all the updates that you want.
7. Close the Update Wizard window and you return to the Internet Explorer screen that started the update.

Step 3: Review

Before Windows 98, getting Windows updates was a game of chance. Users often never knew when Microsoft released an update (Microsoft did not seem to consistently inform registered users of the updates). Even if you knew about an update you probably were not clear where to get it. In addition, some updates (such as Windows 95's Service Release 2 update) were only available for new PCs.

Windows 98 changes all that. You can now routinely log into Microsoft's site and update your system automatically. You can be assured of having the latest Windows 98 components on your system by running the Windows 98 Update Wizard.

Fine-Tune Your System

You've been reading about ways to improve your system's performance throughout this 24-hour tutorial. In addition, subsequent hours describe other ways to increase system speed. For example, Hour 22 explains several tools that improve your disk access.

In the previous section you learned how to maintain the latest Windows 98 drivers and components. As long as you're running the latest Windows 98 version, you might as well keep your system in good shape by running the Windows Tune-Up Scheduler, a program that routinely optimizes your system performance.

The Windows Tune-Up Scheduler monitors the following system areas:

- Disk space
- Memory usage
- Program execution

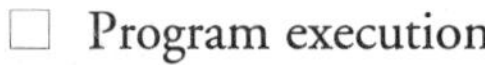

Just a Minute

> You may not fully understand the disk optimizations that Windows Tune-Up Scheduler can perform until Hour 22.

Task 20.3: Using the Tune-Up Scheduler Wizard

Step 1: Description

This task shows you how to run the Windows Tune-Up Scheduler Wizard. The Wizard enables you to specify automatic tune-ups that your PC can perform on its own while you're away.

Step 2: Action

1. Select the Start menu's Programs | Accessories | System Tools | Windows Tune-Up Wizard option to open the introductory Wizard window shown in Figure 20.5.

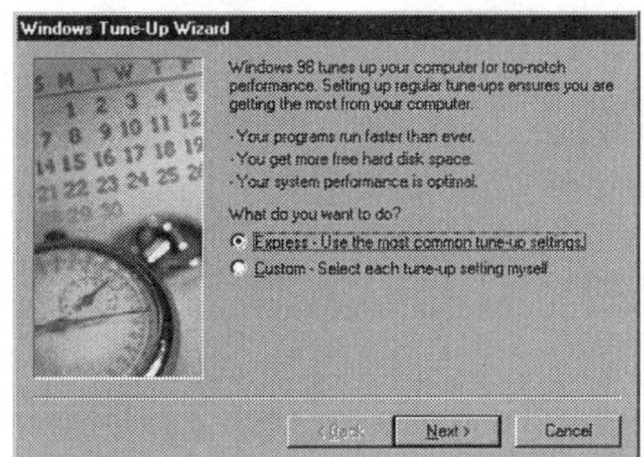

Figure 20.5.
The opening tune-up Wizard window describes Windows Tune-Up Scheduler's operation.

2. Select the Custom option and click Next to begin the Wizard. The Wizard gives a series of prompts, guiding you through the tune-up settings. For example, you are given the choice of changing the tune-up settings for later execution or performing a tune-up now. The Windows Tune-Up Scheduler Wizard also enables you to customize the tune-up or follow preset settings that are common among most Windows 98 users. For example, you'll see a first screen that asks whether you want to optimize your hard disk. As you'll learn in Hour 22, you should optimize your hard disk about every month, and more often if you create and delete a lot of files. The Wizard gives you the choice of optimizing on the Wizard's completion, optimizing at a specific day and time (such as early morning before work), or bypassing the disk optimization step.
3. After you select the disk optimization you prefer, click Next to walk through the selections of a disk drive optimization routine. You'll possibly read about conversion to FAT32 (Hour 22 explains FAT32), as well as other optimization techniques the Wizard supports. Eventually, you'll come to the program execution window shown in Figure 20.6.

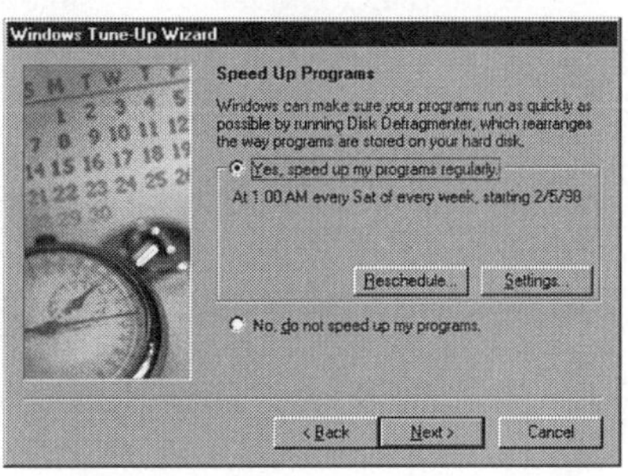

Figure 20.6.
Select a time to speed your programs.

4. The Windows Tune-Up Scheduler will regularly check your hard disk for errors if you select the option. As with any of the tune-up components, you can reschedule the hard disk scan's tune-up for a time different from the default time by clicking the Reschedule button. After you specify the disk scan time, click Next to continue with the tune-up.
5. The window shown in Figure 20.7 is a welcome relief to many Windows users. During its operation, Windows creates several temporary files. Unfortunately, these temporary files often become permanent due to system problems and application programs that don't properly remove the files after using them.

   Pre–Windows 98 users could not safely remove temporary files because Windows could have been using them at the time of the deletion, causing a system crash. The Windows Tune-Up Scheduler takes care of removing those temporary files that are still on your system but not being used anymore. In addition, Windows Tune-Up Scheduler removes backup files, unneeded system recovery files, and older files renamed during system upgrades.

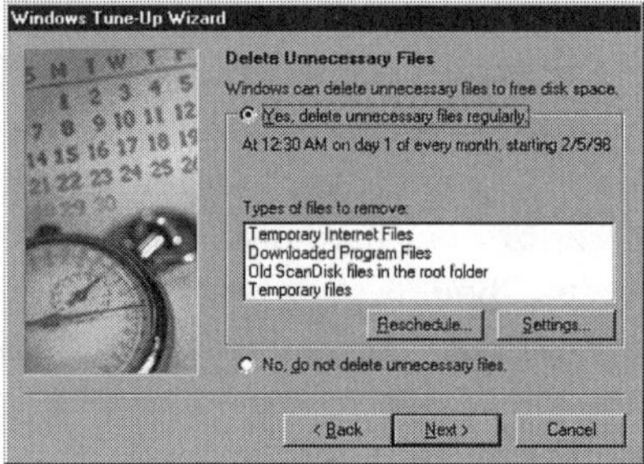

Figure 20.7.
Windows Tune-Up Scheduler safely removes files you no longer need.

TIME SAVER

As with all the Windows Tune-Up Scheduler windows, you can click the Settings button to select various options for the tune-up. At the Delete Unnecessary Files window, you can click Settings and specify exactly which unneeded files you want to get rid of and which to keep. For example, some temporary Internet files are useful for speeding up Web pages you may want to revisit.

6. Click Next and Finish to start the tune-up or to put your tune-up tasks into the Windows 98 schedule.

JUST A MINUTE

The Windows Tune-Up Scheduler uses the Scheduled Tasks program if you schedule tasks to begin at a specific day and time, as opposed to starting right after you finish the Windows Tune-Up Scheduler Wizard.

The Scheduled Tasks program is an updated version of the System Agent that came with the Windows 95-based Microsoft Plus! pack.

Step 3: Review

You can keep your Windows 98 system in top-notch performance by scheduling regular tune-ups. You can schedule the tune-ups to begin any time of the day as long as your PC is turned on. You may want to schedule a tune-up once a week in the early morning hours before you get to work to ensure that your system runs efficiently during work.

Summary

This hour described how you can keep Windows 98 in top condition. The System File Checker helps ensure that your DLL files are not in conflict with Windows 98 or with other applications.

The Windows Update manager makes sure that you have the latest Windows 98 files on your system. To guard against possible application conflicts that sometimes occur with new Windows 98 components, Windows Update enables you to restore from previous updates that you made that might now be causing problems with older software you run. When you have the latest Windows 98 files, keep those files and your hardware running smoothly by scheduling regular system tune-ups with the Windows Tune-Up Scheduler Wizard.

Hour 21, "Manage Your Hard Drives," describes ways that you can manage your hard disk storage and files. Today's data isn't just comprised of numbers and text, but also sound, pictures, and video information. By keeping your hard disk optimized, you can improve your disk's performance.

Q&A

Q How do I know whether I should run System File Checker?

A If you receive no routine errors during your use of Windows 98, you should run System File Checker only after installing new applications.

If you begin to get error messages when you try to run applications or system programs, you may have a DLL file conflict. Run System File Checker to see whether you can circumvent that conflict.

Q I don't leave my PC turned on when I'm away, so how can I schedule tune-ups?

A You cannot schedule tune-ups unless you plan to leave your PC on. Perhaps you can schedule all your system tune-ups for the same day and leave your system on that day only. You don't need to leave your monitor turned on for the tune-ups to run. If you'd rather not leave your PC on, even for one 24-hour period, start the tune-ups before you go to lunch and they should be complete or close to completion when you return. Remember that you can schedule tune-ups to begin as soon as you quit the Windows Tune-Up Scheduler Wizard.

Workshop

Term Review

DLL file A dynamic link library file. A shared routine used by more than one program.

System File Checker A Windows 98 utility program that guards against DLL file problems.

Windows Tune-Up Scheduler A Windows 98 program that routinely monitors your system and makes changes that improve system performance.

Windows Update An ActiveX control that checks your Windows 98 system files to ensure that they match the latest release.

Part VI

Windows 98 Safety at Nighttime

Hour

PART VI

Hour 21

Manage Your Hard Drives

This hour is for everybody and for nobody! Here's the reason for the paradox: *Everybody* wants more disk space, and *nobody* backs up often enough! This hour attempts to help you get more disk space and back up more often.

Windows 98 also contains a backup program that enables you to back up your files. Backups help protect your files from disasters, such as a disk drive failure (called a *disk crash*). You can restore the backup by copying the files from the backup to a healthy disk drive.

Windows 98 contains the *DriveSpace* technology that compresses disk space by as much as 30 to 100 percent. DriveSpace compresses both hard disks and floppy disks. In addition to DriveSpace, you can make better use of your hard disks by considering an upgrade to *FAT32*, Windows 98's advanced disk storage management system.

The highlights of this hour include the following:

- Why backing up with Windows 98 Backup is simple to do
- What precautions you can take to protect your backups
- Why ScanDisk salvages disk files before you know you have problems
- How you can squeeze more data onto your disk drive
- Why FAT32 technology makes better use of your disk

Back Up Often

The Windows 98 Backup program is a backup program that you can use to save copies of disk files that protect you against data loss. If your hard disk breaks down, after you fix or replace it, you will be able to restore the backup and resume your work (you may have to install Windows 98 first if the disk was your C drive). Without Backup, you would have to try to recreate the entire disk drive, which is often impossible because you will not have a copy of every transaction and document that you've created.

JUST A MINUTE

The Windows 98 Backup program both creates and restores backups.

WINDOWS MINUTE

Put It in Reverse—Back Up!

The first time you back up, back up your entire disk drive. After you back up the entire disk, you then can make subsequent daily or weekly backups of only those files that you've added or changed since the most recent backup.

Backup can compress files while backing them up so that you can back up large disk drives to other disks or tapes that would not normally be able to hold all the data. With compression, the backup should take less time and make the backups easier to do.

Backup enables you to select which files you want to back up so that you can make a special backup of a few selected files. Backup can create a full backup of your entire disk drive or an *incremental backup*, which backs up only the files that have changed since the most recent backup. Backup also enables you to direct restored files to a different drive or directory from where they originated.

TIME SAVER

Take your home backup files with you to work every day and bring your work's backup files home each night. If a terrible disaster happens at home or at work, such as a fire, you will be able to restore your data because the backups weren't destroyed.

You must decide on which medium you want to store the backup. Backup creates backups on the following media:

- Network, hard, and floppy disks
- High-density disks such as Zip drives
- QIC 40, 80, and 3010 tapes

To Do

Task 21.1: Backing Up Files

Step 1: Description

This task explains how to use Backup and its major features. This task describes how you can back up a hard disk to floppy disks because readers will have such a variety of backup devices. Today most people will back up regularly to higher-capacity non-disk devices.

Step 2: Action

1. Display the Start menu and select Programs | Accessories | System Tools | Backup. You'll see the opening window, shown in Figure 21.1.

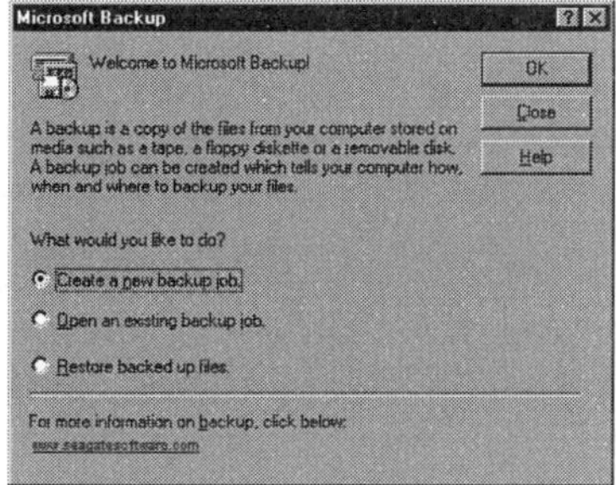

Figure 21.1.
The opening Backup window for backing up a disk drive.

A *backup job* is a description of a specific backup. You won't always want to back up the same folders and drives. You might create a backup job to back up your business files only, your personal files, and your entire hard disk. Instead of specifying the backup details each time, you can save those details in a backup job and select the backup job you want to use in subsequent backups.

2. Select the first option, Create a new backup job, and click OK. The wizard will continue letting you select the files you want to back up.
3. If you are backing up your entire PC, you select the first option, Back up My Computer. This option backs up all your drives. For this task, select the second option to limit the number of files you are backing up and click Next. Backup displays the Explorer-like window shown in Figure 21.2, where you can expand the drive and folder trees and select the files you want to back up.

Time Saver

If you want to back up an entire disk, click the checkbox next to a disk drive instead of expanding that drive's folders and selecting every folder individually.

21

Figure 21.2.
Select the files, folders, and drives you want to back up.

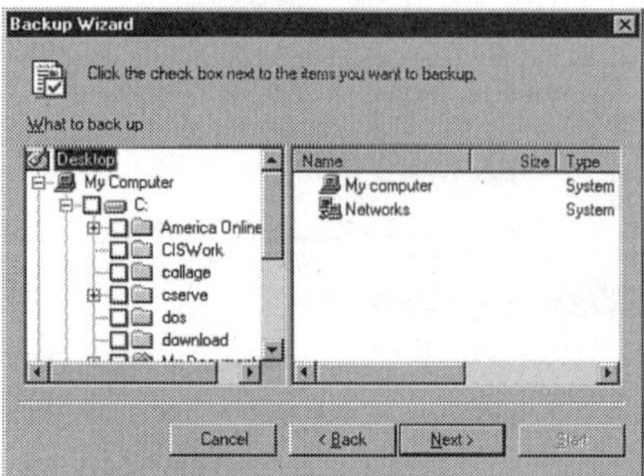

4. Click the C drive to display C's files in the right window pane. Check the `Msdos.sysAutoexec.bak` file and click Next. For this task you back up only that one file.
5. You may want to back up the selected files or perform an incremental backup for only those files that have changed since the previous backup. Select New and changed files if you want to perform an incremental backup, and leave All selected files if you want to back up all the files you've selected.
6. Backup does not start backing up right away because Backup still does not know the kind of backup you want to perform or the type of media to which you want the backup to go. Select where you want to back up. You can back up to a folder, a folder on a different drive, a tape drive, or onto a high-capacity removable disk, such as a Zip drive.
7. Click Next to select a comparison and compression option. If you compare the backup to the original file, the backup takes longer, but you will be assured that the backup matches the original. Although there's rarely a problem, the comparison tells you that the backup properly occurred. The compression option consumes less backup space because Backup compresses the files before writing them to your backup drive. After you select the comparison and compression options, click Next.
8. The final window, shown in Figure 21.3, reviews the backup you've set up and enables you to specify a backup job name for this backup. Whenever you create a new backup job that you'll create again, give the job a name so you don't have to go through the selection process again. Click Start to begin the backup.

Just a Minute

When you want to restore from a backup, start the Backup program and select Restore backed up files at the opening wizard window. You are asked where the backup files reside that you want to restore before restoring the backup.

Figure 21.3.
You now can review your backup, enter a backup job name, and start the backup.

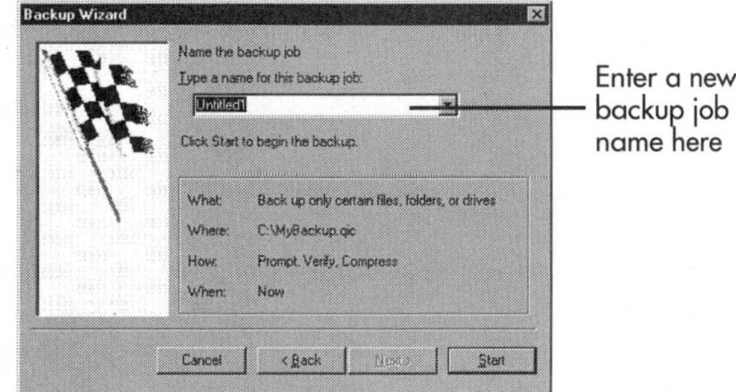

CAUTION

If you cancel a backup or restore wizard, Backup takes you to the Microsoft Backup dialog box. You can still back up or restore, but you have to specify all the options without the wizard as a guide. To start the wizard again, click the Backup Wizard or Restore Wizard toolbar button.

Step 3: Review

Backup contains a complete set of backup, restore, and comparison features. The backup jobs make backing up regularly easy to do because you can create backup jobs that describe different backup settings and open whatever backup job you want to use.

Check the Disk

Windows 98 supplies ScanDisk, which checks your disk drive for problems so that you can avoid future troubles. ScanDisk contains two levels of disk drive inspection: a standard scan and a thorough scan. The standard scan checks your disk files for errors. The thorough scan checks the files and performs a disk surface test to verify the integrity and safety of disk storage.

Run ScanDisk regularly (perhaps once or twice a week). As with most Windows 98 programs, you can multitask ScanDisk while running another program. ScanDisk checks only disk drives, not CD-ROM drives.

Task 21.2: Checking a Disk with ScanDisk

To Do

Step 1: Description

This task explains how to use ScanDisk, which is simple to use and often takes only a few seconds to load and run.

Step 2: Action

1. Display the Start menu and select Programs | Accessories | System Tools | ScanDisk. Windows 98 displays the ScanDisk window shown in Figure 21.4.

Figure 21.4.
The opening ScanDisk window for analyzing your disk drives.

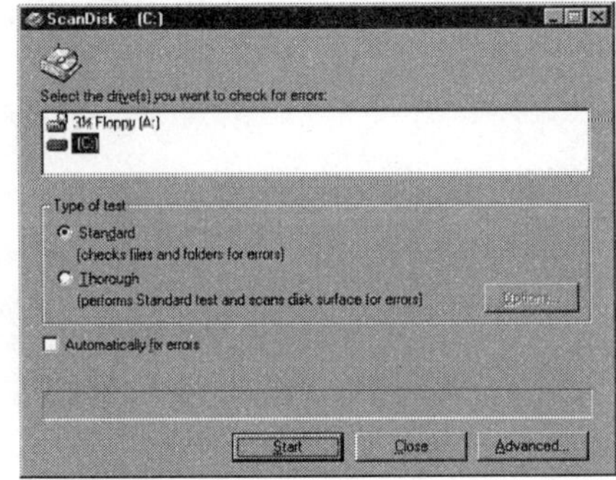

2. The Standard option is initially checked by default. To perform a standard ScanDisk, press Enter to choose the Start command button now. ScanDisk begins its chore of checking your files. Its window displays a moving graphics bar to show how much time remains in each ScanDisk step, as well as a description of each step in the process.

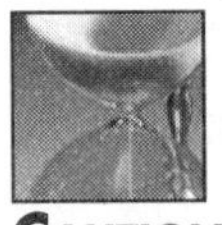

CAUTION

> If ScanDisk finds a problem and you've checked the option labeled Automatically fix errors, it attempts to fix any problems it finds using default repair tools. (You can change the way ScanDisk repairs the disk by pushing the Advanced command button described toward the end of this task.)

3. When ScanDisk finishes, you will see a results window, such as the one shown in Figure 21.5.

Figure 21.5.
ScanDisk reports its results to you upon completion of the disk scan.

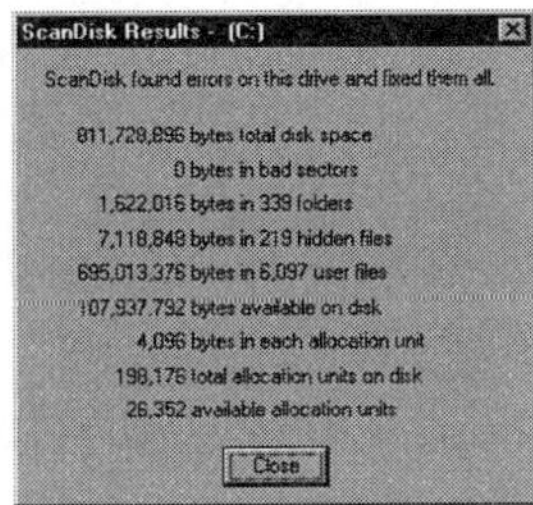

The most important line in the results window is the number of bad sectors. Rarely will the number be anything but zero. If bad sectors appear, ScanDisk will attempt to repair them and report the results. Press Enter to close the results window.

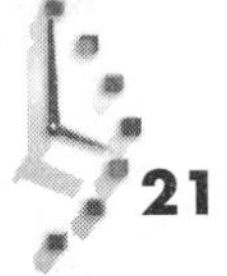

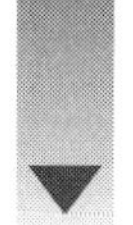

4. Click the Advanced command button. ScanDisk displays the ScanDisk Advanced Options dialog box shown in Figure 21.6. The default values are usually fine, but if you understand disk drive technology and file storage details, you may want to change an option. Click the OK command button to close the dialog box.

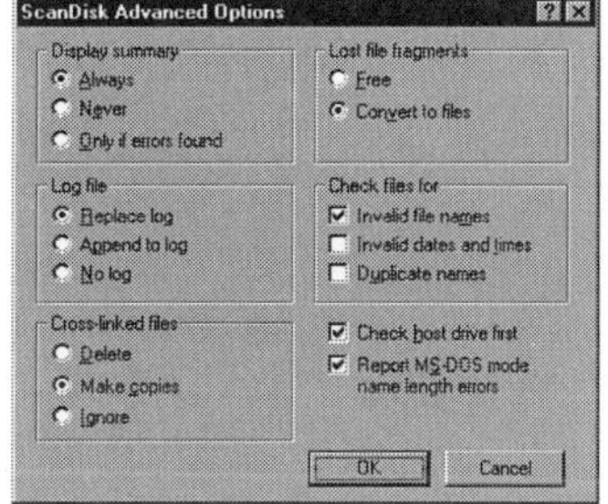

Figure 21.6.
The advanced ScanDisk options that you control.

5. Click the Thorough option and click the Start command button to perform a thorough ScanDisk check. The thorough scan performs a more intense disk check than the standard scan, but it can take up to two hours to finish, depending on your disk speed and size. You see the results dialog box when ScanDisk finishes.

Step 3: Review

ScanDisk is a disk-checking program that searches for disk errors and, optionally, attempts to fix the errors. Run ScanDisk once or twice weekly to make sure your disk is as free from defects as possible.

If you want more control over the ScanDisk process, you can click the Options button to control these options:

- System and data areas: scans your entire disk drive, including the system areas
- System area only: scans your disk's system areas, including the FAT (file allocation table, which controls how your files are placed on your disk) and directory
- Data area only: scans only your programs and data and leaves the system areas unscanned

Fill In the Holes

Disk Defragmenter fills empty gaps on your disks. As you add and delete files, the deleted space leaves free holes around the disk. Over time, your disk response time will slow down as you add or delete document files to and from the disk drive.

WINDOWS MINUTE

Pick Up the Pieces

Windows 98 can store large files on a fragmented disk as long as there is enough free fragmented space to hold the file. Windows 98 stores the files in linked chunks across the disk drive, filling in fragments and linking them.

A large file is stored as one continuous file if enough space exists to do so. But often, Windows 98 tries to reuse fragment space left over from a deleted file. Over time, the number of these file fragments can grow considerably and slow down your PC when you access a file that's fragmented.

Disk access slows down on a fragmented disk drive because Windows 98 must jump to each file fragment when retrieving a file. If you run Disk Defragmenter often enough (once or twice a month for the average user ought to be enough), Windows 98 keeps the fragments to a minimum and, thus, increases the disk access speed.

To Do

Task 21.3: Correcting Disk Fragmentation

Step 1: Description

This task explains how to defragment a disk drive. As you'll learn in this task, Disk Defragmenter not only closes empty disk gaps but also rearranges your disk drive so that often-used programs run faster.

Step 2: Action

1. Display the Start menu and select Programs | Accessories | System Tools | Disk Defragmenter. Windows 98 displays an opening window that asks whether you want a log file that enables you to select the drive to record the defragmentation results.
2. Click the Settings button and the Disk Defragmenter Settings dialog box appears, as shown in Figure 21.7. The dialog box enables you to decide whether you want the program to rearrange your files by selecting your most-used files and putting them at the beginning of your file space for faster access. Disk Defragmenter scans your disk during the defragment process and looks for common files and recently accessed programs to place in the early spaces of your disk. Click Next and the program tells you to quit all running programs. Press Alt+Tab to change to another running program that you can quit before returning to defragment the disk. Click Next when you've closed all open programs.

   In addition, if you select the option labeled Check the drive for errors, Disk Defragmenter checks your files and folders for storage errors before starting to defragment. If errors are found, the Disk Defragmenter stops until you fix them

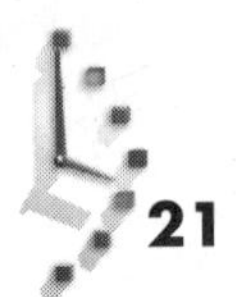

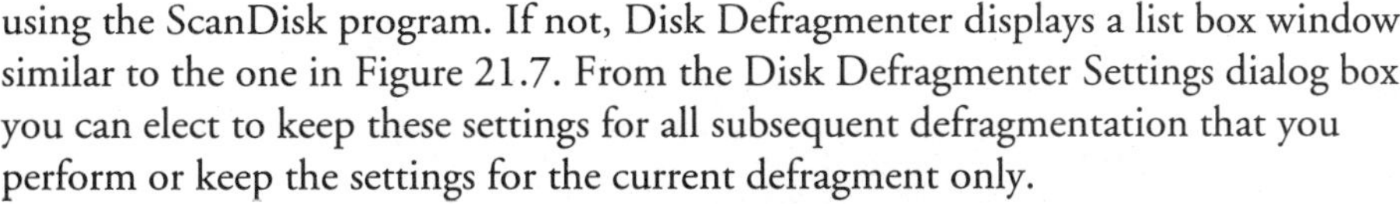

using the ScanDisk program. If not, Disk Defragmenter displays a list box window similar to the one in Figure 21.7. From the Disk Defragmenter Settings dialog box, you can elect to keep these settings for all subsequent defragmentation that you perform or keep the settings for the current defragment only.

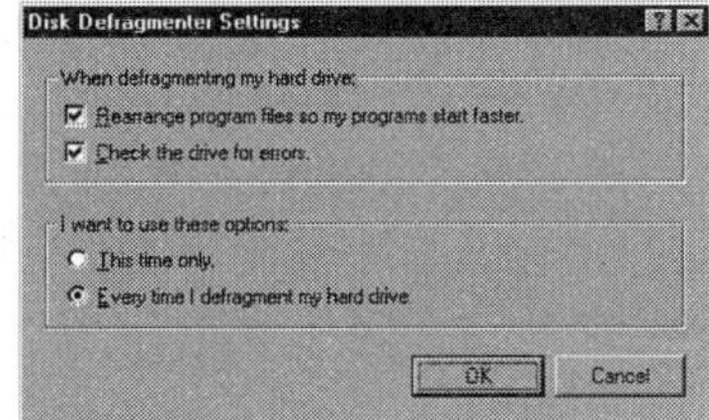

Figure 21.7.
Select the programs you use most often.

3. Disk Defragmenter places the programs you use most often in an efficient disk location so that those programs start faster than the others. Click on one or more programs to select them before clicking Next. If you don't see a program you run frequently, click Other to select one not in the list.
4. Disk Defragmenter then starts each selected program, one at a time, and asks that you close the program after its startup. Disk Defragmenter is able to learn the program and its ancillary files when you do this. After you close all open programs, Disk Defragmenter issues a final wizard window.
5. Click the Finish button to move to the disk-selection process.
6. Select the disk drive you want to defragment. When you do, Disk Defragmenter begins the defragmentation process. In addition to putting your often-used programs in a quick-launch location, Disk Defragmenter also removes the gaps from your disk drive.
7. Click OK to start the defrag process. Windows 98 can multitask while defragmenting your disk space, so you can run other programs while Disk Defragmenter runs. At any point during the defragmentation, you can pause Disk Defragmenter or cancel the process. If the drive is not fragmented, Disk Defragmenter tells you so and asks whether you want to run Disk Defragmenter anyway.

CAUTION

Be careful that you don't work in another window while defragmenting your disk drive. Disk Defragmenter will not be able to defragment your disk, and will keep attempting a restart, until you close all other running programs.

Time Saver

In Hour 22, "Windows 98 Advanced System Tools," you'll learn about Windows 98's Task Scheduler program, which lets you schedule the deframentation at night when you're not at your PC.

8. When finished, click Yes to close the application.

Step 3: Review

The Disk Defragmenter is easy to run regularly because you can run Disk Defragmenter and run other programs at the same time. Disk Defragmenter rearranges information and blank spots on your disk drive, and puts all the data in contiguous disk space and all the empty holes into one large contiguous block. When defragmented, your disk access will speed up and the programs you use most will begin more quickly.

Running DriveSpace

DriveSpace compresses drives and is easy to run. You need to run DriveSpace only once because after compressing the disk drive, the disk stays compressed. You also can reverse the DriveSpace compression if you want to, as long as you have enough space on the uncompressed disk drive to hold all your files.

After you compress a drive, Windows 98 and your computer act as if you've got more disk space. The free disk statistics show the extra drive space, and all programs access the disk as if the disk were originally designed to have the extra space.

Task 21.4: Compressing Disks Using DriveSpace

Step 1: Description

This task explains how to compress a disk drive using DriveSpace. The disk will be a floppy disk. After you've compressed a floppy disk drive, you will more fully understand the process and can then compress a hard disk.

When compressing a disk drive, DriveSpace adds a logical disk drive to your system, called the *host drive*. DriveSpace names the new host drive H, or some other name that falls far down anyone's list of disk drives, so that you'll be able to determine which drive is a host drive and which drive is from your list of real disk drives. The host drive will be uncompressed, and you will never work with the host drive. DriveSpace and Windows 98 use the host drive to hold descriptive information about the compressed drive. All you really need to know about the new host drive is that the host is not an actual drive on your system, and Windows 98 uses the host drive to support the DriveSpace compression scheme. All open dialog boxes you see, as well as the My Computer window, will display the host drive now that you've compressed.

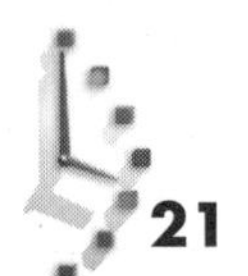

Step 2: Action

1. Display the Start menu and select Programs | Accessories | System Tools | DriveSpace. Windows 98 displays the DriveSpace window.
2. Insert a formatted disk in the disk drive. The disk can have data on it. The disk, however, should contain about 30 percent free space. Before you can compress a disk, the disk should contain some free space so that DriveSpace can write some temporary files during the compression process. If the drive does not have enough free space, DriveSpace will tell you before starting the actual compression so that you can free some space.
3. Select the floppy disk drive from the list of drives.
4. Select Drive | Compress. DriveSpace analyzes the disk and displays the Compress a Drive dialog box, such as the one shown in Figure 21.8.

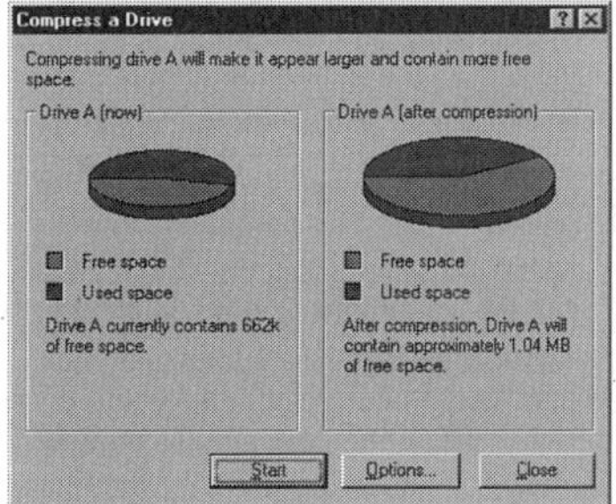

Figure 21.8.
The before and after effect of the disk's compression.

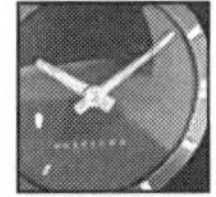

JUST A MINUTE

If you want to decompress a compressed drive, you repeat these steps and choose Drive | Uncompress instead of Drive | Compress.

5. Click the Options command button. Windows 98 displays the Compression Options dialog box that describes the host drive's name (you can select a different name if you want to) and free space (usually there will be no free space). Click the OK command button to close the Compression Options dialog box and return to the Compress a Drive dialog box.
6. Click the Start command button to initiate the drive compression. Before compressing, DriveSpace gives you one last chance to cancel the compression. DriveSpace also offers the option of backing up your files. Although there rarely will be a problem during the compression, it is possible that a power failure during the compression could interrupt the process and cause DriveSpace to corrupt the disk drive (so that the drive would need reformatting). By backing up the drive, you ensure that you can return to an uncompressed drive if needed.

7. When the compression begins, DriveSpace checks the disk for errors and then compresses the disk. The compression can take a while. After finishing, DriveSpace displays a completion dialog box. Close the dialog box and look at My Computer's properties for the compressed drive to see how much disk space you gained.

Step 3: Review

After you compress a disk drive, Windows 98 recognizes the compressed drive and stores up to 100 percent more data on that drive. There will actually be a second disk added to your drive letters, called the host disk, but you can ignore the host disk because DriveSpace uses the host disk to store data tables used for accessing the compressed drive.

CAUTION

If you want to format a compressed disk, you must run DriveSpace and select Drive | Format. The Explorer Format command will not format compressed disks. The disk stays compressed during the formatting procedure.

TIME SAVER

After you compress a drive, you can change the amount of compression by running the Compression Agent program found in the System Tools folder.

FAT32 Adds Space

Today's hard disks are large, and previous operating systems do not adequately handle those large sizes. Pre-Windows 98 operating systems used the FAT16 system to format and manage hard disks. FAT16 (which stands for 16-bit file allocation table) supports disks up to 2 gigabytes (approximately 2 billion bytes). Although you can partition a larger disk drive into smaller logical drives, in doing so, FAT16 wastes a lot of extra space.

JUST A MINUTE

FAT32 supports drives as large as 2 terabytes! That's 2,000 gigabytes, and although 2 terabytes might pose a space limitation some day, it's going to be well into the next millenium when that occurs.

When you create a new file, the operating system reserves more space than the file really needs. Your operating system always reserves disk space in clusters, and a cluster size changes depending on the disk drive size and the FAT you use. FAT16 created up to 32KB clusters. That means that if you create a file and write 5 bytes to that file, the file still consumes 32KB

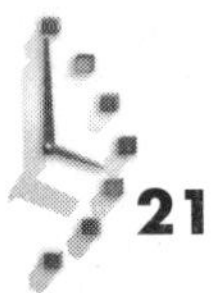

on your hard disk. If you keep writing data to the file and go past 32KB by one byte, FAT16 reserves another 32KB! The bottom line is that when you create a lot of small files, you actually create a lot of 32KB files that are mostly empty.

FAT32's cluster size is only 4KB, a much more efficient cluster size. Therefore, not only does FAT32 support larger hard drives, but FAT32 utilizes your space more efficiently.

The FAT16 system produced another disk anomaly, due to its structure, that designers created years ago. FAT16 supports only 512 files in a root directory. Although rarely will users store that many files in a root directory, as hard drives approach and surpass 10GB, a root directory with more than 512 files is not unthinkable. FAT32 has no root directory file limit.

CAUTION

> Ready to switch to FAT32 and take back control of your hard disk? Don't jump too soon. Although Windows 98 supports FAT32 drives, and although all of Windows 98's programs work with FAT32 after you've converted to FAT32, many other programs refuse to run or install on a FAT32-based drive. Many popular utility programs will not work and neither will older Windows applications. Although software companies are distributing FAT32-compatible programs, you may use legacy programs now (including some games) that fail to work with FAT32.
>
> If you want FAT16 back, you must format your hard disk, repartition the disk for FAT16, and reinstall all your software—including Windows 98. That's why converting to FAT32, although more efficient, causes some users to regret the move.

To Do

Task 21.4: Converting to FAT32

Step 1: Description

This task explains how to convert to FAT32, but before you proceed, reread the previous Caution. FAT32 changes your whole drive structure, and if you can no longer run a program that's important to you, restoring your FAT16 is slow and tedious. At best, you must format your hard disk, partition for FAT16, install Windows 98, and restore your backup. The backup will prove invaluable if you convert to FAT16, so be sure to make a complete backup before you convert to FAT32!

Step 2: Action

Display the Start menu and select Programs | Accessories | System Tools | FAT32 Converter. Windows 98 displays the FAT32 Converter window.

If you want to convert your disk to a FAT32 disk, please remember that you cannot return to the older FAT16 format without reformatting your entire disk in the process. When you select the Start menu's Programs | Accessories | System Tools | FAT32 Converter program, the program begins and walks you through a series of informational dialog boxes telling you

what's about to take place. When you perform the conversion, the FAT32 Converter enables you to back up first; you should back up, although the FAT32 Converter should not harm your files. As a safety precaution, however, make the backup—the power could go out or your disk controller could fail during the FAT32 process.

Summary

This hour described Windows 98's disk utilities. Backup enables you to back up, restore, and compare backups to their original files. This is the most full-featured backup program that Microsoft has offered. You can create backup jobs that quickly initiate specific backup descriptions.

If you have disk trouble, run ScanDisk to see whether the problem goes away. Defragmenter eliminates the empty holes in your drive so that your disk access runs at top-notch performance.

For added space, DriveSpace can almost double your disk drive space. By compressing your files and the free file space, you effectively squeeze more data into the same amount of disk space. You can compress both your hard disk drives and floppy disk drives. In addition, if you convert your drives to FAT32, you will gain extra space due to FAT32's smaller cluster size.

Q&A

Q How often should I defragment and compress my hard disk?

A You should defragment every week or so. Depending on the amount of file accessing you do, you may need to defragment more or less often. If you notice your disk speed slowing down a bit, you'll find that defragmenting speeds the access process somewhat.

Compress your disk drive (or each floppy disk) only once. After the compression, the drive stays compressed. Unless you uncompress the drive, Windows 98 always recognizes the compressed drive.

Q Which kind of backup—full or differential—should I perform?

A The first time you back up you should make a full backup. After you make one full backup, you can make subsequent differential backups of only those files that have changed. Be sure that you save the full backup, however, so that you can restore everything if you need to. If you have a disk failure, you'll restore the entire full backup and then restore each differential backup set of files.

After you've made several differential backups, you might want to make a full backup once again. By making a full backup every once in a while, you can reuse your differential tapes or disks.

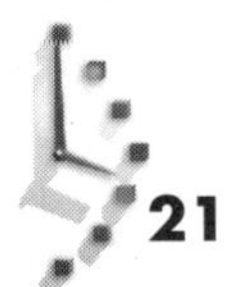

Workshop

Term Review

backup job A description that contains a list of files, folders, and drives you want to back up.

compression The process of squeezing your disk drive so that almost 100 percent more data fits on a disk.

differential backup A backup of only the files that have changed since the most recent backup. Also called an *incremental backup*.

DriveSpace The Windows 98 utility program that condenses the disk space so that more data fits on a disk drive.

FAT File Allocation Table. Describes the layout of your hard disk's files and folders. FAT16 is older 16-bit technology, and FAT32 adds better support for today's large hard disks.

host drive A logical new drive that DriveSpace creates to hold compression information.

incremental backup See *differential backup*.

media The types of storage on which you store and back up data. Examples of media are a disk, a tape, and paper.

ScanDisk A program that monitors your disk for errors.

Part VI

Hour 22

Windows 98 Advanced System Tools

Windows 98 works well but, like a well-made automobile, sometimes gets overloaded with work and gets sluggish. (Nobody wants a sluggish operating system.) When your operating system slows down, your entire computer system slows down because the operating system controls everything else that happens. Windows 98 provides system programs that enable you to monitor Windows 98's performance and determine where bottlenecks reside.

Periodically, you can schedule Windows 98 programs to keep your system running smoothly even when you're not at the PC. By updating your system files, backing up, and scheduling system checking programs to run when you're away, you can help ensure that your system runs in top condition and that you don't have to remember to run important tasks.

The highlights of this hour include the following:

- What system resources are critical for good system performance
- How to check system resources
- When to request a system snapshot
- Why technical support can use your system snapshot to correct problems

- How to schedule tasks to run when you're away from your PC
- How to manage your scheduled tasks

Check Your System

Windows 98 contains two programs, *System Monitor* and *System Resource Meter*, that monitor your system resources. These applications are advanced; many Windows 98 users never run the programs, but they can give insight into problems that may slow down your system.

System Monitor tracks these three items:

- The *file system* comprised of disk access statistics
- The *kernel* comprised of the CPU's activity, as well as some multitasking activities
- The *memory manager* comprised of the various segments of memory that Windows 98 tracks

System Monitor graphically displays one or more of these items and continuously updates the graph to show how your system is being used. You can start the System Monitor and go about your regular Windows 98 work. If the system begins to slow and you want an idea as to which parts of the system are getting the most use, click on the System Monitor on the toolbar to have an idea of your machine's current workload.

When you run the Resource Meter, its program puts a Resource Meter icon next to the taskbar's clock. You can click the icon to obtain statistics on these items:

- *System resources*, which describe the system's resource use percentage (the lower value of the other two kinds of specific resources, User and GDI)
- *User resources*, which describe your resource use percentage
- *GDI* (*graphics device interface*), which describes your graphics resource use percentage

You can see these values if you rest your cursor over the Resource Meter on the taskbar. Task 22.1 demonstrates a simple use of the System Monitor and Resource Meter.

Task 22.1: Checking Resources

Step 1: Description

This task explains how to start System Monitor and Resource Meter. You can use the programs' output to check the efficiency of your computer system.

Step 2: Action

1. Display the Start menu's Programs | Accessories | System Tools menu.
2. Click the System Monitor menu item. (If you don't see it, you have to install the System Monitor option from the Control Panel's Add/Remove Programs Windows Setup option.) Windows 98 displays the System Monitor window. Start another program or two. Click the taskbar to return to the System Monitor graph every so

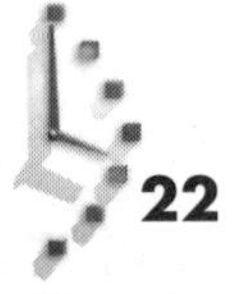

often. As you will see, System Monitor updates its graph, and eventually the graph will fill the window, as shown in Figure 22.1.

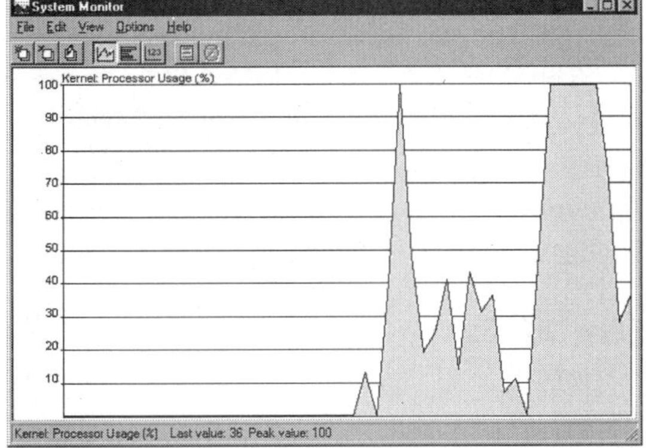

Figure 22.1.
The System Monitor screen updates regularly to show your resources.

3. The default System Monitor displays only the kernel information. Select Edit | Add Item or click the far-left button on the toolbar. Click the File System in the left window and highlight every option inside the right window to request that System Monitor update all the file system statistics. Click OK.
4. Select Edit | Add Item again to add all the detail items for the Memory Manager. When you click OK, the System Monitor displays several small graphs. Watch the graphs for a moment as they update after they check the resources being analyzed. Your System Monitor window can get full, as Figure 22.2 shows.

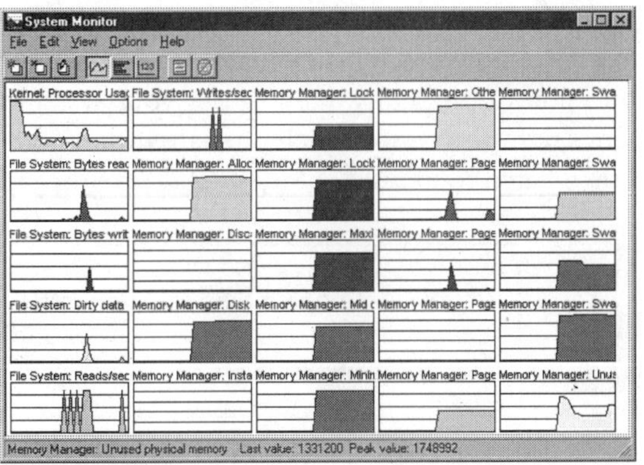

Figure 22.2.
The System Monitor can display statistics for several items.

TIME SAVER

Click over any of the small graphs. System Monitor describes what the graph means in the status bar at the bottom of the System Monitor window.

5. Select File | Exit to close the System Monitor so you can start the Resource Meter.
6. Display the Start menu and select the Programs | Accessories | System Tools menu.
7. Click the Resource Meter menu item. The first time you start the Resource Meter in each power-up session, Windows 98 displays an opening description dialog box. Read the dialog box and press Enter to close the dialog box.
8. Windows 98 displays the Resource Meter icon next to the taskbar clock.
9. Right-click on the Resource Meter icon and select Details. Windows 98 displays a graph showing the current resource usage statistics for the three Resource Meter measurements, as shown in Figure 22.3.

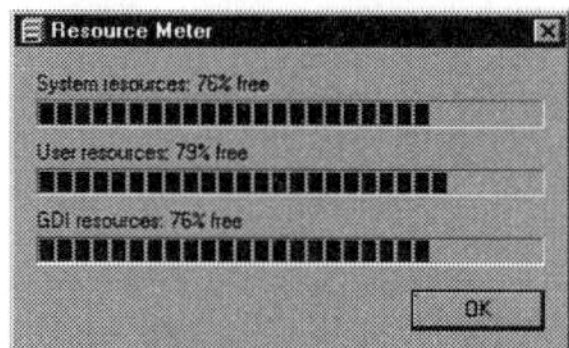

Figure 22.3.
The Resource Meter window available from the taskbar.

As you work in Windows 98, you can check the Resource Meter graphs as often as you want to make sure that you don't get close to running out of resources.

10. Right-click the Resource Meter icon and select Exit to unload the Resource Meter.

Step 3: Review

The System Monitor shows one or more graphs that display usage patterns. The Resource Meter displays a graph of three resource utilizations as you work within Windows 98. If you run graphics- and processor-intensive programs, you can run System Monitor and Resource Meter to see how much load you are placing on Windows 98 and the hardware. If starting a collection of programs often causes your system to slow down or freeze, monitor your system's resources to see which ones are running low right before the problem begins. You can then begin to locate a solution (such as purchasing more RAM or a faster CPU).

Just a Minute

If you use a networked PC, you may see more than the three resource items described in this section. In addition, these meters themselves use some of your system's resources.

Dr. Watson, Come Right Away

Although you won't find it on the Windows 98 menus, a program called Dr. Watson can help you trace severe problems that occur when you run some programs. When you start Dr. Watson, it sits in the background (a new taskbar icon appears) and waits for a problem.

Although Windows 98 is more stable than previous Windows versions, problems can still occur. If your system freezes and you've started Dr. Watson, Dr. Watson will record all pertinent system information right before the error occurred. In other words, if your system freezes or displays a serious system error, you can restart your PC and read the log file that Dr. Watson will have created right before the problem occurred. (Dr. Watson is not foolproof; some system crashes and freezes escape it, but it handles most common situations.)

Dr. Watson's log file will describe the error and often will suggest corrected action you can use to keep the problem from reappearing. If you cannot fix the problem, you can contact Microsoft's Technical Support staff on its Web site (`www.microsoft.com`) or by calling Microsoft's voice support number. The support staff will use Dr. Watson's log to diagnose and correct the problem.

To Do

Task 22.2: Starting and Using Dr. Watson

Step 1: Description

Unlike the programs on your Start menu, Dr. Watson does not appear on the typical Windows 98 menu. Therefore, you must start Dr. Watson from the Start menu's Run command.

TIME SAVER

You can load Dr. Watson every time you start your PC by selecting the Start menu's Settings | Taskbar & Start menu option and selecting Add from the Start Menu Programs dialog box page. Type `\windows\drwatson.exe` for the command line-prompt, select the StartUp group, and type `Dr. Watson` for the shortcut name. All programs that appear in the StartUp menu group begin automatically when you start Windows 98.

To Do

Step 2: Action

1. Display the Start menu's Run command.
2. At the Run prompt, type `Drwatson` and click OK to start the system program. After a brief pause, the Dr. Watson icon appears on the taskbar.
3. Right-click over the Dr. Watson icon and select Dr. Watson to force a snapshot log even though an error has not occurred. The log is created based on your current system information.

JUST A MINUTE

Dr. Watson creates a picture of your PC at a single instant in time, hence the term *snapshot*. Dr. Watson's log shows up to ten of the most recent system snapshots taken due to errors or in response to your request.

4. Although you triggered Dr. Watson when no error occurred, it still recorded a detailed view of your system, just as it would do if a problem *did* trigger its execution. Select View | Advanced to display the full view of snapshot pages.
5. Click System to display the system snapshot shown in Figure 22.4. All this information can come in handy if support personnel need to know the kind of system that you run.
6. Click the rest of the tabs to see the detailed information Dr. Watson determined about your system at the time of the snapshot.

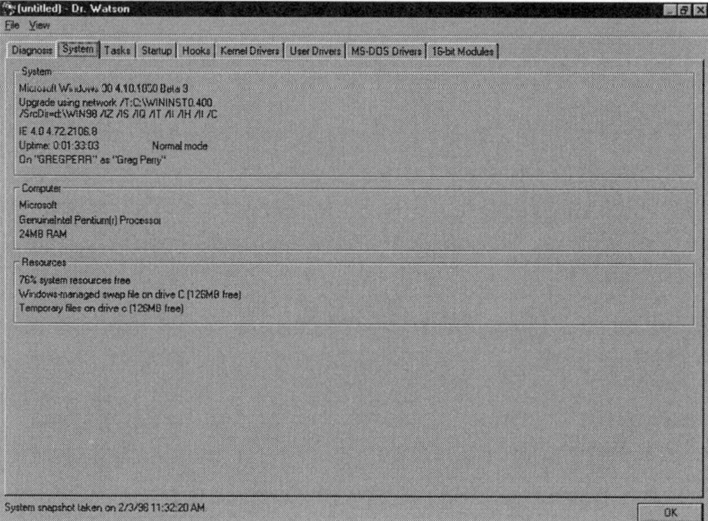

Figure 22.4.
Dr. Watson records all your system's information.

7. Select File | Save if you want to save the current snapshot to your disk. (Right-clicking over the Dr. Watson icon and selecting Open Log File enables you to open the file whenever you need to.)

TIME SAVER

If installing a particular software program seems to cause a freeze-up problem, force a system snapshot before you install the program and then let Dr. Watson record another snapshot upon attempting the install. The software's support staff may be able to use the before-and-after Dr. Watson snapshots to determine the problem.

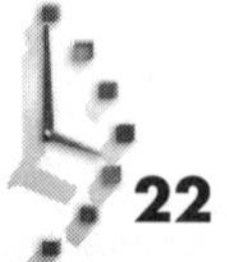

8. Select View | Options to display the Dr. Watson Options dialog box shown in Figure 22.5. You can determine how many logs to save, the folder Dr. Watson uses to save the log files, the number of disassembly instructions (these let the support staff recreate the problem from an operating system level), and the default view that Dr. Watson automatically displays when you first display a log. (You can access this Options dialog box by right-clicking over Dr. Watson's taskbar icon and selecting Options.)

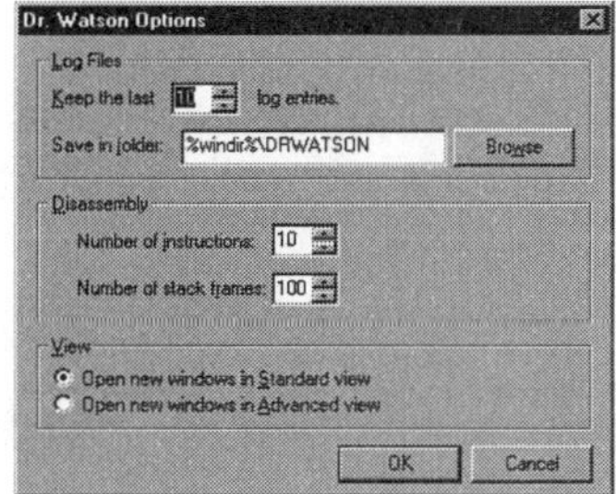

Figure 22.5.
You can change the way Dr. Watson records the system snapshot.

9. Select File | Exit Dr. Watson to close the program.

Step 3: Review

If your system freezes up or displays system error messages such as General Protection Fault, Dr. Watson will be able to record your system's state, automatically, at the time of the error. When you subsequently reboot, Dr. Watson's system log will tell you and any technical support staff what was going on at the error's occurrence.

Scheduling System Tasks

Throughout this 24-hour tutorial, you've seen numerous tools that enable you to manage your Windows 98 system and fine-tune its work environment. Hour 20, "Update Manager and Tune-Ups," explains how to update your system to the latest files and download Windows 98 corrections and upgrades when Microsoft releases them. You saw that, with the Tune-Up Scheduler, you can let your PC fine-tune your disk drives while you're away. Hour 21, "Manage Your Hard Drives," discusses how disk drive tools keep your disk drives running at their most efficient state. In addition, proper system procedures require that you back up your system often, as Hour 22, "Windows 98 Advanced System Tools," explains. To restore your system to its latest and greatest state in case of system failure requires recent backups.

A Windows 98 program called Task Scheduler enables you to schedule these system programs (as well as any other program) to run at preset time periods. You can defragment and back up your hard disk every morning at 4:00 a.m. if you want. You can log into the Internet and retrieve email before work, during lunch, and before you leave work.

When you designate Task Scheduler to run when you start Windows 98, Task Scheduler waits in the background until the time comes to run one of its programs. If you're using your PC when the program runs, you won't be bothered. If, however, a program that you schedule tries to use a data file that you are editing, the Task Scheduler program will be unable to function and will display an error or shut down (as long as the program does not interfere with any you're currently running, which might be the case if they share the same data files).

JUST A MINUTE

One of Task Scheduler's strengths is its scheduling capabilities. You don't have to designate a specific day that a Task Scheduler program runs. Instead, you can specify that Task Scheduler runs a program (or a group of programs) daily, weekly, monthly, or when certain events take place, such as when you start or shut down your PC.

Task 22.3: Working with Task Scheduler

Step 1: Description

Scheduling Task Scheduler is simple. After you set it up, you can easily modify the times or dates your scheduled programs run. In addition, you can easily add and remove scheduled programs.

Step 2: Action

1. Select the Start menu's Programs | Accessories | System Tools | Scheduled Tasks program. Figure 22.6 shows a typical Task Scheduler window. If your taskbar shows the Scheduled Tasks icon, you can double-click that icon to more quickly open the Scheduled Tasks program. (Even when you start Task Scheduler for the first time, the Task Scheduler window contains some entries.)

Figure 22.6.
These programs will run at preset times.

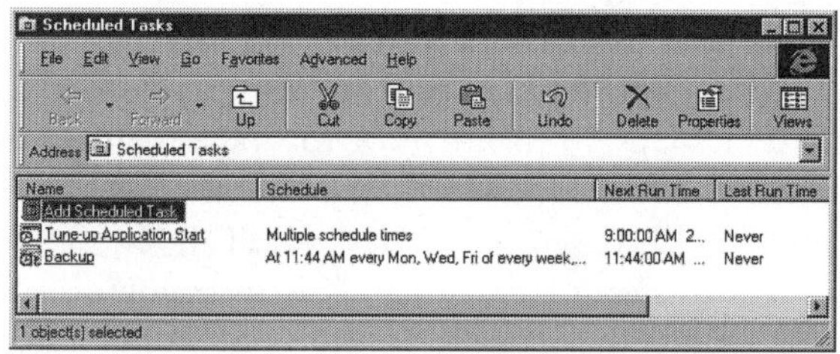

2. Select the first entry, called Add Scheduled Tasks. The Task Scheduler wizard begins, which enables you to set up a scheduled program. Figure 22.7 shows a list of programs the wizard displays for you.

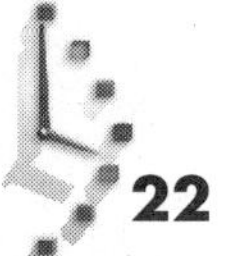

Figure 22.7.
The Task Scheduler Wizard gives you a list of common programs to schedule.

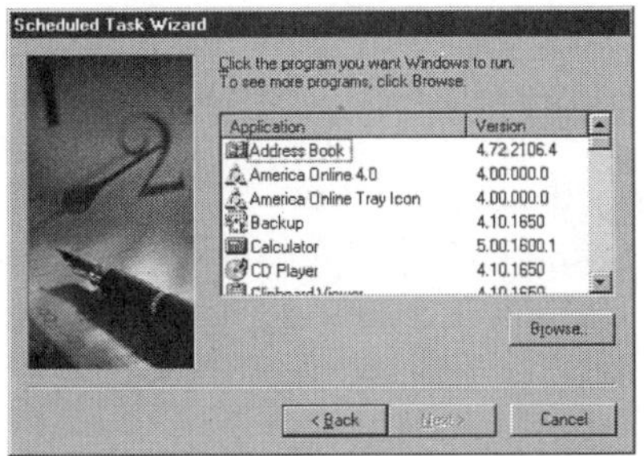

If the program you want to schedule does not appear in the list, click the Browse button to add your own program.

3. Walk through the Wizard and set up Resource Meter to run every time you start your system. The final Wizard dialog box gives you the option of setting up program options available for most programs you schedule. For example, you can set up the scheduled task to stop after running a certain period of time in some cases.
4. To change a scheduled task's scheduled time, open that task (by double-clicking or single-clicking if you've set up a Web view) to display a dialog box that enables you to change the scheduled properties. Click on the Schedule tab to display the Schedule page shown in Figure 22.8 and make any change you want to make. As you can see, Windows 98 gives you total control over a task's schedule, even letting you omit weekend days from the schedule.

Time Saver

Click the option labeled Show multiple schedules to receive a drop-down listbox where you can enter two or more separate schedules for the same task. For example, you may want to run the same program daily before work and at noon.

Figure 22.8.
Change the schedule for a task to suit your requirements for the program.

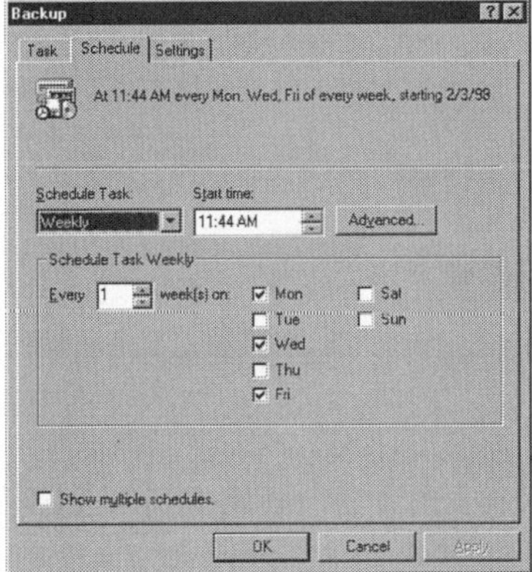

5. To delete a scheduled task, such as the one you added earlier, select the task and click the toolbar's Delete button. Task Scheduler sends the scheduled task to the Recycle Bin where you can retrieve the task, if you change your mind, until you empty the Recycle Bin.
6. To turn off an individual scheduled task without removing the task, open the task (by clicking or double-clicking on the task's entry) and uncheck the Enabled option. The task remains in the task list, but idle, until you check Enabled subsequently or until you remove the task from the list.
7. You can temporarily turn off all scheduled tasks without having to change each one individually by selecting Advanced | Stop Using Task Scheduler.

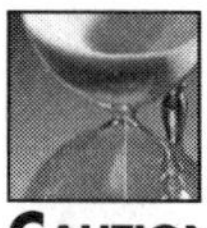

CAUTION

If you select Advanced | Pause Task Scheduler, Task Scheduler stops until you select Advanced | Continue Task Scheduler or until you subsequently reboot your PC.

Suppose you want to run a special disk-checking utility program that you borrowed from a friend. You can temporarily pause your scheduled tasks that might include a disk scan, run the disk-checking utility program, and then resume your scheduled tasks.

8. Select File | Close to terminate your Task Scheduler session.

Step 3: Review

The Task Scheduler program can be there when you cannot be there. Defragment and back up your disk in the middle of the night so your system isn't slowed during the day by those routine operations. Schedule certain programs to run when you start or shut down Windows 98. Task Scheduler gives you complete control over your scheduled tasks.

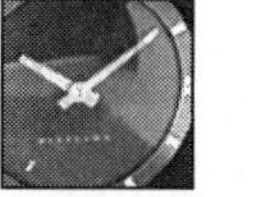

JUST A MINUTE

Task Scheduler adds to a log file every time it runs a task. You can view Task Scheduler's log file by selecting Advanced | View Log. The log tells you whether a task ran successfully and, if not, why.

Summary

This hour described several system tools you can run to manage and monitor your disk, memory, and other system resources. System Monitor and Resource Meter work passively to display statistics about your memory, disk, and system usage. Windows 98 handles resources better than previous versions of Windows, but these tools give you two additional ways to monitor the usage.

Dr. Watson gives you a perfect snapshot of your system, either when you request the snapshot or when trouble occurs. The Dr. Watson program records vital system information when system errors cause your system to shut down, so technical support people can diagnose the problem better. Sometimes, Dr. Watson's log files offer suggestions you can try to eliminate the problem.

You don't have to remember to run routine tasks because the Task Scheduler program runs them for you. You control all aspects of all automated programs that you schedule so that important system check-up and fine-tuning take place when you're not using your PC.

Q&A

Q Should I use Dr. Watson, the System Resource Meter, or the System Monitor when a certain program keeps causing my PC to freeze up?

A Use all three! If you can duplicate the problem consistently, System Monitor and System Resource Meter can help you locate resource problems before they occur. You may be running out of memory right before you attempt to start a program that pushes your memory limits over the edge. Dr. Watson is the program that helps you trace problems that have already occurred. When your system freezes, you can be assured that Dr. Watson recorded all your system's information right before the crash so that you or a technical support representative can eliminate the problem.

Q Does my PC have to be turned on for scheduled programs to run?

A Yes, but you can keep your monitor turned off to save money. The monitor consumes the majority of power in a typical PC system, so you can turn off your monitor when you're not using the PC but leave your PC running so that you won't have to restart your PC the next time you need to use the computer. If you have a laser printer, you should turn off the laser as well because laser printers also consume a lot of power.

Q I want to run a nonsystem program at the same time each day. How can I get my customer-invoicing program to print customer invoices every afternoon at five?

A Task Scheduler is not just for system programs. You can schedule any program to run, whether that program is an accounting program, a game, or a system program. Remember that you're not limited to Task Scheduler's list of choices. You can schedule any program to run at any time.

Workshop

Term Review

disassembly instructions Low-level instructions that describe a program's commands for the operating system.

Dr. Watson A system program that records system information when your PC freezes up.

GDI Graphics device interface consisting of your graphics resources.

kernel The CPU's processor routines.

Memory Manager Controls the various segments of memory that Windows 98 tracks.

System Monitor A Windows 98 program that graphically illustrates your computer's resources as you use the computer.

system resources The amount of CPU, memory, and disk space utilization consumed by Windows 98 and the applications you are running.

Task Scheduler A program that runs other programs at given time periods.

Part VI

Hour 23

Multimedia and Sound

A few years ago, an industry consortium of software and hardware developers led by Microsoft developed a multimedia standard called *MPC* (for *multimedia personal computer*). The MPC standard opened the door for today's wealth of multimedia hardware and software. To use multimedia at its full potential, your operating system must support multimedia, and Windows 98 does just that, as you will see in this hour.

The highlights of this hour include the following:

- How AutoPlay eliminates the CD-ROM startup command
- Where to store the artist, title, and songs for your collection of audio CDs
- How you assign sounds to various computer events
- Why Sound Recorder acts like a digital tape recorder
- How to control the sound and display of full-motion video

Playing with AutoPlay

AutoPlay is one of the Windows 98 multimedia capabilities. If you've ever played a game or an audio CD in your computer's CD-ROM drive, you'll appreciate AutoPlay very much indeed. AutoPlay automatically inspects your audio CD or CD-ROM as soon as you place it in the computer's CD-ROM drive. AutoPlay then does one of three things:

- Starts the installation on your CD-ROM if you've yet to install the program
- Begins the CD-ROM's program if the program is installed
- Starts the audio CD player if it is an audio CD

Microsoft knows that putting a CD-ROM (or audio CD) into your CD-ROM drive almost always means that you want to do something with that CD-ROM. Of course, you might be inserting the CD-ROM in the drive for later use, but that's rare; most of the time when you insert a CD-ROM, you're ready to do something with it right away.

TIME SAVER

If you insert a CD-ROM but want to bypass the AutoPlay feature (perhaps you want to access the CD-ROM later but insert the disc now), press Shift as you insert the CD-ROM. Keep holding Shift until the CD-ROM light goes out. Windows 98 will not start AutoPlay. To turn off AutoPlay, see the last question in Hour 9, "Giving Windows 98 Your Own Programs."

Task 23.1: Using AutoPlay to Play Music from a CD

Step 1: Description

This task demonstrates the AutoPlay feature as it works on an audio CD. Not only does Windows 98 provide for AutoPlay, but it also supplies all kinds of support for audio CDs and CD-ROMs that might surprise you when you see them.

Step 2: Action

1. Find an audio CD that contains music you like to hear.
2. Place the CD in the CD-ROM drive and close the door or push the CD-ROM drive's insert button to close the CD-ROM drive.
3. Windows 98 immediately recognizes that you've inserted the CD into the CD-ROM and begins playing the music! Notice the new CD Player button on the taskbar.

JUST A MINUTE

Depending on the date of your CD's release, something even *more* might happen: You might see a picture of the CD's cover on your screen! If so, move your mouse over the picture and click various parts of the screen to see information about the artist, song lists, lyrics, and other things.

The feature you are viewing is called *Enhanced CD*, and audio CD makers are going to be adding Enhanced CD support to their audio CDs over time so that you can begin to fully integrate your PC and audio and video capabilities. If the CD you place in the drive does not yet contain the Enhanced CD format, you can still add a title and song list, as explained in the rest of this task.

4. Click the CD Player button on the taskbar to display the CD Player window shown in Figure 23.1.

Figure 23.1.
The CD Player window controls the CD's play.

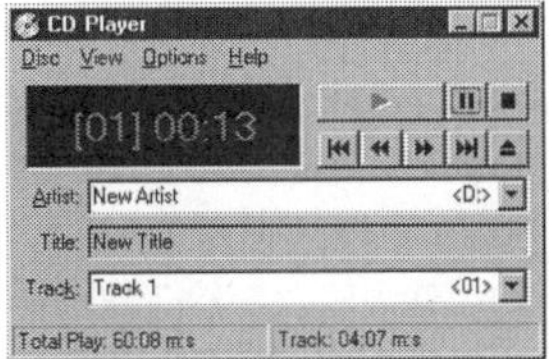

The CD Player acts like a physical CD player that you can control by clicking the buttons. It displays a Play button (grayed out now because your CD is already playing), Pause, Stop, Eject, Previous, and Next track buttons, Previous and Forward time buttons, and an Eject button that you can click when you finish listening to the CD. (Move the cursor over the buttons on the CD Player's window to see a pop-up help box that describes each button.)

Click the Pause button. Click the Play button. Press Alt+K to move the cursor to the drop-down listbox and click the down arrow button to play a different track on the CD.

TIME SAVER

You can adjust the volume control by double-clicking the speaker icon on the taskbar. Task 23.2 describes how to adjust the volume.

5. If your CD is not an Enhanced CD, the CD's information will not show. You must tell the CD Player the artist's name and the songs on the song list.

   Select Disc | Edit Play List. CD Player displays the window shown in Figure 23.2.

Figure 23.2.
Describe the CD to the CD Player application.

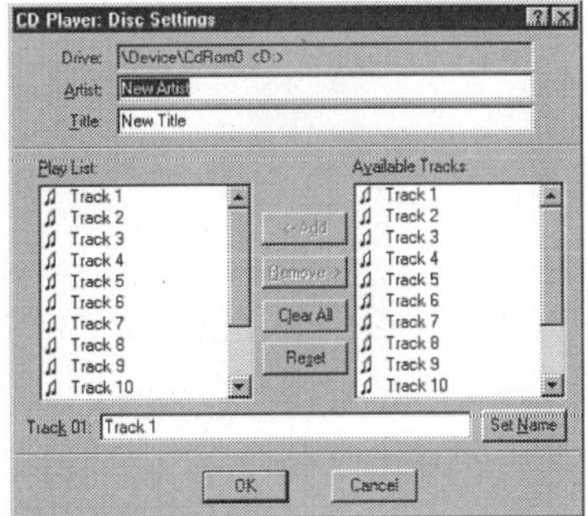

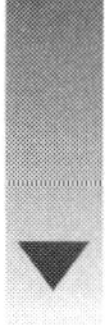

6. Type the name of the artist in the text box labeled Artist. Type the artist's last name first, followed by a comma, and then the first name so that you can later compile an alphabetical list of artists.
7. Press Alt+T to enter the title of the CD.
8. There will be a track listed for each song on the CD. Instead of the default titles of Track 1, Track 2, and so on, you can enter the song titles. Here is the easiest way: Press Alt+K and type the first song title. Press Alt+N to add that title to the track list and enter the second song title. Press Alt+N to add the second title to the track list and enter the third song title. Continue entering all the titles. When you run out of tracks, you have entered all the songs.
9. The Play List and Available Tracks listboxes will now contain the song titles. Don't do so now, but you can later select certain songs from the play list and click Remove to remove those selected songs from the play list (the song titles remain in the Available Tracks listbox). CD Player only plays those songs listed in the play list.

   The CD Player remembers the artist, title, play list, and track lists by storing the information on your hard disk. Click OK to close the window and return to the CD control window. The window now contains a drop-down listbox from which you can select specific songs you want the CD Player to play.
10. Display the various menu commands to see what else the CD Player can do. Display the Options menu to select Random Order | Continuous Play, or Intro Play to play the CD randomly, to play the CD over and over from the beginning to end, or to play only the first few seconds from each track.
11. Select Options | Preferences to display the Preferences dialog box shown in Figure 23.3. You can control what the CD Player does upon completion of playing a CD, as well as several other items, including the amount of time the Intro Play plays each track's introduction.

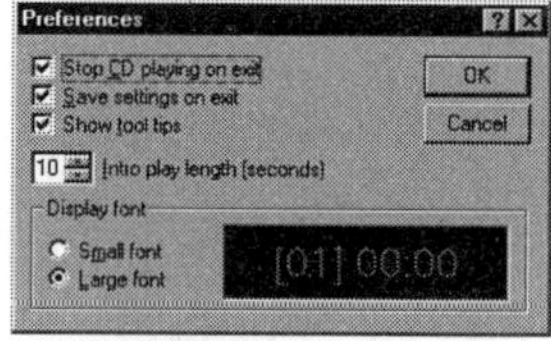

Figure 23.3.
You can set various playing options.

12. Click OK to close the window and eject the CD.

JUST A MINUTE

The CD Player recognizes each individual CD as soon as you've entered the CD's detailed information. In other words, you can, a week later, insert a CD into the CD-ROM drive, and if you've entered that CD's information at any time in the past, the CD Player remembers the CD and automatically displays that CD's title, artist, and song information.

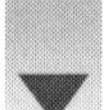

Step 3: Review

The CD Player application not only plays as soon as you insert CDs, but it also keeps track of artists, CD titles, and the CD song lists. After you enter a CD's information, it remembers that information. If you insert a CD that CD Player does not recognize, it still plays the CD, and you can subsequently enter the CD's information.

Just a Minute

More advanced CD Player programs are available through mail-order and software retail outlets. These programs provide more features than the Windows 98 CD Player, such as extra controls and secondary play lists. Some access the *Internet CD Database*, a huge library of audio CD song lists, which eliminates the need to type the titles yourself. Pop in a CD and these programs load the song title list from the Internet CD Database site.

Sounds of Windows 98

You can add sounds to typical Windows 98 *events*. An event is a common task you do while using Windows 98. For example, when you open or close a window, you can add a sound to each of those events, making Windows 98 more fun.

Perhaps you've already heard some sounds coming out of your PC's speakers as you've worked with Windows 98. If you like the sounds, you're going to learn here how to add new sounds and change the ones that you want to change. If you don't want the event sounds, you can also eliminate them.

Just a Minute

The Windows 98 event sounds can help those who are visually impaired. The audio feedback verifies that an event took place, and the sounds can also signal that an error occurred.

Some Windows 98 users do not like sounds attached to events, and others do. The event sounds certainly can be obvious because you can request sounds for all of the following common Windows 98 events:

- Dialog box opening and closing
- User errors
- Starting Windows 98
- Shutting down Windows 98
- Minimizing and maximizing windows
- Starting programs

- Displaying menus
- Displaying help screens

You can assign sounds to several more events in addition to these more common ones. You can even attach sounds to some networking events, such as the appearance of an electronic message.

If you want, you can attach sounds to specific events or use a predetermined set of sounds that comes with Windows 98. The next two tasks describe how to initiate event sounds. Programs written for Windows 98 can access your own sounds; the display of a dialog box from your word processor, then, might produce a sound that you've assigned to that dialog box event.

To Do

Task 23.3: Assigning Your Own Event Sounds

Step 1: Description

If you want to assign a specific sound to every Windows 98 event—or just some Windows 98 events—you can do so. There are many kinds of sounds available, and you can, as you familiarize yourself with the available sounds, customize Windows 98 so that anyone within hearing range will know it's you using Windows 98 and nobody else.

Step 2: Action

1. Open the Control Panel.
2. Open the Sounds icon to open the Sounds Properties dialog box, as shown in Figure 23.4.

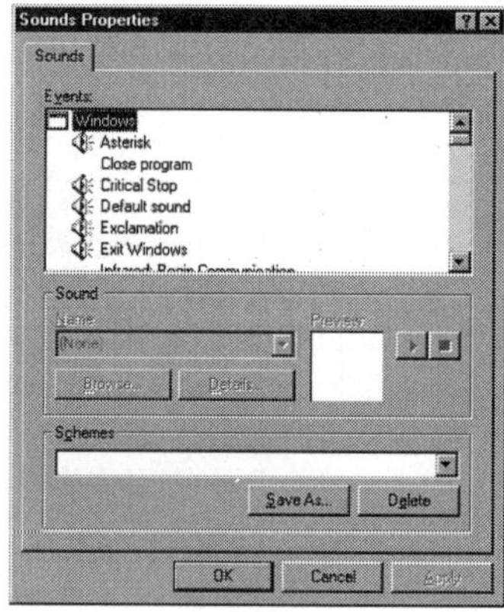

Figure 23.4.
Specify event sounds with the Sounds Properties dialog box.

3. Scroll through the Events list to see all the events to which you can assign sounds. The events are listed by application. The first application is Windows 98. As you scroll through the list, you see specific events listed for Explorer, the Control Panel, and other Windows 98 applications.

Some of the events might seem cryptic to you, but as you use Windows 98 more, you will better understand their purposes. For example, the event labeled Exclamation occurs when an application displays a message dialog box with an exclamation mark, indicating an important message that you need to read.

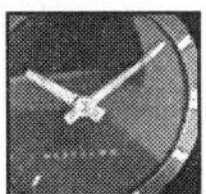

JUST A MINUTE

> The events with a speaker icon next to them have associated sounds. The events without the speaker icons do not have sounds associated with them, but you can add sounds to those, as you'll do in this task.

4. Select the event titled Maximize. You might or might not see a speaker icon next to it.
5. Press Alt+N to move the cursor to the Name drop-down listbox. Click Browse to see the list of choices, and click the Preview button if you want to hear the sound from within the Browse dialog box. Select Chimes. A large speaker icon appears in the box labeled Preview. Click the Play button to the right of the speaker icon to hear the chimes sound. The chimes will sound whenever you maximize a window. If you want to change an event's sound, highlight the event and double-click the sound. You can always preview the sound by pressing Play.

   Finish adding and removing the sounds that you want.

TIME SAVER

> If you see only three or four sounds in the Name list, you might need to run Windows Setup again to install additional sounds from the installation disks or CD.

6. Now that you've customized your own Windows 98 sounds, you can save that customized sound by clicking the Save As command button and entering a name for the sound scheme (your customized set of Windows 98 sounds) in the Save Scheme As dialog box that appears. Figure 23.5 shows the Save Scheme As dialog box.

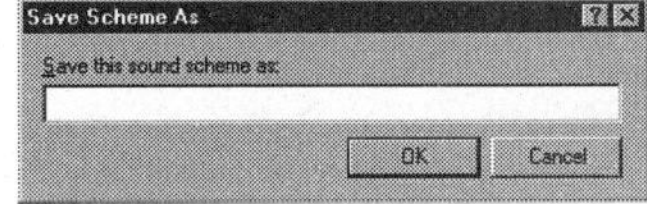

Figure 23.5.
Save your customized Windows 98 sounds to select them in the future.

7. Close the Sounds dialog box by clicking OK and try the sounds out. Open windows, minimize windows, maximize windows, and display message boxes and dialog boxes to hear your sound scheme.

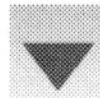

Step 3: Review

The Windows 98 Sound dialog box enables you to attach sounds to various system events. If you don't know what a sound is like, you can preview the sound by clicking the Play button.

WINDOWS MINUTE

Using a Predefined Sound Scheme

The Windows 98 installation supplies you with several predefined sound schemes that add groups of related sounds to your computing environment. When viewing the Sounds Properties dialog box, click the arrow next to the Schemes drop-down listbox to display the list of available sound schemes. You'll find jungle sounds and other sound schemes that give Windows 98 its own voice. You'll enjoy the variety of sounds Microsoft Windows 98 can generate.

If you tire of the sounds, select the sound scheme named No Sounds to turn off all system sounds.

Recording Your Own Sounds

As long as you have a multimedia sound card that accepts a microphone, you can record your own sounds for the event sounds, as well as for other programs that use sound. The Sound Recorder program saves your voice or sounds as digital document files on the disk. The multimedia capabilities of Windows 98 can play back those digitized sounds.

CAUTION

Sound files can take a lot of disk space. If you try to record complete songs but you have only two or three free megabytes of disk space, you might run out of disk storage.

Remember that Microsoft wrote Windows 98 to be a data processing environment and, in today's world, data does not mean just textual and numeric data. Multimedia requires text, numbers, sounds, graphics, and full-motion video. Most of today's Windows 98 word processors enable you to insert a sound (or even a full-motion video file, as you'll see in the next section) inside a document. The word processor places a speaker or some other kind of icon where the sound goes. When the user to whom you give the document double-clicks the sound icon, the user hears your voice!

Task 23.4: Using the Sound Recorder

Step 1: Description

If you've used a tape recorder or a VCR, you'll have no trouble using the Sound Recorder application. This task introduces you to the Sound Recorder application by explaining how to record and assign a sound to a Windows 98 event.

Step 2: Action

1. Display the Accessories menu by clicking Start | Programs and traveling to the Accessories menu.
2. Click the Entertainment menu.
3. Select the Sound Recorder menu item. Windows 98 opens the Sound Recorder window, as shown in Figure 23.6.

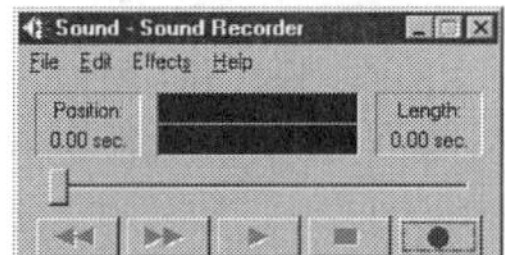

Figure 23.6.
Get ready to record your own sound by using the Sound Recorder.

4. Get your microphone ready. Turn on the microphone (if it has a switch), put the microphone to your mouth, and click the record button. Say the following phrase distinctly and clearly: *I'm a Windows 98 wizard!*
5. As soon as you finish the sentence, click the Stop button. While you recorded the sentence, Sound Recorder displayed the digital wavelength of your voice in the center window.
6. Of course, you now want to hear yourself. Click the rewind button to reset the sound file pointer back to the beginning and then click the play button.
7. Perhaps the quality is not what you'd like to hear. As long as you've got ample disk space, you can improve the quality of the recording. Select File | Properties and select from the drop-down list labeled Choose from.
8. Select Recording formats and click the Convert Now button to display the Sound Selection dialog box. The most important setting appears in the Name drop-down listbox.
9. Click the listbox and select CD Quality. Although your sound files will now consume more disk space, they will sound better.
10. Click the OK command button twice to return to the Sound Recorder window.
11. Click the rewind button to reset the sound file pointer back to the beginning of the file.
12. Click the record button and record the test sentence once again. When you rewind and play back the sentence, your voice should now be clearer. If you want to adjust the volume of the playback, double-click the taskbar's volume control speaker icon and adjust the volume, using the volume control window. Although amplitude increasing and decreasing options are available on the Sound Recorder's Effects menu, the volume control window enables you to adjust your system sound volume in smaller increments.

13. Try adding special effects. Select Effects | Add Echo and play the sound again. Your sound will appear to be coming from a hole. For fun, select Effects | Reverse, rewind the sound, and play the sound again. The sound comes out backward! Straighten things out by reversing the sound again.
14. Select Effects | Increase Speed (by 100 percent) and replay the sound. Decrease the speed once again and replay the sound to make sure that the sound is now normal. You can apply all kinds of special effects and editing actions to sound files that you record. You can also edit songs and sound files from other sources, such as the event sound files. The Edit menu contains instructions for inserting other sounds into your sound files and for removing parts of sound files to shorten sound clips.

    The sound work that you do with Windows 98 is all digitally recorded. Therefore, you can speed up, slow down, reverse, and re-reverse sound files with more accuracy than older recording methods such as tape-based recordings.

    The File | Open menu enables you to load other sound files and edit or change them. For this task, do not load another sound file until you've saved your recording in the next step.
15. Select File | Save. Store the file in the Media folder located within the Windows folder if you want your sound recording file to be saved in the same area as Windows 98's system sounds. Windows 98 stores all sound document files using the .WAV filename extension. If you want to assign your own sounds to events, do so from the Control Panel's Sound Properties window.

Just a Minute

For fun and frolic in the office, secretly assign a voice message to one of your coworker's Windows 98 events. Once you do, however, be sure to assign a password to your screen saver to prevent retribution while you're at meetings!

Step 3: Review

The Sound Recorder application records your own voice. After you create sounds, you can embed those sounds in other document files or save the sounds in the Windows Media folder so that you can add the sounds to the Windows 98 repertoire of possible sound events. The Sound Recorder works just like a tape recorder but enables you to add special effects and even cut and insert sections of sounds within one another.

Full-Motion Video

Windows 98 supports full-motion video better than previous versions of Windows. Windows 98 can display video in a full-screen resolution or smaller windows, if you prefer.

The video is smoother than previous Windows versions because of the way Windows 98 handles the playback. Windows 98 supports *DirectX 5.0* and *ActiveMovie* multimedia formats that take advantage of Intel's MMX multimedia-based CPU. In addition, Windows 98 supports extended video support, such as multiple monitors on a single PC, as well as broadcast and digital video.

No matter how much Microsoft improves the Windows 98 video playback software, the ultimate quality of video playback depends on your computer's hardware speed. If you notice your video is sluggish, you might have to get a faster computer with a faster CD-ROM drive.

TIME SAVER

> Television cards are becoming more popular and less expensive. With such a card you can watch cable or digital television on your PC screen. Watch the television by using the Windows 98 new *TV Viewer* program available on your Start menu's Multimedia option. (If you have the proper hardware for viewing television but do not see the TV Viewer program, run Windows Setup again from the Control Panel's Add/Remove Programs icon and add the TV Viewer program.

Windows 98 uses the Media Player application to play video and the ActiveMovie control that you can use to take advantage of MMX technology if your PC supports MMX. Both Media Player and ActiveMovie are capable of playing all of the following kinds of items stored on the disk:

- Sound files
- Microsoft Multimedia Active Movie Player files, including MPG and AVI files
- Video for Windows files
- MIDI Sequencer files

Most full-motion video clips fall within one of these categories. Rarely do you have to know anything about the details of these files. Windows 98 recognizes the file formats and plays any of them. As a matter of fact, if you type a multimedia file's name at the Start menu's Run command prompt or select a multimedia file from an Explorer or Windows 98 window, Windows 98 starts ActiveMovie or Media Player and automatically plays that file.

To Do

Task 23.5: Looking at a Full-Motion Multimedia Video

Step 1: Description

This task demonstrates the full-motion video and sound that Windows 98 supports. Before starting, insert your Windows 98 CD-ROM into the drive and hold down Shift while the drive first settles to override AutoPlay.

Step 2: Action

1. Select ActiveMovie or Media Player from the Start menu's Programs | Accessories, Entertainment option.
2. ActiveMovie automatically requests a file. If you use Media Player, select File | Open to display the Open dialog box.
3. Select your CD-ROM drive from the Look in drop-down list.
4. Open the cdsample\Videos folder. A list of video files appears.
5. Select the MPG file named Greeting from the list. After a brief pause a video window appears.
6. Click the Play button to watch (and hear) the video. Figure 23.7 shows the video in progress.

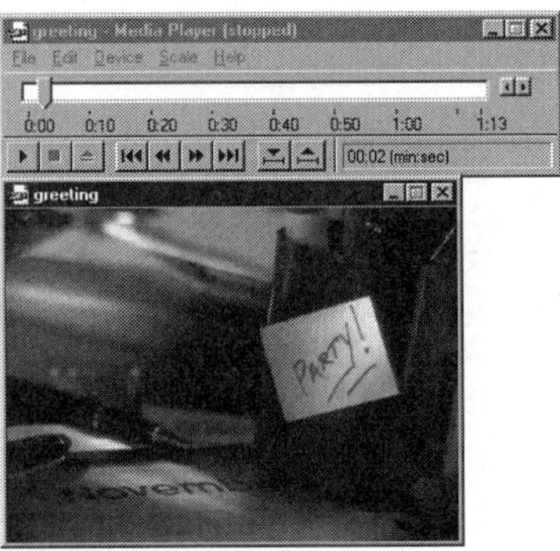

Figure 23.7.
Watch video while you work!

7. Resize the window to full-screen size by dragging the window's edges to the sides of the screen. Depending on your video card and monitor's resolution, the video might look better in a smaller window. Use the play and pause buttons at the bottom of the video clip's window. You also can adjust the position of the play by dragging the play meter's indicator left and right.
8. If you want to adjust the volume, double-click the taskbar's speaker to see the series of volume controls and left and right balance controls. Depending on the type of multimedia sound you're listening to, you can adjust these volume and balance controls:
   - *Volume* Controls the entire system's volume, no matter what is playing.
   - *Wave* Controls wavetable sound volume. Wave sounds are realistic sounds, unlike FM synthesis, which cheaper sound boards and older PCs use. This is the same kind of sound you worked with earlier in the "Recording Your Own Sounds" scction.

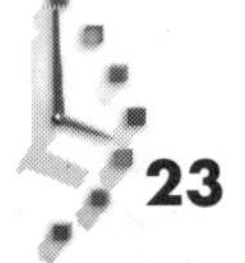

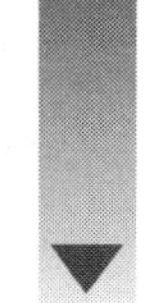

- *MIDI* Controls MIDI sound (stands for Musical Instrument Digital Interface) that reproduces musical instruments and other sounds.
- *CD* Controls the volume of your audio CDs when played with CD Player.
- *Line-in* Most sound cards contain a line-in port to which you can connect an outside sound source such as a stereo's output.

9. Close the window to close the video player program.

Step 3: Review

Full-motion video is a lot of fun to see on a computer. For too long, computer graphics have been low quality. Full-motion video requires ample storage space, so most video resides on CD-ROMs that can hold a lot of data. The Windows 98 Media Player and ActiveMovie applications control all full-motion video, and the volume control window lets you adjust the different kinds of volumes to the best levels.

Summary

This hour described how Windows 98 contains integrated multimedia in its windowed multitasking environment. The multimedia capabilities of Windows 98 are advanced and provide for smooth video and sound. As computer hardware gets faster, Windows 98 will support better multimedia that uses the extra speed.

Audio is only part of the multimedia glitz. Full-motion video capabilities enable full-screen viewing of video clips by using the Media Player. The video is smoother than previous versions of Windows.

This hour discussed multimedia hardware. The next hour explains how you can manage other kinds of hardware connected to your PC.

Q&A

Q How do I know if my computer is MPC-compatible?

A Your PC's manual should state if the computer is MPC-compatible or not. Most likely, you have an MPC-compatible computer if you've purchased your computer within the past few years and your computer has a sound card, speakers, a microphone, and a CD-ROM.

Q Why would I want event sounds?

A Event sounds can be fun, but they also can, over time, get irritating in the wrong environments. Some people, understandably, do not want to hear a bell ring every time they see an error message. Other people like to hear sounds to help reinforce certain events that take place. There are visually-impaired individuals who can benefit from event sounds, because the sounds provide audible feedback that certain events took place, either successfully or unsuccessfully. (If you use screen savers, you still hear event sounds so you know if you get an email message.)

If you don't want to hear sounds every time you start a program or maximize a window, you might do one of two things: Turn off all event sounds, using the Control Panel's Sound dialog box or remove sounds from common events but keep them available for those rare events that you really want to know have happened.

Q I share my computer with my family. My kids like system sounds but we, the parents, don't. How can we coexist in harmony?

A I'm not sure that I can tell you how to coexist in perfect harmony, but I can solve the computer sound conflict. Open the Sound dialog box and select No Sounds. Save your scheme under the name Dad and Mom. Let your kids then assign their favorite sounds to Windows 98 events and save their sound scheme under the name Crazy kids. When you use Windows 98, open the Sound dialog box, and select your sound scheme. You'll be able to work without the sounds. When your kids use the computer, they can select their sound scheme, so they can beep and chime all they want while computing.

(You know that Windows 98 event sounds aren't the real problem, don't you? It's all those games they play that really make noise!)

If you set up user profiles for each member (see Hour 3, "Take Windows 98 to Task," for a description of user profiles), Windows 98 keeps track of each user's sound event settings based on the password that each one uses to sign in to Windows 98.

Q Why can't I use the CD volume control to adjust a video playing from my CD-ROM drive?

A The volume control labeled CD is useful for controlling audio CDs that you play by using the CD Player application. When playing videos, the computer uses one of the other volume controls such as the Wave or MIDI volume control.

Q Why are there so many kinds of sounds (CD, Wave, FM synthesis, and MIDI)?

A The different sounds produce different qualities of audio. Your hardware and software determine the kinds of sound that come out of your computer's speakers. Luckily, you probably won't have to worry about the different sounds because Windows 98 recognizes most sound sources and selects the proper playing software accordingly.

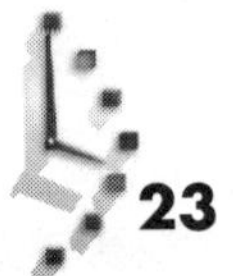

Workshop

Key Terms

Review the following list of terms:

- ☐ *ActiveMovie* A multimedia player that supports MMX technology.
- ☐ *AutoPlay* The capability of Windows 98 to install or start a program from a CD-ROM as soon as you place the CD-ROM in the drive. AutoPlay plays audio CDs as well.
- ☐ *DirectX* A set of internal Windows 98 system files that performs direct writing of video and sound hardware for smoother playback of multimedia files and games.
- ☐ *Enhanced CD* A new audio CD standard that puts graphics and text on the same CDs that your stereo plays.
- ☐ *event* Windows 98 actions you perform, such as opening and closing windows or displaying a menu.
- ☐ *FM synthesis* An older sound standard that produces non-realistic computer-generated sounds.
- ☐ *Internet CD Database* A vast collection of audio CD titles and song lists available from some CD player programs.
- ☐ *Media Player* The Windows 98 application that plays video clips.
- ☐ *MIDI* Stands for *Musical Instrument Digital Interface* and reproduces musical instruments and other sounds.
- ☐ *MPC* (*Multimedia Personal Computer*) A computer hardware and software standard that determines the minimum hardware and software requirements for a product to be called MPC-endorsed.
- ☐ *MMX* A type of Intel CPU that supports multimedia technology.
- ☐ *Sound Recorder* The Windows 98 application with which you can record and edit sounds.
- ☐ *sound scheme* A collection of customized Windows 98 event sounds. After you add sounds to Windows 98 events, you can save that collection of sounds in a sound scheme file.
- ☐ *wave* Also called wavetable. Sound that produces realistic sounds from your computer's speaker.

Advanced Windows 98 Tips

You've worked hard to master Windows 98! You've already mastered the basics, so now you're ready to move up to the level of *Windows 98 guru*. This hour teaches several practical tips that you are ready for now that you understand the ins and outs of Windows 98.

Due to the nature of tips, you won't find step-by-step tasks in this hour. Instead, this hour presents its Windows 98 tips in several categories. For example, if you are comfortable with Windows 98's interface, you can now turn to this hour's first section for some advanced tips that will help you manage the desktop.

The highlights of this hour include the following:

- How to use desktop tips to more quickly manage Windows 98
- When Internet Explorer shortcuts save you online time
- Where to look for Outlook Express shortcuts
- How to improve your computing efficiency when on the road with a laptop

Windows 98 Desktop Tips

When you master this section's desktop tips, you'll more quickly select programs and manage your desktop.

Rearrange Start Menu Items

If you don't like the location of a menu item on one of your Start menus, drag the item to another location. When you've opened one of the Start menus, such as the Programs | Accessories menu, you can click and drag any menu item to another menu.

Suppose you use Notepad a lot to edit text files and want to placc the Notepad program at the top of your Start menu so you don't have to traverse all the way over to the Accessories menu. Open the Accessories menu and drag the Notepad option to your Start menu. You'll notice two things:

- The menu option's name does not drag, but the mouse cursor displays a box showing the movement.
- You cannot drop the item onto the lower section of the Start menu (the section with the Settings and Programs options). The cursor turns into the international *Don't* symbol as you drag the Notepad over the Start menu's lower portion.

When you release your mouse button, the menu option will appear on the Start menu.

CAUTION

The menu item does not move. Instead, the item appears in both places. If you want to move an option instead of copying the option, you must delete the menu item from its original menu location.

Delete Menu Items

To remove a menu item, drag the item to the Recycle Bin. If you change your mind about removing the item, you can restore it from the Recycle Bin up until the time that you empty the Recycle Bin.

JUST A MINUTE

Your desktop does not have to be set up as the Windows Classic interface to drag menu options, as you do when dragging items to the Recycle Bin. Although Windows 98 becomes a single-click selection environment when in the Web view, it can tell the difference between a single click and a click that initiates a drag session. Select View | Options | Classic style to convert windows and the desktop to the classic view. If you want to delete items when your desktop is set up for Web view, you must do so from the item's properties dialog box described in the next tip.

TIME SAVER

If you want to rearrange more than one or two items from your Start menu, consider selecting the Start menu's Settings | Taskbar & Start Menu option, clicking the Start Menu Programs tab, and clicking the Advanced button to display the Explorer menu shown in Figure 24.1. The two panes enable you to move and rearrange entire menu groups. The click-and-drag approach to menu management works well if you need to move or remove only a few menu items because you can select only one item at a time.

Figure 24.1.
The Start Menu Explorer window enables you to perform advanced menu editing.

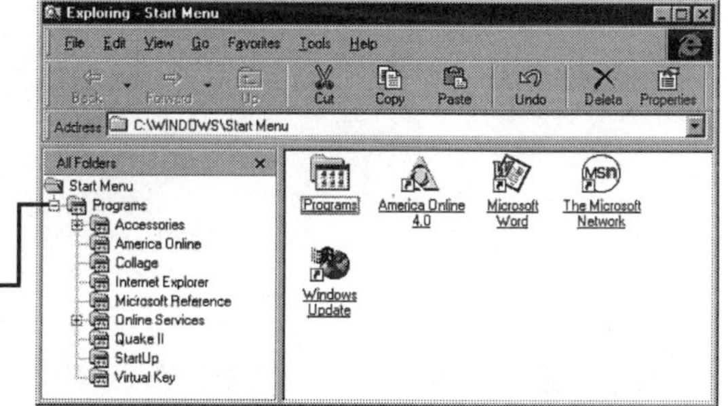

WINDOWS MINUTE

Menu Items Are Shortcuts

You can move menu options and send them to the Recycle Bin because the Start menu contains shortcuts to programs. A shortcut is just a pointer to a program, not the program's filename. Therefore, when you drag a shortcut from one location to another, the pointer moves but not the file itself.

You can even drag a menu item to your desktop. Subsequently, if you want to launch that program, you need only to open the desktop's icon. You won't have to traverse the Start menu every time you start the program.

Right-Click Menu Options

When you right-click over a Start menu option, Windows 98 displays a pop-up menu similar to the one in Figure 24.2.

You can delete or rename menu items with the pop-up menu as well as view the item's properties. The Properties option describes the menu option and its underlying file information.

24

Figure 24.2.
The pop-up menus give you control over a menu option.

Start Windows Explorer Quickly

If your keyboard is a Windows keyboard—that is, your keyboard has a key with the flying Windows logo that displays the Start menu when you press it—you can press the Windows key along with the letter E, as in Windows+E, to start Windows Explorer. (This is not Internet Explorer but the Windows Explorer program you use to traverse disks, folders, and files.)

Adjust the Toolbar in Any Window

With the Web view active, you can right-click over any Windows 98 window's toolbar to display a menu of toolbar options, as shown in Figure 24.3, that determines how the toolbar appears. You can display or hide any of the following on your toolbar:

- *Standard Buttons* Displays the toolbar buttons using the icon-based standard.
- *Address Bar* Displays the Web Address text box in which you can type a Web URL or any pathname to a folder you want to work in.
- *Links* Displays hyperlink buttons (they appear next to the address bar if you display the address bar) that quickly point the window to a Web or folder location. You can drag other shortcuts to the links to add your own buttons and you can also right-click over a link button to change its property or rename the button.
- *Text Labels* Displays the button name beneath the toolbar buttons so you do not have to rely on the icons alone to determine the button's purpose.

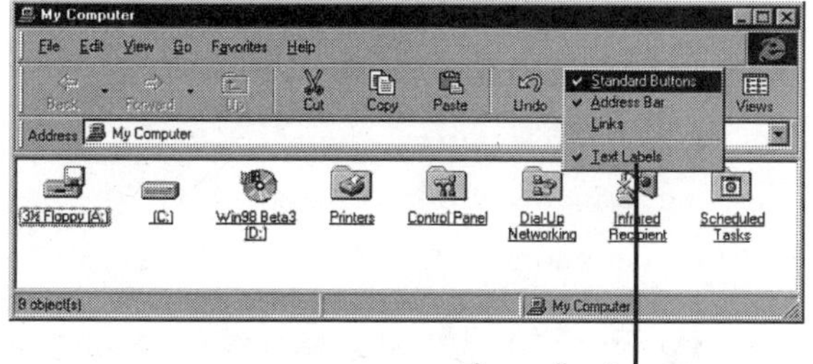

Figure 24.3.
The pop-up menus give you control over a menu option.

Internet Explorer Tips

If you load Internet Explorer 4 and the Web view, Internet Explorer becomes such an important part of the Windows 98 interface that you find yourself using it more and more when you upgrade to Windows 98. Therefore, the more shortcuts you learn about Internet Explorer, the more efficient and effective you are with the Internet Explorer program interface.

Start Internet Explorer from Any Window

Any time you open a window you have the immediate option of starting Internet Explorer and signing into the Internet. Simply click the Internet Explorer icon in the window's upper-right corner (see Figure 24.4).

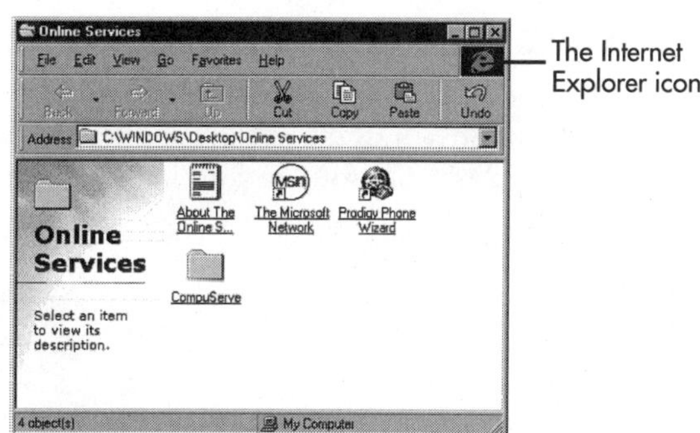

Figure 24.4.
Click the Internet Explorer icon to surf the Internet from any open window.

Learn the Web as You Use It

After you start Internet Explorer, select Help | Web Tutorial, and Internet Explorer starts an interactive Web tutorial that teaches you about the Web.

Where Do You Want to Go?

Keep Internet Explorer's Go menu in mind as you traverse the Web and use Internet Explorer. The Go menu gives you quick access to these items:

- ☐ Email
- ☐ Newsgroups
- ☐ Your My Computer window
- ☐ Your Windows Address Book
- ☐ Internet phone calls with NetMeeting

Quickly Enter Web Addresses

If you often type URLs in Internet Explorer's Address text box, you'll find yourself having to click the Address box first to place your text cursor there to type an address. The Address text box appears to have no shortcut key because no letter in the label Address is underlined indicating any kind of Alt+key combination.

Although no Alt+key combination exists, Internet Explorer does map a shortcut key to the Address text box. When you press F4, the text cursor instantly moves to the Address text box so that you can enter a new address there.

Speaking of the Address text box, all addresses that appear in the Address text box have a small icon to the left. You can drag that icon to your desktop, email message, or anywhere else you want to place that address for later reference. If, for example, you visit a Web page that you want to remember, you can drag its icon to the toolbar's link buttons to create a new link button (assuming you've turned on the toolbar links, as previously described in the section entitled, "Adjust the Toolbar in Any Window").

Set Up Internet Explorer Security

When you select View | Internet Options, Internet Explorer displays a dialog box that enables you to adjust Internet settings. Click the Security tab to display the dialog box shown in Figure 24.5. The four options in the center of the box determine how secure you want to be with your Web browsing.

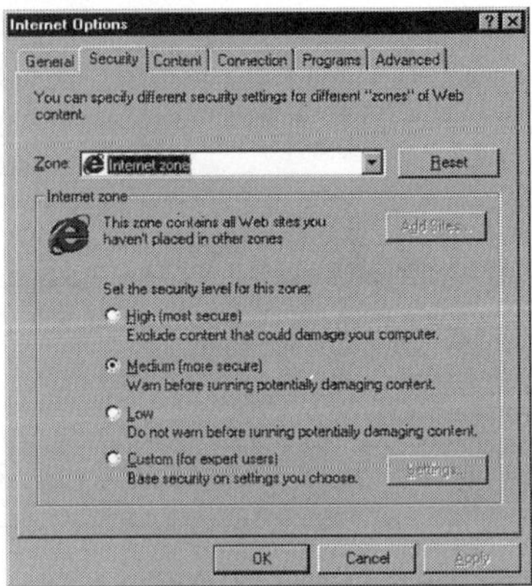

Figure 24.5.
Select the security with which you feel most comfortable.

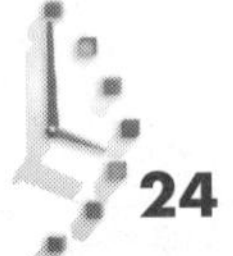

A high security level protects your PC from incoming information that could possibly contain virus-laden files. A virus is a computer file that destroys other files. The problem with this high security level, however, is that you often access secure sites and want to purchase something or give other information, and Internet Explorer will not let you send that information. You can always lower your security level when you know that a site is secure.

Keep More History for Faster Access

The General tab of the View | Internet Options dialog box enables you to enter a value that determines the number of history days to keep track of. As you traverse the Web, Internet Explorer saves each Web page that you visit in a history area. By adjusting the value in the option labeled Days to keep pages in history, you can make Internet Explorer keep more pages in case you return to recently visited pages.

CAUTION

> The more days of history you keep, the less disk space you will have. Some Web pages consume a lot of disk space.

Take a Look at Advanced Internet Explorer Options

Select Internet Explorer's View | Internet Options menu and click the Advanced tab to display the customization list shown in Figure 24.6. Each item in the list describes a different aspect of Internet Explorer that you can control, from browsing tasks to toolbar information.

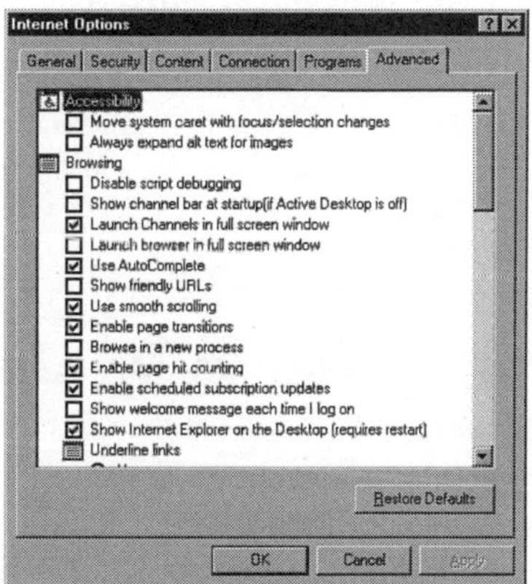

Figure 24.6.
You can completely customize Internet Explorer.

It pays to return to this dialog box every month or two. As you use the Internet in different ways, and as you develop procedures you routinely follow, set options that help Internet Explorer work the way you do.

Change Your Home Page

If you begin traversing to a particular site, such as your company's Web page, as soon as you sign into the Web, you might want to make that page your home page so your browser automatically displays that page when you first start. Instead of using the Edit menu to change your start page, drag the Address text box icon to the Home button to change your browser's home (start) page. The next time you start your browser, the page will appear as soon as you sign into the Internet.

Refresh Occasionally

If you view a Web page for a long time, as you might do if you are working in a different window but you return to the Web page for information as you work, refresh the Internet Explorer window often. For instance, suppose you are tracking stock quotes throughout the afternoon as you work on a word-processing document in another window. You can press Alt+Tab to switch to the Internet Explorer window that displays your stock portfolio page. If the Web page provider updates its stock prices throughout the day, you need to update the Web page contents to reflect the latest prices.

Although you can click the toolbar's Refresh button to refresh the page with its current contents, you can also press F5 to refresh the page. By using F5, your hand does not have to leave the keyboard to grab the mouse, move the mouse to the toolbar, click the Refresh toolbar button, and then return to the keyboard.

Just a Minute

> On some pages that contain numerical information, such as a stock price page, you sometimes get a dialog box that asks `Refresh from data?`, to which you should answer Yes by clicking the Yes button. When you click the button, only the data will refresh and not surrounding graphics or frames that don't change throughout the day, and your refresh will occur more quickly.

Check for Windows 98 Updates on New PCs

When you or your company installs a new PC, make sure that the operating system includes all the latest updates. Get in the habit of selecting the Start menu's Windows Update and go to the Web to install all the updates since the PC's version was created. (Windows Update is also available from the Start menu's Settings menu in case someone already removed the option from the top portion of the PC's Start menu.) If a PC has been in inventory for a month or two before arriving at your site, the chances are good that a new operating system update is now available from the Web.

Disconnect Quickly

To disconnect your Internet dial-up connection, whether or not you are using Internet Explorer, double-click the taskbar's Web icon next to the clock to display a small connection dialog box window. (The Web icon may show two PCs connected by a wire or a different symbol, depending on your Internet connection.) Select Disconnect and Windows 98 immediately signs you off from your Internet provider.

Outlook Express Tips

You'll often work in Outlook Express due to the prevalence of email in today's online world. You can make Outlook Express more enjoyable by utilizing some of the following tips.

Compress Files

If you store many sent and retrieved email messages or subscribe to a lot of newsgroups, your disk space can fill up fast. To help, you can reduce the amount of space consumed by messages and newsgroup files by selecting Tools | Options | Advanced and clicking the Clean Up Now button. When you click the Compact button, Outlook Express compresses your message and file space.

If you click Remove Messages instead of Compact, Outlook Express removes the message bodies but retains all message headers (descriptions) so that you'll know which messages you've already read. (Outlook Express places a read icon next to your read messages as long as you've saved the headers.)

If you click Delete, you save the most space because Outlook Express removes all newsgroup messages and files from your disk; but you have to download those newsgroup messages and files if you ever need them again.

Clean Up Your Deleted Folder

Like files that you delete to the Recycle Bin from within Windows Explorer, email messages that you delete from your Inbox and Outbox don't really go away but go to your Deleted Items folder. If you want to free space completely of unwanted, old email messages, routinely open your Deleted Items folder and delete the messages from there. You have to confirm the delete because Outlook Express knows that the files are truly gone when you delete them from the Deleted Items folder.

If you decide not to delete one or more messages from the Deleted Items folder, you can drag messages from the Deleted Items folder to any other folder at the left of the Outlook Express screen. Feel free to create new folders, from the File menu or by right-clicking over the list of folders, if you want to create an organized set of folders. You can create a folder for your business correspondence and one for your personal correspondence. You then can keep your Inbox, Outbox, and Deleted Items folders free from messages that should appear in other folders.

Create a Personal Signature

You cannot sign your email with your handwriting, but Outlook Express's signature feature is the next-best thing. An email signature is text that appears at the end of your email. Your signature might be just your name, or you might want to close all correspondence with your name, address, and phone number.

JUST A MINUTE

> You can choose not to enclose your signature with certain email messages.

Outlook Express enables you to add a signature to your email messages, your newsgroup postings, or both. To create the signature, select Tools | Stationary. Select the Mail or News page depending on where you want to add a signature. You can select a default font to use for the message as well as a signature if you click the Signature button to display the dialog box shown in Figure 24.7.

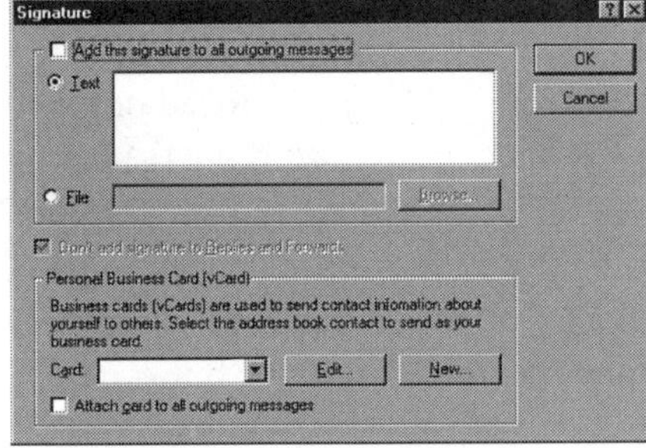

Figure 24.7.
Create a signature for the bottom of your messages and postings.

Your signature can come from text you type at the Text option or from a text file on disk that you select at the File option.

TIME SAVER

> Outlook Express supports a special vCard (virtual card) format for electronic business cards. Some Internet sites and applications support the new vCard standard, from which you can send and receive business card information easily and in a standard format. You can create a vCard-based signature or edit one that's already on your system from the dialog box's Personal Business Card section.

Check Email Often

If you receive lots of email throughout the day, select Tools | Options and decrease the time that Outlook Express waits before checking for new email. If you read your email only once or twice a day, you may want to check for new email less often than the 30-minute default so that your system runs more efficiently when you don't want email. You must have Outlook Express running before it can check for new email.

Outlook Express emits a sound if you get email. When you hear the sound, it to check the Outlook Express Inbox for new messages. Check or uncheck the second option on the Options General page that reads Play sound when new messages arrive to request or cancel the new message sound. (Open the Control Panel's Sounds icon to change the sound that plays when you get a new message.)

Printing Tips

Windows 98 adds advanced printer support that enables you to manage the documents you send to the printer. As you probably know, you can begin printing a second (or more) document even before the first one finishes printing. Windows 98 stores the output in memory and on disk until all the documents are on the paper. Have you ever printed two or three long documents and then wished you could cancel the first one? You can, as the next tip shows.

Manage Printer Jobs

As soon as you print, Windows 98 sends the output to the print queue. The *print queue* is a temporary file that resides partially in memory and partially on disk. The print queue holds the document or documents that you've sent to the printer but that have not finished printing yet.

From the time you issue a print command until the time the document is completely printed, Windows 98 displays a printer icon on your taskbar. If you double-click that icon, the printer window appears like the one in Figure 24.8.

Figure 24.8.
Manage your print jobs from your system's printer window.

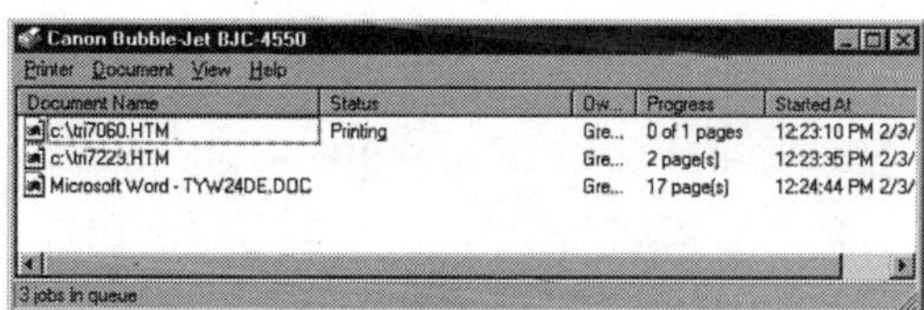

The printer window tells you which jobs are printing and their status, including the number of pages printed for the current job. If you change your mind and want to cancel a job that's started or one that has yet to start, right-click over the job's name and select Cancel printing.

Rearrange print jobs when you want to move a more important job up in the queue. Drag a job up or down to change its priority and printing order.

Cancel All Print Jobs Easily

Select the printer window's Printer | Purge Print Documents to remove all jobs from the print queue.

JUST A MINUTE

> Select one or more print jobs (Ctrl+A selects all print jobs in the printer's window) and select Printer | Pause Printing to temporarily suspend printing in case you need to change printer forms. Select Printer | Resume Printing to restart the output.

Multiple Users Should Print Separator Pages

If you share a networked printer with others in an office setting, make sure that you've specified a separator page for your networked printer. A separator page prints before or after every print job. If several people print at the same time, the separator pages help you determine where one print job begins and ends.

The separator page can contain text, but if you select a large graphic image (the image must end in the graphic file extension `.wmf`), you can more easily locate the separator page when sorting through a list of printed output.

Miscellaneous Tips

Although Windows 98 offers hundreds of shortcuts and tips that you'll run across as you use Windows 98, your 24 hours is about up, and the day must end. The following sections round out the final Windows 98 tips offered here.

QBasic Is Hidden but Still There!

Many programmers got their start writing simple QBasic programs. QBasic is a programming language designed for text environments. You cannot write Windows 98 programs with QBasic, but you can run QBasic programs inside an MS-DOS window.

Learning programming takes some time and effort. If you begin with a simple programming language, such as QBasic, you don't have to wade through a complicated window environment and you can concentrate just on the programming language. If you want to try QBasic, insert your Windows 98 CD-ROM, start Explorer, and copy the two files that begin with QBasic from the CD-ROM's `\Other\oldmsdos` folder to your `\Windows\Command` folder.

To start QBasic, select the Start menu's Run menu, type `QBASIC`, and press Enter. QBasic begins with a Parameter dialog box. Click OK to close, and then QBasic actually begins, as shown in Figure 24.9.

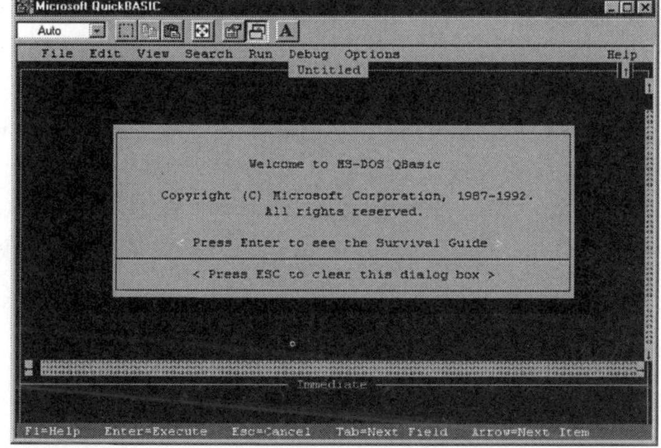

Figure 24.9.
QBasic appears on the Windows 98 CD-ROM.

JUST A MINUTE

If you want to learn how to write programs in QBasic, check out *QBasic Programming 101* from Sams Publishing.

Press Esc to remove the opening instruction screen and begin programming. When you finish, you can select File | Exit to return to Windows 98.

Save the Scraps

Suppose you work within a word processor and want to copy a paragraph or two from the word processor to several different programs over the next few days. The Windows 98 clipboard will hold data only as long you don't replace the clipboard with additional contents or until you shut down Windows 98.

You can create a *scrap,* a portion of a data file, by dragging selected text and data from an application to your desktop. When you release the data, a scrap icon appears on the desktop. Keep in mind that a scrap is not a complete document but only text you've selected and copied to the desktop.

The scrap stays on your desktop until you delete it. Therefore, as long as the scrap remains on your desktop, you can copy to any file.

Stop a Copy or Move

Sometimes you begin a copy or move operation with your mouse by dragging something from one location to another, and you realize that you want to cancel the copy or move. Press Esc to cancel the current copy or move in process.

See All of the Start Menu

Over time, your Start menu can fill up. (If you use a 15-inch monitor, your Start menu and its cascading submenus quickly overflow the screen size so that you must scroll the menus to see all their items.) To see more Start menu items at one time, select the Start menu's Settings | Taskbar & Start Menu option and check the option labeled Show small icons in Start menu. Windows 98 then devotes a smaller amount of screen space to each item in your Start menu and you see more items at one time on your screen.

Delay On-the-Road Printing

Without a laptop printer you cannot get a hardcopy (a printout) of your data. You can, however, print all your data to an offline printer. When you print to an offline printer you appear to print but your laptop stores the printing for later.

To convert your laptop to offline printing, open your Control Panel's Printers folder and select File | Work Offline to check the offline printing option. All subsequent printing goes to the disk. You can print as much as you want and Windows 98 stores the output for when you eventually connect a printer to your laptop. When you get back to the office, plug a printer into your laptop, select Printers File | Work Offline again, and the laptop will print every file you sent to the printer while on the road.

Time Saver

If you want to back up your files and you have a laptop modem, email your files to yourself! When you get home you can download the mail or ignore it if your laptop files made it home safely.

Purchase a Desktop Infrared Transmitter

If you transfer files between your desktop and laptop more than once a week, you'll soon tire of the cable connection that you have to make. If you use a network, plug the network cable into your laptop's PC Card slot, perhaps also removing your PC Card hard disk or modem first and inserting the network PC Card. If you use a Direct Cable Connection, you may have to unplug your desktop's printer or modem before you can cable the desktop to your laptop.

An infrared device frees you from the cables. People who use an infrared transmitter to transfer files between their laptop and desktop are more likely to keep their files up to date than users who must mess with cables.

Summary

This hour wrapped up your 24-hour tutorial with some tips that help you streamline your work. As you work more with Windows 98, you'll find many other tips that lighten your workload. Windows 98 itself is there to help you, not to hinder you. As you've learned throughout this 24-hour tutorial, Windows 98 often provides several ways to accomplish the same purpose. Although Windows 98 is powerful, it tries not to get in your way; instead, it is there to help you get your work done faster.

Q&A

Just a Minute

Due to the nature of this hour's material, questions and answers don't appear.

Workshop

Term Review

hardcopy Another name for printed output.

offline printing The process of printing to a disk file when no printer is attached to your PC.

print queue A combination of memory and disk space that temporarily holds printed output until the printing completes.

QBasic A simple programming language designed for newcomers to programming.

scrap A part of a data document you place on the Windows 98 desktop.

separator page A page that contains text or graphics that prints between print jobs.

shortcut A pointer to a program or file.

signature A text message that follows the email and newsgroup postings you send.

vCard A standard format that represents common business card information.

virus A computer file that destroys other files.

INDEX

Symbols

A

B

C

E

I

N

O

P

Q

R

S

T

U

V

W-Z